How to restore VOLKSWAGEN BEETLE

YOUR step-by-step illustrated guide to body, trim & mechanical restoration
All models 1953 to 2003

Jim Tyler

VELOCE PUBLISHING
THE PUBLISHER OF FINE AUTOMOTIVE BOOKS

Also from Veloce Publishing –

Practical
4-Cylinder Engine – How to Blueprint & Build a Short Block for High Performance by Des Hammill
Alfa Romeo DOHC High-performance Manual (SpeedPro) by Jim Kartalamakis
Alfa Romeo V6 Engine High-perfomance Manual (SpeedPro) by Jim Kartalamakis
BMC 998cc A-Series Engine – How to Power Tune by Des Hammill
The 1275cc A-Series High performance Manual (SpeedPro) by Des Hammill
Camshafts – How to Choose & Time them for Maximum Power by Des Hammill
Classic Cars, How to Paint by Martin Thaddeus
Cylinder Heads – How to Build, Modify & Power Tune Updated & Revised Edition by Peter Burgess
Distributor-type Ignition Systems – How to Build & Power Tune by Des Hammill
Dune Buggy, Building a – The Essential Manual by Paul Shakespeare
Fast Road Car – How to Plan and Build New Edition by Daniel Stapleton
Ford SOHC 'Pinto' & Sierra Cosworth DOHC Engines – How to Power Tune Updated & Enlarged Edition by Des Hammill
Ford V8 – How to Power Tune Small Block Engines by Des Hammill
Harley-Davidson Evolution Engines – How to Build & Power Tune by Des Hammill
Holley Carburettors – How to Build & Power Tune New Edition by Des Hammill
Jaguar XK Engines – How to Power Tune New Edition by Des Hammill
Mazda MX-5/Miata 1.6 Enthusiast's Workshop Manual by Rod Grainger & Pete Shoemark
Mazda MX-5/Miata 1.8 Enthusiast's Workshop Manual by Rod Grainger & Pete Shoemark
MG Midget & Austin-Healey Sprite – How to Power Tune Updated Edition by Daniel Stapleton
MGB Electrical Systems by Rick Astley
MGB 4-Cylinder Engine – How to Power Tune by Peter Burgess
MGB V8 Power – Third Edition by Roger Williams
MGB, MGC & MGB V8 – How to Improve by Roger Williams
Mini Engines – How to Power Tune on a Small Budget 2nd Edition by Des Hammill
Motorsport – Getting Started in by SS Collins
Nitrous Oxide High-Performance Manual by Trevor Langfield
Rover V8 Engines – How to Power Tune by Des Hammill
Sportscar/Kitcar Suspension & Brakes – How to Build & Modify Enlarged & Updated 2nd Edition by Des Hammill
SU Carburettors – How to Build & Modify for High Performance by Des Hammill
Suzuki 4WD by John Richardson
Tiger Avon Sportscar – How to Build Your Own Updated & Revised 2nd Edition by Jim Dudley
TR2, 3 & TR4 – How to Improve by Roger Williams
TR5, 250 & TR6 – How to Improve by Roger Williams
V8 Engine – How to Build a Short Block for High Performance by Des Hammill
Volkswagen Beetle Suspension, Brakes & Chassis – How to Modify for High Performance by James Hale
Volkswagen Bus Suspension, Brakes & Chassis – How to Modify for High Performance by James Hale
Weber DCOE & Dellorto DHLA Carburettors – How to Build & Power Tune 3rd Edition by Des Hammill

Those were the days ... Series
Alpine Rallies by Martin Pfundner
Austerity Motoring by Malcolm Bobbitt
Brighton National Speed Trials by Tony Gardiner
British Police Cars by Nick Walker
Crystal Palace by SS Collins
Dune Buggy Phenomenon by James Hale
Dune Buggy Phenomenon Volume 2 by James Hale
Motor Racing at Brands Hatch in the Seventies by Chas Parker
Motor Racing at Goodwood in the Sixties by Tony Gardiner
Motor Racing at Oulton Park in the Sixties by Peter McFadyen
Three Wheelers by Malcolm Bobbitt

Rally Giants Series
Ford Escort Mk1 by Graham Robson
Lancia Stratos by Graham Robson

Enthusiast's Restoration Manual Series
Citroen 2CV, How to Restore by Lindsay Porter
Classic Car Body Work, How to Restore by Martin Thaddeus
Reliant Regal, How to Restore by Elvis Payne
Triumph TR2/3/3A, How to Restore by Roger Williams
Triumph TR4/4A, How to Restore by Roger Williams
Triumph TR5/250 & 6, How to Restore by Roger Williams
Triumph TR7/8, How to Restore by Roger Williams
Volkswagen Beetle, How to Restore by Jim Tyler
Yamaha FS1-E, How to Restore by John Watts

Essential Buyer's Guide Series
Alfa GT Buyer's Guide by Keith Booker
Alfa Romeo Spider by Keith Booker & Jim Talbott
Jaguar E-Type 3.8 & 4.2 Litre Essential Buyer's Guide by Peter Crespin
MGB/MGB GT Essential Buyer's Guide by Roger Williams
Porsche 928 Buyer's Guide by David Hemmings
Triumph TR6 Essential Buyer's Guide by Roger Williams
VW Beetle Buyer's Guide by Ken Cservenka & Richard Copping
VW Bus Buyer's Guide by Richard Copping and Ken Cservenka

Auto-Graphics Series
Fiat & Abarth by Andrea & David Sparrow
Jaguar MkII by Andrea & David Sparrow
Lambretta LI by Andrea & David Sparrow

General
1½ litre GP Racing 1961-1965 by MJP Whitelock
AC Two-litre Saloons & Buckland Sportscars by Leo Archibald
Alfa Romeo Giulia Coupe GT & GTA by John Tipler
Alfa Tipo 33 Development and Racing History by Ed McDonough & Peter Collins
Anatomy of the Works Minis by Brian Moylan
Armstrong Siddeley by Bill Smith
Autodrome by SS Collins & Gavin Ireland
Automotive A-Z, Lane's Dictionary of Automotive Terms by Keith Lane
Automotive Mascots by David Kay & Lynda Springate
Bahamas Speed Weeks, The by Terry O'Neil
Bentley Continental, Corniche and Azure by Martin Bennett
BMCs Competitions Department Secrets by Stuart Turner, Marcus Chambers & Peter Browning
BMW 5-Series by Marc Cranswick
BMW Z-Cars by James Taylor
British 250cc Racing Motorcycles by Chris Pereira
British Cars, The Complete Catalogue of, 1895-1975 by David Culshaw & Peter Horrobin
BRM V16 by Karl Ludvigsen
Bugatti Type 40 by Barrie Price
Bugatti 46/50 Updated Edition by Barrie Price
Bugatti 57 2nd Edition by Barrie Price
Caravans, The Illustrated History 1919-1959 by Andrew Jenkinson
Caravans, The Illustrated History from 1960 by Andrew Jenkinson
Chrysler 300 – America's Most Powerful Car 2nd Edition by Robert Ackerson
Citroen DS by Malcolm Bobbitt
Cobra – The Real Thing! by Trevor Legate
Cortina – Ford's Bestseller by Graham Robson
Coventry Climax Racing Engines by Des Hammill
Daimler SP250 'Dart' by Brian Long
Datsun Fairlady Roadster to 280ZX – The Z-car Story by Brian Long
Ducati 750 Bible, The by Ian Falloon
Dune Buggy Files by James Hale
Dune Buggy Handbook by James Hale
Ferrari Dino – The V6 Ferrari by Brian Long
Fiat & Abarth 124 Spider & Coupe by John Tipler
Fiat & Abarth 500 & 600 2nd edition by Malcolm Bobbitt
Ford F100/F150 Pick-up 1948-1996 by Robert Ackerson
Ford F150 1997-2005 by Robert Ackerson
Ford GT – Then, and Now by Adrian Streather
Ford GT40 by Trevor Legate
Ford in Miniature by Randall Olson
Ford Model Y by Sam Roberts
Ford Thunderbird by Brian Long
Funky Mopeds by Richard Skelton
Honda Acura NSX by Brian Long
Jaguar, The Rise of by Barrie Price
Jaguar XJ-S by Brian Long
Jeep CJ by Robert Ackerson
Jeep Wrangler by Robert Ackerson
Karmann-Ghia Coupe & Convertible by Malcolm Bobbitt
Land Rover, The Half-Ton Military by Mark Cook
Lea-Francis Story, The by Barrie Price
Lexus Story, The by Brian Long
Lola – The Illustrated History (1957-1977) by John Starkey
Lola – All The Sports Racing & Single-Seater Racing Cars 1978-1997 by John Starkey
Lola T70 – The Racing History & Individual Chassis Record 3rd Edition by John Starkey
Lotus 49 by Michael Oliver
MarketingMobiles, The Wonderful Wacky World of, by James Hale
Mazda MX-5 Miata Roadster by Brian Long
Mazda MX-5 Miata – The Book of the World's Favourite Sportscar by Brian Long
MGA by John Price Williams
MGB & MGB GT – Expert Guide (Auto-Doc Series) by Roger Williams
Mini Cooper – The Real Thing! by John Tipler
Mitsubishi Lancer Evo – The Road Car & WRC Story by Brian Long
Montlhery by William 'Bill' Boddy
Motor Racing Reflections by Anthony Carter
Motorhomes, The Illustrated History by Andrew Jenkinson
Motorsport in colour, 1950s by Martyn Wainwright
MR2 – Toyota's Mid-engined Sports Car by Brian Long
Nissan 300ZX & 350Z – The Z-Car Story by Brian Long
Pass Your Theory and Practical Driving Tests by Clive Gibson & Gavin Hoole
Pontiac Firebird by Marc Cranswick
Porsche Boxster by Brian Long
Porsche 356 by Brian Long
Porsche 911 Carrera – The Last of the Evolution by Tony Corlett
Porsche 911R, RS & RSR, 4th Edition by John Starkey
Porsche 911 – The Definitive History 1963-1971 by Brian Long
Porsche 911 – The Definitive History 1971-1977 by Brian Long
Porsche 911 – The Definitive History 1977-1987 by Brian Long
Porsche 911 – The Definitive History 1987-1997 by Brian Long
Porsche 911 – The Definitive History 1997-2004 by Brian Long
Porsche 911SC Super Carrera, The Essential Companion by Adrian Streather
Porsche 914/914-6 The Definitive History Of The Road & Competition Cars by Brian Long
Porsche 924 by Brian Long
Porsche 944 by Brian Long
Porsche 993 'King of Porsche' – The Essential Companion by Adrian Streather
RAC Rally Action by Tony Gardiner
Redman, Jim – Six Times World Motorcycle Champion by Jim Redman
Rolls-Royce Silver Shadow/Bentley T Series Corniche & Camargue Revised & Enlarged Edition by Malcolm Bobbitt
Rolls-Royce Silver Spirit, Silver Spur & Bentley Mulsanne 2nd Edition by Malcolm Bobbitt
Rolls-Royce Silver Wraith, Dawn & Cloud/Bentley MkVI, R & S Series by Martyn Nutland
RX-7 – Mazda's Rotary Engine Sportscar (updated & revised new edition) by Brian Long
Singer Story: Cars, Commercial Vehicles, Bicycles & Motorcycles by Kevin Atkinson
SM – Citroen's Maserati-engined Supercar by Brian Long
Subaru Impreza – The Road Car & WRC Story by Brian Long
Taxi! The Story of the 'London' Taxicab by Malcolm Bobbitt
Triumph Motorcycles & the Meriden Factory by Hughie Hancox
Triumph Speed Twin & Thunderbird Bible by Harry Woolridge
Triumph Tiger Cub Bible by Mike Estall
Triumph Trophy Bible by Harry Woolridge
Triumph TR6 by William Kimberley
Edward Turner – The Man Behind the Motorcycles by Jeff Clew
Velocette Motorcycles – MSS to Thruxton Updated & Revised Edition by Rod Burris
Volkswagen Bus or Van to Camper, How to Convert by Lindsay Porter
Volkswagens of the World by Simon Glen
VW Beetle Cabriolet by Malcolm Bobbitt
VW Beetle – The Car of the 20th Century by Richard Copping
VW Bus – 40 years of Splitties, Bays & Wedges by Richard Copping
VW Bus, Camper, Van, Pickup by Malcolm Bobbitt
VW Golf – Five Generations of Fun by Richard Copping & Ken Cservenka
VW – The Air-Cooled Era in Colour by Richard Copping
Works Rally Mechanic by Brian Moylan

First published in 2004 by Veloce Publishing Limited, 33 Trinity Street, Dorchester, Dorset DT1 1TT, England. Fax: 01305 268864/e-mail: info@veloce.co.uk. Reprinted May 2006.
web: www.veloce.co.uk or www.velocebooks.com. ISBN: 1-903706-90-4. ISBN 13: 978-1-903706-90-9. UPC: 6-36847-00290-9

Readers with ideas for automotive books, or books on other transport or related hobby subjects, are invited to write to the editorial director of Veloce Publishing at the above address.
British Library Cataloguing in Publication Data - A catalogue record for this book is available from the British Library.
Typesetting, design and page make-up all by Veloce Publishing on Apple Mac. Printed in India by Replika Press.

Contents

Acknowledgements Introduction, Using this book & Safety

ACKNOWLEDGEMENTS

This book is very much the richer thanks to the help and goodwill of Simon and Barbara of the Beetle Specialist Workshop of Worcestershire, England, and most especially the encyclopedic knowledge and vast experience of all things Volkswagen of BSW workshop chief Terry Ball. It is a rare privilege to be invited to spend a substantial length of time in such a quality professional restoration workshop.

INTRODUCTION

As recently as the 1990s, the Beetle was easily the most prolific classic car on the roads of Britain but, in the following years, the situation altered and, in the 21st century, the Beetle has become quite a rare sight on our roads. The decline in Beetle numbers is almost certainly due to many having failed their annual road worthiness test due to body rot, consequently being scrapped or left to rot away; not just a few, but tens of thousands. The reason why Beetles have been scrapped in such awesome numbers is that the cost of restoring them professionally has been greater than the car's end value, and too few owners have been prepared to undertake (or have started and abandoned) DIY restorations.

In recent years, countless Beetles will have had shoddy welded repairs necessary to keep or make the car roadworthy, giving it another year or two of life on the road but ultimately leading to the car's demise as the cost of properly repairing the growing number of such temporary repairs rises. Many people will have started DIY restorations on their unroadworthy Beetles but, as is so often the case with DIY restoration, enthusiasm and/or money will have petered out partway through the job.

One factor which has undoubtedly exacerbated the reasons why so few Beetles are restored, either professionally or by enthusiasts, has been the availability in the UK of brand-new Beetles imported from Mexico, which have been available for far less than the cost of a good professional Beetle restoration. The ending of production in Mexico in 2003 might well cause a sea change, and encourage owners of old or laid-up Beetles to embark upon a DIY restoration, or commission a professional restoration.

Another factor that might prompt a reversal in the fortunes of classic Beetles is that, as the number of Beetles decreases, the car becomes rarer. Sooner or later, the monetary value of the remaining cars will rise - possibly to the point at which professional restoration becomes financially viable, and the incentive to finish those stalled DIY restorations increases. The very fact that the Beetle is a less familiar sight on the roads should, in itself, provide the motivation for owners of out of commission Beetles to get a restoration underway. The need for a book that helps the DIY restorer is stronger than ever.

The apparent shortage of Beetles is the reason for a change of emphasis in this book. In 1993 when Beetles were still commonplace, the emphasis was very much on restoring Beetles properly and against 'patch' repairs, on the basis that properly restored Beetles have a long life ahead of them whereas patched cars usually last just a few years. However, in the current climate, ANY repair - however temporary - which keeps a Beetle on the road rather than it being crushed has to be considered acceptable.

Like any other car, many older Beetles suffer extensive body rot and/or near-terminal mechanical problems which render them unfit for the road. Some of these cars are hastily smartened up for sale to an unsuspecting buyer, others will be given a thorough restoration which returns them to their former glory. A few of the Beetles which come to the market are unsafe for use on the road due to extensive but expertly camouflaged rot or uncorrected collision damage. It can be difficult for the aspiring Beetle buyer to establish which treatment a viewed car has received.

This book should arm the prospective buyer with the knowledge needed to sort the good from the bad, help the would-be Beetle owner find the right car, bring it to the desired condition - whether the car is intended as a workhorse or a 'classic' or show car - and keep it in good condition and where it belongs - on the road. This is not a workshop manual, but is, perhaps, a companion to a workshop manual. It is strongly recommended that the book be used in conjunction with a good manual.

USING THIS BOOK

As stated in the author's introduction, the primary purpose of this book is to guide you through the selection, purchase, repair and home restoration of a classic Volkswagen Beetle. The book is not intended to be a workshop, operations, or spares manual, but is intended to supplement these invaluable sources of information. Consequently, you would be well advised to purchase the manual(s) relevant to your Beetle before embarking on a significant repair, and certainly before starting a complete restoration.

All of the components/service prices are approximately those prevailing in the UK at the time of publication. These prices will be subject to normal market forces, and will, of course, tend to rise with economic inflation. You would be well advised to allow for these factors when calculating your budget.

It is possible that the goods and services mentioned will become unavailable, or alter with the passage of time. Dimensions given in the illustrations are in millimetres, unless otherwise stated. Line illustrations are not to scale. References to right side and left side are from the point of view of standing behind the car.

The author, editor, publisher and retailer cannot accept any responsibility for personal injury, mechanical damage or financial loss, which results from errors or omissions in the information given. If this disclaimer is not acceptable to you, please immediately return your unused, pristine book and receipt to your retailer, who will refund the pruchase price paid.

SAFETY

Important! During work on your car of any type, your personal safety MUST always be your prime consideration. You must not undertake any of the work described in this book yourself unless you have sufficient experience, aptitude, and a good enough workshop and equipment to ensure your personal safety.

Veloce Publishing Ltd

Chapter 1
Buying a Beetle

The acronym MoT (Ministry of Transport) appears throughout this section, and refers to an annual roadworthiness test of cars in the UK. Most countries will have a similar test.

Finding a Beetle to buy is fairly easy because, with over 20 million manufactured, there are a fair number to choose from. Finding and buying a reliable, rot-free, safe and sound Beetle is anything but easy, however. So many are unreliable, rotten, unsafe and unsound because of patch-repair and cosmetic work, which only make them appear roadworthy. What's more, the most recent European-manufactured Beetle is now over a quarter of a century old ...

Although the Beetle is rightly renowned as a rugged and long-lived vehicle, many examples (especially older cars) will be suffering from acute, chronic, widespread - and usually camouflaged - rot in the bodyshell and chassis, and/or serious mechanical problems, both of which render the cars totally unsafe for road use. Sometimes cars with dangerous body rot are sold honestly at low prices as 'restoration project' cars, although experience suggests that, quite often, the problem areas are hastily and shoddily covered up, and the car sold dishonestly - and sometimes at quite a high prics - as being roadworthy.

It can be difficult for even an experienced person to assess the true condition of a car with expertly camouflaged body rot, although mechanical problems are often self-evident in those cases where they noticeably affect some aspect of the car's performance, such as poor braking, road-holding or acceleration. Some mechanical faults, however, are less evident and demand an expert knowledge of the car and how to properly appraise it.

Body rot and failing major mechanical components can both prove expensive

A Mk I GP Buggy and a 'Splittie' pickup share the workshop with a 1972 Beetle.

to rectify, and render a car unsafe for use on the road; failings in the electrical and hydraulic components can prove almost as bad. The hydraulic fluid used in the braking system is highly flammable and leakage is both a fire risk and, of course, a reason for loss of braking. Old electrical components, their wires and terminals can not only be unreliable but are also the cause of the majority of car fires. The state of even small components is vitally important when buying a car.

Many of the Beetles which come onto the market may be advertised as 'restored,' and offered at an appropriately high price when, in fact, they have been incompetently repaired by a DIY enthusiast or back-street body shop. Price is no guarantee of quality. Many of the customised examples offered for sale may have been converted in a similarly slipshod manner, and even the best-looking and highest-priced restored and customised cars can actually be in poor condition - and a few may even be death-traps.

Another pitfall awaits the unwary buyer: thieves, using a variety of devices - including giving the cars new identities - fraudulently sell stolen cars to honest buyers who will lose both car and their money when the true identity of the car becomes known to the authorities.

So, despite the Beetle's exceptionally robust construction and reliability, finding a genuinely good example can be just as problematic as finding a good example of any aged car.

The first question to be addressed is: which Beetle? The Beetle world appears to be split into two camps, which can be summed up as the 'traditionalists' and the 'radicals:' both love the Beetle, but in different ways. The traditionalists like the Beetle just the way it is, and, whilst some might consider the whole topic of customisation to be slightly infra dig, most will accept the custom enthusiast as a kindred spirit; the radicals favour one or other of the various schools of customisation, and might consider that the standard car is quite okay for those who like that sort of thing - but not for them.

The Beetle can be all things to all men: some might be looking for an honest, roadworthy and reasonably-priced example, and demand no more of it than reliable daily transport with a little more character than a modern car has; there are those who seek an early car for restoration or customisation, whilst others may wish to by-pass the countless hours of hard labour which go into such projects and buy an already restored or customised example.

Amongst restored Beetles there's a choice between early and late, convertible or closed, original spec or mildly customised. Amongst customised examples there are Cal lookers, Bajas, Beach Buggies, and a host of kits, plus innumerable one-off specials - the range of available options is huge.

RESTORATION/RE-SHELLING CARS

The flitch panels (inner front wings) and the associated reinforcing pressings of the 1302S, 1303 and 1303S were not available as repair panels when the first edition of this book was written. Thankfully, both full assemblies and some repair sections are again available, though the full assemblies are very expensive to buy at the time of writing.

The alternatives are to use repair pressings to renew rotten structural steel, or to fabricate repair pressings for the structural pressings from heavy gauge steel. However, such work is outside the abilities of all but the most experienced restorers, and the process is so time-consuming to have carried out professionally that it is financially questionable.

Another drastic alternative is to graft a frame head capable of taking the earlier beam axle onto a 1302S with the flat windscreen, then to renew the front end of the car using the flitch, other panels, and suspension components from non-McPherson cars.

If you're looking for a Beetle to be the basis of a restoration (or to re-shell or build up into a buggy or other kit) then it will pay you to look for a particular type of car. This will be one which has been in daily use, with a predominance of excellent (recently replaced) mechanical components and good trim, but a shell/chassis that's in need of some welding. Such cars usually come onto the market when they fail the annual road worthiness test (MoT) on bodywork grounds, and they usually come very cheaply, even if the hapless owner has recently spent a small fortune renewing mechanical and electrical components. Never pay a high price for any car that needs welding to make it roadworthy, because, until the car is stripped right down, it's impossible to estimate the extent of the repair work. Such cars have usually been patch-weld repaired over rotten steel for many years; rot which can prove extensive and, in many cases, difficult to repair.

If major mechanical assemblies such as the engine or gearbox are claimed to have been replaced recently, ask to see the invoice/receipt to ensure that the reconditioning was carried out by a reputable company. The price you pay for such a car should be a fraction of the sum of the costs of the new and usable components. The advertisements for these cars usually include the pitiful words 'some welding needed...'

If you intend to find a restoration project car and repair its rotten bodyshell, be very careful when checking for previous collision damage, and also for rot in the most structurally important areas, which might have allowed a suspension mounting point - or even the frame head - to move out of alignment. Restoring a straight bodyshell is usually within the capabilities of the enthusiastic amateur, but straightening a bent one is most certainly the province of

There comes a point at which restoration is simply uneconomic. This car has been standing outdoors for over a decade, and its only value is as a source of spares.

the professional bodyshop equipped with a jig, because misalignment of suspension mounting points can make a car dangerous to drive, and it's doubtful that a bent Beetle spine could be straightened.

The Beetle spine chassis is particularly strong, although rot in the front end of the spine can allow even a minor bump to move the frame head. Checking chassis alignment precisely needs a jig, but taking perpendiculars from suspension points front and rear (mark crosses on the ground underneath), and then moving the car away, allows you to check that the front to back measurements are the same each side of the car and the diagonals are also equal. This method is not precise, but it will certainly reveal all but a tiny misalignment; if you're not sure that the chassis is straight, reject the car. The cost of professionally straightening such a car can be prohibitive, and another chassis (floors and spine) might be the only option.

Whilst it's true to say that any car - no matter how badly the body has rotted - can be rebuilt, there comes a point when it will be uneconomic, and so difficult to do unless you have access to jigs to help align panels, plus a deep enough pocket to buy in a lot of quite expensive body repair and replacement panels. Such cars are best considered as candidates for either re-shelling or conversion into one of the kit cars which come complete with their own chassis.

Mechanical components are widely available and not too expensive in comparison with components for more recent cars, but in the course of a restoration many of them will need at least refurbishment and some will need replacement. The cost of renewing mechanical, electrical and hydraulic components can add up to a sizeable bill on cars in generally poor condition, so check out as many components as possible before negotiating a price for the car.

Check that the car has been maintained properly by examining the state of the engine oil. If the oil is black, the cylinder bores and piston rings, and/or the valves, are probably worn, and have allowed carbon to mix with the oil. If the oil is a cream colour, then oil changes have been infrequent, and the car used mostly for short runs (water condensing onto the crankcase has formed an emulsion with the oil); neither of which are good for the engine. If the oil smells of petrol then a new fuel pump is needed and, if the leakage has been occurring for any length of time, expect increased wear of engine components due to the reduction in lubrication.

Engine oil plays an important role in preventing the engine from overheating. If a car has black or cream oil, poor oil pressure or a low oil level, and has been used in that condition, it will have run far too hot, and component wear will have been high.

Check whether the engine bay and engine ancillaries (especially the distributor cap and other elements of the ignition system) are clean or covered in dirt or oil; if the car has been properly maintained they will be clean. A car on which maintenance has been skimped will mainly have dubious spares, and the last thing you want is a freshly restored car which keeps breaking down whenever another old component decides to quit.

If you want a quick and easy re-shell, or kit car build-up, avoid cars which have been standing idle for any length of time.

The state of the oil clinging to a dipstick tells a lot about the condition of the engine. Although rather black, this is not unusual, and it's not thick and full of carbon, which can happen when the engine is burning oil.

If you find an emulsion of oil and water (a creamy substance not unlike mayonnaise) sticking to the oil filler cap, or within the filler neck, this indicates that the car has been used mainly for short journeys. Not a good sign as engine wear is highest during short trips.

Many mechanical, electrical and hydraulic components appear to deteriorate more quickly when the car is left standing than if the car is regularly used. Another point against cars which have not run for some time is the likelihood that many of the nuts and bolts will have seized solid, making the initial strip-down far more difficult and frustrating than it need be, and giving you no option but to cut, drill or grind away seized fittings, which must, of course, be replaced with new ones at increased cost. Even worse, there's always the danger that, when dealing with a recalcitrant fitting, you will damage the associated component.

It's a good idea to look for a car which, although in poor condition bodily, is sound enough be used on the road for however short a period before the test certificate expires. Using the car on the road will help to highlight any looming mechanical problems which can then be dealt with at leisure during the restoration.

The very best Beetle for a restoration is one which, although it may have some body rot, has not been 'bodged.' When, in 1992, the author asked the folk at the Beetle Specialist Workshop to keep an eye out for a Beetle for him, they managed to find a 1970 1500 (RVJ 403H) which had failed the MoT on bodywork, but which had no evidence of previous bodywork repair apart from some body filler on external panels. This car, according to BSW workshop manager, Terry Ball, had 'not been got at,' meaning that cover patches had not been welded over areas of rot. When patches of steel are welded over rotting bodywork, the underlying rot accelerates, because it is encapsulated - ideal conditions for the rot to spread. The rot quickly reaches the edges of the cover patch, then carries on to infect surrounding steel.

The rot on RVJ 403H included the heater channel rear ends, sections of the floor pans, the rear body mounting points within the wheelarches, and the rear bumper mounts. Plenty of rot - but honest rot. If you can find such a car then your restoration will be so much easier.

THE WORKHORSE

If you want a low-cost Beetle to put into immediate daily use, then the condition of mechanical and electrical components automatically assumes greater importance than in the case of the restoration car. If you were to buy an older car with mostly tired and worn components, these would inevitably fail, one-by-one, at unpredictable intervals, and the car would never be reliable.

The best advice is to concentrate on finding a low mileage, garaged recent car with documentary evidence of a good service history, or one which has been owned for a long time by a competent and consciousness DIY (do-it-yourself) mechanic who has not skimped on regular servicing. Proper maintenance includes anticipating at what point various components are likely to give problems, and replacing them before they fail. The vendors of such cars should be able to show you a series of invoices for spare parts (and labour charges if the maintenance has been carried out professionally) to prove that the car has been properly cared for.

The state of the bodywork in such cars is even more important than that of the mechanical components because, whilst a mechanical fault can mean taking the car off the road for, perhaps, one or two days whilst the fault is rectified, the rectification of body rot entails taking the car off the road for far longer - sometimes weeks, sometimes months, if the work has to be carried out on a DIY basis.

All European Beetles are now old enough to have had some bodywork repair, so assume that a viewed car will either have had such work, or will need it. As much as with any other Beetle, be vigilant when looking for camouflaged body rot and poor repair.

Accept from the outset that it's very unlikely you'll find a cheap solid and reliable Beetle: when setting a price, owners of such cars will bear in mind the maintenance, repair, new component and/or bodywork costs they have incurred on it. In the long run, it usually works out cheaper to pay a fair price for a good car than buy the cheapest you can find and suffer a constant stream of repair bills every time another tired old component breaks down.

Avoid cars which have been off the road for any length of time because, as stated previously, most mechanical, hydraulic and electrical components actually age far less when the car is in regular use than if the car is left standing. Also best avoided are cars on which the vendor has recently spent a lot of money in mechanical repair; this indicates that many components reached the end of their useful life at the same time; maybe the rest of them will similarly be in need of repair/replacement before too long?

Most large motoring associations will - for a fee - undertake mechanical and body surveys on cars on behalf of members. Motor engineers usually offer the same service. Both will give you a written report on the state of a viewed car and, if you're not confident about your ability to properly assess the condition of a prospective purchase, then the survey fee could repay itself many times over.

Be wary of cars with brand new roadworthiness test certificates: some - but by no means all - may have had the minimum of work done in order to scrape through the test (which makes them easier to sell). They could also be on the market because they are unreliable, or the owner wants to avoid looming repair bills.

A dwindling number of companies sell Beetles which they have 'sorted' the mechanics of in-house, and these usually come with a guarantee and can be safe buys. Other companies sell Beetles which they have fully restored and these, too, are a good option for those who want a reliable car. In both cases it pays to deal with companies fairly close to home; you don't want to have to drive (or trailer) the car for miles if you have problems with it.

RESTORED CARS

A good quality professional Beetle restoration will generally cost more than the car will be worth afterwards. A full and conscientious DIY restoration not only costs a lot of money, but usually involves thousands of hours of work - not all of it pleasurable. It's little wonder, then, that many would-be Beetle owners seek a ready-restored car, nor that the vendors of good restored cars very often ask high prices.

The first fact to consider is that you will not be able to buy a well restored car cheaply. If a restored car is offered at a low price, this should arouse suspicion regarding the quality of workmanship and/or the extent of the restoration work - not to mention the possibility that the car could be stolen. Apart from the vendor's natural desire to recoup as much as possible of the financial outlay involved in the restoration, a genuinely good restored car will usually attract other potential purchasers, one of whom may want the car badly enough to try and outbid you.

You should also accept that a high price is no guarantee of quality, and that a number of 'bodged' cars will inevitably come onto the market place dressed-up as quality restorations, and priced accordingly.

With professional and amateur restorers alike, it's now almost universal practice to keep a full photographic record of the work-in-progress, and it's recommended that you don't buy a 'restored' car unless you can see such a record (and satisfy yourself that the car pictured is actually the car you are buying). Don't buy unless you can see photographs of the separated body and chassis assemblies - you can't restore a Beetle to a good standard without splitting the two.

Because there is usually so much money at stake when you are buying a restored car, it may be worth commissioning a motor engineer's survey before parting with your money. Alternatively, take along a knowledgeable friend when you view cars; if you don't have a knowledgeable friend, join the nearest Beetle owner's club and quickly make friends with the most knowledgeable person you meet there!

In addition to the points made in this chapter about assessing cars, there are a few extra checks to be made in the case of restored cars. A restoration basically comprises two parts: the bodywork and the mechanical elements. It is common practice when commissioning a professional restoration, for owners to have the body restoration work carried out professionally, but to undertake the mechanical build-up themselves. It's vital that you attend to small details when examining the mechanical components and, more particularly, their fastenings. Look at the screw slots, the nuts and bolt heads. If the screw slots are distorted, if nuts and bolt heads are rounded, then the person who carried out the rebuild obviously did not possess a very good set of tools, and the state of the fastenings could well be reflected in more important, hidden areas.

Irrespective of whether the bodyshell restoration was carried out professionally or at home, it goes without saying that your inspection of it should be thorough. Rather than try to assess the body inch-by-inch, concentrate on the areas where repair panels (as opposed to full body panels) and home-made patches are commonly used. There is nothing wrong about the use of repair panels, but some people will try to weld them to existing metal which has thinned through rusting (and which will therefore be weak and/or will rust completely through in the fullness of time) instead of replacing the entire affected panel. Where you do find welded joints, assess them, and look for pores, poor penetration, and the usual welded joint faults. (See Chapter Four.)

Welded joints on external panels are usually well finished and should be invisible, so, whenever possible, try to get a look at the inside of the seam. If you find rust there, expect all repaired welded seams on the car to rust out before too long.

It doesn't matter how good a Beetle looks, you should check all of the areas described in this chapter to ensure that the restoration work is of a high standard.

CUSTOMISED CARS

There's such a wide range of off-the-shelf customisations for Beetles that it is difficult to give advice which is strictly relevant to all types. The main concern must be the build quality (because many such cars are built by amateurs), not only of the bodywork, but especially of fuel, brake, engine, and electrical components. Bear in mind that these are all possible causes of fires, which are even more serious with GRP-bodied cars than with steel-bodied cars.

All Beetle-based kit cars fall into two basic groups. Some utilise the Beetle spine/floor pan assembly and others are built up onto a special chassis. When assessing the former, always pay special attention to the spine/floor pan assembly - it could have started to rot even before the kit body was bolted on, or, in the case of a shortened chassis (Beach Buggy), the welding could be of a very poor standard and the chassis spine consequently weak. The author has seen shortened chassis/floor pans on Buggies which appear to have been crudely 'stick' (arc) welded, and which still showed evidence of burning through: the inappropriate welder burns holes through the steel which it is meant to be joining!

Begin by visiting a large Beetle gathering, so that you can see the various customs in the flesh and make a proper decision about which best suits your needs. This will also allow you to see both good and bad examples of the build quality of the custom, and enable you to quickly decide whether a car you subsequently view is a badly or well-built example. Talk to the owners of customs which take your fancy, because they will be able to give you valuable information on what to specifically look for when assessing the cars.

When viewing a customised car, be it a kit or a one-off special, try to establish whether the car meets all legal requirements, bearing in mind that, in some countries, these include the positioning of lights, number plates, etc. Also, check the car over for anything which might cause it to fail the government roadworthiness test (MoT test in the UK), which can include any projections that the tester feels might pose a hazard to other road users or pedestrians, moving parts which are exposed, or an insecure battery, etc.

The availability of any single type of custom Beetle is a fraction of that of standard cars, and the pressure to buy a viewed example 'before someone else gets it' is greater. Don't rush into a purchase as to do so is nearly always a mistake. If you have any cause for doubt about a viewed car and the vendor begins to get pushy, leave the car alone and console yourself with the thought that: A) You could probably build a better one yourself; B) There will probably be a better example available next week; and C) Pushy vendors want you to buy before you find the fault which led to the car being on the market in the first place!

Quite a few customised Beetles come onto the market as unfinished projects. This can happen for a variety of reasons; it's important to establish which it is. Many people simply run out of money before they complete the car, a familiar occurrence in the kit car world, where those essential items - sometimes listed by the kit manufacturers as 'optional extras' - can add up to rather more than the cost of the kit, and lead to financial embarrassment for the builder. Some projects are unfinished due to a lack of time, others due to a lack of motivation to see the job through. All of these perfectly plausible reasons for selling an unfinished project custom or Beetle-based kit could be given as a cover-up for a more sinister one; the knowledge that the work done to date is in some way inferior, or the fact that the kit or custom is based on a weak chassis.

When viewing an unfinished project custom car, you really have to be very careful when assessing the build quality of the job to date. Check the floor pan (and any standard body panels which have been retained) for rot and even light rusting. Check GRP panels for signs of damage and/or repair, because someone might have accidentally dropped something onto one.

Buying an unfinished project can save a lot of money in comparison with completing a build-up yourself, but it can also lead to heartache, so tread carefully.

In the case of kit cars, you might also

Cabriolet bodyshells are rather different from those of fixed-head Beetles, having strengthening members above and below the heater channels. This is at the base of the 'A' post.

This is part of a large bracing pressing situated at the base of the 'B' post on cabriolets.

care to acquire the manufacturer's build manual (most will sell this separately) in order to familiarise yourself with the kit and the way in which it is built. This should help you to properly appraise built examples.

CONVERTIBLES

Convertible Beetles come in three varieties: Karmann originals, professional conversions, and DIY jobs. Karmann convertibles are always towards the very top end of the Beetle price range, so expect to have to pay a lot for one and assess the car as carefully as you can for the usual signs of accident damage and corrosion. Do check for authenticity, because there is money to be made from dressing up a DIY conversion as a Karmann original and selling it at a high price.

Many companies today offer a professional conversion service for the standard Beetle and, whilst cars converted in this way will not be so expensive or exclusive as a Karmann, they offer exactly the same function at a far lower price. Because the roof panels of saloon cars generally contribute greatly to the strength and rigidity of the cars, it is vital that a saloon which is made into a convertible receives some extra strengthening. In the case of a Beetle, the immensely strong chassis/floor pan assembly arguably lessens the need for extra strengthening, but the author would recommend that widely available strengthening members are welded to the heater channel assembly, and to the A-post (to prevent scuttle shake), and the rear crossmember. Professional conversion companies should do this as a matter of course, but it pays to check. The strength afforded by the sill/heater channel assembly of converted cars is vitally important in preventing the bodyshell from twisting, so this area should be assessed very thoroughly. Karmann originals also have a strengthening pressing running under the heater channel; something similar would be reassuring on a aftermarket or DIY conversion.

Most DIY saloon-to-open-top conversions will be based on a commercially manufactured kit. If you

The Karmann convertible has extra longitudinal pressings running under the heater channels to stiffen the car and make up for the absence of a roof.

are looking for a car which is based on a particular kit, then a visit to one of the larger Beetle events will enable you to talk to existing owners of converted cars, and learn enough about them to be able to assess the build quality. If you are thinking of buying a home-built convertible the first thing you should ask is whether it is based on a kit and, if so, which one? Treat non-kit DIY conversions with caution.

'LOOKERS'

By definition, a 'looker' will have a very smart external appearance, and some might even appear to have an almost perfect finish outside and in. Irrespective of the plushness and quality of the interior, and the deepness of the gloss of the paint work, cars like this can be heavily bodged examples of basically rotten bodyshells. Because the cars look so good, the asking price - and therefore the stakes - are high. Try to ignore the flash and get down to basics: give the car the most thorough bodywork and mechanical examination you can.

Check that beautiful bodywork with a magnet to discover whether it is steel or GRP and body filler! There's nothing wrong with body filler per se, but if the magnet shows no attraction whatsoever to a panel, this tells you that the thickness of the filler is such that: A) The car has been bodged; and B) The filler is likely to drop out at some point in the future because filler this thick cannot flex with the panel.

The price asked for a looker which has a lot of expensive accessories will sometimes be a reflection of the cost of those accessories, rather than the car. Apart from the very finest exceptions, the value of a non-standard Beetle rarely exceeds, and sometimes falls far below, that of a standard car in similar condition.

There's always a wide selection of custom Beetles offered for sale in the UK, so don't hurry when making a buying decision.

BAJAS

Because Bajas consist of the basic Beetle chassis and body, with sundry GRP bolt-on and bonded panels which contribute nothing to the strength of the body as a whole, the body/chassis can be appraised using exactly the same routine as for a standard Beetle.

The main point to bear in mind when looking for a Baja is that some - but by no means all - will have seen some fairly heavy duty off-road use, and the worst of these could have camouflaged underbody/steering/suspension damage. In addition to this, breathing in dust-laden air will have done nothing for the engine unless good air filters were fitted. Check for off-road damage (including camouflaged damage to the roof and pillars, which results if the car is rolled and, of course, damage to the floor pans, frame head, suspension and steering). Because it is nigh-on impossible to clean all traces of fine dirt from a car, check for this in nooks and crannies. A lot of Bajas are probably - like most off-road vehicles - used only on tarmac, and it's better to go for one like this than one which has been used in the rough. There is a good selection of cars with the popular Baja modification, so don't be rushed into buying.

Because the Baja is usually raised to increase ground clearance, the effects of transaxle jacking on single-joint drive shaft cars are exaggerated, and the presence of a 'camber control' device should be reassuring! The so-called 'Z' bar fitted to the 1500cc Beetle is not, as widely supposed, an anti-roll bar, nor is it an 'equaliser' (as the author has seen it erroneously described). The Z bar only acts when the transaxle tries to lift itself from the axle shafts and, as such, is an anti-jacking device. The 1500cc Beetle is a good candidate for the Baja conversion because of this.

Be especially careful when assessing a Baja for road legality. In particular and with regard to the UK MoT roadworthiness test, the wheels must not protrude beyond the wheelarches, and no moving part of the engine should be exposed.

WHERE TO LOOK

When you have decided which variety of Beetle you want, the problem arises of where to begin looking for your dream car, who to buy it from, and roughly how much to pay for it.

Beetles for sale are, of course, widely advertised in national magazines and on the Internet, and might, at first sight, seem as good a place as any to begin your search. Unfortunately, because such magazines are distributed nationally, they attract advertisements from all over the country. If you are in the market for a comparatively rare, original UK RHD Karmann convertible, then the national press might be the best (perhaps only) source because it will be the only place where you can find a reasonable selection to choose from. If you're seeking one of the more common variants, then you might as well begin looking nearer to home, and with good reason.

Vendors of Beetles often arrive at an asking price by reference to one of the published classic car value guides in a classic car magazine (although some are misled by agreed value insurance figures - more on this later). This can cause the buyer certain problems. Firstly, the guides often differ from each other in the values they ascribe to particular cars (the author has seen valuations of the same car in two guides, published at the same time, where one valuation is 50 per cent higher) and, secondly, they generally value the cars in one of three groups, according to condition. Group '1' or 'A' usually refers to very clean and original cars with little or no rust, and reliable mechanical and electrical components (but not pristine concours winners). Group '2' or 'B' usually includes cars which run and possess the relevant certificate of roadworthiness (the MoT certificate in the UK), but which would benefit from a certain amount of mild mechanical repair and/or a small amount of bodywork attention. Group '3' or 'C' cars are described as those which may or may not be runners, and may or may not possess a current certificate of roadworthiness, but which do require fairly extensive mechanical and body repair to make them really usable.

Problems arise because a vendor often wrongly assumes that his or her group 3/C car is actually a group 2/B, and asks the appropriate price as indicated in a value guide. It will not be until you come to actually examine the car that the mistake - or sometimes the deliberate misrepresentation - will come to light. This is not too annoying if you have travelled only a short distance to view the car, but following a long and totally wasted drive, it can be infuriating.

If you are looking for a reasonably common Beetle variant you'll save much time, money and temper by only travelling to view cars fairly close to your home. In this case it's best to confine your search initially to local newspapers and other local publications. Word-of-mouth is also an excellent way of finding a local car. Going out and finding a Beetle before it is advertised for sale also has the advantage of allowing you to make an offer without having other potential buyers hovering in the background, ready to outbid you, which can often happen if you and they both answer an advertisement and turn up for a viewing at the same time. Another advantage of viewing locally is that many of the cars you see advertised will not be owned by Beetle enthusiasts, and the prices asked can sometimes be far more reasonable, because the non-enthusiast does not always attach any special 'classic' or other value to his or her Beetle: to such people, their Beetle is simply an old car - not a classic, nor a cult car.

In the UK, regional advertisement-only publications which specialise in used cars offer another useful media. These usually feature far more Beetles than local media, giving a much better selection at the cost of having to travel further within the region to view likely cars.

You could always place a 'wanted'

advert yourself, which should generate a selection of available cars for you to choose from. The greatest benefit of placing an advert yourself is that you will often attract responses from people who would not advertise their Beetle for sale, but who would part-exchange the car, or perhaps sell it to a relative or friend. You may also attract responses from people who were not previously thinking of selling their Beetle; in both cases, you alone will be viewing the car and there won't be other potential buyers around.

The author has noticed particular pricing trends, depending on where the cars are advertised. National magazine advertised cars tend towards the top end of their expected price range, especially cars which are advertised in the more 'upmarket' magazines, which have pages full of ads for affordable classic cars, as well as glossy editorial features on Ferraris and pre-war blown Bentleys. There are some 'man-in-the-street' type classic magazines which seek to assure readers that their own car is a classic (and that, therefore, they should continue to buy the magazine), and the advertisements in these tend to feature less extravagantly-priced cars. At the time of writing the UK Beetle/VW press appears to include the widest selection of sensibly-priced cars, and is probably the best national shop window.

The prices asked for cars in regional advertisement-only publications - in common with local newspapers - are, in general, realistic, although the occasional silly price creeps in from time-to-time.

If you want to see the very largest selection of Beetles for sale, visit one of the larger Beetle shows held throughout the summer months. Rather than having just a photograph by which to judge the car before embarking on a buying expedition, the cars are there in the flesh. Don't, incidentally, hand over money at the show (unless buying from a known bona fide dealer), but arrange to visit the vendor and carry out the transaction at his or her own house. The reason for this advice will become clear later in this chapter.

WHO TO BUY FROM

There are five sources from which to buy Beetles. 1) The vast majority of Beetles are bought and sold privately. 2) An increasing number of Beetles are sold by dealers who specialise in classic cars, a particular marque or, preferably, a particular model. 3) Relatively few Beetles nowadays find their way on to general car dealer pitches. 4) The classic car auction is a relatively modern, but growing, phenomenon at which more and more classic cars seem to be traded. 5) General motor auctions very occasionally include a good Beetle. Each source has points for and against, and is briefly discussed in the following text.

Private; looking for a bargain?

The private vendor is often sought out by potential purchasers because it's assumed that the asking price will always be lower than that asked by dealers. This is not necessarily so, for a variety of reasons.

Many vendors, misinterpreting (genuinely or otherwise) classic car value guides or insurance agreed values, ascribe ridiculously high values to their cars. Many sellers - loathe to sell their beloved Beetle but forced to do so because of financial or other reasons - add a degree of 'sentimental' value to the actual value of the car when arriving at an asking price. Some private vendors are simply avaricious, prepared to keep their Beetle on the market until they find a buyer foolish enough to pay their inflated asking price.

Buying from a private vendor can sometimes result in your getting a bargain, but the practice does carry huge risks. Private vendors of many products, certainly within the UK, are not subject to the stringent consumer protection laws by which a business selling the same item would have to abide. In the case of a privately sold motor vehicle, it is still (at the time of writing) an offence to misrepresent it, but unless the misrepresentation has been published in an advertisement, there's no proof of this. If the vendor gives a verbal rather than a written assurance that the bodywork is sound, yet the car breaks its back on the first humpback bridge you drive over, you won't be able to claim that the car was misrepresented. It is, however, an offence in the UK to sell a motor vehicle which is in a dangerous, unroadworthy condition, but unless you can prove that the car was unroadworthy at the actual time of purchase, it is very difficult to take any action against the vendor. A private vendor will usually take the position that, once money has changed hands, the car is your property, and you have driven it away, he or she has no further liability for it. If you put your foot through the floor the first time you use the brakes, you may have to resort to the legal system for redress.

Beetles are now extremely tempting targets for thieves. Not only do the cars command attractive prices, and usually find a ready market, but, even broken down for spares, they're worth real money. Most classic cars that are stolen and offered for sale (certainly in the UK) seem to be the target of a type of organised crime called 'ringing,' where a car of a specific year and colour is stolen. In order to sell the car, the thief has to give it a new identity, which he can do in one of two ways. Firstly, he can take the registration document and number, engine, and any other identification numbers of a scrapped example of the vehicle and simply replace the various identification plates on the stolen car (the 'ringer'). Secondly, he can apply for a duplicate registration document for an existing and perfectly legitimate example of the car (usually one which lives many miles away from the scene of the sale), then buy number plates and other identification plates to create another seemingly legitimate example.

Ringing is far more likely to occur with later cars, because there are so many still in circulation. Of course, with the value of all Beetles likely to continue increasing, there could come a day when it would be financially viable for a thief to respray a ringer - if unable to steal one in the right colour - to match his seemingly legitimate documentation. At the time of writing, however, Beetle values are such that there does not seem to be a real threat of this happening.

Your best guard against buying a ringer is to ask to see not only the current owner's receipt of purchase, but also a current or last tax disc, test certificate, and insurance document, relevant to the vehicle and owner respectively. A vendor who cannot immediately supply these documents can't have used the vehicle for some considerable time, or may never have run it at all if it is a ringer.

Perhaps the safest private vendor to buy from would be a member of a local Beetle club, or a local branch of a nationally-based Volkswagen owners' club. The enthusiasts who belong to these clubs will often have already verified that the car was legitimate when they bought it. Alternatively, few thieves would risk advertising in club literature, so cars offered for sale through advertisements in club magazines should also, in theory, be safer buys.

To summarise: buying from a private vendor rarely means getting a car at a bargain price, and can be risky.

Specialist dealers

There are certain to be a few rogues among specialist Beetle dealers, just as there are in any other trade or calling, although the dodgy specialist car dealer is usually fairly easy to spot. A good dealer will have repair, and possibly restoration, facilities with which he can honour the terms of whatever guarantee he gives. A dubious dealer will not. A good dealer will usually have proper premises, whilst a dubious dealer will often be found operating from a barn, a small lockup, or even his own front room.

A good dealer will usually specialise in a particular marque, model or type of car, which he knows well enough to properly appraise, whilst a dubious dealer will take anything that comes his way. Without specialist knowledge, he will be vulnerable to being sold poorly restored cars, fakes, and unroadworthy vehicles. A good dealer will avoid such cars, because he knows that, to sell just one, could cost him his reputation.

It's important to establish whether a dealer is honest and reputable. You'll also want the assurance of a worthwhile guarantee to the authenticity, legality, and roadworthiness of a car before you part with your money. If you buy from a rogue, redress will be difficult to achieve.

There is another type of dealer which should be avoided at all costs. This is the individual who trades cars from his own residential premises, usually unofficially. These people often come from the ranks of classic car enthusiasts who, having bought and sold a few cars and made a profit from the activity, try to build it up into a lucrative sideline. They cannot offer guarantees, which would be worthless in any case as they have no facilities to repair the cars. These people are probably breaking various trading laws, as well as avoiding taxes; if they quite happily defraud the authorities, they will just as happily cheat you, the customer. Avoid them at all costs.

Be guided by other Beetle enthusiasts in your choice of dealer, because there are a number of very competent and totally honest small businesses which restore Beetles and offer them for sale. These companies are well known, and their reputation is a pretty good guarantee.

General car dealerships

General used car dealerships do not usually welcome a Beetle on their forecourts, or in their showrooms, for the simple reason that it would probably be the only one amongst a sea of modern vehicles, and therefore very unlikely to sell. General dealers will take Beetles in part-exchange against newer cars, but are often then disposed of through the trade, i.e. sold on to a business that specialises in this type of car, or sent off to the nearest car auction.

The fact that Beetles do occasionally enter the mainstream used car trade can be an advantage for anyone who lives in or near a large town. Simply visit or telephone the car dealer(s) and explain that you wish to buy a particular type of Beetle. The dealer will be certain to let you know the moment he has one, because he can sell it to you for a far higher price than he could get through the trade. The price in question, incidentally, would almost certainly be negotiable, and you may be able to haggle the price down and get a bargain in this way.

Classic car auctions

Classic car auctions have been around for years, but it's only since the start of the classic car boom of the 1980s that there have been so many. In the UK there seems to be an auction taking place somewhere every weekend in summer.

The drawbacks to buying from an auction are that you do not have the opportunity to test drive the car, or place it on ramps or over a pit for a close inspection. However, a practised eye can rule out many cars on the grounds of poor bodywork with a minimal visual inspection, and most auctioneers seem to build a 'cooling off' period into their terms of business contract so that, if the loom catches fire when you turn on the ignition to drive the car away, you can back out of the deal.

Classic car auctions attract many very knowledgeable people (and a great number who merely kick tyres and check to see whether the ashtray is full). By listening to the comments of the more expert appraisals, you can glean much useful information about individual cars. Be careful not to get caught doing this, just in case the person giving you a free lesson in car appraisal notices and starts giving out false information!

Auctions are terrible places for impetuous people to shop. In the heat of the moment many buyers get completely carried away, and really need a level-headed companion to keep them in check. Try to take along an experienced Beetle enthusiast who can give you reasoned advice, just in case your enthusiasm takes over completely!

General car auctions

Nobody visits general car auctions expecting to see good examples of the Beetle, so nobody much bothers to enter them in general auctions. Occasionally, a company liquidation, or the auctioning of goods and chattels from an estate, might be the reason a Beetle is entered in a general car auction. In the main, though, a Beetle will be in a general auction because it has proved impossible to sell elsewhere. Avoid these events.

HOW MUCH TO PAY?

A Beetle, like any classic car, has three values: the value to the seller, the value to the buyer and, usually somewhere in-between, the purchase price. Beetles cannot have such accurate published value guides as current and recent cars; Beetles are now old cars, and the value of the individual example will be most heavily influenced by its condition, irrespective of any arbitrary figure which might be ascribed to its year and which model it is.

The entire classic/recreational car market is in a constant state of flux, and so it is important that your cash offer is based on current pricing trends. There are several ways of obtaining current information. Some classic car magazines include value guides and, whilst these can sometimes prove slightly out, they do, over a period of some months, serve to show which way the market is moving.

Some vendors will base their asking price on an insurance valuation. Valuations carried out for insurance purposes are not to be taken too seriously. Some of the figures involved are arrived at by a valuer whose only experience of the individual car is a set of photographs - and you can't tell the condition, and hence the value of a car, simply by looking at photographs. Apart from any other consideration, who is to say that the car in the photographs is not another example in better condition, and only wearing the number plates from the actual vehicle? Some agreed values might be based on some kind of report prepared by a garage business, or other valuer, on behalf of the insurance company, but they cannot be relied on either as it's not possible to rule out collusion between the vendor and the valuer.

More accurate pricing information is usually available from owner's clubs, which may either be published by the club magazines or, in some circumstances, given out on request. Alternatively, a local club will doubtless have some members who keep an eye on Beetle prices, and they may be persuaded to share their information with a fellow member.

If you have the time and inclination, monitoring adverts across a wide range of platforms (Beetle/VW magazines, local newspapers, and regional advertisement-only publications) will enable you to build up a picture of what money is being asked for what cars. Concentrate only on the particular Beetle which interests you, and within a couple of months you could be as knowledgeable about Beetle values as any authority.

The author prefers to use the following method to value cars. Firstly, he decides how much he can afford, then what he would regard as a fair price to pay for the car he is seeking in the condition he requires. When viewing a car, he lists all of the components which need renewal, plus any other work required (or which will require attention in the near future). He prices this and subtracts the total from the figure he considers a fair value for the car when all of the repairs have been carried out, to arrive at the value of the car to him.

ASSESSING BODYWORK

Because the Beetle is blessed with that rugged spine chassis, the strength of many pressings and assemblies - particularly the sill/heater channel assemblies - is arguably not quite as vital as it is on monocoque-bodied cars. However, the only real difference between the two (apart from

It's important to learn to distinguish between rusted steel and rust stain, which can be seen here. The rust that caused this stain is nothing to do with the heater channels but has washed from inside the door.

The heater channels and front and rear crossmembers form a strong framework for the bodyshell. The fact that they sit on a spine chassis does not diminish their contribution to the overall strength of the car.

perpetually misted windscreens on Beetles with rotten heater channels!) is that the Beetle which has rotten sills but a sound spine chassis is unlikely to suffer distortion capable of moving suspension mounting points, whereas the monocoque bodyshell with rotten sills can easily be bent to the point that the suspension mountings front and rear move, making the car unsafe to drive and necessitating the aid of a jig for the repair work. The work involved in rectifying body rot on the Beetle can be as difficult and time-consuming as the same work on any car. When assessing the bodywork of a Beetle which you intend to buy, therefore, it pays to be thorough. The suspension mounting points of the Beetle can, it should be noted, be bent in a frontal collision. A bent or misaligned front axle is a sure sign that, not only has the car been involved in a heavy collision, but also that the damage repair was less than thorough. Do bear in mind that it is usually more difficult and time-consuming to repair bodged bodywork repairs than it is to deal with honest-to-goodness rot. Furthermore, there can be little more dispiriting than to discover that a car is heavily bodged only after you have started work on what you believed to be a straightforward restoration. Once you discover just one shoddy bodywork repair, you really have no option but to strip the entire body in order to find all similarly bodged panels.

One last point in this preamble: Beetles with sound floor pans, front crossmembers, A and B posts, rear body mounting panels, bumper brackets and heater channels, etc., will never come cheaply, and, in the experience of the author (and this is confirmed by BSW worshop manager Terry Ball), Beetles that are offered at low prices always require welded repair or replacement of one or more of these components. Beetles sound in these vital areas, but which may have poor paintwork and tatty interiors, can often be found advertised at prices similar to those of cars with plenty of rot on the inside but gloss on the outside and plush interior trim. Given a choice between the two, take the former.

When you go to view a car, you will

Check the rear roof pillar area for rivelling, which might indicate that the car has been rolled and badly repaired. The swage line and the seam are difficult to make look good, so pay especial attention to them.

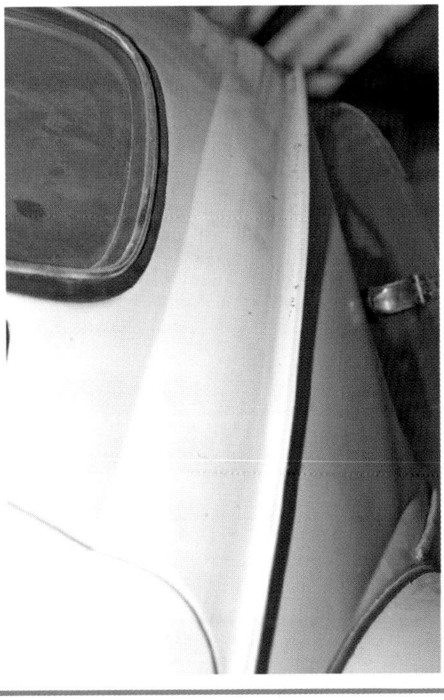

Test the front screen pillar for body filler using a magnet. Anything other than the thinnest skim of filler indicates either collision damage or non-welded rot 'repair.' If the magnet is not in the least attracted to any area of the roof pillar, reject the car.

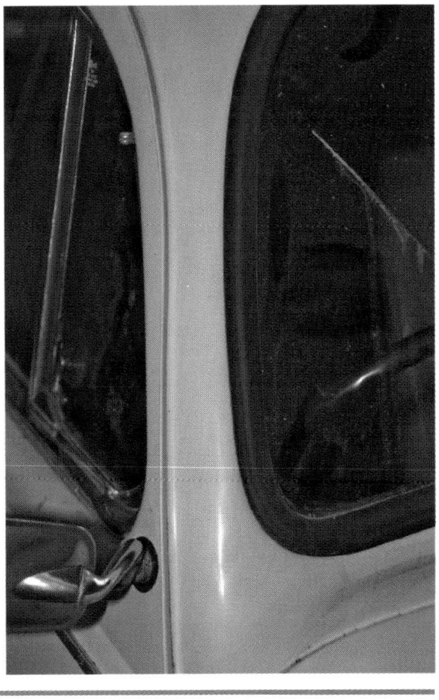

need to take the following: a notebook and pen to note down any faults you find (this list of faults may ultimately be long enough to put you off a car - or give you a useful bargaining tool); a magnet to test for body filler; a jack and a pair of axle stands; a torch to help you see into dark crevices, and a sharp implement, such as an old screwdriver, which you can prod into suspect metal to see whether it is sound or rotting. A pair of goggles, gloves and overalls will be needed if the inspection gets serious and you climb under the car. Before getting dirty, however, you might care to examine the external panels; what you discover there may rule out the car before you have to don overalls.

Begin your inspection by examining the visible external body panels for signs of rivelling - corrugations usually caused by heat build-up during gas welding, but also possibly a sign of badly finished body filler which is hiding collision damage. You can spot rivelling best by looking along the panel concerned just a few inches above its surface; this will also allow you to see dents more clearly. If the paintwork is covered with a thin layer of grime (giving it a matt finish), you won't be able to see any but the largest dents, so ask the vendor to give dirty panels a wipe with a damp cloth in order for you to be able to examine them.

Pay particular attention to the roof panel and pillars. Because quite a few Beetles have been rolled onto their roofs, courtesy of the back end breaking away on hard cornering, some cars will have dents that have been roughly beaten out and filled with body filler. Some bodgers don't bother to beat out roof dents because this entails removing the head lining - and the worst won't even clean and key the surface for the filler. If there's more than the thinnest skim of filler on the roof panel (or, indeed, any other panel), suspect that the work is of a very poor standard. If you find any evidence of filler in the roof pillars other than a very thin skim covering a welded repair to the windscreen aperture lip, the car has probably been rolled and should be avoided.

On de-seamed cars check for heavy use of filler around the areas where the seams used to be. If a thick layer of filler is found here, chances are that de-seaming the car entailed hammering the seams inwards and flushing over the body filler! Check de-seamed roof pillars with a magnet, because many will have been brazed rather than welded, and braze is not nearly strong enough. In fact, it would be advisable to steer clear of any de-seamed car unless the vendor can provide a photographic record of the de-seaming, clearly showing the standard of workmanship and the materials and methods used.

The proper way to de-seam is to cut/grind away a short length of seam and weld the two edges together before grinding the next length of seam. However, some people might braze the joint, and that's simply not strong enough, so check the de-seamed area with a magnet to establish that there is weld underneath rather than brass.

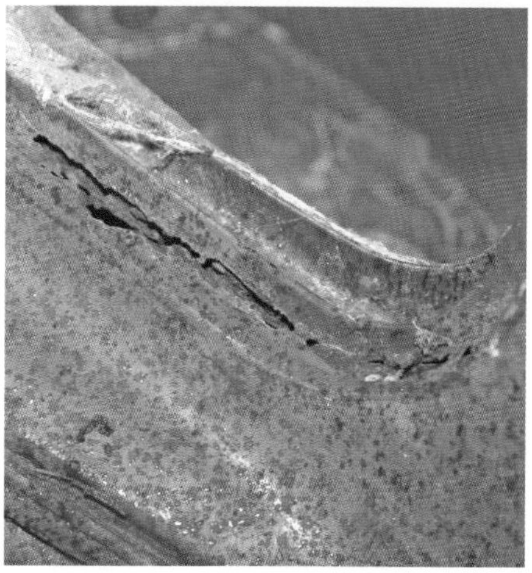

This rotten area is typical (not only on the Beetle, but on most old cars) and is usually caused by perished window rubbers.

Perished window seals allow water in which, inevitably, leads to rot.

Whilst checking the roof and pillars, check the metal near the window rubbers, because if the window has been replaced without sealant, water will have entered the rubber seal and caused rusting of the metal lip underneath. In time, this will spread under the paintwork surrounding the rubber. If this area is freshly painted, incidentally, it's probably hiding rusting of the metal lip - not too difficult a repair apart from refitting the screen afterwards, but nevertheless an indication that the car has been 'tarted-up' for sale. If the window seals are in poor condition, expect to find some rusting from within on panels underneath; if the door window rubber is perished, for instance, then rusting out of the door skin and door bottom is likely.

On the subject of doors, check for filler and GRP repairs right in the middle of the door skin, because there is a panel behind this which holds water against the skin. Carefully check door gaps and the hinges and their surrounds for evidence of force being used to make the door fit - tell-tale signs are spacers or even washers hammered in front of the hinge to force it backwards, buckling of the skin adjacent to the hinge (either crash damage or extreme force when fitting the door), and obviously damaged paintwork on the hinges.

Lift the front (luggage compartment) lid: if you are immediately greeted by the smell of petrol either the fuel tank or filler/expansion pipes are leaking, and the car should not be run until the problem has been identified and cured. Disconnect the battery immediately and inform the vendor of the problem and the dangers of using the car, smoking in the vicinity, etc.

Check that the lid seal is in position and in good condition, and examine the edge seams for rust; if you discover any, you may well also find that the luggage

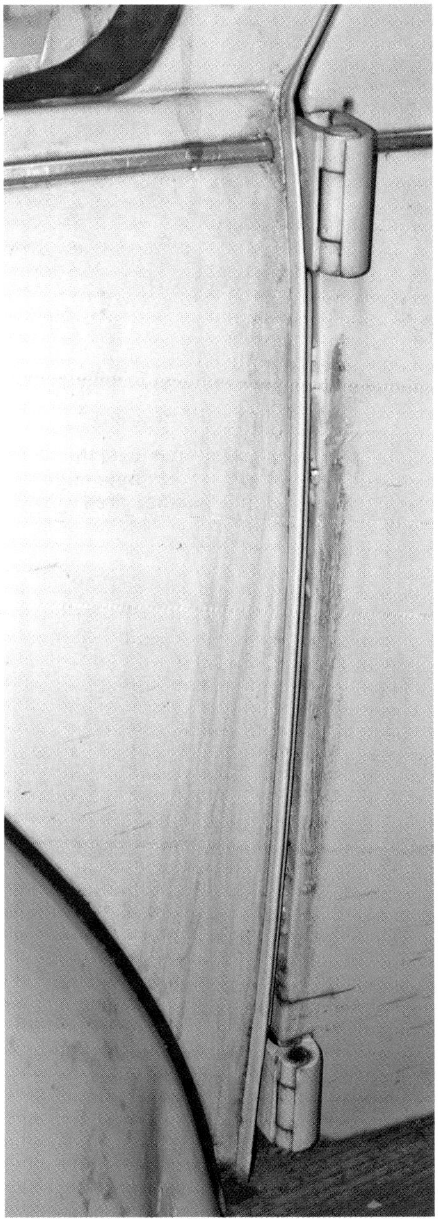

Door hinges rust. If you find a rust stain like this you can safely assume that the car has not been smartened up to deceive you, but has been standing for a long time.

Under the luggage bay lid check the state of the wiring, the spare wheel well floor for rot, the flitch panels, and washer bottle recess. See text for what to do if you smell fuel here.

This front indicator feed wire and earth should run through a grommet that prevents them chafing against the edge of the hole in the flitch. If they're not, it should set alarm bells ringing, because a breakdown of insulation caused by chafing can blow a fuse or - on a non-fused circuit, start an electrical fire.

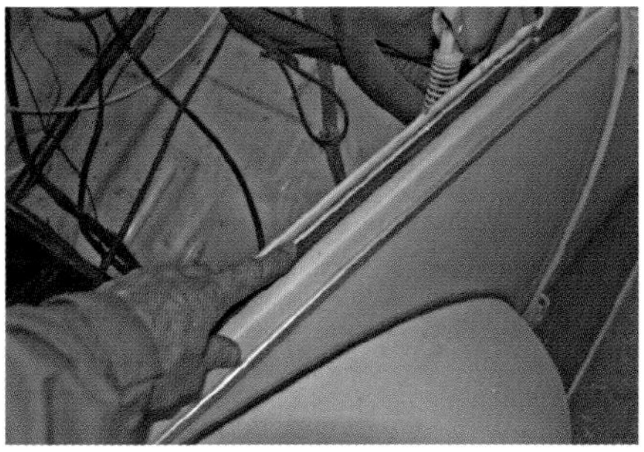

The luggage bay side seal retaining strip is a common victim of rust and, unless the strip is cut away and a new one fitted, sooner or later rust returns.

Brake fluid is a very effective paint stripper, so spillage around the reservoir gives rust an easy way to get established. The rust stains on the flitch panel above the reservoir are due to condensation. The rust visible in this photograph is only surface rust, so can be dealt with by sanding back to bare metal and repainting.

floor and/or the side channels are rusted. If rusting of the visible section of the luggage floor is bad, expect to have to either patch or replace this pressing (the latter is a difficult task, because only LHD versions appear to be available), and probably also the inner wing/flitch panels at the same time (a task for only advanced DIY-ers). The spare wheel well will normally also be rusted if the luggage floor is, and, if you find that the spare wheel well has recently been replaced on a car which has bad rusting of the adjacent pressings, you will probably also discover that all bodywork

Remove the spare wheel and check out the bottom and sides of the spare wheel well, which rusts from the top and from underneath. If this area has been sprayed recently, check carefully to ascertain whether the paint is covering new steel or a non-ferrous bodge, and reject the car if it turns out to be the latter.

Typical rot inside the spare wheel well means that a difficult repair is needed, which will include the front valance, spare wheel well, washer bottle platform, and lower front flitch repair panels. What you see here is a mixture of rot and GRP.

This windscreen washer bottle platform is thoroughly rotten. Repair panels are available.

Above: The area surrounding the strut top on McPherson strut Beetles should be carefully examined, because it needs to be immensely strong. When it rots it is often plated, and the proper panels are either expensive or not widely available.

Incredible. Various patches have been welded around the - presumably - rotten remains of the 'A' post. Not only does this weaken the bodyshell, but also means that rot will spread to the new steel very quickly. When you see evidence of butchery of this level on a car you MUST assume that other areas which have received this sort of attention will be equally poor.

Below: 'Repairs' like this are, sadly, not uncommon. The heater channel has had a patch welded along the top section under the door aperture, the side of the heater channel appears to be largely body filler, and the 'B' post does not even reach the terrible repair sections - yet the car has been resprayed.

The surface rust in the doorstep could be a problem, and a prod with a screwdriver will reveal if it is rusted thin.

"The demisters don't work" is a familiar cry of anguish from owners of elderly Beetles, and this picture shows why they often don't. Note the huge pile of rust flakes on the floor and the cover panels welded onto the heater channel.

Although the front end of the heater channel air duct on this car was all but rotted away at the 'A' post, the duct under the 'B' post is remarkably sound. However, the heater channel has had at least one new base welded on, and probably two.

If you see anything resembling this don't buy the car! Outer and inner 'repair' sections have been welded over rotten heater channels, and the repairer has not even bothered to try and hide the welded seam before giving this unfortunate Beetle a complete respray.

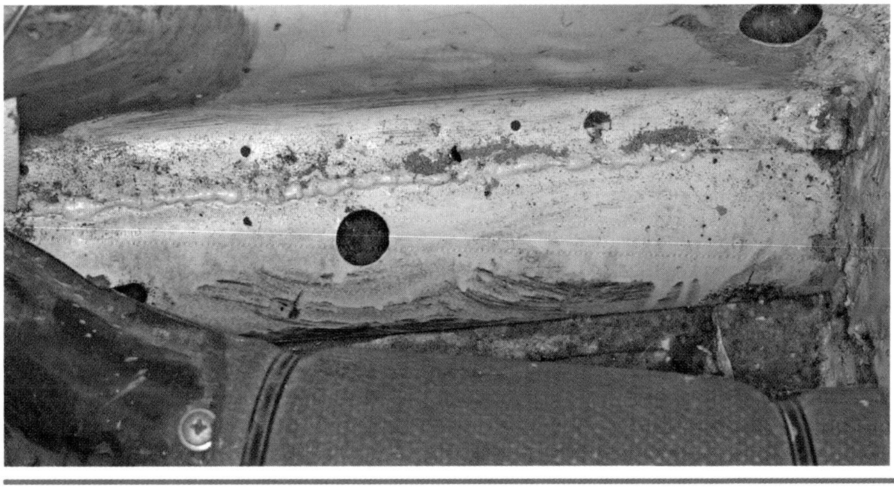

This car was not given a bare-metal respray, but does have good, renewed heater channels. It's not unusual to find a car with a first-class paint job but rot in the structural steel, so never buy a 'restored' car without checking the heater channels, spine, and frame head.

repairs throughout the car have involved welding good metal next to bad, so that a total rebuild is called for.

On cars fitted with McPherson strut front suspension, the loadings from the concentric spring damper unit (i.e. the shocks transmitted from bumps in the road) are fed into the flitch panels. Any rusting or signs of patching/bodging in these panels – especially in the vicinity of the strut top mountings – is to be considered very serious. Don't go by looks alone, because it is not unknown for these vital areas to be smartened with GRP and body filler – check for metal using a magnet and, if you have any cause for doubt regarding the strength of the area or if you find any evidence of body filler it is best to reject the car or to consider it as a restoration project only. Flitch panel replacement for McPherson strut cars is possible but the panels are very expensive and the repair is one of the most difficult (and expensive) jobs in Beetle restoration, and in reality the province of the professional and specialist restorer.

Open the doors, and examine them for signs of rusting; in addition to the centre of the panel as already described, also check the lower quarter of the skin and the door base. Attempting to lift the doors will reveal whether there is too much play in the hinges. The A and B posts rot at their bases, so check for signs of rusting and for camouflaged rot and shoddy welded patch repairs. If the sill/heater channel assembly appears to be in better condition than the bottoms of the A and B posts, this indicates that the heater channel was welded onto rusted steel, and means that both will probably have to be renewed together - a time-consuming task. The side of the car between the B post and rear wheelarch tends to rot at its base, so, again, if the heater channel appears to be in better condition than this panel, the car has been bodged.

Inside the car, the most obvious area to find rust is the sill/heater channel assembly and the floor pans. It's common (though not good) practice to patch repair the heater channels, especially on cars which have rot in adjacent bodywork, such as the door posts and car side. If the heater channel is patch repaired, expect to find rot in the whole assembly; if the heater channel alone has been replaced, count on having to rebuild the lot at a future date. If the heater channel has been repaired or replaced, look for signs of burnt rubber, which will be the remains of the belly pan gasket! If the car is carpeted, this will have to be lifted out; if you discover that the carpet is glued to the heater channels, either ask permission to remove it so that the channel can be examined thoroughly, or assume that new heater channels will be required. The same goes for the floor pan and, if the carpet is glued down, at the very least you should be able to lift the outer edges (which is where rot is most likely to be).

The one area where rot is considered terminal on a Beetle is the spine, so you must be able to lift the inner edge of the

If the carpets have been glued over the heater channels, this is what they might be hiding, so don't buy unless you can lift the carpet, or are prepared to renew the heater channels.

The bulk of the parcel shelf - seen here from underneath - rusts but rarely rots, though the outer edges are suspect and should be prodded to check for weakness, GRP 'repair,' and the like. Fortunately, the panel can be checked from inside the car.

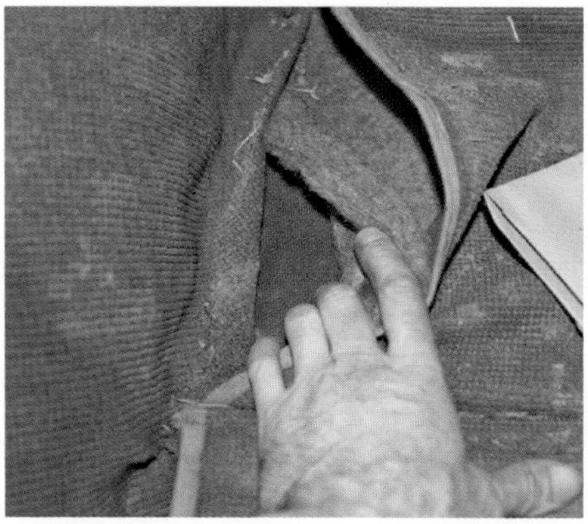

The boot floor panel is situated behind the rear seat. Lift the carpet and check the outer edges; if you find rot there, the inner rear wing will probably also have it.

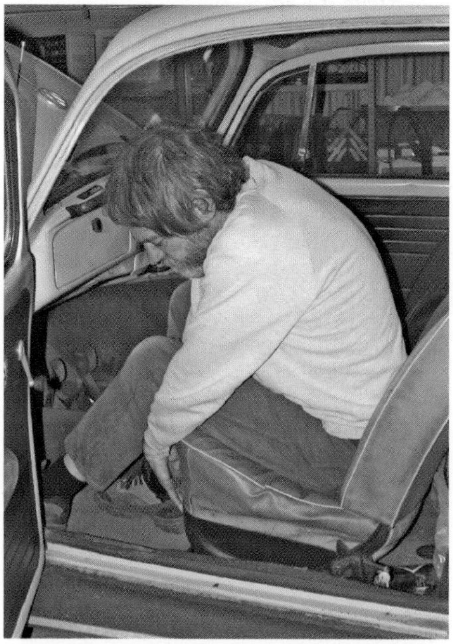

Check the floor pan strength by sitting in each of the front seats, grabbing the lower front edge of the seat with both hands, and pushing on the floor with your feet.

There's a drain hole immediately above the jacking point and, when it rusts, many people weld a plate over it. Plugging a drain hole, of course, accelerates rusting, which is why so many jacking points crumble when you attempt to use them. Major surgery is then called for, meaning a body-off restoration.

Raise the car using the jacking point - gently, because it's common for the metal above the jacking points to be so weak that the jacking point crumples upward. Some mechanics won't use the proper jacking point on the Beetle because so many on old Beetles simply crumple! Always chock the wheels that remain on the ground.

carpet to inspect it. The spine rots in a line just above the floor pan inner edge. If you find rot here then the car needs a new rolling chassis.

Lift the carpet and/or sound-deadening material from the rear parcel shelf and check the state of the metal. Rust here indicates a long-term problem with a leaking rear window rubber, and is usually dealt with by patching - far from ideal. The only really satisfactory way to deal with a rotted parcel shelf is complete replacement, along with the adjoining panels which will usually also have rotted - in other words, a bodyshell-off restoration.

If the floor is suspected of being weak, but a close inspection is not possible because of carpet glued to the topside and underseal underneath, sit in each front seat in turn, hold the sides of the seat firmly and push downwards with your feet. A rotten floor pan will flex considerably under such provocation, and you might even hear cracking sounds as rust flakes break loose. A rotten floor pan, or even a partly rotten one, means a bodyshell-off restoration. As an example of the lengths some people will go to in order to dress up a rotten Beetle, Terry Ball tells me he has found floorpans on an outwardly respectable Beetle that consisted largely of GRP - beautifully finished to match the contours of the original, but GRP nonetheless, and a sign that the car needed extensive bodywork repair.

Still on the subject of the sill/heater channel, one thing you can check without getting your hands dirty is the condition of the jacking point. When rotten, these collapse up into the heater channel. A common 'repair' is to weld a sturdy steel

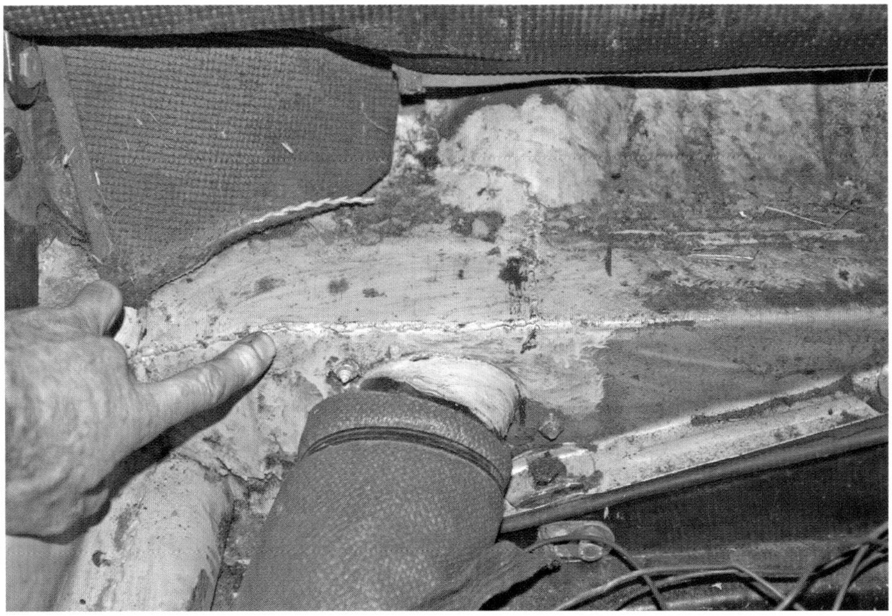

The heel board/rear crossmember outer edge has been repaired using steel plates - not ideal.

This battery platform appeared okay at first sight from inside the cab, but a good wire brushing revealed perforations, most easily visible from underneath. The only way to find this on a car you're thinking of buying is to poke at the steel with a sharp instrument - if the vendor objects then reject the car. This will have to be renewed: a battery must be securely held.

plate onto the heater channel base above the jacking point; this panel will effectively have sealed off the drain hole and the heater channel can be expected to rust through in record time afterwards! Later in the examination of the car you will have to jack it up in order to see underneath; if you hear crunching sounds as the jack begins to take the weight of the car, find alternative jacking points rather than risk being blamed for pushing up the jacking point and crushing the heater channel, which is likely to happen. In fact, if the jacking point does start to creak as you attempt to raise the car, reckon on having to renew heater channels, and probably much more besides.

Before leaving the subject of the heater channel assembly and floor pans, it's been known for these to be welded together, whereas they should really be bolted. If you discover that the heater channels are welded to the florpans, this indicates that the car has been most horribly bodged and is worth very little because of the amount of work required to put it right.

When heater channels are replaced, the correct method involves lifting off the bodyshell, complete with remnants of old channels, bolting new channels onto the floors, then cutting the old channels from the bodyshell and lowering the shell back onto the chassis for welding to the heater channels. If this sequence is not followed, the holes in the floor pan and heater channel assembly don't line up, with the result that either the heater channels are welded to the floor pan as already described, or new holes are drilled in the floor edge to accept the heater channel fixing bolts. Some cars have extremely enlarged or multiple holes along the floor pan edge because of this. Not a problem in itself, but a sure sign of shoddy restoration which will, no doubt, be repeated throughout the rest of the car.

Still inside the car, examine the rear crossmember at its outer edges where the heater ducting is connected to the heater channel; this is one of the most frequently encountered Beetle-bodge areas, and rust

Splits in the engine bay rubber seal can allow exhaust fumes to enter the engine bay, and hence the air intake. Best renew it.

This is the major rear bodyshell mounting. The panel, as a whole, is a notorious rot-spot, so probe with a screwdriver. This is all you can see with the wheel in place.

This rust stain looks dreadful but is really nothing serious. The rear lamp unit and mount can easily be removed, and the steel underneath cleaned bright and repainted.

The rear crossmember (heel board) edges are a common spot to find bodged repairs. If this area is weak, expect to find rot in vital adjacent panels.

This is the whole of the rear bumper mounting panel. Replacing it is not an especially difficult job but, if this panel has rotted, except the adjacent panelwork to be rotten, also. You can't weld to rot!

This is the whole of the reinforcing panel, which includes the rear body mounting point. If you find rot anywhere on this panel, but the rear body mounting bracket appears okay, it has been bodged to make it look good.

Right: When placing axle stands, watch out for anything that could be damaged when the car is lowered onto the stands, such as this grease nipple.

here is commonly dealt with by GRP, or even body filler and wire mesh! Welded repairs to this area would certainly destroy the belly pan gasket, so, for a proper repair, the body has to come off the car.

Lift the engine lid and examine the seal, then the folded lips for signs of rusting; also examine the air intake grille. The rear panel (valance) is prone to rot, so check for the use of filler and GRP. Check the fit of the engine bay to valance gasket - gaps indicate that a new rear valance has at some time been welded on in the wrong position.

Before jacking the car, clean all of the dirt from the rear body to damper casting mounting points within the rear wheelarches. This is a prime rot spot, so give it a good stabbing with a blunt instrument. If rot is found here, expect to also find it in the rear bumper mounts, the heater channel closing panels, and most probably the heater channel/sill assemblies. Be extra careful when feeling for rot around the bumper mounting points, because sharp edges can make a mess of your hand.

Crumpled bumpers obviously indicate collision damage: perhaps less obviously, you should look for distortion of the flitch panels and engine bay/rear inner wing areas, which can also reveal collision damage. If you find evidence of collision damage, check the fit of the doors carefully, because heavy damage will have dictated that, if the door gaps are to look right, the hinges and idoor surround would have come in for some heavy duty bodging.

UNDERNEATH

Apply the handbrake, chock the rear wheels and raise the front end of the car with a jack placed under the track control arm pressing, then support the car on axle stands. Examine the frame head. Rot here is very expensive and time-consuming to deal with and, in most cases, will entail a full strip down to a bare chassis before it can be properly dealt with. Any sign of collision damage on the frame head or axle (torsion bar cars), or the flitch panels of McPherson strut cars, should be taken very seriously because suspension mounting points could have been disturbed. In cases such as these, it will pay to commission a motor engineer's report if you are still interested in the car.

Turn the wheels from lock-to-lock so that you can examine the flitch panels (inner

Raising and supporting the front end of the car. The jack is a lifting device, and should not be used to support the car while you're working on it - use axle stands. I favour placing the stands under the beam axle, which is very stable, yet gives plenty of working space around the wheels/brakes.

The lower edge of the flitch panel rots and will, at some stage, have been replaced or repaired - most are repaired. Your job is to determine how well the repair was done. If the rot was simply covered up by repair panels, putting matters right will be a very difficult business. If the rot was cut out and new steel welded in, as here, it's a fairly straightforward job to repair it.

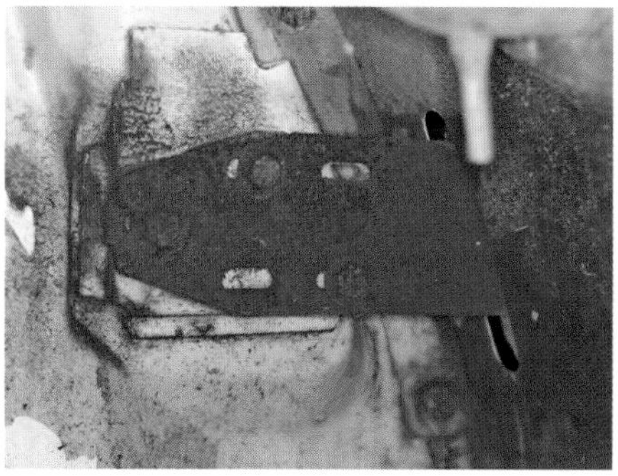

The front bumper mounting. The steel to which the mounting bracket is welded is rot-prone, being the side of the spare wheel well, so have a prod with a screwdriver to check the steel is sound. The base of the panel is usually the first area to rot. Also check for signs of collision damage, which will buckle the area.

wings); rotted flitch panels are not only a very difficult repair, but also indicate a strong likelihood of serious (and perhaps camouflaged) rot in adjacent panels.

Using a torch for illumination and a blunt instrument to stab with, check as best you can the underside of the luggage compartment/spare wheel well. Also check the insides of the front wings; if you find an area which appears to be thicker than the rest, this is filler.

Whilst the front of the car is raised, check the wheel bearings, brakes and steering (see mechanical examination).

Slacken the rear wheel nuts, transfer the chocks to the front wheels, raise the rear of the car and remove the road wheels. Examine the inner wheelarch area closely, probing for rot and checking for body filler or GRP, and look for creases in the panels which indicate poorly corrected rear collision damage. The rear body mounting brackets and bumper iron panels

The heater channel and floor pan edge are prime rot-spots. Be suspicious if either are covered in fresh underseal; give them a good prod to make sure they're sound.

are common rot spots, so probe around them for rot. Similarly, check the outer rear crossmember and the underside of the decking (internal rear parcel shelf). Check the inside of the valance. Check the small horizontal panels each side of the engine bay.

MECHANICAL EXAMINATION/ TEST DRIVE

Whether you undertake the mechanical examination or the test drive first is your choice. In favour of test driving first is the fact that some mechanical faults might come to light which allow you to rule out the car without getting your hands dirty! More seriously, a mechanical examination might reveal faults that would make a test drive risky, even dangerous. For this reason, the author recommends that you check the car before taking it on the road.

MECHANICAL/ELECTRICAL

Inside the car

Begin your inspection inside the car where you can remain clean and (hopefully) dry. Check all of the electrical equipment; lights, wipers, and horn. Grasp the steering wheel and try to lift and lower it; movement indicates poor mounting. Turn the steering wheel and try to ascertain how much the perimeter moves before the front wheels react. If the steering wheel turns by more than an inch or so, it could be due to slack wheel bearings, worn kingpins, a worn or maladjusted steering box/rack, or a loose mounting. If a car has a lot of null steering wheel movement, the front wheels can react freely to bumps in the road and you will have no way of knowing which way the car will jump when a front wheel hits a bump or pothole.

Check that the windscreen is free of cracks and scratches (a possible cause of roadworthiness test failure, depending on country and current standards), and that all

Strong though they are, the engine mounting legs can break. This chassis is best considered scrap.

This rusting of the bumper mount pressing area looks bad but, in reality, it's only surface rust which can be cleaned off and the area painted.

of the rubbers are in good condition (not perished and free from cracks).

Press the brake pedal and hold it down. If the pedal is spongy rather than firm, there is air in the system, which will have to be bled and the source of the air found and rectified. If the pedal sinks slowly to the toeboard the master cylinder is faulty.

Remove the rear seat base and check the condition of the wiring and the battery. Wire insulation must be intact and free from signs of scorching (indicating a short to earth fault which, if not cured, can result in the loom catching fire), and the battery should be clean, free from spillage and securely fastened. Check the electrolyte level in each cell, and use a torch to see whether the plates are buckled, in which case the battery is on the way out. Check the condition of the wiring in the vicinity of the voltage regulator (under the rear seat base, left hand side of the car), not only for damaged insulation, but also for melting of the insulators of sleeves, which happens when new heater channels, or a lower quarter repair panel, are welded in wrongly or carelessly. If you find welding damage to the wiring, reject the car.

Check all seat belt mounting points by tugging on the belts, and also check the condition of the seat belt fabric and mechanism because frayed or damaged belts are an MoT failure point.

Establish that window winders, screen washers, and all instruments work. Are the sun visors firmly held in the upright position (you don't want them dropping down

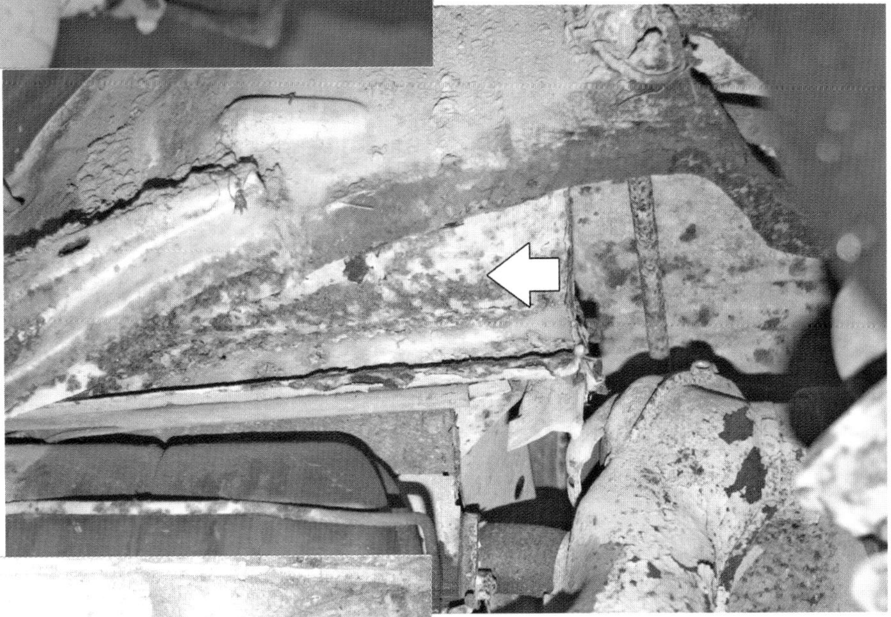

This is the underside of one of the panels that runs along each edge of the engine bay, but which cannot be seen from inside the bay because it's covered by sound-deadening material. Checking the condition means getting down under the car. Rust is normal - check for rot by proding the panels with a screwdriver.

This is the battery platform on the author's car after it had been standing for a couple of years. It looks dreadful, but all that rust is only on the surface, so all that's needed is a clean up and a lick of paint.

unexpectedly), and do winding windows open and close without too much winding effort - renewing winder mechanisms isn't easy? Check that the doors close properly and stay shut.

Outside the car

'Bounce' each corner of the car; push it sharply downwards and let go so that the suspension pushes upwards. If the corner rises, falls and rises again then the damper is faulty. This is a very unscientific test, and damper problems are more readily detectable on the road (vague handling and a tendency to rock backward and forward on acceleration or braking). If, however, bouncing the car indicates ineffectual dampers, don't drive the car on the road, because worn dampers reduce tyre grip to an unbelievable degree.

Then move to the engine bay. Firstly, if there's a strong smell of petrol, and the fuel delivery system is leaking, immediately disconnect the battery and don't run the engine until the cause has been found and dealt with. Grasp the crankshaft pulley firmly and try to move it backwards and forwards; if the movement (crankshaft end float) is much greater than 0.005in (0.13mm) the engine requires attention. An alternative way to test the end float is to get a helper to depress the clutch pedal whilst you watch for movement of the pulley. Try to lift the crankshaft pulley to test for worn mains; if the pulley can be pulled up and down, the crankcase will probably have to be align bored and the crankshaft probably reground - an expensive repair.

If you have a compression tester, use it! Remove all four sparkplugs (marking the leads if you are unsure of which goes where), and pull the king HT lead from the coil turret. Have an assistant turn the engine over on the starter motor whilst you check in turn the compression for each cylinder. This normally runs in the range of 100-142 pounds per square inch. If one or more cylinders are lower than the rest, apply a little engine oil through the plug hole (to seal the piston rings) and recheck. If the pressure is now okay, the problem lies with leakage between the piston rings and cylinder bores. If the low pressure persists this means that the leakage is past a valve stem, and a cylinder head overhaul will be needed.

Check the engine oil level and the condition of the oil; if you don't know what signs to look for, take along someone who does! Check the condition of the sparkplugs, leads, distributor cap (look for minute splits), and the points (check that the surfaces are level and not pitted). The general condition of the engine bay can tell you a lot about a car. If it's dirty and covered with oil, maintenance has obviously been a low priority. The Beetle

If the crankshaft pulley can be moved up and down an engine build might be on the cards, because this indicates worn main bearings. Forward and backward movement of more than 0.13mm (0.005in) also indicates a worn engine.

Left: Take a look inside the distributor cap. That condensation is not a good sign because it can lead to misfiring by redirecting the HT charge. Also, it's clear that this is a fairly old cap, which suggests that maintenance intervals have not been observed.

More maintenance issues. The rotor arm is almost a museum piece, yet the condenser seen bottom left is almost new. This indicates that the condenser has been replaced to cure a misfire, and that other aged ignition components will probably also soon be causing problems.

This fuel line should be securely held by a clamp. If the line comes off, there's the potential for an engine bay fire.

Remove the oil filler cap and look at the underside of the cap and down the filler tube. If you see a creamy emulsion this is oil mixed with the water, caused by too many short trips, which result in high engine wear.

Rusting on the crankshaft pulley is common, but the rust in the channel where the belt runs tells you that the car has been off the road for a long time.

engine is good for well over 100,000 miles if cared for, but a neglected engine will have a much shorter life.

Check the condition of the wiring, looking for burns and abrasions. If your bodywork inspection reveals that the rear chassis mounts have been replaced, lift the sound deadening material from the engine bay side and check that the wiring insulation is not burned. Check that the wiring is original and that it has not been added to, or otherwise tampered with.

Check that the tinware is all properly fastened in place. This might not seem terribly important, but the author has seen a shattered dynamo pedestal which was broken by violent vibration caused by unfastened tinware.

Whilst the rear of the car is raised for the bodywork/chassis inspection, check the rear brakes, suspension, and wheel bearings. There are small inspection holes in the brake back plate through which, with the help of a torch, you can see the thickness of the brake lining. If there appears to be less than 1in of frictional material on the brake shoes, they will have to be renewed. Using a screwdriver (preferably with an angled blade), or the proper tool, check that the brake adjusters are not seized and that the brakes are correctly adjusted (see Chapter Four). Maladjustment indicates shoddy maintenance; sticking adjusters indicates a total absence of maintenance!

Check the brake back plates for signs of brake fluid, or, perhaps more commonly, oil contamination. The former means getting and fitting wheel cylinder seal kits; the latter entails getting and fitting a hub oil seal kit.

Check the rear tyres for uneven wear. Excessive wear in the centre, or at the outside edges of the tread, indicates over or under inflation respectively. If the tyres are worn on one side only, ask whether they have previously been fitted at the front of the car (indicating ill-adjusted front tracking). If not, suspect that the spring plate has, at some time, been unbolted from the hub and replaced in a different position, which will cause toe in or out. In addition to increasing tyre wear, wrongly tracked rear tyres will suffer reduced grip; this is a problem that needs resolving before the car is used on the road.

Check the condition of the handbrake cables and, if they're frayed, or if they stick, make a note to that effect. Check the brake pipes for corrosion, kinks or damage, and the flexible hoses for signs of damage or perishing. Check the condition of the drive shaft gaiters/boots. Splits are an MoT failure point; leaking gaiters on swing axle cars must be rectified before transaxle oil is lost.

Check the transaxle and the underside of the engine for obvious oil leaks, which

If the crankcase has been painted green, this usually signifies that the engine has been built for use with unleaded fuel (hardened exhaust valve seats in the cylinder heads).

must be traced and rectified. If the entire underside of these units is covered with oil, and you are seriously interested in buying the car, wipe off as much of the oil as you can and recheck to establish the cause of the leakage following the test drive. An oil leak from the clutch housing could emanate from either the gearbox input shaft seal, or the rear engine oil seal - the latter is more common but both require removal of the engine, and the latter location means removing the clutch as well.

Check the condition and correct adjustment of the clutch cable, and check that the clutch return spring is not broken.

Check all visible wiring - most especially the starter and solenoid feed wires - for insulation damage. Check the bump stops and all visible bushes for perishing. Check the heater ducting for damage and the exhaust/heat exchangers for leakage and general condition. Exhausts are not too expensive but are an MoT failure point; good quality heat exchangers cost rather a lot.

Most importantly, use a torch to illuminate the visible section of the fuel

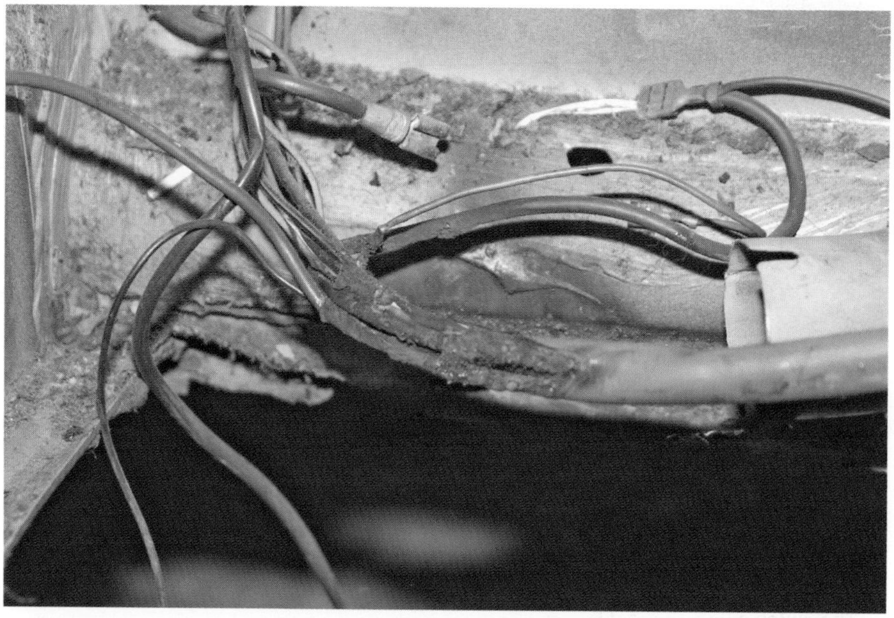

This loom damage must have occurred when the welded 'repair' to the heater channel (visible in the background) was carried out. It's a wonder none of the wires in the loom shorted and started an electrical fire.

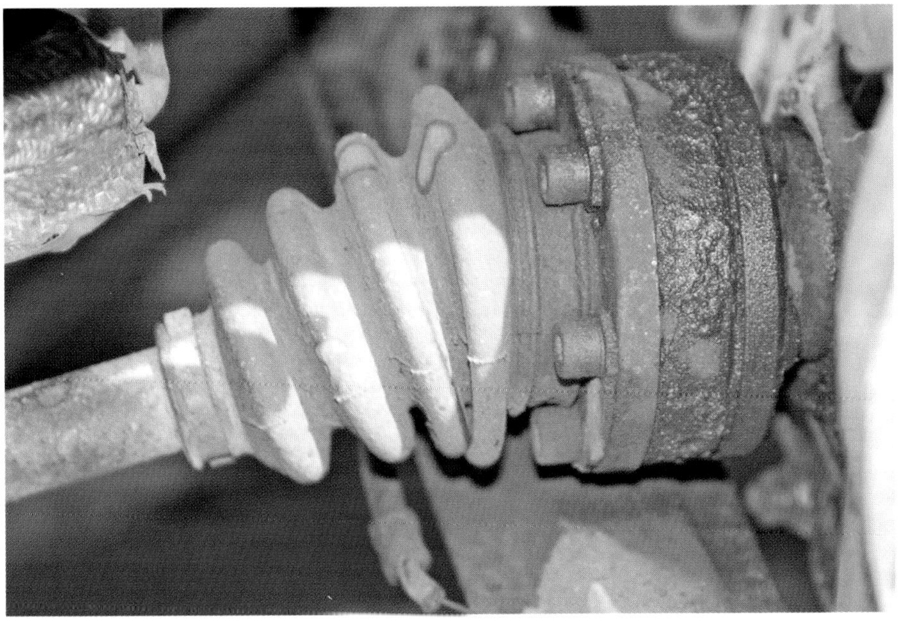

Check there's no oil on the driveshaft gaiter.

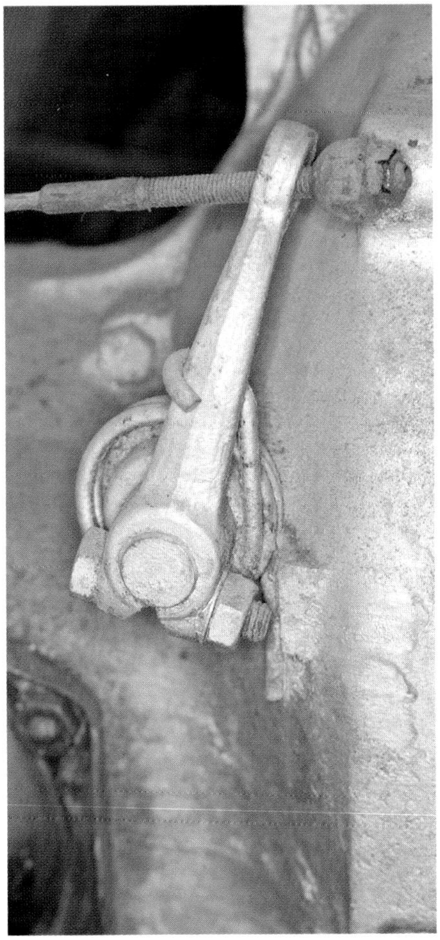

The clutch cable on most Beetles has a wing nut. Check the condition of the operating cable, and that the return spring is not broken.

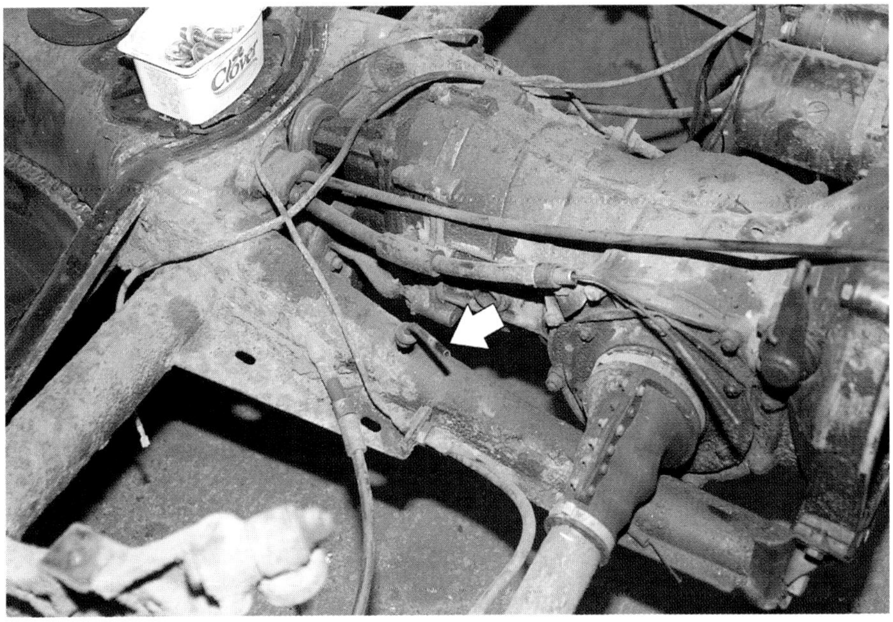

Check the short length of fuel line for damage and corrosion. Replacing the fuel line is probably the most difficult Beetle repair going; a bodyshell-off job, as well.

line; if you have the slightest suspicion that it may be corroded, you must budget for immediate replacement. This is neither a cheap or pleasant task and, in fact, verges on the impossible.

Whilst the front of the car is raised for bodywork/chassis inspection, take the opportunity to check the front brakes, wheel bearings, suspension, and steering gear. Check drum brake back plates for fluid leakage, use a torch to check the shoe material thickness through the hole provided. On cars with disc brakes, check the thickness of the pad frictional material, and also the condition of the disc - a disc which is thin, or has grooves or pitting on its surface, must be renewed, Check the condition of the lines and flexible hoses (check that the hoses don't foul the tyres when the steering is at full lock), and check for fluid leakage at unions. Again using a torch, examine the visible portion of the fuel line (see previous comments). Check the dampers for leakage and visually inspect all rubber components for perishing.

Check the tyres for uneven wear. Wear concentrated on both sides of the tread pattern, or in the middle of the tread pattern can indicate simple under or over inflation respectively; wear on one side of the pattern could indicate either that the tracking is wrongly set (an easy adjustment which should be carried out professionally), or that more serious problems lie elsewhere in the suspension. On cars with torsion arm front suspension, check that the beam is not damaged, because it is possible for the suspension to be thrown out by frontal collisions. Check the two vertical pressings on the beam for rot; the beam axle is not cheap or easy to fit, and any rot automatically means renewal. Check that both notches in the large, hexagonal eccentric bushes located in the top of the stub axle assemblies are facing forward. These set the front wheel camber, and, if inserted wrongly, handling will be adversely affected and tyre wear will be high.

You can see the thickness of brake pads.

Place a lever under each tyre and try to lift it - taking care not to unbalance the car from the axle stands supporting it! Vertical free movement indicates kingpin problems. Grasp each tyre at the nine o'clock and three o'clock positions, and try to rock it; movement indicates worn wheel bearings. To double-check that the fault lies with the wheel bearings and not the suspension, have a helper apply the foot brake and repeat the test; if the movement disappears with the brake on, the wheel bearing is definitely at fault. Turn the wheels lock-to-lock, feeling for roughness in the steering box (expensive), and/or stiff/loose points probably caused by the steering damper (easy repair).

Check the beam axle assembly for rot like this; a new beam axle will be required.

A little probing with a sharp implement shows the extent of the rot. Replacing beam axles is hard work.

TEST DRIVE

If the car has passed all of the tests so far, a road test will enable you to discover many of the possible drive/suspension faults without getting your hands dirty.

Please note that the author and publisher cannot accept responsibility for the consequences of any of the following advice. It's up to the individual to ensure that the car is driven in a safe manner with full regard to the safety of yourself and other road users, and that the car is legally fit to drive. The car must be roadworthy and taxed, and you must be properly insured. If, at any point during the test, you have doubts about the efficiency of the brakes or suspension, it is best to discontinue the road test.

Start off at a moderate speed, and don't try anything fancy until satisfied that the road holding, handling and brakes are up to it. If you're unfamiliar with the on-road behaviour of the Beetle, it's recommended you arrange for an experienced Beetle driver to undertake part or all of the test drive. The experienced Beetle driver will be able to detect problems with the engine, unusual noises from the drive train, and deficiencies in the handling and braking which may not be apparent to the uninitiated.

With each front wheel in turn raised from the ground, grab the tyre each side and turn the wheel lock-to-lock. If the steering feels rough, count on having to fit a new steering box or, if there's play, adjust the steering box (an easy job). If the car is fitted with a steering damper you should feel consistent resistance throughout the travel - if not, the damper needs renewal (fuel tank out).

With each front wheel in turn raised from the ground, use a lever as shown to raise and lower the suspension arms. If there is play, repeat the test while a helper applies the foot brake; if the play disappears, a new wheel bearing is needed.

If the car shows signs of 'floating' at speed, the dampers are worn; if the front of the car nose-dives as the brakes are applied, and/or if the bonnet pitches up and down as the car moves away from a standstill, expect to find worn or leaking dampers. A car with worn dampers is unsafe to drive at speed, so continue the test - if at all - slowly.

On an empty stretch of road, brake to a standstill from about 30mph, and note whether the car pulls to one side (sticking, worn or contaminated brakes). If the brakes have to be 'pumped' before they will operate properly, there is air in the system. A clonk on braking could indicate suspension problems or a loose brake caliper (disc brake models only). If a clonk can only be heard when the car is first braked when travelling either forwards or in reverse, the caliper pistons could be sticking. Repeat this test using the handbrake.

In all gears, accelerate and decelerate sharply to see whether the car can be encouraged (under provocation) to jump out of gear! Reverse the car a short distance and again brake to a halt, listening for clonks which could indicate suspension problems or a loose brake caliper.

Increase to normal road speed and repeat the braking and gear change tests, when any deficiencies in the engine, transmission or suspension not previously noted will be accentuated.

Stop somewhere off the public highway. Engage the handbrake, then slowly let the clutch out, depressing it again immediately the engine begins to labour. If the car begins to creep forwards, the handbrake is out of adjustment, or the rear brakes are worn or contaminated. If the engine does not labour appreciably, the clutch is slipping and in need of attention.

Back on the road slow down to 25-30mph in fourth gear and press the accelerator pedal fully down. If the engine misses or is hesitant, this could indicate a weak mixture, as could pinking (otherwise known as pre-ignition). Pinking has a host of other possible causes, including wrongly set ignition timing, an overheated engine, air induction, or pre-ignition caused by very hot carbon or tiny metal burrs on the cylinder head, which ignite the mixture ahead of the appropriate time. The pinking sound is made by the pistons tipping in the bores. In time, pinking wrecks an engine. If the engine' knocks,' it is almost certainly due for new big-end bearings and a crankshaft regrind; a 'bottom end' rebuild or engine exchange, in effect.

When exiting a corner check that the steering wheel returns to the straight ahead position; if not, suspect partial seizure in the kingpins.

THE FINAL ANALYSIS

While you carry out the bodywork and mechanical checks, note down whatever work you think might need doing, and list all the spares that will be needed. Rather than try to haggle a price there and then, it's better to go home and price the spares and labour needed to bring the car to the desired condition; then (if you're still interested) contact the vendor with an offer which reflects the car's worth to you.

Equally important as the financial aspect is your gut reaction. While you examine and drive the car you will slowly but unconsciously form an overall opinion - a 'gut' feeling - about the car. Your gut feeling should override any other consideration: if you're not happy with the car or the vendo, the best advice is not to proceed with the purchase. Another car will always come along.

A CAVEAT

Don't accept a receipt for your cheque or cash (pay by cheque if possible) from the vendor of the car which includes the words 'sold as seen.' This is a rather tacky and not entirely effective get-out which some people employ when they want to shift a car they know to have some serious (but undisclosed) fault, intended to put you off pursuing your complaint when said fault comes to light. In the UK, it is an offence during a transaction for anyone to misrepresent an unroadworthy vehicle as fit for the road, so keep hold of any published advertisement as proof of misrepresentation should a car described as being in 'good' condition turn out to be unsafe.

WHEN YOU HAVE BOUGHT YOUR BEETLE ...

There's a great temptation to load friends and family into a newly-acquired Beetle and set out on a long 'test' drive, but this is not the smartest way to begin your relationship with the car. It would be tragic if your car were to suffer a breakdown - or worse - a fault which leads to an accident on that first drive. No matter how thorough your pre-purchase inspection of the car was, there's always the chance that the car has a fault or faults you might have missed; something so obvious, perhaps, that you will kick yourself when it results in a breakdown.

The vast majority of people are honest, but the vendor could turn out to be a rogue, maybe forgetting to mention that intermittent electrical fault which knocks out the headlights, or occasionally blows a fuse which he uprated so much that the fault is now entirely capable of setting fire to the loom if the driver happens to switch on the wrong combination of electrical devices ...

You might even discover that, during the period between your inspection and collection of the car, the vendor has swapped some of the good components which passed your inspection standards for worn out ones from another car - perhaps something as fundamental as brake pads or dampers. The components which might most typically attract this sharp practice are usually those which are reasonably easy to swap and fairly expensive to replace. You could discover that the reason why the engine bay was spotless when you previously inspected it was because it had just been steam cleaned, and that plenty of fresh oil has, by now, found its way past the cylinder head gasket during the drive home, leaving the engine oil level low.

It is better to begin your acquaintance with your new car in the workshop rather than on the road, and to give it a thorough check-over followed by a service. In addition to tools and consumables, you'll need a good workshop manual.

Bear in mind that many of the Beetles which come to the market have received some mechanical attention just before they are offered for sale. The work could have been carried out to a poor standard; in particular, fixings might not be correctly torqued, or were fitted without shake-proof washers, and these can come loose in a short space of time - perhaps even when driving the car home.

If, at this stage, you don't feel qualified to carry out the checks yourself, get your local professional mechanic to give the car a once-over. An experienced mechanic should be able to spot a potentially dangerous fault; alternatively, subjecting the car to an MoT test should unearth any faults/problems and list them on the failure sheet.

The following checks and service routines recommended here are all covered in detail later in the book. As ever, the author recommends that you also refer to a good workshop manual.

INSPECTION

Under the car

Begin by chocking one pair of wheels, loosening the wheel nuts and hub nut (drum brakes) on the other pair, disengaging the handbrake, and taking the car out of gear. Raise the non-chocked side of the car and rest it on axle stands. Remove the road wheels and check the tyres for cuts, abrasions, and bulges. Check the condition of the pads and examine the discs for scoring (disc brakes), back off the adjusters on drum brakes, remove the hub nuts and drums, and check the shoes for wear, the drum for scoring, the back plate for oil or brake fluid contamination (hub seal or wheel cylinder seal kit needed), and (rear wheels), the handbrake components for free operation. With disc brakes, check for fluid leakage from the piston seals.

Visually inspect the dampers for signs of leakage, and condition in general. Check the brake hoses for bulges, cuts, abrasions or collapse. Gaiters on the drive shafts must be free from cuts, and will have to be replaced if damaged.

If you discover that any of these vital components have been swapped for worn out alternatives following your inspection, contact the vendor immediately and confront him/her with the facts. Contact your bank with a view to putting a stop on the cheque, and, if the vendor denies any skulduggery, the trading standards office, police, any motoring organisation or owner's club to which you belong, and anyone else that you feel may be able to help.

Whilst the car is raised, take the opportunity to check the exhaust for signs of blowing, the visible sections of the fuel line for damage, and the main battery/starter solenoid feed wire for signs of damage. Check any other wiring which runs under the car and inside the engine compartment. If you find wires with damaged insulation, these should be replaced before the car is used, and the battery earth should be disconnected there and then just to be sure that no wires can short to earth.

Rear of the car

Whilst you have access to the rear underside of a Beetle, check the transaxle oil level, and top up, if necessary, with the correct oil. If the oil level IS low, keep an eye on it when you begin to use the car in case there's a serious leak.

Remove the thermostat cover (rear offside of the car) and measure thermostat length with the engine hot and cold. If the thermostat does not alter in length the cold running flaps in the ducted air cooling system will not open, and the engine will overheat, causing accelerated wear and damage to the engine. See Chapter Three for more details about this check. Finally, check the torque of the nuts and bolts which hold the suspension together. Repeat the checks for the other side of the car.

Engine compartment

Establish firstly that the engine compartment and underside of the engine/transaxle are in the same condition as when you examined the car prior to buying it. If everything was spotlessly clean then, but is now covered with oil, there's little doubt that either the engine and transaxle were steam cleaned for your inspection, and the test run (if any) was too short, or that the engine you saw during your inspection has been replaced with another. It is easy to carry out an engine transplant on the Beetle.

Check the generator drive belt for deflection. Check that all the tinware set screws are in position, and that they have been tightened correctly.

Trace back any mysterious lengths of wire which do not appear on the circuit diagram in your workshop manual; they are probably add-ons and might well at some stage in the future overload the fuse for the circuit they are tapping. A blown fuse might not, at first, seem too dangerous, but if your lights went out whilst you were driving the consequences could be terminal ...To be really thorough pay special attention to all earth connections - most intermittent electrical faults can be attributed to poor earths.

Not necessarily a problem in itself, this surface rusting on the generator drive belt pulley indicates that the car has been standing idle for a long time. Expect problems with ignition components, possible gumming in the carburettor, and a seized handbrake.

GENERAL

Move the front wheels to full lock in each direction, and check that they don't foul the bodywork; it may be as well to 'bounce' each corner of the car to simulate suspension travel when you check this. If the front wheels DO foul the bodywork, chances are that larger or wider wheels and tyres have been fitted. If both prove to be standard, either extremely poor bodywork repair has resulted in badly aligned panels, or the front suspension geometry has been altered because the car has been involved in a front-end collision. In either case, confront the vendor with the evidence.

INTERIOR

Lift the rear seat base and check the battery for condition (ensure it is the one you saw during your inspection of the car), and especially for stability. Were a battery to tip over, at best, leaking electrolyte will make a mess of paintwork, at worst, an electrical fire could be the result. Check the wiring in the vicinity.

Check the seat belts by tugging quite violently; these are anchored to the tops and bottoms of the B posts; it's better to discover that the mountings are weak with rust (or have been bodged) at this stage then when you're headed towards the windscreen following a head-on collision, or even partway through an MoT. Weak seat belt mountings make a car unroadworthy, so seek redress from the vendor.

Check the steering by feeling for lost movement; that is, movement of the steering wheel perimeter which does not move the front wheels. If it is much more than about 1in, check that none of the fixings in the steering mechanism have come loose. This can happen when a car has received attention to the steering prior to sale, but nuts and bolts have come loose since. Void steering wheel travel can indicate that the steering box components require adjustment: this is covered in Chapter Four. Also pull and push the wheel to check for play; lift it then push down to check that the steering column fixings have not come loose.

Sit in each front seat in turn, grab the seat firmly and push down on the floor pan with your feet to check that the seat fixings and floorpans are sound.

FIRST SERVICE

It's recommended that a full lubrication/ ignition system service is carried out on a newly-acquired car, irrespective of evidence of the fabled full service history, or claim by the vendor that the car is perfect and freshly serviced. Apart from giving you the peace of mind which comes from knowing that the job has been properly done, it might also unearth some latent fault which has so far escaped your attention. It also gives you a clean starting point for future servicing.

These are the jobs. Change the engine oil and clean the strainer. Even better, flush the system with a proprietary cleaning fluid before replacing oil and filter.

Top up the transaxle oil. Go over the car with a grease gun and fill every nipple until clean grease emerges, then wipe off any excess. Get out the pumping oil can and attend to the hinges, locks, window winding mechanisms, etc.

It's advisable to change the brake fluid, not only to get new fluid pumping through the lines, but also to establish that the bleed nipples are not seized. Then adjust the handbrake and handbrake lever travel, and check the efficiency of the brakes against the engine before venturing out onto the public highway. To check the brakes, simply let the clutch pedal out slowly with the engine at tick over, the car in first gear, and either the handbrake or foot brake engaged, ready to depress the clutch pedal the moment that the engine begins to labour. If the engine does not labour, the clutch is slipping, UNLESS the car happens to be moving forwards, in which case the brakes are not functioning proprely.

The tracking should be checked at a service centre.

AND FINALLY ...

Before setting out on your first drive in the car, do check that you have a jack and wheelbrace - and that there is air in the spare tyre!

Chapter 2
Mechanical restoration & repair

Every car owner should have the relevant workshop manual for their vehicle, if only to use as a reference source to check whether work carried out on the car professionally was necessary, and completed to a satisfactory standard.

Workshop manuals don't cater well for the owners of very old cars, because they are usually based on work carried out on nearly-new examples of the cars concerned. Gleaming, spotless, almost showroom condition cars on which nuts, bolts and screws are not seized solid, or screw slots, nuts and bolt heads distorted so that screwdrivers and spanners cannot grip them, clean components come apart easily, and the use of brute force is never needed. With older cars of all types, life is rarely as easy as shown in workshop manuals, so this book covers as many of the typical Beetle problems as possible, giving the best solutions to those problems, based on the advice of experienced Beetle mechanics, and from the author's own experience of working on a wide range of classic cars.

As far as possible, this chapter covers mechanical and other repair work as if the individual jobs were being dealt with during the course of a restoration, rather than as a series of one-off running repairs, though each job is covered in such a way that, hopefully, the chapter can be used in the absence of a workshop manual.

Beetle numbers and variety of specification does not allow truly comprehensive coverage of a mechanical repair, and readers are strongly advised to obtain a good workshop manual specific to their Beetle. Bear in mind that the more limited the scope of the manual (the fewer model years and varieties of Beetle it covers), the more comprehensive it should be. A manual which covers half a dozen different varieties will be very limited in specific detail on any of them.

The author strongly recommends that restoration novices use a camera to record stages in the strip down of mechanical components as a reminder of how they fit together during reassembly! Not even the most detailed of workshop manuals - let alone a restoration guide - can illustrate absolutely everything and, although the author has included as many illustrations as possible, the 80,000 or so production modifications to the Beetle preclude the chance of any book every being truly comprehensive in this respect.

WORK PLACE AND TOOLS

A dry, warm place of work is very desirable when working on your car, because some of the work is less than pleasant and very time-consuming, and your own comfort has to be a priority. In addition, you will be dismantling components that are prone to rusting if left for any length of time in damp conditions (as will your tools).

The ideal premises will have a strong workbench and lots of dry storage, yet still with ample room for you to work on the car. One metre clearance all around the car is really an absolute minimum for basic repair work, and a clearance of two metres or more each side is preferable for restoration, or a strip down and rebuild if you opt to do the mechanical work yourself, and trailer the car away for bodywork restoration.

A solid and level floor is essential to support the jack and axle stands. The Beetle is not an especially heavy car, but, if the axle stands supporting it tumble and the car lands on you, it will result in severe injury. The building should be secure; it's unlikely a burglar will steal a Beetle in bits, but tools are always sought-after by the criminal fraternity - especially power tools. A mains electricity supply is essential because some jobs can only be accomplished using power tools.

Your basic household or car maintenance tool set will be found wanting for many mechanical repair tasks. Not only will the number of different tools that you need grow with the range of repairs you undertake, but some of the tools will have to be fairly heavy-duty if they are to survive the rigours of a full mechanical restoration.

In addition to a normal metric socket set it pays to have a set of deep sockets (preferably hexagonal), perhaps a speed brace and extension bars if your current set does not have these, and a torque wrench is vital. When dealing with large and rusted nuts and bolts, a breaker bar is needed.

The socket set is best viewed as a

long-term investment which will not only see you through the restoration, but also subsequent repairs. Good quality sets, though more expensive, will give many years of service and prove cheaper in the long run than several inferior quality sets. As with many tools, it's cheaper to buy sockets and associated items in sets rather than individually. Also, try to buy spanners and screwdrivers in sets and, if you cannot afford top quality, buy the best you can and replace any that are damaged - which will be those that receive the greatest use: 13mm, 14mm and 17mm sockets and spanners, for instance - with better quality alternatives.

Many of the fasteners (screws, nuts and bolts) which you will have to remove may be seized almost solid. These are best dealt with by using an impact drive, which will come with a set of screwdriver bit heads, and should have a detachable half inch square drive adapter which allows it to be used with hexagonal impact sockets when necessary. (If you have a large enough air compressor, an air impact wrench is obviously better.) The Beetle, in common with most cars, has a small number of large, and usually stubborn, nuts ranging in size up to 42mm. The author always prefers to buy hexagonal rather than twelve-point sockets in larger sizes, because they are far less likely to 'round' the nut or burst in use.

Still with heavy-duty tools, a set of general-purpose pullers (2 and 3 legged) will be necessary, along with a ball joint splitter, a coil spring compressor (McPherson strut cars only) and, perhaps, a nut splitter. There will be occasions when power tools - angle grinder, electric drill and pneumatic tools - are useful.

A vice is often essential when stripping components that have been removed from the car; if you can, get one with an anvil surface, because hammering anything held in the vice jaws can damage the vice. You can make padded jaw inserts from sheet copper or wood so that the jaws don't mark whatever you hold in them, and a couple of lengths of angle iron can be held in the jaws for folding sheet steel.

You will need a car jack capable of safely raising the rear of the car high enough to allow you to pull the engine out under the rear panel. To achieve the lifting height you will need and remain stable, there's no substitute for a trolley jack. A two-ton trolley jack will suffice, though, ideally, you should buy one which has a good lifting range for raising the car high enough for engine removal. You'll also need a pair of axle stands with the same height and weight capabilities as the jack. A pair of car ramps is not really a viable alternative for restoration, because at some point the wheels will have to come off.

A number of less heavy tools are needed, including internal and external circlip pliers, a vernier caliper, Allen keys, an inspection lamp, hose clamps, electrical crimping tool, and a selection of electrical connectors. Some Beetles have many non-insulated spade connectors which can easily short to earth and pose a fire hazard if they drop off their terminal. These should be renewed during the restoration with insulated terminals. A soldering iron can be used as an alternative to a crimping tool.

Depending on the extent of work you wish to carry out, you may also require a number of highly specialised tools specific to the Beetle, or perhaps even to a particular model or year. These tools are not all essential but can make life very much easier when working on the engine, drive train, and suspension.

As ever, buy the very best tools you can afford, because poor quality tools will cost you more in the long run. Of course, this doesn't mean you should blow half your budget on a set of top-end spanners, and then not have enough money to buy a decent socket set! If your budget is limited, ensure you get all of the basic tools mentioned previously, and borrow or hire more specialised tools as and when necessary.

SAFETY

Safety - yours and others - is of paramount importance before starting a job. Whilst every care is taken to point out the potential hazards in the jobs described, the author and publisher cannot accept responsibility for any loss, injury or damage which occurs whilst any of the instructions in this book are being followed.
Disconnect the battery earth strap before working on or near the electrical and fuel system; for bigger jobs, remove the battery from the car, disconnecting the earth strap before the positive lead.

When disconnecting the battery, always disconnect the earth terminal first and, when reconnecting it, connect the earth terminal last. Why? If you disconnect or reconnect the live terminal while the earth terminal is connected, and the spanner you are using touches an earthed metal object (including the bodyshell) then you create a short circuit across the battery, which can cause it to explode.

If you have to work under the car, ensure that it is properly held aloft by solid axle stands, and that the wheels which remain in contact with the ground are properly chocked so that the car cannot roll and tumble off the axle stands. If you're starting work on a job which may involve using a naked flame, or will generate a spark anywhere on the front of the car (welding, grinding, or using heat to help 'start' a reluctant nut or bolt), remove the fuel tank and line first. Before using a naked flame or generating great heat (as in welding) anywhere on the car, remove the fuel hoses/brake hose or pipe, and any combustible material in the vicinity.

Petrol is not the only highly flammable substance: brake fluid is equally dangerous and apparently more easily set alight; plastics and rubber also burn well. Petrol fumes are more dangerous than the actual petrol as they are heavier than air and can fill an inspection pit with a potentially explosive mix - so no smoking, welding, or naked flames in the pit.

Always make full use of appropriate safety clothing. You only have one pair of eyes so protect them with goggles whenever you are working under the car, or doing anything which causes sparks or rust flakes to fly through the air, including a cutting, filing, or drilling operation. The author has firsthand experience of the consequences of not wearing goggles when, during a simple and apparently innocuous job hacksawing steel, a sliver of steel became embedded in his eye. In hospital, this had to be dug out with the needle of a hypodermic syringe, under a particularly ineffectual local anesthetic.

When removing components that require a deal of force to get them started, try not to use just the strength in your arm muscles, but bring your whole body into play, instead. If you do use just your arm muscles, and the spanner you are holding slips off the nut you are trying to undo, your hand will fly forwards with great velocity and may smash into one of the hard and invariably sharp components that car designers position with this very eventuality in mind. For the same reason, it pays to keep a pair of strong leather gloves handy whenever you have to use brute force to undo a fastening.

Some mechanical restoration jobs entail lifting fairly heavy weights, often from a position that makes the lifting very awkward, and puts the operator at risk of serious back injury. If you are not comfortable about lifting a weight, always seek help or use lifting equipment.

When replacing components which are held by bolts, it's good practice to put a little copper-based grease, or alternative aluminium-based product, on the bolt threads, because this will make subsequent removal much easier. Do not, however, use grease on fittings which have to be torqued, because they reduce the natural friction to the point at which fitting can be over-stressed when torque is applied. On nuts and bolts which are to be torqued, use a light oil instead.

AVOIDING TROUBLE

If you possess a digital camera it's worth photographing components and their

This Beetle has been fitted with a gizmo (arrowed), which is supposed to allow the use of standard valves and seats with unleaded petrol, without damaging the exhaust valve seats due to loss of compression. It's in the workshop to have new cylinder heads fitted, as compression has been lost from no. 4 cylinder. If you want, or have to use unleaded, fit heads with hardened exhaust valve seats and valves.

surroundings before you start to strip them, because the photographs can immediately tell you where everything ought to go - even which way up - when you come to the rebuild.

Another good policy is to place all the components and fixings (nuts, bolts, set screws) that come off the car in the course of a job in a single container. Not only does this save hours of rummaging around to find the right part during the rebuild but, if there are any components left over when you've finished, you'll know the job's not been done correctly.

If you cannot fathom out how a component should be removed or dismantled, resist the temptation to resort to force. Instead, ask a mechanic at your local service station, or a fellow Beetle owner; someone will know the answer, and often there's a 'trick' to it that you'd never discover by yourself. Don't hesitate to ask for advice because most people are flattered to be asked for advice.

Order all the spares catalogues from Beetle spares suppliers. Not every supplier stocks, or will have in stock, every single spare, so having alternative sources is good policy. Another reason for getting all the catalogues is that the diagrams and photographs, along with part numbers, often help to ensure that you order the correct spare for your car - verbal descriptions of parts can easily be misunderstood.

ENGINE TESTS AND REMOVAL

Before starting a restoration, there are a couple of simple tests that can be carried out with the engine *in situ* to give you a rough idea of its condition.

It's worthwhile borrowing a compression tester to use on all four cylinders to ascertain whether any have low compression due to leakage past the piston rings or valves. Remove the sparking plugs and disconnect the HT king lead from the coil turret to ensure there's no spark near the sparkplug holes. In turn, fit or hold the compression tester in each sparkplug hole,

Using a decent trolley jack with a high lifting height, single-handed engine removal is easy, as Terry demonstrates.

The lower engine mounting bolts are not too difficult to get at. Remove the lower bolts before turning to the top two.

Having pulled the engine from the first motion shaft, it's simply a matter of tilting the engine slightly to clear the rear panel seal ...

... not forgetting, of course, to pull the throttle cable out of the fan housing ...

(above right) ... then gently lower the engine. Ideally, someone to help steady the engine would have been much more useful than someone standing around taking photographs!

At this point, raise the car a fraction and pull the engine out on the trolley jack.

With care, you can even move the engine into the workshop on a trolley jack.

while an assistant spins the engine on the starter motor.

The desired compression varies between 100-142psi, according to engine type. If all four cylinders give similar readings of in excess of 100-110psi, and within 10psi of each other, compression is probably okay. If one or more cylinders give low readings, expect to find leakage, either past the piston rings (worn or damaged rings or bores), past the barrel and cylinder head, or from a valve (burnt valves/seats). If one or more readings are low, put a little engine oil into the bore via the sparkplug hole and re-test. If the reading is now normal, chances are that the leakage is past the piston rings (the oil temporarily seals the piston ring to cylinder wall gap); if the compression is still low, suspect burnt valve seats.

Also before removing the engine, try pulling and pushing the crankshaft pulley to check for excessive end float (over 0.005in), and lifting and lowering it to check for play in the mains; if you can feel play here then a bottom-end overhaul is called for. A very quick and easy way to check for crankshaft end float is to have a helper depress the clutch pedal whilst you watch the crankshaft pulley. If the pulley moves noticeably when the pedal is depressed, the end float is probably excessive.

If the engine displays both compression problems and crankshaft end float, it's probable that the engine is generally tired and will require quite a lot of work to make it good. Consider whether it might be better to opt for an exchange reconditioned engine rather than refurbish the existing one.

Another test well worth doing is to check (or have checked) the ignition dwell angle, which is simply a measure of the length of time that the points are closed. The reason for having it checked is that, if the reading fluctuates, the distributor drive shaft bearing is shot and the timing will never be spot-on. Also, check the generator output by measuring the voltage (you should see circa 14.5V on a 12V system and over 7V on a 6V system) at the battery terminals with the engine running at a fast idle. It's difficult to renew the generator when it's *in situ*, so if it is at all suspect, renew it while you have the chance.

ENGINE REMOVAL

The Beetle has to be the most DIY enthusiast-friendly car of all, because engine removal can be accomplished more quickly and easily than with any other car. In fact, so easy is it to drop out the Beetle's engine that it's tempting to remove it for some jobs which can be accomplished - albeit with some difficulty - with the engine in place.

In addition to a trolley jack and either axle stands or ramps, the tools needed are: a 17mm open end and ring spanner; an 8mm combination spanner; straight and cross-head screwdrivers, and a fuel hose clamp.

It is obviously easier to remove the engine after the bodyshell has been lifted off the chassis, but lifting the bodyshell off if the engine is in place means lifting the bodyshell that much higher to clear the engine; too high for many workshops, which is why the following describes engine removal with the bodyshell on the chassis.

Basically, engine removal involves raising the rear of the car, unbolting some of the tinware, disconnecting everything which connects the engine to the rest of the car (wiring, fuel line, throttle linkage, etc.), supporting the engine on a trolley jack, unbolting the four engine mounting bolts, pulling the engine back clear of the gearbox input (first motion) shaft, then lowering it onto the trolley jack and pulling it out from under the rear valance.

Begin by disconnecting the battery earth strap. Because engine removal becomes easier the higher the rear of the car is raised, you may prefer to - and it is advisable - disconnect both battery terminals and remove the battery to prevent spillage as the car tilts. You can also remove the engine lid if required, although this only improves access and is not essential.

Chock the front wheels fore and aft (it is good practice to engage the steering lock, where fitted, to prevent the wheels from turning side-to-side), raise the rear of the car as high as possible (using a piece of soft timber to protect the sump), and support the car on axle stands placed under the side members, again, using wood packing to prevent damage. Check that the car is raised high enough for the engine, when balanced on top of the (lowered) trolley jack, to be drawn out from under the rear valance.

If you cannot raise the car high enough to slide the engine out under the rear panel, an alternative is to have a sheet of plastic-faced board under the jack, to support the engine after it and the jack have been lowered, and then to remove the jack and lower the engine onto the plastic-faced board, on which it should slide. More clearance can be gained by removing the heat exchangers before tackling the engine, but this can be a difficult operation *in situ* if all the fastenings are seized (which they usually are).

After raising the car and placing the axle stands in position, establish that the axle stands are secure by lowering the jack until the stands are taking the combined weight of the engine and body. Check that the front wheel chocks are correctly positioned and holding the car, because the trolley jack tends to pull the car backwards slightly due to the arc described by its arm, which can cause the chocks at the rear of the front wheels to push the car forward unless the chocks are repositioned. Finally, raise the jack so that it takes the engine's weight but does not lift the bodywork off the axle stands.

Remove the air filter assembly, pre-heater and oil breather hoses. You can drain the oil if desired, although this is optional. Use masking tape and a biro to make up tags for wires as you remove them if not completely sure of remembering where each goes. Remove the wire from the oil pressure switch, and the low tension lead, any wires attached to the carburettor, plus wiring which runs to the generator.

Remove the accelerator cable from the carburettor, and push it back through the hole in the fan cowling. Remove the heater hoses from the exhaust shield plate, then remove the exhaust shield plate itself, taking care not to damage the engine bay rubber seal, which is easily damaged and very difficult to replace. The exhaust shield plate is secured by cheese-headed set screws, and some run into nuts (typically, the one that holds the hot air intake) which have to be held while the screw is turned.

Make absolutely sure there are no possible sources of ignition in the vicinity and, from underneath the car, clamp the flexible fuel hose and disconnect the flexible fuel hose from the rigid fuel line, plugging the latter to minimise fuel leakage. (The potential for fuel leakage is greatly reduced if the fuel tank has already been removed.)

Disconnect the heater control cables from the levers at the front of the heat exchangers. The fastenings are usually seized, and soaking the threads in penetrating oil sometimes helps, though the operation usually ends up needing a self-locking wrench to hold the assembly still while the nut is turned. Disconnect the heater ducting from the heat exchangers.

Ensure that the jack is taking the weight of the engine but not of the bodywork. Remove the top engine mounting nuts and bolts. These cannot normally be seen, so you'll have to work by 'feel' alone. On pre-1971 Beetles there's a nut on each bolt, and removal, ideally, is a two-man job, though it can be achieved solo with considerable difficulty. On later cars the bolts run into captive threads and the task can be easily accomplished single-handed. Check again that the engine is fully supported by the jack before removing the lower engine mounting bolts - it is essential that weight is not allowed to fall on the gearbox first motion (input) shaft. Check that no wires, cables or hoses connect the engine to the rest of the car. Try to arrange

Behind the fan shroud there's just enough room to get a 13mm spanner onto this nut, which serves as an engine mounting, and also secures the starter.

This engine mounting bolt head (arrowed) is not easy to get at, though it is possible with a socket and a short extension.

for two helpers to steady the engine - to balance it on the trolley jack - before proceeding. Pull the engine and trolley jack rearwards together until the engine is clear of the input shaft, then lower it and finally drag it out from underneath the car.

Refitting is the reverse of removal; the same cardinal rule of not allowing engine weight to hang on the gearbox first motion shaft applies. The engine bay side seal may need replacing - one of the less pleasant tasks of Beetle restoration! The rubber locates in rails and, whilst in theory it should be possible to work its lips into the rail, in practice you may succumb to the temptation to open up one of the metal lips, slip in the rubber and then tap back down the lip. The drawback to this is that the paint cracks as the steel bends, and you can bet on rusting occurring before very long ...

If you have previously removed the sound-deadening material from within the engine bay, replace this before the engine goes back in. The panels have wire reinforcing, which is all too easy to stab your hand with, so be careful! Whilst on the subject of trim, the engine lid seal can either be clipped or fed into place; in either case be sure to leave plenty of slack so that the trim lies flat and does its job. Do remember to feed the throttle cable through the hole in the fan casing before fitting the engine, and ensure that it cannot kink or become trapped in-between the engine back plate and the bell housing.

Raise the car just high enough to allow the engine on a trolley jack under the valance and support it on axle stands, noting the safety advice given previously. Then, with an assistant to help balance the engine, raise it up to the same height as the first motion shaft, align it correctly, and ease it backwards. Take care not to rip out the engine bay seal!

If the engine will not locate easily then the chances are that the clutch assembly is out of alignment with the first motion shaft. Do not try to force the engine into position but remove it and check the clutch alignment, and also that there's nothing else to get in the way of the engine as you try to fit it.

HEIGHT RESTRICTION

If your trolley jack and axle stands don't have the range to lift the car high enough

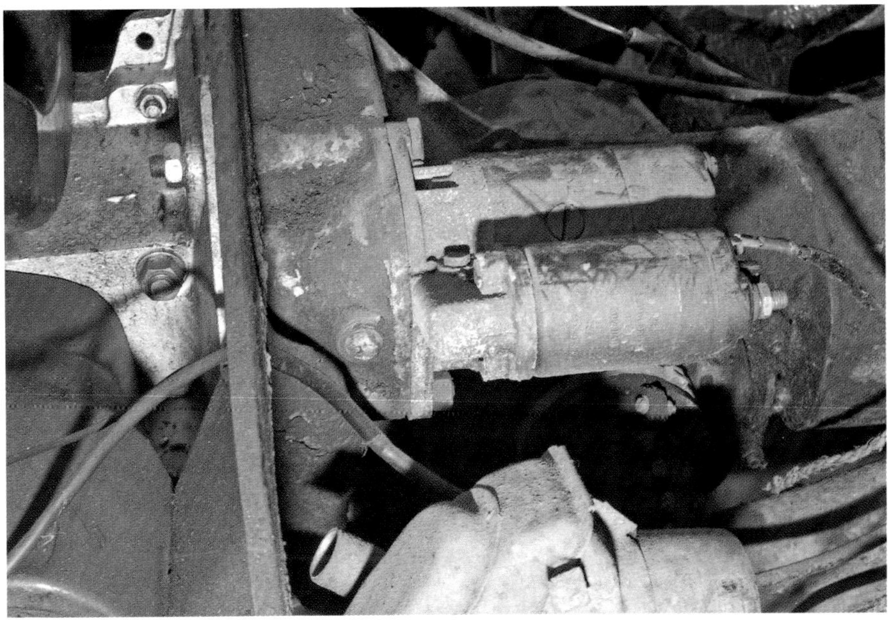

The starter motor fixings, both visible with the bodyshell off. When removing or refitting the engine mounting nut on the engine bay side, take care not to drop the washer.

for you to slide the engine out from under the rear panel, you might care to consider an alternative method of engine removal. It involves more work than the traditional method, but is safer because the car remains nearer the ground and is more stable than it would be if perched on axle stands at the very top of their travel.

Remove the engine bay lid (cut the rear number plate light wires and fit crimp bullet connectors), and the brackets to which the hinges bolt, then the air filter and carburettor. Remove the distributor and fuel pump. Remove the tinware at the rear of the engine. Unbolt the inlet manifold. Remove the set screws from either end of the fan cowling, and remove the nuts from the generator pedestal.

It is now possible to lift the fan cowling (and, with it, the generator) sufficiently to allow removal of the generator pedestal, after which, the manifold can be removed. The generator can be unbolted from the fan cowling and removed and, finally, the fan cowling can be lifted away - it's tight, but it can be done. (An advantage of this method of engine removal is that the top two engine mounting nuts are then very easy to reach.)

You can also unbolt the oil cooler, which will further reduce the height of the unit, and allow you to pull it out on top of the trolley jack.

It's not easy, but if you strip everything away from the top of the crankcase, engine height is lowered sufficiently to remove what's left, even if you can't raise the car very high.

The easiest way of turning over the engine is to use a 21mm socket on the generator pulley nut. Alternatively, engage a gear and push the car, or remove the crankshaft pulley tinware and turn the crankshaft pulley nut using a spanner.

ENGINE STRIP, INSPECTION & REBUILD

During a restoration, if you have only one building in which to work there is a strong case for leaving the engine rebuild - and, in fact, most of the mechanical work - until the bodywork has been completed, and the shell sprayed. This is because working on mechanical components usually involves using various fluids - especially aerosol cans of releasing fluids and silicones - that can react with paint and ruin an otherwise blameless paint job. An equally strong argument for finishing the bodywork before starting work on mechanical repairs is that flatting undercoat and filler fills the air with fine dust, and gets into every nook and cranny; air-dry paint dust is no better.

Having a split crankcase and separate cylinder barrels gives the flat four more in common with a motorcycle engine than the average car engine, and stripping and rebuilding the Beetle engine is much easier than working on most other car engines. To properly inspect the internals, however, requires that you have access to highly accurate measuring equipment, which is expensive to buy and can usually only be found at an engineering business. This measuring equipment can reveal whether certain engineering operations should be carried out, again, using equipment which is unlikely to be available to the amateur.

If the checks outlined at the start of the instructions on engine removal indicate that the engine needs a lot of work - or if you have doubts regarding the general condition of the engine - bear in mind that it can prove cheaper to buy a reconditioned engine than to have your own engine reconditioned. If you were to strip your engine and take the components to a professional engineering shop for inspection, and any machining work found to be necessary, you may discover that the cost of the work, plus any components which have to be renewed, by far exceeds the cost of a straight replacement reconditioned unit.

Because of this, it's strongly recommended that you give serious consideration to replacing your existing engine with a reconditioned unit. In addition to being a hassle-free, straight swap, it gives you the option of buying a more powerful unit, or one modified to withstand use with unleaded fuel.

If you do decide to work on the engine yourself, a dry work area is vital, and cleanliness is of the greatest importance generally. You can strip the Beetle engine on any flat surface such as a workbench, or even the floor, but the task is much easier if you can buy or borrow one of the special bench or floor standing mounts which bolt onto one half of the crankcase, and allow the unit to be swivelled for improved access.

Before starting to strip the engine, drain the oil.

Remove the sparkplugs and turn the engine over by pulling the generator belt until the notch in the front half of the generator pulley aligns with the screw in the generator. Use a screwdriver between the two to lock the generator, then undo the pulley nut, remove the drive belt and replace the pulley nut with its shims. Undo the clamp which holds the generator and the set screws which hold the fan shroud, then lift the assembly clear of the crankcase.

If you find a creamy substance in the lower section of the generator pedestal, and in the crankcase directly underneath it, this is an emulsion of engine oil and water. The emulsion forms as a result of the vehicle being used predominantly for short journeys, which do not give the condensation - that forms overnight in the engine - time to evaporate out of the oil

What looks like a mixture of tar and mayonnaise is actually carbon mixed with an emulsion of oil and water.

Undo the inlet manifold nuts and lift the manifold and carburettor clear. Unbolt and remove the oil cooler, then blank off the oil feed and return holes in the crankcase to prevent anything from entering.

Remove the thermostat. Remove the distributor and fuel pump.

Unbolt the heat exchangers/exhaust assembly complete. Remove the crankshaft pulley bolt, and use a puller to remove the pulley. Remove the clutch.

The flywheel nut should be tightened to 200ft/lbs, and can take some shifting! The flywheel has to be locked before the nut can be undone, and this is best achieved by using a steel bar at least four feet long with two holes drilled to correspond with clutch bolt holes, to which the bar is bolted. Using a 36mm, three-

Two bolts hold the sides of the fan shroud - slacken, but don't remove them because they pass through a slot - then the shroud can be lifted away.

To remove the fan shroud (or the generator), remove the nut on the generator clamp.

The two slackened bolts, and one removed nut, are all that hold the fan shroud in position.

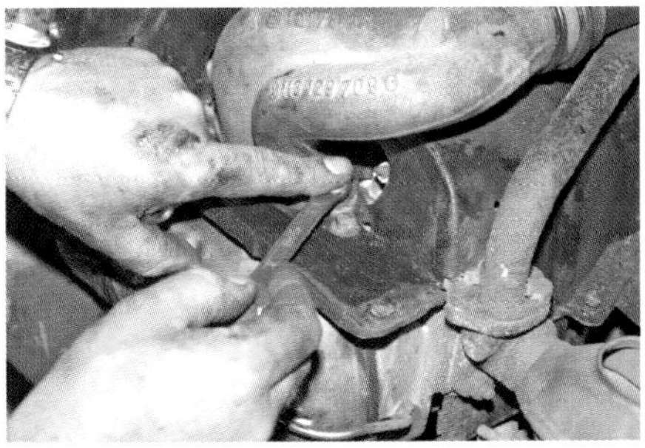

Two of the inlet manifold nuts don't have much clearance, and it can be a problem getting a ring spanner onto them.

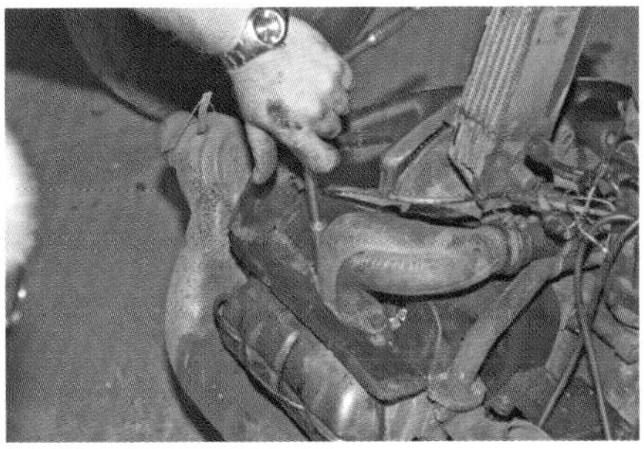

The other manifold nuts have unobstructed access.

The hot spot nuts are often seized solid. Take as much time as necessary to free them, because the studs break quite easily.

and be drawn out through the breather pipe. This emulsion builds up and can finally choke the crankcase breather system, raising crankcase pressure which, in turn, forces oil past the piston rings into the combustion chambers on the induction stroke. Result - blue smoke.

The small cavity under the engine oil filler plate can become almost completely blocked by carbon. The only way to treat an engine in this state is a complete strip down and rebuild, because any attempt to clean away the carbon will result in much of it getting into the engine oil, possibly blocking off oilways and leading to terminal bearing damage.

quarter inch drive hexagonal socket, and the best leverage you can obtain, slacken the nut. It may be necessary to have an assistant or two to hold the engine still while force is applied; a better method is to arrange the two levers so that you can push them together. If one lever end rests firmly on the workshop floor, the second can be

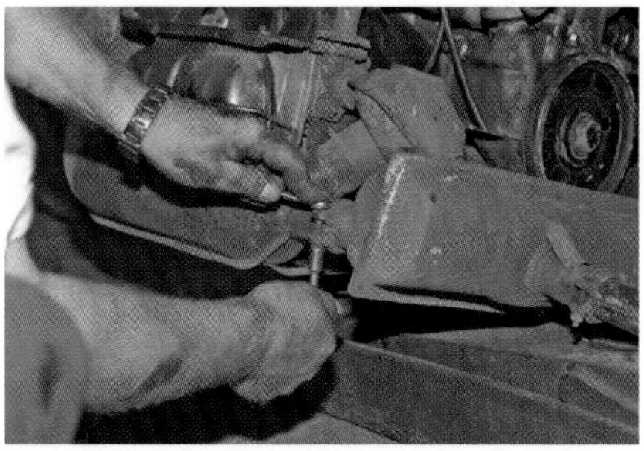

The exhaust clamp nuts and bolts are also prone to seizing solid - happily, new clamps are cheap.

Even with the engine out of the car, removing the heat exchanger nuts can be difficult. Try cleaning the exposed stud threads and soaking the nuts in penetrating fluid to avoid shearing them.

Corrosion between the exhaust clamp nut and the threaded stud in the cylinder head can cause the stud to come unscrewed when you try to remove the nut. You can remove the stud by splitting the front exhaust port to silencer pipe from the heat exchanger, allowing the exchanger to be pulled away from the head and the stud to be unscrewed.

pressed downwards, without any of the force being applied moving the engine. It is still advisable to have an assistant to hold the engine still.

If this fails, it may be as well to take the engine to a garage and ask a mechanic to start the nut - a powerful air impact driver can sometimes work.

Mark one dowel peg and the adjacent area of the flywheel with a dab of paint so that the latter can be replaced in the same

Remove the two rocker assembly nuts (arrowed) and lift away the

Remove the push rods. Unlike with other engines, it's not necessary to label the push rods as they can go back in any order. Check that they're all straight by rolling them on a flat surface.

relative position, then remove the flywheel. A little help from a rubber mallet may prove necessary.

Clean, then remove, the rocker box covers by prising off their spring clips. Clean away all traces of the gaskets (which, like all other gaskets, must be renewed). Undo, as evenly as possible, the two rocker gear retaining bolts, then lift the rocker gear clear and mark it in some way to show which cylinder it corresponds to. From now on, all components should be marked or stored in such a way that they can be replaced in the correct location. Remove and mark the push rods, or (alternatively) place them in a piece of stiff cardboard with suitable holes and make your marks on this.

Slacken, then remove, the cylinder head nuts in the sequence shown, turning each nut a fraction before progressing to the next, repeating the process until all are loose and can be removed. Lift the cylinder head from the cylinders, giving the underside of the head a tap or two with a rawhide mallet if necessary (it usually is). NEVER use any kind of lever in-between the head and the cylinders, because this would ruin the seal between them. As the head comes free, remove the push rod tubes and mark them.

Pull each cylinder in turn away from the crankcase until the piston pin and gudgeon clip can be seen. Remove the gudgeon pin, gently drift the pin until it is free of the connecting rod small end, and then remove the cylinder and piston complete. You can remove the cylinder first and then the piston if you wish, but

Top: Initial tightening and final loosening order. Bottom: Final tightening and initial loosening order.

Even on a head that's being renewed, follow the correct nut slackening order, because the head will usually be repairable and of use to someone.

The Beetle cylinder heads usually lift away easily, though sometimes a light tap with a soft faced mallet is needed to free them.

With any luck, the cylinder heads will lift off without disturbing the cylinders.

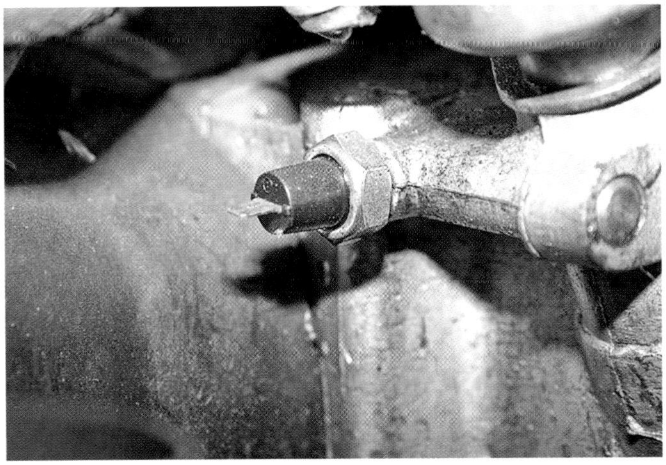

The engine oil pressure switch operates the warning light if pressure drops too low, which can result in a wrecked engine. Renew it during the course of an engine build.

removing both together reduces the chances of cylinders and pistons becoming mixed up.

Remove the oil pump cover plate. The oil pump is gripped between the two crankcase halves, and removal requires a special tool or, alternatively, can happen when the crankcase halves are split. Remove the six nuts which secure the oil strainer plate, then remove the oil strainer.

Remove - where applicable - the generator pedestal/oil filler assembly. Remove the oil pressure switch. The crankcase may now be split. Ideally, the crankcase assembly will be held in a special mount of the type already described; if not, support it so that it leans to the left (viewed from the crank pulley end).

Remove the nuts and washers from the join seam, plus, on 1200cc engines, the two bolts at the flywheel end. There are six large nuts on the right hand side of the casing. Remove these and, if no fastenings remain, the crankcase halves should begin to part when LIGHTLY tapped with a rubber mallet. Remove the cam followers (tappets) and mark them.

The crankshaft and camshaft simply lift out of the crankcase half. Remove the distributor drive shaft and the fuel pump push rod assembly.

INSPECTION

It is strongly recommend that further stripping and inspection is carried out professionally. Unless there's something obviously wrong (such as a crack in a casting), the cylinder barrels and heads, pistons, crankshaft, camshaft and crankcase should be taken to an automotive engineer for proper inspection and measuring. There is no point in rebuilding an engine with renewed bearings, piston rings, and so on, if there's excess wear of, or unseen damage to, any of the retained components, because the life span of the rebuilt engine would be greatly reduced, perhaps to just a few thousand miles.

Some faults which can be spotted easily are wear in the cylinders, which leaves a lip at the top of the piston ring's travel that can be felt with a thumbnail; traces of carbon where it shouldn't be, such as on the rocker gear (worn valve guides and possibly valve stems), and scoring on the cylinder wall, which is visible or might be felt by dragging a thumbnail across it. What simple checks won't reveal is whether components which should be perfectly round have become oval, so even if the components seem okay it's best to have them measured by a competent engineer.

Sometimes, depending on its condition, it is necessary to have the crankcase halves assembled and align-bored - that is, the holes for the main bearings are bored true. If the crankcase is out of true, the centre bearing will come in for very heavy wear. When the time comes to grind the crankshaft, the engineer should firstly measure the crank to ensure that it is straight - if not, crankcase align-boring might be necessary.

You can't really tell whether the crankcase needs align-boring until it has been thoroughly cleaned - which is no easy matter. The centre web (which holds the centre main bearing) might show wear in the form of a raised rough ridge down the centre, where the oil relief groove was in the mains bearing half shell. The web each side of the ridge might be very smooth, indicating that the main bearing has been 'fretting' - moving.

If you're unsure whether or not to opt for a crankcase align-bore, have it checked by an engineer; if the cost of this, or a new crankcase, is prohibitive, my friend, Terry Ball, suggests using 'bearing lock' to seat the bearing half as an alternative. Bearing lock - which might be called 'Stud and bearing lock' (available from most motor factors) sets very hard and bonds bearing shells when it is compressed - as the crankcase halves are pulled together. This can 'take up the slack;' hardly precision engineering but it seems to work.

Align-boring means stripping the crankcase completely - removing the studs - then sending it away for perhaps a month, unless you are lucky enough to live near one of the very few engineering companies that carry out this work. The boring cost will probably constitute the largest part of the price of a new set of crankcase halves, and this is possibly the better route to take. If you do have your crankcase align-bored and the crank reground, remember that the new mains bearings should be larger on the outside and smaller on the inside! Ask the company that carries out the align-boring to also supply the correct mains bearings.

The final check is to reassemble the reground crankshaft, with its new bearings, into the crankcase, tighten the two halves together and check whether the crankshaft spins freely - if not, the crankcase will probably need align-boring.

When working on an engine, always cover any external holes - even the small oilways leading to the oil cooler - so you don't drop anything inside.

The single punch mark on the camshaft gear should be between the two marks on the crankshaft drive gear (arrowed in yellow - the marks arrowed in red). Note the distributor drive gear (arrowed in blue).

CRANKSHAFT GRINDING

Each journal in turn will be measured, ground, re-measured, and reground until it is the correct size. The company that carries out the grinding will then supply the correct sized bearings, though you must inform it if you have had the crankcase align-bored, because bearings with a larger external diameter will be needed.

Having a crank ground can prove slightly more expensive than obtaining an exchange reground crankshaft from a Beetle spares specialist, probably because the spares companies have cranks ground in batches, thus reducing the unit cost.

A point worth remembering if your crank proves too far gone, or has already been ground to the limit, is that the crankshafts in competition cars are rarely ground more than once, and are considered scrap even though there's still plenty of 'meat' on the journals and crank pins. If you can find an engineering shop that does a lot of work on Beetle engines, and on those used in competition, you might be able to pick up a serviceable, ex-competition crank for very little more than the price of a straight 'grind.'

If the engine needs a new crankshaft and the engine casing needs align-boring, don't overlook the alternative of finding an engine in better condition than yours from a scrapper, ideally, a fairly recently fitted reconditioned unit.

REBUILD

Begin by assembling the crankshaft, connecting rods, and big end bearings. Remember that rods and caps, rods and crank pin journals must all be rebuilt in the correct locations - don't mix them up. Use new engine oil to lubricate the big end bearing shell halves before pressing them firmly into the connecting rods and caps, then place each rod in turn in position on its crank pin and fit its cap, ensuring that the tongues and notches of the bearing halves align correctly. Torque the nuts to 24ft/lbs, and check that the rod turns freely on the crankshaft; if not, dismantle and examine it to identify the problem, then gently peen the cap nuts with a light hammer to prevent them from working loose.

Fit main bearing three into position (oil hole nearer the flywheel end of the

When the crankcase halves have been bolted together, stuff rags into any apertures so that nothing can drop down into them.

A small arrow stamped into the piston top should face the flywheel.

crankshaft), and heat the gear assembly gently until it can be located on the crankshaft. Don't use a flame to heat the gears but place them in a hot oven until they have expanded sufficiently. Immersion in hot oil is an alternative, but take care, because of the dangers of fire and also spillage of hot oil.

Spread the snap ring and slide it into position, followed by number four main bearing (oil hole toward crank pulley), and finally the oil thrower. Refit number one main bearing on the flywheel end of the crankshaft.

At this stage, set the crankshaft end float before assembling the engine. To do this, fit the rear main bearing, then two standard end float shims, then the flywheel. You will need to hold the crankshaft in a heavily-padded vice whilst applying a torque of perhaps 80ft/lbs to the flywheel nut. Using a set of feeler gauges inserted between the bearing and the flywheel, measure the gap, then subtract from it 0.0027-0.005in (0.07-0.13mm) to find the thickness of the third shim required.

Refit the split number two main bearing halves into the crankcase halves. Replace the cam followers into the crankcase halves with a little grease to (hopefully) hold them in position, and oil to lubricate them.

Fit the crankshaft shims and a new oil seal, and place the crankshaft assembly in the left hand crankcase half, feeding the connecting rods through the appropriate holes. Without disturbing the bearings, turn the crankshaft until the two punch marks on the timing gear coincide with the axis of the camshaft. Fit the camshaft half bearings to the left hand side of the crankcase, then the camshaft so that the notch on its tooth is in-between the two marks on the crankshaft timing gear. This ties the opening and closing of the valves to the rise and fall of the pistons - get it wrong and you'll be kicking yourself for at least a month!

Fit new rubber seals onto the six crankcase studs. Fit the camshaft half bearings to the right hand side of the crankcase, then put a bead of sealing compound on the crankcase half lips and offer the right hand half into position on the left, again, feeding the connecting rods through the holes. Replace the lip nuts but don't tighten them until you have replaced the oil pump body. Then progressively tighten the nuts, checking that the crankshaft and camshaft are free to turn, until the two lips are pressed tightly together. Using sealing compound, fit the six large crankcase nuts to the threaded studs, again, checking that the crankshaft is free to turn and, on 1200cc engines only, replace the two large bolts near the flywheel end of the crankcase.

The lip nuts should be progressively tightened and torqued to 10ft/lbs; the six large nuts to 20ft/lbs. Recheck the crankshaft, then torque the lip nuts to 14ft/lbs and the six large nuts to 25ft/lbs.

Pistons & cylinders

It is taken as read that you will have had the pistons, piston rings and cylinders examined for damage, measured for wear or ovality, perhaps the pistons weighed by an automotive engineer, and everything machined or renewed as appropriate.

Fit new cylinder gaskets to the crankcase halves. You can fit the pistons alone and the cylinders afterwards, or the pistons with the cylinders already attached, as long as the gudgeon pin hole is clearly visible. Lubricate each bore with a little engine oil, then use a ring compressor to fit the pistons into their respective cylinders. Offer the pistons into position on the small ends - ensuring that the arrows stamped into the crown face the flywheel - then gently press home the gudgeon pins and fit the circlips. Use oil to lubricate the cylinder seals before pushing the cylinders fully home.

Cylinder heads: refit

Pull the push rod tubes to stretch them to a fraction over seven inches, and fit new sealing rings. Slide the cylinder head onto the studs and position the push rod tubes (seam upwards), before pushing the cylinder head fully home. Check that the push rod tubes are correctly located, and torque the cylinder head nuts in the correct progressive sequence. Fit the push rods, then the valve gear.

Cylinder heads: repair

You can diagnose some existing and potential cylinder head problems easily. If your engine tends to run very rich, the cylinder head combustion chambers and valves become coated in a matt black layer of carbon (not to be confused with oil leakage which gives a shiny black layer), and the sparkplug ends will have an equivalent covering. Carbon conducts electricity and, when the carbon coating has built up sufficiently to breach the ceramic insulation of the sparkplug end, it won't fire and you'll have uneven running, misfiring and non-starting problems to sort out. Cleaning the plug end will get the car going, but the problem - carbon build-up - needs attention in the form of a head de-coke. You also need to do something about the rich running problem ...

Having combustion chambers and valves covered in carbon is not a great problem in itself, but can give rise to real trouble if the cause is not dealt with. The process of removing cylinder heads and cleaning off the carbon is called a 'de-coke,' and used to be a fairly regular maintenance job before the advent of modern petrol which contains detergents that reduce carbon build-up. But a carbon build-up can still occur - if the choke mechanism is faulty, for instance - and have serious consequences. When the engine runs, carbon deposits in the combustion chamber can glow red hot, which can prematurely preheat and/or ignite the next incoming charge of fuel/air mixture - known as pre-ignition - which causes the head and inlet valve to become very hot, making it even more prone to pre-ignition. It's a vicious circle.

Pre-ignition can be evident as pinking - a harmless-sounding 'tinkling' noise which is actually the pistons tipping in the bores. Pinking can quickly wreck an engine. A covering of carbon on the cylinder head assembly components can also contribute to 'knocking,' which is more serious, because the noise is that of a shock wave resulting from a detonation - an explosion rather than a controlled burn - of the fuel/air mixture. The problem faced by Beetle owners is that the rear-mounted engine is so far from the driver, and so noisy, that pinking, or even knocking, may not be noticed.

What actually happens with both pinking and knocking is that the mixture ignites so early in the firing cycle that the piston tries to travel upwards and compress the mixture. Suddenly, there's a burn (pinking), or an explosion (knocking), fighting to stop it rising. Because all the energy cannot be dissipated as it usually is by pushing the piston, it damages the engine components instead.

Other non-terminal cylinder head assembly problems can concern the rocker gear, the valves, their guides, and their seats. Valves and seats can be damaged through sheer old age or - especially the exhaust valve seats - if an engine is allowed to run far too hot (generally caused by pre-ignition). Exhaust valve and seat damage can be exacerbated if unleaded fuel is used and the valve seats aren't hard enough. Such damage causes a loss of compression, and you can buy meters to measure the compression within each cylinder.

Valve guides wear, which, in itself, causes overheating problems because the contact between valve stems and their guides is important in dissipating heat. If the guide wears, contact between the two is reduced, the valves become too hot, and this can cause or contribute to pre-ignition. Valve stem wear can also allow hot gasses into the rocker box, where it 'cooks' the oil. Lastly, the valve stems can become bent. This can cause extreme wear of the guide, or can result in the valve not closing fully.

All the faults described so far can be rectified, but some head damage is terminal - if the cylinder head is cracked

This is what oil looks like after it's been mixed with carbon and cooked. Gas has escaped from the exhaust port between worn valve guides and stems, so a complete head overhaul is called for. The amazing thing is that the engine ran perfectly before it was stripped.

Many Beetles cannot run on unleaded petrol because the exhaust valve seats erode. If you have to remove the cylinder heads, consider exchanging them for modified heads with hardened exhaust valve inserts which will allow the use of unleaded petrol.

(usually between the valve seats or a valve seat and the sparkplug hole), it really needs renewing. Some specialists can effect welded repairs but, having had one such repair fail as soon as the engine was restarted, I'd recommend renewing the head, expensive though it is. I'd also recommend buying new cylinder heads, which should be guaranteed to withstand use with unleaded fuel.

Rocker gear

It's best to strip the rocker gear while you have the chance so that it can be thoroughly cleaned. To strip a rocker shaft, simply remove the end spring clip using circlip pliers, then the three washers, first rocker, pedestal, and second rocker, then the other end fittings. Two rockers slide on from each end of the rocker shaft, so you can strip one end at a time, then rebuild it after cleaning before you strip the second end.

If the rocker adjuster screws or their lock nuts appear seized, don't use force to try and undo them as this risks damaging the screw adjuster slot. Heat the rocker end to expand it slightly, and everything should come apart very easily. One common obstacle to setting the rocker gap is damaged adjuster end slots, usually caused by a tapered screwdriver being jammed into them. If they're bad, renew them along with their lock nuts.

A common rocker gear problem - which, in my experience, seems not to affect the flat four to any great degree - is wear of the rocker shaft, or the rocker itself. It's not really a huge problem, but does make setting the valve clearances a little more hit-and-miss if the rockers are a slack fit on the shaft. If there's a lot of play, or the engine is to be 'hotted-up,' I recommend you renew the rocker gear assemblies.

Valve guides

Having cleaned, stripped and examined the cylinder heads, the next step is to fit new valve guides. With most engines, you can do this at home by using a long bolt, a nut and washers to 'pull' the old guides out and pull the new ones in. With the flat four, the fact that the valves are set at an angle, their length (and especially the amount of contact area between the exhaust valve guide and the head), and the consequent amount of force needed to budge the guides, means that your only hope is to have the old guides either pressed or drilled out by an engineer. We managed to remove Beetle inlet valve guides using a ten-ton press, but not even this, coupled with heating the head to make it expand, could move the exhaust guides.

Sometimes, the only way to remove valve guides is by using specialist and very expensive drill bit guide systems to drill out the centres of the old valve guides, to weaken the grip on the head that the, by then, very thin walls have to the extent that they can be pressed out. Beetle cylinder heads are prone to cracking when the valve guides are pressed out. All in all, I strongly recommend you have this work carried out professionally.

A tip for those who do opt to fit their own guides is to put the new guides in a sealed plastic bag and leave this in the freezer overnight. Leave the head in a warm (not hot) oven for an hour or so; the guides contract, the head expands, and the valve guides are easier to push into position - if a little cold to the touch! However, if new guides are fitted, the chances are that the valve stem axis will move fractionally, which will move the valve head slightly to one side, with the result that it won't sit in its seat and will probably be too poor a fit to be dealt with by lapping. In such cases, the valve seat must be re-cut.

Valve seat cutters have guides that fit snugly in the new valve guides so that the seat is cut in the right place, and at the right attitude, and cutters can be bought at not too high a cost. Whether the expenditure can be justified when you're unlikely ever to have to use them again is another matter - I prefer to have seats cut professionally.

Modifications

Working on the cylinder heads gives you an opportunity to 'tweak' engine power. You can have larger valves and seats fitted to move more fuel/air mixture, or you can have the ports 'gas flowed' (often referred to as 'porting'). Both modifications are the province of the engineer; you can acquire DIY equipment capable of grinding ports, but the chances are that, if you attempt the work yourself, you'll either end up with the ports out of balance or - worse - will grind away too much material and weaken or ruin the head. One engineer specialising in cylinder head gas flowing suggested that removing some of the 'meat' from around the exhaust valve guide in the exhaust port would give a worthwhile power boost in itself.

If you're serious about getting more power, consider fitting performance components - camshaft, carburettor etc. - in conjunction with cylinder head modifications or - best of all - simply increase the capacity of the engine by fitting big bore pistons and cylinders, available in sets at reasonable prices.

Increasing engine capacity increases power but, unlike other power modifications, keeps the essential character of the engine; you still get bags of torque low down, and the bhp/revolutions relationship remains the same, so that the car is tractable in normal town traffic. The more you modify an engine, the more you reduce the useable revolutions power band, so that you have to keep the revs up all the time. Modifications can also affect slow running to the extent that you might not - with a highly modified engine - be able to get it to tick over evenly at under 1000rpm, and if your country of residence has vehicle emission tests, the car might fail as a result of not being able to maintain a proper tick over.

One very worthwhile, if not essential, modification is fitting hardened exhaust valve seats, which allows you to run the Beetle on unleaded fuel. The question of whether you can run your air-cooled VW on unleaded is by no means a simple one, and you may get different advice from different authorities, though the question is a bit academic if you cannot be sure whether your Beetle is fitted with the original cylinder heads.

The easiest modification if you want to be 100 per cent certain that your engine will suffer no ill-effects from being run on unleaded fuel is to acquire new cylinder heads. Alternatively, you can have the existing exhaust valves and seats replaced with harder ones as part of the head overhaul. In either case, you may need 'fat' head gaskets, scalloped pistons or re-profiled compression chambers to lower the engine compression ratio.

On the subject of unleaded petrol, one thing is clear. There are many products on the market that claim to make your car compatible with unleaded fuel, but the author has never found any that work ...

HEAD OVERHAUL

The first job is to clean the external surfaces of the cylinder heads thoroughly, and a proper cleaning bath makes the job slightly easier. On the Beetle cylinder head there are fins and holes which assist cooling, and these can become filled with a mixture of what seems like burnt oil and dirt. The finned areas take some cleaning, but it's worth the effort. If you don't possess a cleaning bath, try a proprietary cleaning fluid and a toothbrush to work it in.

The Beetle combustion chambers are easily gouged if you try to scrape off carbon deposits (the usual method of cleaning heads), and the sharp edges of gouges, or even scratches, in the chamber will glow red hot when the engine is running, causing pre-ignition. To clean out the combustion chamber in the head, therefore, use spray-on gasket remover and a toothbrush to work it in - leave it for ten to fifteen minutes whilst it loosens the carbon, then scrape it away with a plastic scraper, or wipe it off with a cloth. The gasket remover has to be used with caution; wear rubber gloves to protect your hands, and use some form of eye protection in case of splashes.

Once the head is clean the valves can be removed. Removing a valve involves using a compressor to compress the spring, removing the collets from each side of the stem, then releasing the pressure. The valve and spring can then be removed. It's usually necessary to give the valve spring cap a tap with a hammer to free it from the collets before the spring can be compressed.

As you remove the valves, store them in such a way that you can replace them in the correct cylinder positions - don't mix them up. You can use pieces of cardboard with holes punched in to hold the valve stems and write the location of each valve on the board; an alternative is to use a centre punch to make small marks in the valve face but, because the tiny raised edges around a centre punch mark can glow red hot when the engine is running and cause pre-ignition, I no longer recommend this method.

Check the head for cracks - cracked heads can be welded but renewal is a better option, in my opinion. Check the valve seat visually for pitting and damage, and also check the part of the valve that sits in it. Damaged seats can be lapped (ground) or re-cut if the damage isn't too bad - if there's deep pitting then they have to be machined out and new ones pressed in; damaged valves may be lapped in, although if the damage is severe, they'll have to be renewed.

To check a valve stem and its guide, place the stem in the guide from the top of the cylinder head and feel for slackness between the two. If the valve stem is slack, the guide will have to be renewed; if the stem sticks in the guide it is bent, and both valve and guide will have to be renewed: replace all valves and guides as a set. If the valve guides have to be replaced, the valve seats will have to be recut; DIY cutters are available but it's probably best to leave this work to an engineer.

To check a valve spring you need one good or, preferably new, spring for comparison, a length of ½in diameter threaded rod, nuts and washers (you'll find these at any DIY store). Thread the good spring onto the rod, then a washer, then the spring you wish to check. Place a washer and a nut each side, then tighten one of the nuts so that the springs compress. Simply compare the lengths of the compressed springs to determine whether the old one is still okay; if it's much shorter than the new one, renew it.

Lapping valves

If the valve faces and their seats aren't damaged, you have simply to lap them in, for which you need a tub of grinding paste and a grinding tool (both available at low cost from any motor factor). The 'tool' is no more than a short stick with a rubber sucker on the end; most people use saliva to wet the sucker which can then be stuck to the valve end, the tool held between the palms and the hands rubbed together, so that the valve rotates.

Place a little coarse paste (there will be both coarse and fine paste in the tub) on the valve contact area, then position it, rotate it for a couple of seconds, lift the tool and valve slightly, turn them through 60 degrees and repeat. The paste grinds both the valve and the seat.

Check the valve and seat by wiping off the paste and visually inspecting them; there should be an unbroken matt ring on both. If not, repeat the grinding. When the unbroken ring is visible, change over to the smooth paste and repeat.

The final check that the valve and seat are okay is to drop the valve into position from a height of a couple of inches above the seat. If it bounces back up, it's okay; if it doesn't bounce, lap it some more.

As an alternative to the traditional grinding tool, you can acquire tools that fit into the chucks of electric drills and speed the process. Whether the expense of buying the tool justifies the small amount of work it saves is a decision for the individual. I've never seen a need for one, and I work on engines more than most people.

REBUILD CONTINUED

There is another recommended pre-assembly test. If you have purchased new cam followers, measure the depth of the head flanges because they might be thicker than the originals, which could result in a camshaft lobe jamming. If the flanges on the new cam followers are thicker, refit the cam followers, then the cam bearings and camshaft, and check the cam lobe/follower clearance using a feeler gauge; this should be 1-2mm. If there's less than 1mm of clearance, the crankcase under the cam follower flanges needs relieving to give adequate clearance; not a difficult job but one I'd always hand over to an engineer.

An engineer friend gave me a useful tip for engine rebuilding, which is to pack the oil pump with petroleum jelly. This effectively 'primes' the pump so that it starts to draw oil from the sump as soon as the engine spins. I always make a point of removing the sparkplugs (pull the leads well away from the sparkplug holes or, ideally, disconnect the king lead at the distributor), and spinning an engine on the starter (maybe five, 5 second bursts - don't overdo it, because the battery can be damaged if it's drained too much, too rapidly) until there's some oil pressure after the engine has had major work done, or even after it's lain unused for any length of time. You can also use either petroleum jelly or grease to hold the camshaft followers in position in the right hand crankcase half while you assemble the two crankcase halves.

On the subject of the oil pump, your workshop manual will show you how to measure for wear, but I recommend you ignore this and fit a new pump regardless. They don't cost a lot and give you the peace of mind of knowing that the oil pump should, if anything, outlast the rest of the reconditioned engine. And, on the subject of engine oil, there's no harm in and, in fact, a lot to be said for, increasing the frequency of engine oil changes for a reconditioned engine.

Before reassembling the engine, you have the option of lightly grinding the cylinders into the heads using a fine valve lapping paste. This should give a better seal but I'm not entirely convinced it's always necessary. If there are carbon marks where the cylinder end sits in a head, by all means lap in the cylinders; just be sure to get every scrap of abrasive paste off afterwards.

FUEL PUMP

The fuel pump pressure should be 3.5psi at 3400rpm, and equipment with which to take this measurement can be found at

The oil cooler (arrowed) is the Beetle's radiator, responsible for keeping the engine temperature within bounds. If you go to all the trouble of reconditioning an engine, it's worth renewing the cooler; they're not too expensive.

most repair shops. However, the Beetle fuel pump is not too expensive, and most people will renew the pump as a matter of course during a restoration. When a fuel pump fails, it allows fuel to enter the crankcase, diluting the oil and damaging the engine: early signs of this are a rise in oil level and a smell of fuel on the dipstick.

Replace the fuel pump push rod assembly and the pump, and refit the distributor drive shaft if you have not already done so. When fitting the thrust washers, use grease to hold them together, and fit them with a thin length of rod to ensure that they don't drop down into the crankcase.

Refit the oil pressure relief valve (two on cars after 1969), and the oil strainer and its cover plate. Check the flywheel ring gear teeth for damage, replace the gasket and offer the flywheel into position, remembering to line up the dowel and hole which you marked when stripping the assembly. Refit the crankshaft pulley and the flywheel, torquing the former to 33ft/lbs and the latter to 253ft/lbs - okay, let's be honest here, we DIY-ers don't usually possess a torque wrench which goes quite as high as that! The sensible solution is to take the engine to a garage for final tightening of the flywheel nut - most people use a long lever on the end of a 36mm hexagonal socket - but the former method is recommended.

Replace the heat exchangers and exhaust system, then the generator pedestal, inlet manifold and carburettor, oil cooler and, finally, the generator and fan shroud.

You can test run the engine on the floor, if desired, and can get hold of an early transaxle half casing complete with starter motor. However, few enthusiasts will possess this, and so will have to refit the engine and hope for the best!

TINWARE

On any Beetle 'of a certain age' the tinware will probably be starting to look a little rough, courtesy of scratches made by slipping screwdrivers during maintenance, overspray in the body colour or a primer following minor repairs. It all adds up and, however smart the external paint job, every time you lift the engine bay lid the lacklustre tinware is there to greet you. Not a few proud owners of smart-looking classic cars hide their scruffy engine bays from prying eyes, like a guilty secret. It only takes a relatively short time to clean and repaint tinware, and its not exactly what you'd call hard work. Getting the tinware out of the engine bay is, however, and so the tinware receives attention usually only when the engine has been removed.

Before starting work on the tinware paintwork, check out the vital air flaps that direct cooling air to the oil cooler matrix. If the air flaps stick in the open position, the engine will take a long time to come to proper operating temperature, and fuel consumption will be high and engine wear accelerated. If the air flaps stick in the closed position, the engine will overheat to the point at which engine damage becomes likely.

You can check the flap mechanism (even with the engine in the car) by pushing the thermostat connecting link toward the tinware, simulating what happens when the engine warms up and the thermostat expands. The two flaps should move easily to the open position, and return when pressure on the thermostat link rod is eased. If the flaps do not move easily, it's worth removing them and cleaning out the dirt that's causing the problem; left unattended, the problem would become worse.

Never remove the thermostat to try and 'cure' an overheating problem, because that leaves the flaps permanently closed and exacerbates overheating. Many people remove the flap mechanisms and thermostat together, thinking that this reduces overheating, but all it does in the long run is increase the time the engine takes to come to normal operating temperature, which also happens to be the time that engine wear is at its highest - in other words, it accelerates engine wear.

Tinware with sound paint can simply be cleaned, thoroughly degreased and repainted. Cleaning involves carefully chipping or scraping away any thick deposits such as underseal (which shouldn't be there anyway), then degreasing the tinware. Degreasing involves using a substance which dissolves grease and oil - spirit wipe (available from automotive paint suppliers) is probably the best product. Paint on the cleaning fluid and then wipe it and the grease away with a clean rag - if the grease is thick, you may need to scrub the tinware with an old toothbrush or similar tool. It's good policy to give the new paint something to grip by keying the existing paint - use a fine wet 'n dry emery paper wet to lightly score the surface.

If no bare metal is exposed you can do without undercoats - too great a thickness of paint can cause problems - and apply the topcoat. Do take time to test spray a small, out of sight area of tinware first to ensure that your chosen paint does not react with the paint that's already there.

Tinware which has rusted is another matter. Ideally, clean away all the rust. Deal with flat areas using a 40 grit abrasive 'production' paper disc powered by an electric drill. Convex areas and corners are more of a problem. Cup brushes which mount in an electric drill rarely seem to be up to the task, and flap wheels might prove a better option (go for the coarsest grade abrasive you can). Alternatively, if you possess an angle grinder, you can buy cup brushes for these which are made effective by the 11,000rpm or so speed of the angle grinder - but be very wary of using abrasive discs with the angle grinder, because they can prove very fierce, and will chomp their way through the steel if you're not very careful.

After cleaning/degreasing comes priming. Use a fairly inert - in that it doesn't react with tiny traces of other paint types - primer, preferably a rust-resisting type.

Safety is paramount. The thinners used with all paint types is both flammable and injurious to health. You don't need to drink paint or thinners to suffer ill-effects, simply breathing in the fumes is enough. With some paints and thinners, the effects can be very serious indeed, because they can be both toxic and corrosive - primers for aluminium being a case in point. Don't spray automotive paint in a confined space unless you have breathing apparatus - dust masks are useless, you need a filtered air supply and a helmet to spray safely in a booth. If, like me, you don't possess breathing equipment, don't take chances - spray outdoors. Don't get paint or thinners on your skin - thinners suck the natural moisture out of your skin and leave it wide open to infection.

The dangers of fire and explosion should be taken very seriously indeed. Thinners are flammable, and their fumes - if allowed to build up, can be explosive - again, don't spray in a confined space. Spray booths have air circulation systems to stop fumes building up, but don't try and cobble an extractor system together yourself, because sparks between the brushes and commutator arms of the fan's electric motor can be quite sufficient to trigger an explosion - air circulation systems MUST force air into the building rather than suck it out.

Unless your workshop has superb natural ventilation, spray outdoors. Pick a fairly still, warm and dry day. There's a chance that dust, leaves or insects will land on the still-wet paint, but that's a lot better than risking a fire, explosion or internal damage through breathing in fumes.

Topcoat paints

The majority of tinware acts only to seal off the engine bay so that the hot air cannot be drawn up into the engine bay and taken in by the cooling system. It, like the fan cowling, doesn't get very hot, so I favour radiator enamel, which is proofed to far higher temperatures (200 degrees Celsius) than will be necessary. The cylinder shrouds are another matter; their close proximity to the cylinder and head cooling fins means they could get very hot indeed, and a black gloss exhaust paint is probably best for these.

Radiator enamel is available in aerosol cans from most DIY stores, along with suitable primers if you don't have spray equipment. Aerosol spray cans are very useful for spraying small areas, but not so good for large areas. With a spray gun you can usually adjust the width of the spray up to around 8in, which means that you have to make far fewer 'passes' than when using a spray can with a narrower spray width. What's more, the paint is distributed in a more elliptical shape with the spray gun, whereas aerosol cans spray paint in a circle, which deposits many times more paint in the centre than at the edges when you make a pass with it, so it's difficult to achieve an even layer of paint.

However, the largest tinware area you'll have to spray is the fan cowling, and so the shortcomings of aerosol cans is not so important.

After the paint has been applied, leave it to harden for as long as possible before refitting the tinware - 'soft' paint is easily damaged. Therefore, you should deal with the tinware BEFORE you start the engine reconditioning, so that the paint can carry on hardening while you wrestle with the engine internals.

Whatever you do, don't handle recently-painted tinware with greasy hands - you'll leave indelible fingerprints all over it.

ENGINE ELECTRICS

Coil and condenser

Intermittent condenser and coil faults can occur and are very difficult to pin down, so renew both the coil and condenser when

The condenser or capacitor bolts to the side of the distributor. The condenser can fail, and cause the low tension current to short circuit to earth, and then the sparkplugs won't fire. However, if the condenser fails by going open circuit, the sparkplugs will still fire and the engine run, but excessive sparking will occur between the contact breaker points, causing a build-up of carbon which, long-term, will damage the faces of the points and cause erratic ignition. Capacitors can fail without warning, so carry a spare.

refitting the engine (and every couple of years afterwards). You can test the coil and condenser and, given that even brand-new examples of both can be faulty, I'll tell you how.

Test the coil using a multimeter set to measure resistance. The primary winding can be measured at the two low tension terminals, and should be very low - around one ohm. The secondary winding is measured between the coil feed (+) terminal and the centre HT contact, and should be in the region of 10Kohms (10,000 ohms). To test the condenser, turn the engine so that the heel of the points is not on a cam and the contact points are touching. Turn on the ignition and separate the contacts using a non-conductive implement. There should be a small flash between the points as they separate. If not, check that the points are receiving a charge and, if so, change the condenser. If, when separating the contact points, there's a bright flash and a loud crack is audible, renew the condenser.

Distributor

The original distributor will be either Bosch or VW, according to the model and year. These are the original distributors:

1200cc
1967-70 .... 0.231-137 0091029
1970.................... 0231-137 009/039

1300cc
1968.................... 0 231-137 009/029
1969-70 .... 0 231-115 0731082
1970-71 .... 0 231-167 049
1972.................... 0 231-146 101/170 034

1302, 1303
1970-71 .... 0 231-167 049
1972.................... 0 231-146 101/170 034

1300, 1302 and 1303 (automatic)
1970-72 .... 0 231-167 051
1972.................... 0 231-115 094/170 036

1300S, 1302S (1970-73), 1303S
(1974 on)
1970-71 .... 0 231-167 049
1971.................... 0 231-146 101/170 034

1300S, 1302S (1970-73), 1303
(automatic)
1970-71 .... 0 231-167 051
1971.................... 0 231-115 094/170 036

Most Beetle spares suppliers today offer only the famous '009' distributor, which suits most models but does not have a vacuum advance, using centrifugal force to vary the timing instead. If you fit an 009 distributor be sure to blank off the vacuum take-off on the inlet manifold or you'll have a weak mixture.

When the rotor arm aligns with no. 1 plug lead, it's also aligned with the notch in the distributor rim ...

... and the crankshaft pulley timing mark will align with the mark on the crankcase or the split line of the crankcase halves.

Vacuum units for Beetle distributors are available and, if this is the only faulty component, then by all means renew it. However, one of the most common problems with old distributors is worn bearings, which give variable dwell angle (the length of time the points are closed), and therefore variable ignition timing. If a distributor has worn bearings, the easiest solution is to fit an 009 distributor.

HT components

Examine the HT leads for cuts or abrasions. These would allow moisture (including light condensation) on the outside to form an electrical pathway which the HT charge would take in preference to jumping the sparkplug electrode gap - causing misfiring - and damaged leads (and caps) must be renewed.

Both the HT leads and the distributor cap benefit from a light covering of silicone, usually in the form of WD40, Damp Start and similar spray-on products. Remove the leads and distributor cap from the engine bay before spraying.

Moisture can also cause problems if the distributor cap is cracked (the crack holds moisture which diverts the HT voltage), and a cracked cap must be renewed. Examine the inside of the cap for etched, rough-edged black lines, these are filled with carbon, a good conductor of electricity able to divert the HT voltage. In the short term, the carbon can be scraped out but renew the cap at the earliest opportunity.

C/B (contact breaker) points

Examine the contact faces: if they are merely dirty clean them gently; if they are pitted, renew them. You can test the points accurately if you possess a suitable electrical test meter; set it to measure ultra-low voltage (0-1V) and connect it across the closed points, then switch on the ignition - the reading will show the voltage drop across the points: if it is greater than a third of a volt, clean or renew the points.

Using a 21mm socket on the generator pulley nut, turn the engine until the points' heel is resting on a cam lobe and the points are fully open, and then check the gap using a 0.016in (0.4mm) feeler gauge. The gauge should enter and move with just a little drag. To adjust the gap, slacken the screw on the baseplate and use a screwdriver as shown before pinching up the screw and rechecking.

Rotor arm

Check the rotor arm contacts and gently clean if necessary. Before replacing the rotor arm, place a dab of grease on the distributor drive shaft cam, to help lubricate and reduce wear in the c/b points' heel.

TIMING

Whenever the points gap has been altered, it will be necessary to reset the ignition timing - and this is where things become complicated. Setting the timing means checking that the appropriate timing mark (on the crankshaft pulley) is aligned with the join line in the crankcase, at the exact point at which the sparkplug is to ignite the mixture, usually expressed as so many degrees before the piston reached the top of its travel ('X' degrees BTDC - Before Top Dead Center or ATDC - After Top Dead Center). Problems arise because different Beetles have different ignition timing requirements and various combinations of notches on the crankshaft pulley, according to the year and model.

Even worse, you often cannot be sure that the crank pulley fitted to your engine is the correct one; a previous owner may have fitted a non-standard one, or an uprated camshaft or distributor (which will require different timing settings). If you're in any doubt about which crank pulley notch is the right one to use, have the timing set at a garage using a Crypton or similar, and ask the mechanic to mark the correct timing mark for future reference.

Timing is as follows:

1200
(1954-July 1960), 10 degrees BTDC
(Aug 1960-1970), 7.5 degrees BTDC,
(after August 1970) TDC

1300
(Aug 1965-1970), 7.5 BTDC
(1970-July 1971 with double vacuum unit 5 ATDC)

1500
7.5 BTDC, Auto with AA dist. TDC

1600
(pre-August 1971), 5 ATDC
(August 1971 on), 7.5 BTDC

There are two popular DIY methods of setting the timing - static and dynamic. Static timing is carried out with the engine not running, is easy and requires no specialist equipment, but it's not as accurate as the dynamic timing method. Dynamic timing is carried out with the engine running and requires a stroboscopic timing light (£10-£20).

Static timing

This entails turning the crankshaft until piston number one is on its compression stroke, aligning the appropriate timing notch, and then checking that the points open at this precise point.

Remove the distributor cap and, using a 21mm socket on the generator pulley nut, turn the engine over until the rotor arm is pointing at the position occupied by number one cylinder plug lead - there is a very small notch in the distributor body rim at this point. Now turn the engine until the crankshaft pulley timing notch is in line with the split in the crankcase, when the points should just be starting to separate. You can check this by connecting a test bulb to the points' live side and an earth, such as the distributor body. Switch on the ignition, and the bulb will illuminate the moment the points open. To adjust the timing, slacken the distributor clamp nut and turn the distributor until the light illuminates, then tighten the bolt.

Dynamic timing

This is inherently more accurate than static timing, and can reveal problems with the vacuum advance system.

Connect the stroboscope leads to number one HT lead and the distributor HT socket. Highlight the timing notch using Typex or white paint, to make it easier to see. Ensure that the strobe leads cannot become fouled in the generator drive belt, then start the engine and run it long enough for the engine to come to normal operating temperature.

Disconnect the vacuum advance pipe and plug it. Slacken the distributor clamp nut just enough to enable you to turn it by hand. Start the engine and point the strobe light at the crank pulley wheel; the light flashes every time number one plug fires, and this appears to arrest the motion of the pulley, allowing you to clearly see the timing mark and the crankcase split line - they should be aligned. If you cannot see the timing marks clearly enough, stop the engine and place a dab of white paint on the marks. If the marks do not align, adjust the timing by rotating the distributor body, and finally pinch up the distributor clamp nut.

When the timing is correct, reconnect the vacuum advance pipe. There should be an advance in the timing - if the timing does not advance when the pipe is reconnected, the pipe could be leaking (check), the points' base plate could be sticking (check, clean and lubricate), or the vacuum diaphragm could be damaged (renew the unit).

Dwell angle

Some automotive test meters are able to measure dwell angle, and this is very useful. The dwell angle is a measure of the time the points are closed; if the points are opening early or late, this affects the dwell angle, so measuring the dwell angle allows you to double-check whether the points are opening on time. However, the main advantage of measuring the dwell angle (48 to 52 degrees for the Beetle) is that it can reveal distributor wear - especially in the drive spindle bushes. The reading should be steady; if it fluctuates, the cam bearings are worn. This wear gives a fluctuating dwell angle and hence variable ignition timing, causing generally rough running.

A DIY dwell angle meter is connected to the coil (+) terminal, in addition to which it needs an earth and feed to power it.

Vacuum advance

Irrespective of which method you use to set the ignition timing, you can easily check that the vacuum advance is working properly, by pulling the pipe from the diaphragm unit with the (warmed up) engine running. If the vacuum advance is okay the revs will drop markedly.

ENGINE WON'T START!

As soon as the engine, fuel and ignition components have been refitted, it's a good idea to ensure that the engine runs before continuing with the last stages of the restoration. It is very common for engines in newly restored cars to fail to start.

The following advice might seem pedantic and overly safety-conscious but, in the few minutes it takes to connect the battery or fire up the engine, you could inadvertently start a fire that could easily wreck the wiring loom, or reduce your newly-restored car to a burned-out wreck.

Before connecting the battery, put petrol in the tank and check there are no fuel leaks. Petrol gives off highly combustible fumes, and connecting the battery often causes a small spark at the terminal, so get down under the car, get your nose right into the engine bay and sniff around. If you cannot smell fuel it's time to connect the battery.

DO NOT carry out the following test if the battery has recently been charged, because the charging process generates gas which can cause the battery to explode (covering everything in the vicinity in a weak, but potentially dangerous, acid). If you've had the battery on charge, allow a wide margin for safety and consider doing this test the following day.

Always connect the positive battery lead first, then touch the negative lead momentarily against the negative post - if there's a small spark in between the two, something's wrong with the vehicle wiring. Check that nothing is switched on, or that a current-drawing accessory is connected; if there is, disconnect it and try touching the earth lead to the negative battery terminal again. If you still get a spark then either a wire or terminal is shorting to earth, or an electrical component is faulty. Start disconnecting wires one-by-one until you find the faulty circuit.

Earth leakages aren't always dangerous; most cause wires in the affected circuit to become hot, but then the circuit fuse should blow. However, not all circuits are fused, and a short circuit to earth in one of these causes the wire to become so hot that it first melts its insulation and, within seconds, can be on fire. Many Beetles have non-insulated spade terminals, especially under the luggage bay hood behind the dashboard, and any one of these could have been accidentally knocked off, causing a short, as could damaged insulation on a wire.

If you cannot track down the short to earth, disconnect the battery and call in a mobile auto-electrician to sort it out. This is not cheap but is cheaper and less traumatic than setting the car ablaze.

DIAGNOSTICS

The mechanical fuel pump should have filled the carburettor bowl whilst you were spinning the engine on the starter to get oil pumping around the engine, so the engine should fire up with no problem - give it a go! If it won't start, don't sit there spinning it on the starter and running down the battery, stop and diagnose what's wrong.

When trying to diagnose a fault that prevents the engine from starting, it's important to keep an open mind and not take anything for granted, especially in the case of new ignition components. Just because the high tension leads are brand-new it does not mean that they can't be faulty. The same goes for other ignition components, so don't blinker yourself by confining fault-tracing to testing old components and ignoring the new stuff.

If the engine won't fire at all then the fault affects all four cylinders, which could mean that fuel is not getting through, or that a component in the ignition system between the distributor cap centre terminal and the low tension feed to the points is faulty. If the engine fires but won't run, there could still be a fuel delivery problem (insufficient delivery), but it's more commonly caused by the ignition.

Just after turning over the engine, if you can smell petrol near the exhaust tailpipes you obviously don't have a fuel problem (unless the engine is flooding, which is far less likely to be the problem than an ignition fault), so concentrate on the ignition.

Carry out the simplest and quickest tests first.

Is there a spark?

The first task is to establish whether there's a spark at a sparkplug. There are variations on the method described here, but the procedure I describe means you won't experience the sensation of 25,000 volts of HT pulse through your arm!

Pull one sparkplug lead from its plug and connect it to a spare sparkplug. Grip the sparkplug in the clamp of one standard battery jump lead, and connect the other end of the lead to earth on the car. Ensure that the plug lead and jump lead cannot become entangled in the generator drive belt or either of the pulley wheels, then have a helper turn over the engine and look to see whether there is a spark visible across the plug gap. If there is a spark, check out the fuel system (see 'Fuel'). If there's no spark, read on.

Low tension circuit

Remove the distributor cap and check that the points heel is not on a distributor drive shaft lobe (the points are closed). If it is, turn the engine using a socket on the crank nut, or put the car in gear and push it until the points are closed. Switch on the ignition and manually open the points using a non-conductive implement. There should be a small spark visible as the points part. If there is, move on to testing the coil. If there's a bright spark accompanied by an audible 'crack' when the points open, the condenser is faulty and must be renewed. If there's no spark, either the LT circuit is dead or the points are corroded/covered in dirt.

Use a bulb tester to check for power at the points. If there is power, remove and clean or renew the points; chances are the contact faces are either corroded or covered with carbon from sparking, the latter indicating that the condenser isn't working and requires renewal. If there's no power, you will have to trace back through the LT circuit to the ignition key to find the break.

Next check out the coil. Disconnect the low tension wires and meter the resistance of the primary winding (measure across the two terminals) using a multimeter set to measure ohms. The primary winding resistance varies but it should be low, anything from under one ohm to four or five ohms. If it's higher or infinite (open circuit), renew the coil.

High tension (HT) circuit

Measure the coil secondary winding resistance (from the coil '+' terminal to the centre contact) with the multimeter set to record kilo (thousands of) ohms. The reading should be maybe seven to fifteen kilo ohms. If it's low or infinite (open circuit), renew the coil.

HT leads, distributor cap and spark plugs

If you service your own car you ought to have handy a spare distributor cap and set of leads which you renewed during a service, so check these HT components by substitution. HT faults are usually caused when the HT voltage finds an easier route to an earth than jumping the sparkplug electrodes. When this happens, you can usually see what's called 'tracking' along the HT leads, though tracking can occur within a faulty distributor cap, in which case it leaves rough-edged grooves containing carbon within the distributor cap head - check for this.

Fuel

If a fault can't be found with the ignition system, the engine may be flooded; remove the sparkplugs and check if the electrodes are soaked in petrol. If they are, dry them, remove the King lead from the coil (to prevent sparks jumping from the HT leads near the sparkplug holes), and spin the engine on the starter for twenty or so seconds to clear excess fuel from the cylinders. Then refit the plugs and the engine should start.

If the engine repeatedly floods, the cause is either the float chamber needle is stuck or being held open (strip and clean), or the float is jammed.

If you cannot smell fuel near the exhaust tailpipes after turning over the engine, fuel starvation could be the problem. Check the fuel pump by disconnecting the fuel line at the carburettor (wrap a cloth around the end first just in case there's any residual pressure). Place the end in a jar, and turn over the engine for a couple of seconds. Fuel should be pumped into the jar and, if not, it's possible that the fuel pump diaphragm is shot (the engine oil level will rise and the oil will smell of petrol), or there's a blockage in the fuel lines or the filter (check visually). It's more likely that the cut-off valve in the carburettor is faulty (remove and apply a voltage to test it), or its feed wire has been knocked off.

If the fuel pump is okay, visually check the cold start enrichment mechanism; the throttle stop screw should be resting on the top step of the cam. As a last resort, strip and clean the carburettor float chamber, needle valve, and jets.

RUNNING IN

A rebuilt engine does, contrary to popular belief, benefit from a 'running-in' period; that is, a period of use on the road when revolutions are restricted to, perhaps, 3500rpm, and the engine is not allowed to labour in too high a gear. In other words, drive slowly and be gentle with a rebuilt engine.

In a rebuilt engine both new and machined engine components will appear to fit very snugly with neighbouring components, but will still have to be completely 'bedded-in' by being run in the assembled engine. During this bedding-in period, component wear (journals, crankpins, bearings, piston rings, and cylinders, etc.) is initially very high, but will progressively reduce. This wear produces tiny pieces of metal, which the oil carries and - hopefully - dumps in the sump, so extra oil and oil changes are essential.

Before putting the car on the road, the author strongly recommends that you warm and run the engine for, perhaps, ten minutes at around 1500rpm, and then a further ten minutes at 2000rpm. Change the engine oil and clean the filter. These running periods can be longer, and many authorities advise that both number of times they occur and revolutions are increased. The idea of this is to start bedding-in the engine components before the extra stresses of feeding power through the wheels is brought to bear, especially on the mains and big end bearings.

Remember that component wear is also always higher when the engine is cold, so take it very easy on the road for the first few miles each day. If your daily journey begins with a long uphill climb, warm the engine through before tackling this.

The author recommends that, for the first 500 miles on a rebuilt engine, top speed is limited to around 50mph, that you accelerate as slowly as possible, and that you tackle steep hills - if at all - in a suitably low gear. At that stage it would be a good idea to change the engine oil and filter to get rid of any tiny fragments of metal which the oil should have cleaned from bedding-in new components. During the second 500 miles he would recommend a revolution limit of, perhaps, 4000rpm, terminating again in an oil change and filter clean. The next two 500 mile intervals should be marked with oil changes if you want your rebuilt engine to enjoy the longest possible life; when you've gone to the trouble of restoring your car, why wouldn't you?

Remember that, during the running-in period, you are effectively 'blueprinting' some of the most important and stressed components in the engine. An engine that is abused during this period will inevitably last for less time, and will usually give less power and use more fuel than one which is run-in correctly. However, don't be so single-minded during the running-in stage that you are a danger to other road users. Don't crawl along the motorway at 35mph; avoid such roads until your engine is run-in.

THE FUEL SYSTEM

Fuel tank

The first step in a restoration, or any welding job, is to make the car safe, not only disconnecting - and preferably removing - the battery, but the fuel tank and lines, too.

The fuel tank is situated within the front luggage compartment, usually covered with carpeting or trim. It's usually removed before a full restoration, although it can be necessary to remove it to check suspected leakage, as well as to allow access for replacement of the front axle beam or steering damper.

Disconnect the battery, and pull the petrol gauge wire connector from the terminal on the sender unit.

To reduce weight, the tank can be partially drained, which can be accomplished in two ways. It's feasible to clamp the flexible hose under the tank, disconnect the fuel line and connect another line which leads to a suitable receptacle. Most people will opt to siphon out the fuel. Whichever method is used, it's essential that the tank and receptacle (if it's metallic) are earthed, and are connected by a length of wire which will prevent any chance of static electrical discharges between the two, which could ignite the fuel/air mixture. The quickest way to achieve this is to use a battery jump lead.

To remove the fuel gauge or the fuel tank, begin by disconnecting the battery and then the sender wire.

The sender unit on most Beetles is held by a number of set screws.

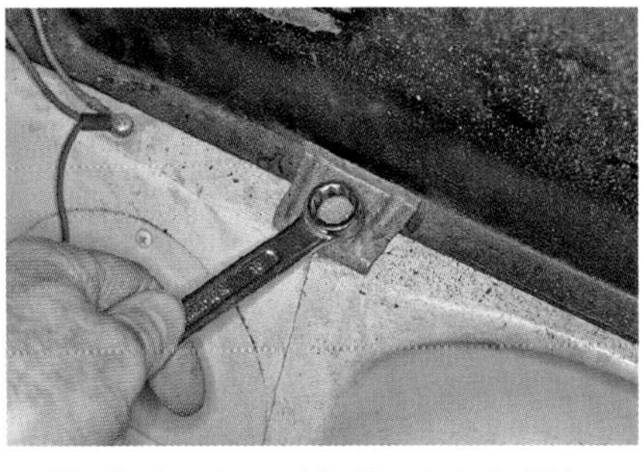

The fuel tank on this Beetle is held by clamps fixed by bolts running into captive nuts.

Access to the rear fuel tank clamp bolt heads is not good with a spanner, but easy if you use a socket.

The fuel filler neck will probably be secured by a jubilee clip.

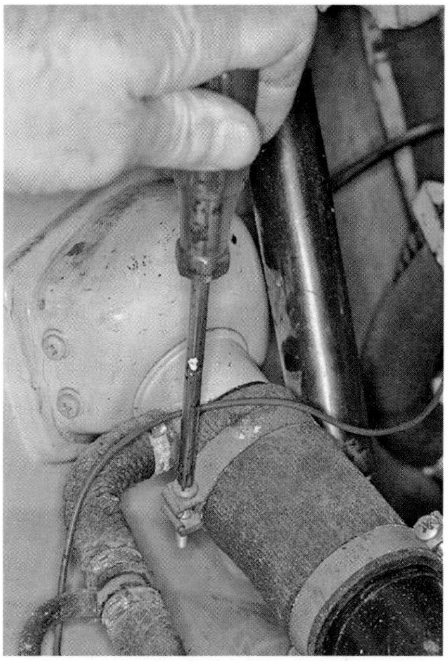

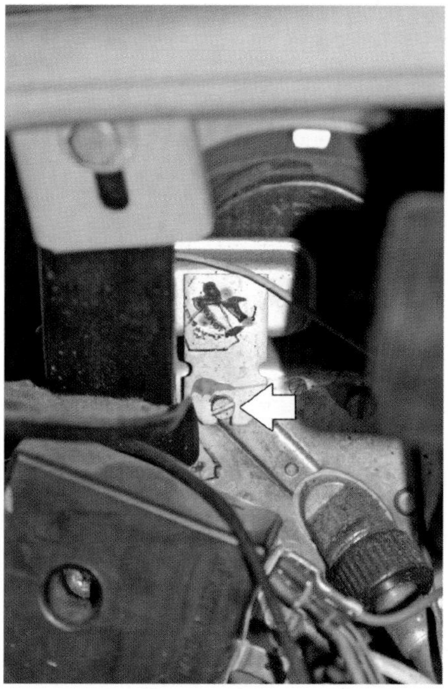

The fuel gauge sender varies the voltage it passes to the gauge, according to how much fuel is in the tank. Battery voltage varies according to whether the battery is run down or being charged. Stabilising the voltage between the battery and sender is the voltage stabiliser or trembler. The trembler regulates battery voltage to around 7-8V by making and breaking contact points very rapidly (via a bi-metal strip), and the fuel gauge is designed to work at this lower voltage. If the trembler stops working, so does the fuel gauge, and the trembler (held by the screw arrowed) must be replaced. DO NOT simply bypass the trembler, because the winding in the fuel gauge will burn through in a matter of seconds if full battery voltage passes through it.

Undo the set screws which secure the tank and lift it just high enough to get a clamp (a brake hose clamp is ideal) onto the flexible hose on the outlet, if you've not already clamped it. Undo the fitting which holds the fuel filler pipe to the tank, and pull this from the tank, then stuff the tank filler hole with rag to prevent spillage. The tank may now be carefully lifted out, preferably by two people, one each side of the car.

Do not store the fuel tank in the workshop, or any place where fire or sparks might occur. Even if drained of petrol, the tank will still be full of highly combustible petrol fumes, so store it in a separate outbuilding.

Inspect the fuel tank minutely (especially the underside and seams) for signs of rust, or tiny perforations. Never attempt to repair a fuel tank; if it leaks, replace it. Fill the old tank with water and ask your local garage to dispose of it safely.

Fuel tank sender unit

To remove the fuel gauge sender unit with the tank *in situ*, begin by disconnecting the battery and checking there are no potential sources of combustion anywhere near.

Disconnect the feed wire, then undo the five fixing screws. The sender unit can now be pulled from the tank. If the unit is not to be replaced immediately, tape plastic sheet over the aperture.

When refitting the sender, renew the gasket.

The fuel gauge on older cars can be problematic, but the fault might not necessarily concern the fuel gauge sender, nor the gauge - the 'trembler' (a voltage regulator) could be the culprit. The fuel gauge system uses a variable resistor in the sender unit to alter the voltage sent to the fuel gauge and, if unmodified battery voltage was used, the reading would vary according to the state of the battery: a run-down battery would result in the fuel gauge recording that a nearly full petrol tank was nearly empty! The voltage fed to the fuel gauge sender is regulated by a bi-metal voltage gauge, often called a 'trembler,' which quickly heats when current flows through it, causing the bi-metal arm holding one of the contact points to bend, breaking the circuit. The bi-metal arm cools very rapidly and straightens so that the contact points meet again, and the process repeats many times a second.

The trembler rapidly switching the current on and off effectively regulates the voltage - if the points were open half the time, the voltage would be 6V. Beetle tremblers are very expensive for what they are but, if they fail, NEVER bypass them, because the coil in the fuel gauge will burn out in a matter of seconds, and new fuel gauges are also expensive!

If you're troubleshooting a non-functioning fuel gauge outside of a restoration, switch on the ignition, pull the wire from the tank sender unit. and earth it. The fuel gauge should read FULL and, if it doesn't, the problem lies with the gauge, trembler or the system electrical feed, rather than the sender.

To test the sender during a restoration, first remove the sender from the tank (no smoking, naked lights or sparks); make a note to order a new sender gasket and take it well away from the tank before testing it. Plug the tank sender hole with rag so that fumes cannot escape. Attach a multimeter to the sender and earth, then operate the sender float - you should see a steadily rising resistance as the float moves towards the top of its travel, at which point there should be little or no resistance.

If the sender unit tests okay, refit it with a new gasket and look elsewhere - the trembler and gauge - for the problem. The gauge can be tested by connecting it to a battery of 6V or less and, if the needle responds to the voltage and the wiring is sound, the trembler is the cause of the problem.

Fuel lines

The petrol tank and carburettor are connected to flexible fuel hoses, which are in turn connected to a metal fuel line that runs inside the chassis spine. Old fuel hoses can become brittle and crack, and should be renewed during a restoration unless they are obviously in good order. The metal fuel pipe is rather problematic.

The fuel pipe can, in time, corrode from the outside to the point at which the wall becomes weak and cracks. Furthermore, the bulk of the pipe is hidden inside the chassis spine and cannot be viewed for assessment. It is possible to remove the fuel pipe from the chassis and fit a replacement, though it can prove very difficult, even when the body is off the chassis during restoration. The trouble involved is worth it, though.

Try fixing a line or a length of wire to the end of the pipe before pulling it out of the chassis, and fix the end of this to a replacement pipe to help guide it during fitting - this usually works. New metal fuel pipe comes in coiled lengths, and gently straightening it out before attempting to fit it can make the task easier. If it proves impossible, run the fuel pipe under the floor pans alongside the brake lines, using clips to hold it - NEVER run the fuel pipe through the passenger cab - that's a recipe for disaster should it ever spring a leak.

Carburettor

Well-worn carburettors will never be as fuel efficient as good carburettors, and may cause a reduction in performance. Some faults, such as worn jets and needles, can be put right fairly easily using widely available carburettor service kits, but others - including air induction past throttle butterfly spindle bushes - require specialist equipment and are not DIY jobs.

Some carburettor faults are not easy to pinpoint because their effects/symptoms can vary according to what the engine is being asked to do. Effects can be difficult to measure, in any case: air induction through a worn butterfly bush, for example, initially gives a weak mixture at low engine revolutions, but the ratio of the leakage to the 'normal' air reduces as engine revs rise. If the mixture is set correctly at low revs, then, the engine will run too rich at higher revolutions, giving high fuel consumption and increased engine wear. The problem is that you cannot measure whether the mixture is lean or rich unless you have access to a meter able to analyse the exhaust gasses. For less than the cost of having a tricky carburation fault professionally diagnosed (which needs a rolling road), you could buy a new carburettor.

If a high mileage Beetle is suspected of still having the original carburettor, it might pay to have this refurbished, buy an exchange reconditioned example, or a new carburettor. If the carburettor is believed to be generally good, there are still a couple of jobs that you should do.

Sediment in the fuel bowl can partially block the fuel chamber jet, especially if the carburettor is not stored upright whilst off the car. If allowed to build up, it can cause the main jet to become blocked, stopping the engine, often when the car is driven over rough terrain and sediment is thrown into the suspension. Regardless of whether or not the jet is blocked, it's good practice to clean out the fuel bowl and blow air through the jet.

Disconnect the cold-start wire,

To remove the air filter, remove the chesse-head screw (arrowed) and slacken the screw on the filter clamp, as shown here.

These two wires (combined on some cars) are live when the ignition is switched on. The upper terminal attaches to the fuel enrichment device (choke), and the other to the fuel cut-off device.

To clean out the fuel bowl, remove the carburettor and the five screws holding on the top section of the carburettor.

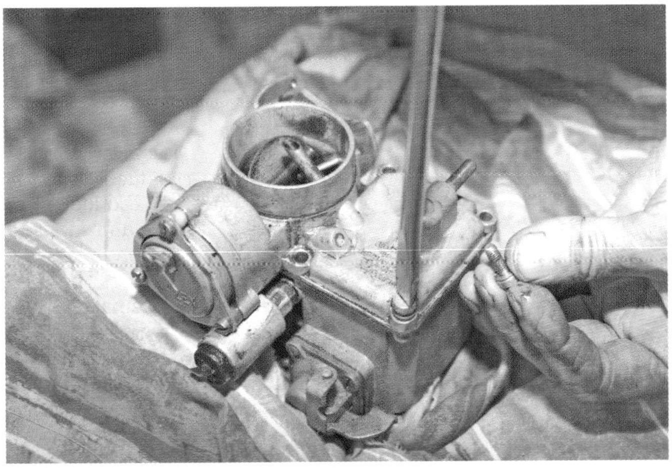

The upper carburettor section contains the fuel enrichment device, and the float chamber needle and jet.

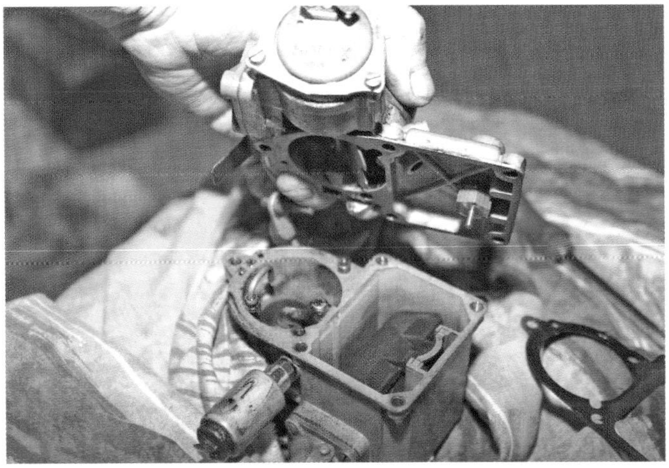

This float chamber is actually fairly clean. Loosen the crud and wash out with fuel. Inspect the float for damage.

The fuel enrichment device (white arrow) is adjusted by slackening the three screws surrounding it, and twisting the body until the top notch of the stepped lever on the other end of the choke spindle aligns with the throttle stop (ignition off). If faulty, the fuel cut-off valve (grey arrow) is removed using a 9mm spanner. Accelerator pump failure (black arrow) makes the engine unresponsive to acceleration.

If the mixture cannot be set properly and the car runs rich at speed and lean at tickover, suspect air induction. Try running a little oil onto the throttle butterfly shaft ends as indicated by the arrows. If the problem persists, you've tracked down the air induction: a new carburettor is probably the easiest solution.

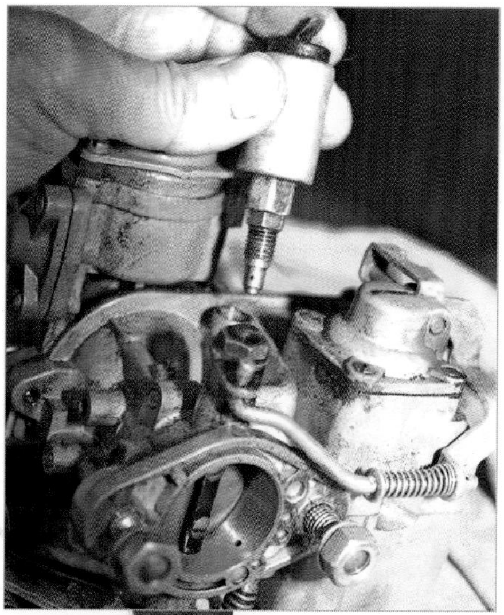

The most common fault with the fuel cut-off valve is the feed wire falling off. If the valve fails it's not too expensive to renew.

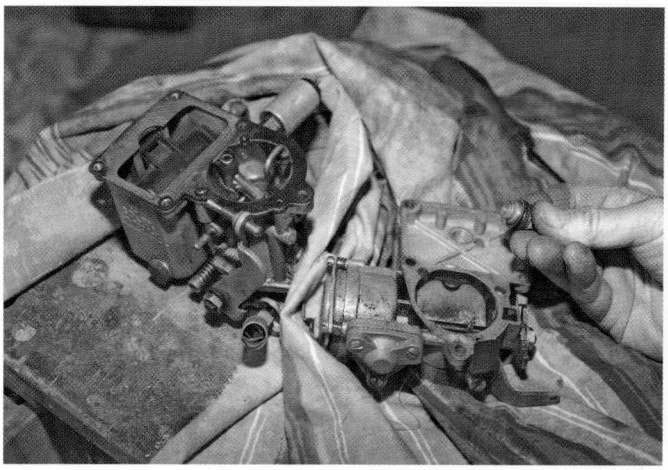

The fuel inlet jet simply unscrews. Blow compressed air through it to make sure it's clear.

When the carburettor is removed, be sure to block the down pipe with rags.

remove the air cleaner, and remove the screws securing the upper section of the carburettor body. Carefully lift out the float and remove the jet plug from the bottom of the float chamber, which will allow any fuel in the bowl to drain.

Clean the fuel bowl using a jet of air or a rag. Use compressed air to blow out the jet, and replace the jet, then the float and carburettor body gasket.

Check the float needle valve for leakage, by blowing air through the threaded end (fit a length of pipe to it rather than get a mouthful of petrol vapour), and pressing on the needle to shut the valve. If the valve leaks, renew it, but retain and refit the original packing washers, because the packing determines the fuel level.

The carburettor originally fitted to your Beetle varies according to the model and year of manufacture. The original carburettors are as follows:

1200
To August 1970 .... Solex 28 PICT 2

1200
August 1970 on .... Solex 30 PICT 3

1300
To August 1970 .... Solex 30 PICT 2

1300/1302
Aug 1970-Nov 1972 .... Solex 30 PICT 3

1300
Nov 1972 on .... Solex 31 PICT 3

1302S
Aug 1970-1972 .... Solex 34 PICT 3

1303
August 1972 on .... Solex 31 PICT 4

1303S
August 1972-1975 .... Solex 34 PICT 3

1303S
August 1975 on .... Solex 34 PICT 4

1500
Jan 1968-Aug 1970 ..... Solex 30 PICT 2

SPECIFICATIONS

It has long been common practice to uprate carburettors by fitting non-standard components and, if you wish to bring your Beetle to original specification, these are the correct internal components for each of the carburettors.

Solex 28 PICT 2
Choke tube 22.5mm
Main jet 122.5
Slow running jet 55

Solex 30 PICT 2 (as fitted to the 1300)
Choke tube 24mm
Main jet 125
Slow running jet 55

Solex 30 PICT 2 (as fitted to the 1500)
Choke tube 24mm
Main jet 120
Slow running jet 55

Solex 30 PICT 3
Choke tube 24mm
Main jet 112.5
Slow running jet 55

Solex 31 PICT 3
Choke tube 25.5mm
Main jet 130
Slow running jet 52.5

Solex 31 PICT 4
Choke tube 25.5mm
Main jet 130
Slow running jet 52.5

Solex 34 PICT 3
Choke tube 26mm
Main jet 145
Slow running jet 65

Solex 34 PICT 4
Choke tube 26mm
Main jet 127.5
Slow running jet 55

Today, most spares suppliers seem to offer just one carburettor for the single port and one for the twin port engine. These should function well, though it's advisable to seek professional advice on whether the most appropriate jets for your car are fitted.

When refitting the carburettor, do use a new gasket because air induction past a reused gasket will mean the reconditioned or new carburettor will perform no better than the original. When fitting the washers and nuts that hold the carburettor to the inlet manifold, take care not to drop them as they have a knack of bouncing behind the crankshaft pulley.

INLET MANIFOLD

The Beetle inlet manifold is prone to a phenomenon called 'icing,' whereby ice builds up inside and partially plugs the manifold, causing the engine to miss and even stop at tick over. The pressure of air passing through the manifold is low, which chills it and the manifold, causing moisture in the air/fuel mixture to condense onto the wall of the manifold and freeze.

To counteract this, VW equipped the manifold with a 'hot spot,' a tube that connects the two exhausts so that hot exhaust gasses pass back and forth inside, warming it and the inlet manifold. Problems arise when the hot spot end gaskets leak

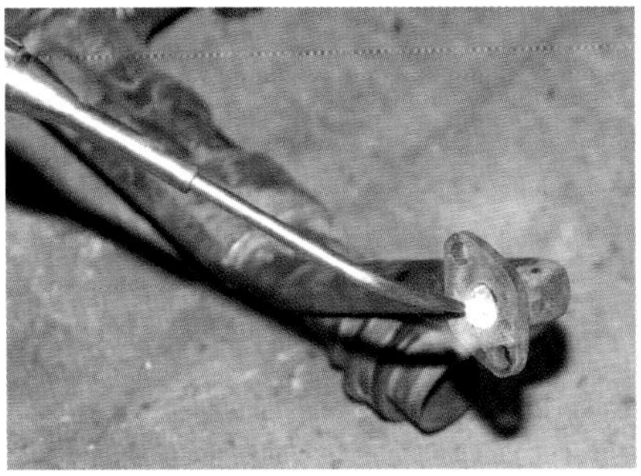

Blocked hot spot pipes are difficult to clear because the blockage is usually a mixture of (mainly) carbon with a touch of rust scale from the wall of the pipe. One way to clear it (which could be the ONLY way) is to burn out the carbon.

After preliminary heating of the end of the pipe, a few sharp blows will dislodge mainly rust scale and a little carbon.

Now the serious stuff begins. Terry 'turns up the heat' to get the carbon burning ...

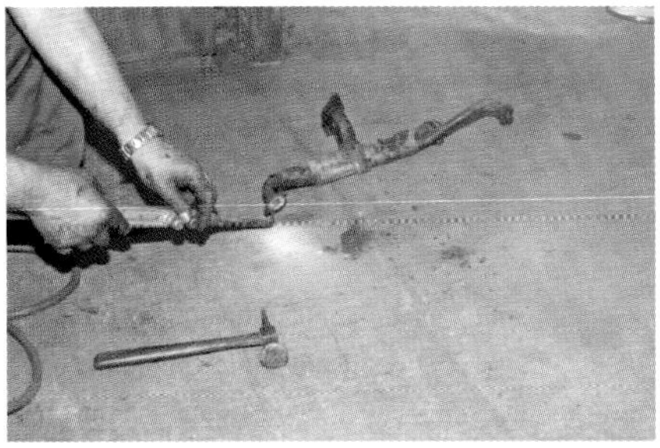

... then the acetylene is turned off and oxygen is fed into the pipe.

Eureka! (or words to that effect). It took, perhaps, fifteen minutes to clear the hot spot blockage but, because the assemblies are no longer made, it's worth it.

The clutch operating shaft and arm of an early car, and the clutch release bearing and its retaining spring, are all different on early cars. Take the old one with you when you go to get spares to avoid misunderstanding.

The finger-type clutch found on later Beetles. The hole in the driven plate (arrowed) must be centred so that, when it slides onto the gearbox first motion shaft, the engine is in the correct position and the engine mounting bolt holes line up.

or - long-term - when the inside of the hot spot becomes clogged with carbon.

Carbon cannot simply be brushed out of the hot spot as a chimney is swept. The best method of removing it is to burn it out, as shown in the photographs.

CLUTCH

The clutch is a very simple mechanism. The driven plate has frictional material on its surfaces and is located on the gearbox input shaft (first motion shaft) splines so that, when it turns, the input shaft also turns. The driven plate is normally gripped tightly in a 'sandwich' between the flywheel and the pressure plate (the latter contained within the clutch cover, and the pressure provided either by diaphragm or coil springs, depending on the type of clutch), so that when the engine turns over, the clutch assembly - and hence the driven plate and gearbox input shaft - also turn.

When the clutch pedal is pressed downwards, the clutch operating lever moves the release bearing which, in turn, pulls the pressure plate away from the driven plate, so releasing the driven plate from the sandwich between the pressure plate and flywheel, and disengaging drive to the gearbox.

During a restoration it's as well to replace the clutch driven plate and cover, unless they're in very good condition. If, in daily use, the clutch develops problems, such as failing to disengage, dragging or slipping, try adjusting it via the large wing nut on the clutch operating lever before removing the engine!

If you need to replace the clutch or its operating lever, and/or release bearing, outside of a restoration, it's possible to replace the clutch components by simply lowering the engine and turning it to give access to the clutch assembly, rather than having to drag it out from under the car. (See Engine Removal.)

With the engine removed from the car, lock the flywheel using a large screwdriver wedged against the flywheel teeth and the starter motor aperture. Loosen the clutch bolts evenly in a diagonal pattern - a few turns at a time - to avoid causing distortion of the pressure plate. Release the pressure from the springs slowly until the clutch assembly comes free.

Examine the driven plate frictional material. If this has worn down so that it is close to the rivet heads, replace the plate. If it shows contamination (oil), replace it and ascertain whether the oil has come from a leaking crankshaft seal or gearbox input shaft seal, and replace the leaking seal before reassembling the clutch. If the driven plate shows signs of burning, renew it, and ensure that, in future, the clutch is correctly adjusted and not prone to slipping.

If the driven plate rivets have become exposed they can severely score the flywheel and pressure plate, in which case the affected components should be closely inspected for marks and replaced if necessary. The flywheel can be refaced if the scoring is minor: check with an automotive engineer.

Check the condition of the diaphragm or coil springs, and replace the pressure plate assembly if wear or damage are apparent.

When refitting the clutch, it's important that the driven plate is gripped exactly concentric with the gearbox input shaft, otherwise the plate could be damaged during engine refitting. There are many clutch alignment tools available for this purpose; they hold the driven plate in line with the other components whilst the pressure plate is bolted tight. Some people use a spare input shaft to achieve this; others can assemble the clutch accurately by eye alone.

The clutch thrust bearing (arrowed) mechanism on later cars. Examine the forks on which the thrust bearing sits; the welds can weaken and break, so look for hairline fractures.

Clutch fork shaft

The clutch fork shaft can be a weak point - specifically, the welds that hold the two arms to the shaft can break (visually check the welds), and the semi-circular cutouts that hold the release bearing can distort or wear, so visually inspect these and renew the operating arm if necessary while you have the opportunity.

The clutch operating arm is secured on splines at the end of the fork shaft, and might simply pull off, though it will normally prove reluctant to move. Don't try to lever it away as you risk damaging the transaxle casing. Use a small, two-legged puller or, as I have done, a scissors-type ball joint splitter and a small socket as a spacer.

Next, remove the set screw that holds the bush and sleeve in position. The bush has to come out from the nearside of the car in order that the fork assembly can be angled for removal. Move the fork assembly back into its usual position, then push the sleeve out (and with it, hopefully, the bush) in the direction of the nearside of the car; with a bit of luck the oil seals and bush will come out and can be pulled from the fork shaft. The fork assembly can then be pushed backwards slightly so that the offside end can be pulled forwards, then the fork shaft can be pulled out.

The usual problem when trying to remove the assembly is that the bush grips the plastic sleeve, so it can be tricky to get the bush out. If the bush is to be renewed, you can push the two into the bell housing together, then cut open the length of the old sleeve and peel it away, so that the bush can be pushed out easily.

Clutch spares

Whenever a repair dictates engine removal, it's worth renewing the clutch thrust bearing and its retaining clips at the very least. When buying clutch spares take the original components with you to a spares supplier to ensure that you get the correct parts. I once ordered a heavy-duty fork shaft assembly for my Beetle, but, when it arrived, I immediately saw I had been sent the wrong type. It was fully 4mm greater in diameter than the original, and would have fitted my Camper van, though this thought was of no comfort at the time.

The clutch fork operating shaft bush (arrowed) is apt to stick to the plastic sleeve.

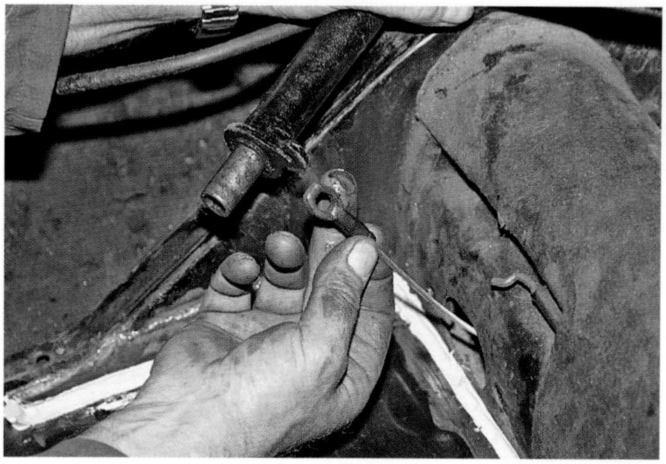

The clutch cable will locate on this hook.

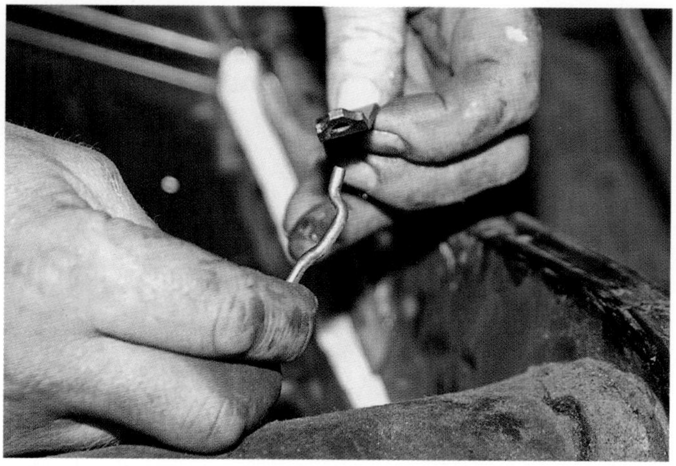

The throttle cable end and lever.

I then ordered another assembly from a different supplier, and this time was sent the correct part, although it had no fewer than three faults. Firstly, one of the arms had been welded onto the shaft at an angle, which meant that the clutch release bearing would have jammed in-between the two arms as the lever moved. I cured this using heat, a large vice, and brute force to twist the offending leg into the right attitude. Secondly, the offside end of the shaft was mushroomed and would not fit into the bearing. I gently removed the mushrooming using a small abrasive stone. The third problem was worrying. The arms were more than twice as deep as the originals, and, in trying to stretch the thrust bearing springs over them, one 'lost its temper,' as it were, in that its springiness suddenly went, it became malleable, and didn't grip the thrust bearing. I reshaped it, heated it to red hot using a blowtorch, then plunged it into some engine oil to see whether this might restore the springiness - it did, but I didn't have enough confidence in my understanding of metallurgy to actually install it in the car.

I contacted the supplier of the release arm assembly, informed it of the problem, and asked whether it stocked a different release bearing spring clip more suitable for use with the release arm assembly. It didn't and, what's more, didn't seem too bothered!

I did consider deepening the 'V' slots at the rear of the arms and, with hindsight, rather wish I'd done this. In the event, I'd already fitted the assembly and had to use so much force to get the bush and sleeve into position that I would not have been able to get it back out without damage; I was stuck with the assembly as it was.

Clutch fork shaft rebuild

When fitting the clutch release lever assembly, apply grease to the bearing surfaces - I use a grease with molybdenum.

Fit the assembly, then refit the inner circlip, washer and oilseal. Fit the bushes, then the locking bolt, and finally the outer oil seal, spring collar, return spring, and lever.

Getting the clips onto the release bearing is one of those jobs where it's very possible to injure yourself, as pliers or small, self-locking wrenches slip off the clip and your hand can smash into the release arm assembly. There is a better way.

Take one old, flat-bladed screwdriver, and cut and/or file a small 'U' into the end. Grip the spring clip using a small, self-locking wrench and position the clip so that its end is located just inside the hole in the release bearing. Place the notch in the screwdriver blade against the other arm of the clip and push - the clip should easily push back and locate over the arm. Make sure that the clip is properly positioned over the arm before refitting the engine; if the clip isn't fully home, gentle leverage with a screwdriver does the trick.

Before refitting the engine, make sure

Connect the throttle operating lever to the throttle cable end, then fasten the lever to the pedal assembly end.

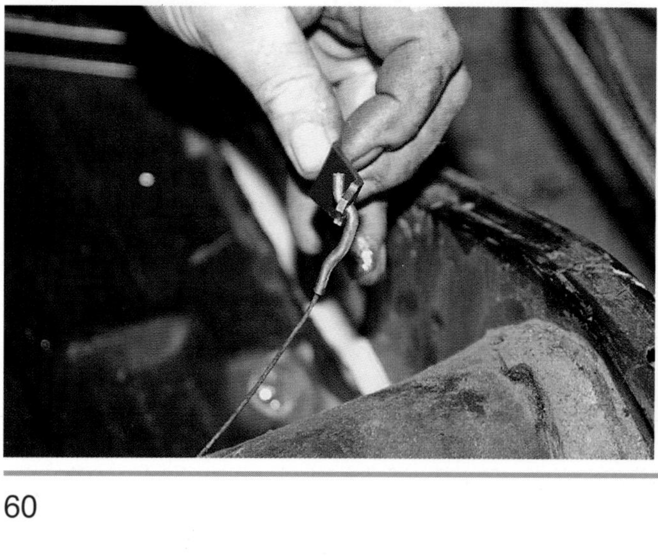

To dismantle the pedal assembly, remove the external circlip.

that the release bearing pivots freely on the shaft arms, and that the shaft turns freely.

GEARBOX (TRANSAXLE) REMOVAL AND REFITTING

The gearbox and differential share the same housing, and the complete assembly is called a transaxle. The transaxle cannot be removed until the engine has been taken out; the swing axle and double- jointed drive shaft Beetles each have their own routines, and are covered separately.

Because the engine will have been removed before the transaxle, it is assumed that normal safety precautions - especially battery disconnection - have already been taken. Some time before starting work it's advisable to clean and apply penetrating oil to all fixings which will have to be undone, so that the oil has plenty of opportunity to do its job.

If your Beetle has an early transmission with the split casing, you have to decide whether to retain it or replace it with the later, one-piece unit. Later units are inherently stronger, and the obvious choice if you intend to increase engine power. However, in order to mount the one-piece transaxle on the early chassis, you will need to locate the front casting from an early 'Splittie' Type 2, which can prove difficult to find now, and will become increasingly rare.

Swing axle cars

The transaxle must be removed complete with axle tubes. This job is much more complicated and long-winded than on later cars, so careful consideration should be given to whether or not to replace the gearbox with a reconditioned unit as a matter of course during a full restoration, when the car will be stripped down completely and the task accomplished more easily with the bodyshell off the chassis.

Remove the oval cover plate at the rear top of the spine chassis, and remove the 8mm square selector rod coupling bolt, which may be wired (wire it during the rebuild). Chock the front wheels, apply the handbrake and place the car in gear, then remove the hub caps and slacken the hub nuts, preferably with a burst-proof hexagonal socket and a very long lever! Slacken the wheel bolts. Disengage the handbrake and select neutral gear, then raise the rear of the car and support it on axle stands.

Remove the road wheels and the hub nuts. Slacken the brake adjusters and remove the drums, then strip the brake components as detailed in the section headed 'Brakes,' using clamps on the lengths of flexible hose to prevent leakage of brake fluid.

Slacken the clutch cable nut and

The 8mm square gearshaft coupling bolt. Early Beetles have a more basic gearshift rod coupling than later cars but, as you can see from the developing gap between the metal and rubber, they can fail. When they do, there's no gear selection, so renew the coupling whilst you have the chance.

disconnect it from the clutch operating arm.

Use a sharp chisel or centre punch to make a mark on the suspension trailing arm next to the mark on the hub casing to enable accurate rebuilding, then unbolt the hub from the trailing arm and pull away the axle shaft. Undo the lower damper nut and bolt and pull this away from the hub casing. Support the transaxle and remove the four nuts at the front, followed by the two large nuts at the rear. The transaxle, axle shafts and hub assemblies can now be pulled rearwards and lowered.

When refitting, offer and bolt the transaxle into position before tackling the axle shafts. Ensure that the mark you made on the trailing arm aligns with the hub casing mark, otherwise the rear tracking will be out, causing accelerated tyre wear and adversely affecting road holding. There is a special tool which clamps to the torsion tube and to the swing axle shaft to correctly position the latter. If you are unsure whether the spring plate is correctly positioned, take the car to a VAG workshop or Beetle specialist and have the job done properly.

Renew the gearshift rod coupling.

Diagonal arm suspension cars

Check the fixings used on the inner drive shaft CV flanges, and, if necessary, obtain the correct tool for their removal from a specialist Beetle spares supplier.

Remove the oval cover plate at the rear top of the spine chassis, and remove the 8mm square selector rod coupling bolt, which may be wired. Chock the front wheels, raise the rear of the car, and support on axle stands.

From underneath the car, undo the drive shaft inner CV joint fixings both sides of the car, using the appropriate tool. It usually pays to clean out Allen heads and splined fixings beforehand. Slacken the clutch lever cable wing nut until it can be unhooked, and remove the two nuts on the transaxle side cover which hold clutch cable clamps to free the cable from the transaxle.

Remove the earth strap from the transaxle casing, then undo the single nut which now holds the starter motor, and remove the starter motor. Check that nothing is left which connects the transaxle to the chassis legs.

Support the transaxle. Slacken the two front mounting bolts (nearest the front of the car) and remove the two main bolts. The gearbox can be withdrawn from the car, or lowered onto the chassis legs until you are ready to manoeuvre it out.

Refitting is pretty much the reverse of removal: be sure to check the transmission oil level and top up if necessary.

GEARBOX

The Beetle gearbox is very long-lived provided that it's not abused. In time, though, even this robust unit can develop annoying noises when under way. Gearbox noises do not necessarily indicate serious problems, and many people learn to live with them as long as they don't become too loud. A noisy gearbox can last for years.

Some gearbox problems, however, are more serious and, after you've gone to the trouble of restoring your Beetle, it would be heartbreaking to have to remove the engine and transaxle because of a progressive fault. Stripping, inspecting and rebuilding a gearbox is no task for a novice,

The main transmission mounting bolts are quite shallow relative to their size, so use a ring spanner if possible to start them - sockets want to slip off.

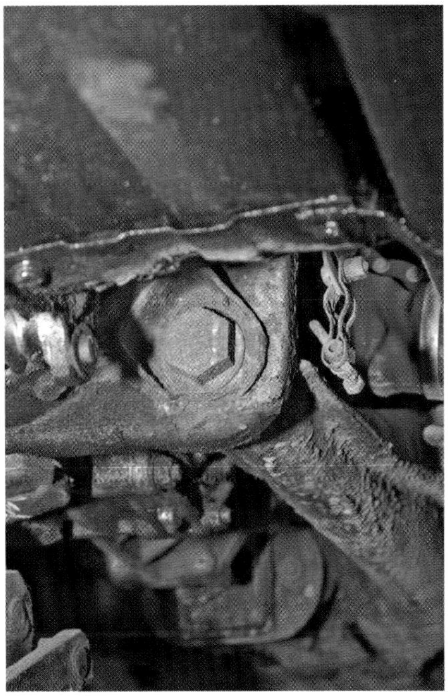

and there are convincing arguments for opting, instead, for an exchange reconditioned unit.

The individual gears in a gearbox mesh with the laygear cluster, and excessive or uneven wear in just one gear in time wears the laygear teeth out of true. If you replace a noisy (damaged) gear, you should really also replace the laygear cluster because this meshes and has worn with it, which means replacing all of the other gears as well, because the laygear teeth will have worn in concert with the teeth of each of the gears! In short, a complete rebuild using all-new components is required, which is always more expensive (assuming that you can obtain the components) than an exchange reconditioned unit.

A cheaper cost alternative is to fit another gearbox salvaged from a scrap Beetle. Buying such a unit privately from a classified advertisement is risky; buying from a general breaker gives a guarantee of replacement if the 'box turns out to be faulty. The best option is buy from a specialist Beetle restorer or breaker.

When replacing the gearbox, consider fitting urethane axle gaiters and a urethane gearshift coupling, which are more robust and long-lived than the original rubber items.

The starter motor support bush is located in the transaxle casing and, if worn, the starter can become at first noisy and may later jam. Offer the starter front spigot into this bush and feel for excess play. It may be necessary to replace the bush - easily done whilst the transaxle is out of the car or the bodyshell is off, more difficult *in situ*. (See 'Starter Motor.')

The differential shares the transaxle housing with the gear assembly. Again, it is recommended that any problems here are dealt with by a transmission specialist. These businesses can be found in many large towns and, although some will refuse to work on the Beetle transaxle, the better ones will be happy to inspect your transaxle and undertake any necessary repairs.

When you come to box up your Beetle, pay special attention to the condition of the plate which sits on the spine around the gearshift lever aperture. The two folded protrusions must point upwards and the pressing must be replaced if worn. One of the two lugs prevents the driver from shifting into reverse unless the lever is pressed firmly downwards; when the lugs are worn it's all too easy when changing down from third gear to inadvertently go straight across the gate to reverse. This is not only embarrassing but hard on the gear teeth and downright dangerous!

On early cars with split transaxle casings, the gearshift operating rod coupling - essentially a block of hard rubber

To remove the gearshift lever simply undo the two bolts.

The gearshift lever can then be lifted away. Try not to disturb the position of the selection plate (arrowed) unless you've been having problems with gear selection, or the car jumping out of gear, in which case, the plate could be wrongly positioned.

The selection plate has two raised flanges (arrowed) which limit the travel of the gearshift lever and, for instance, prevent the driver from changing from third gear to reverse instead of second gear. When the plate is correctly positioned, the gearshift lever MUST be pushed downward in order to select reverse gear; position the plate by trial and error until this is right. Also, a tendency for the car to jump out of gear can be caused by the selection plate being too far forward or backward; again, experiment until it's right.

with steel plates glued onto each side - that lives under a removable plate on the spine at the rear of the car, is inherently weak. When these units fail, gears cannot be selected or deselected, so check that the coupling is in good condition. Original equipment replacements do not appear to be available, but after-market ones certainly are. The alternative is to switch to the newer type of coupling, though, in order to fit it, you'll also need a link rod from a later Beetle.

The gear linkage rod connects the gearbox to the gear selection lever. To remove a rod, disconnect the rear coupling, remove the cover plates in the front panel and spine chassis end, and remove the gearshift lever. It should now be possible to work the rod toward the front of the spine and out through the front panel.

The gear linkage rod runs through a guide that's welded into the spine. If the guide wears through, the linkage rod drops down to the bottom of the spine, disconnecting itself from the gear lever - result, no gearshift. Guides, along with the sleeves that fit inside and their clips, are available, and have to be welded into place.

BRAKES - OVERVIEW

Beetles manufactured prior to May 1950 had mechanically-operated brakes; all Beetles produced from that date have hydraulic braking systems. Because of the comparative rarity of pre-1950 cars, this book covers only hydraulic systems. Owners of Beetles with mechanical brakes will find the details they need in the specialised workshop manuals dealing with early Beetles.

In essence, the Beetle - in common with most cars - has two separate brake operating mechanisms. The handbrake is operated mechanically and acts only on the rear wheels, whilst the foot brake acts on all four wheels using hydraulic pressure. When the brake pedal is depressed, a piston moves within a cylinder (the master cylinder), which contains non-compressible brake fluid. Because this liquid cannot be compressed, this action pushes it along a series of pipes and hoses to smaller cylinders containing pistons (wheel cylinders and pistons in the case of drum brakes, and calipers and pistons for disc brakes), so applying pressure against the secondary pistons, causing them to move.

The secondary pistons press shoes (drum brakes) or pads (disc brakes) against the drum or disc respectively; these are mechanically fastened to the rotating road wheels. The friction between shoe/drum pad/disc causes the road wheel's speed of rotation to reduce, so slowing and stopping the car.

If you are undertaking a bodyshell-off restoration then, unless the brake pipes have obviously been recently replaced (and are not kinked), it is worth renewing them whilst access is good. If you intend keeping the car for any length of time, consider fitting the more expensive nickel-copper alloy brake pipes, which should last as long as the car does. By the same token, it's better to spend a little extra in order to renew wheel cylinders, master cylinders, and calipers rather than buy repair kits for the originals.

Because most people who restore a Beetle will wish to completely overhaul the braking system, this entire section is devoted to a full brakes overhaul. It is important to stress that, when working with the braking system, cleanliness is vital; keep all lubricants well away from discs, drums, shoes, and pads, and do not allow the brake fluid to become contaminated.

REAR BRAKES

The rear brakes of all Beetles are drum brakes. The drums are secured to the axle by a large, castellated nut torqued to 253lbs/ft. This nut should be slackened before the car is raised from the ground. Select first or reverse gear and engage the handbrake, chock the rear wheels, and remove the hub caps and the split pin from the castellated nut. Then slacken off the nut, using a large, square T drive (preferably a three-quarter inch drive), a strong, 36mm socket, breaker bar, and a long steel pipe (the longer the better - a two metre pipe is ideal) to gain the necessary leverage to start the nut. If the nut stays stuck fast and the car moves when you apply pressure, try jacking up one side of the car at a time, removing the road wheel and chaining a (spare) wheel nut to the chassis. If all else fails, soak the nut in penetrating oil, or try applying gentle heat to make the nut expand.

When both axle nuts have been loosened, slacken the rear wheel nuts, engage the steering lock (wheels dead ahead), chock the front wheels, raise the rear of the car, and support it on axle stands. Remove the axle nuts. Slacken off the brake adjusters until the drum turns freely, and pull the drums from the splined axle shafts, tapping the drums with a rawhide mallet to centre the shoes. Use a puller if necessary.

Some brake shoes contain dangerous asbestos, so wear a dust mask and gently wipe the drum and the shoes clean outside. If there's less than 1in of frictional material left on the brake shoes, they will have to be renewed. If a brake drum is scored internally it should be replaced.

To strip the brakes, use a pair of pliers to remove the shoe retaining springs and clips. Ease out the lower ends of each shoe from the slot in the adjuster tappet, and then ease out the top ends from the wheel cylinder tappets. If the wheel cylinders are to be left alone, run a zip tie around them through both tappet (piston) bifurcations to prevent the pistons from dropping out. Ease out the handbrake cable end and

Brake pipes are fairly vulnerable during restoration, and easily flattened. You can sometimes buy cut-to-length pipes and end fittings, but almost any car workshop should be able to make them up for you as needed. Take the opportunity to clean out the unions.

Fit new brake hoses and bleed nipples throughout.

To remove the rear brake drum, first remove the hub cap and split pin which passes through the large castellated hub

To move the hub nut - which should be tightened to over 200lbs/ft - you will need a 36mm socket - preferably hexagonal - and a lever of between four and six feet! Also slacken the wheel nuts.

When the hub nut is slack, raise the wheel from the ground and support the car on axle stands. Remove the wheel. I usually place the wheel under the heater channel, because, if the car rolled off the axle stands, the wheel would prevent the car dropping to the ground

Even after backing off the brake adjusters, or if one is stuck fast, when trying to pull off the brake drum, hitting it each side with a rawhide mallet can help by moving the shoes slightly.

This is what you see when you take a brake drum off a car that's been standing idle for a long time - rust. The best way to remove all the brake dust and fine rust is with a cylinder vacuum cleaner.

Not surprisingly, the pistons were seized into the wheel cylinder, but not badly. Light turning pressure on a screwdriver blade located in the piston bifurcation was all that was needed to free them. If pistons are badly seized, the wheel cylinder can be removed, drained of fluid, and heat used to free the pistons. If the wheel cylinder bore is pitted it can be cleaned with a honing tool, but renewal is the best policy.

Then pull free the lower end of the other shoe.

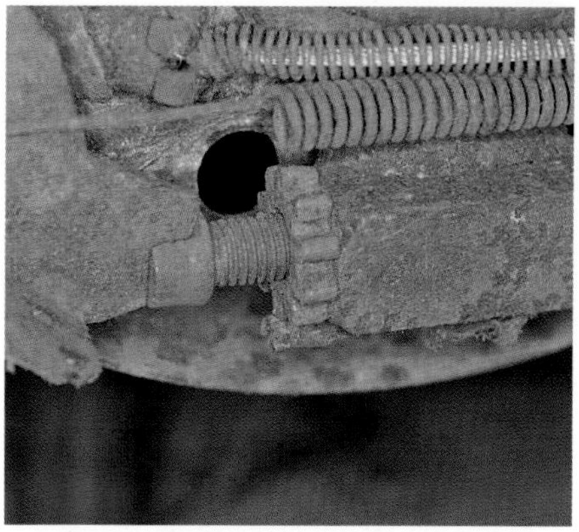

This brake adjuster was seized solid. The thread could turn, but the body of the adjuster was seized into the block. Don't try to hammer it free - a little heat is all that's needed.

To remove the shoe holders, grab the end washer using a pair of pliers.

Push the washer in, twist, and remove both it and the spring.

At this point the lower spring will probably come free.

The brake shoes are secured by these pins and springs.

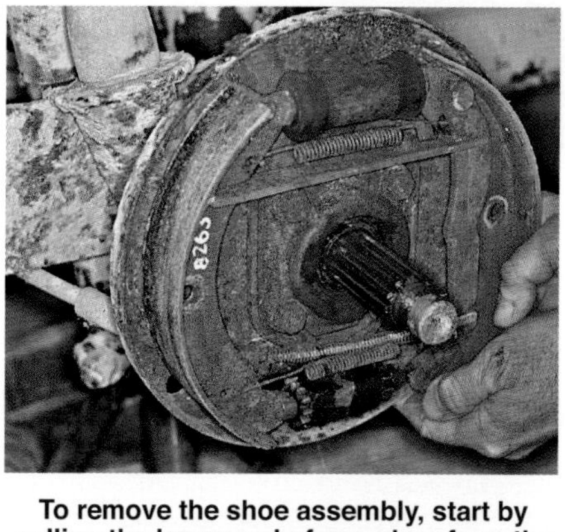

To remove the shoe assembly, start by pulling the lower end of one shoe from the adjuster bifurcation.

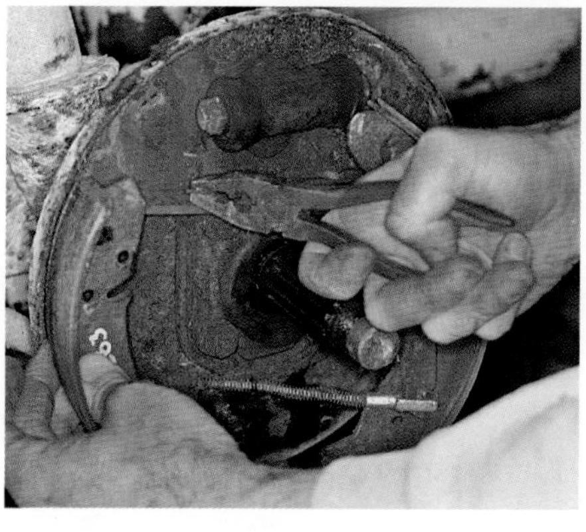

The shoes can then be freed from the wheel cylinder. At this stage you can unclip one end of the upper spring.

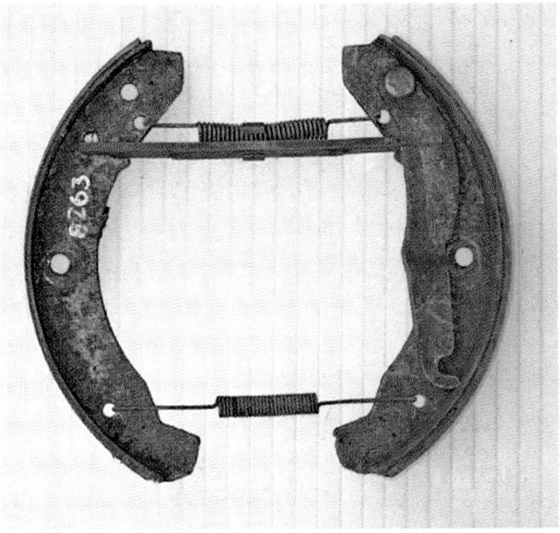

I prefer to assemble the brake components for storage as shown, because it prevents individual components being mislaid.

The handbrake cable end is secured by a pressing, in turn held by a 13mm bolt.

When the handbrake cable is refitted, first attach the bracket, then feed the bracket into the hold in the back plate, ensuring that the steel 'ear' locates inside the back plate.

Disconnect the handbrake cable end fastening from the rear shoe lever.

Run a little oil down the end of the handbrake cable to help prevent sticking.

The rear brake assembly. Note that the two adjusters are fully backed off to facilitate fitting of the drum.

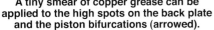

What was once surface rust on this brake back plate is now rust scale. You can chip it away with a hammer, but the steel will be thin so it's better to renew the plate. It is a good idea to fasten a zip tie around the wheel cylinder to prevent the pistons from popping out before you rebuild the brakes. A tiny smear of copper grease can be applied to the high spots on the back plate and the piston bifurcations (arrowed).

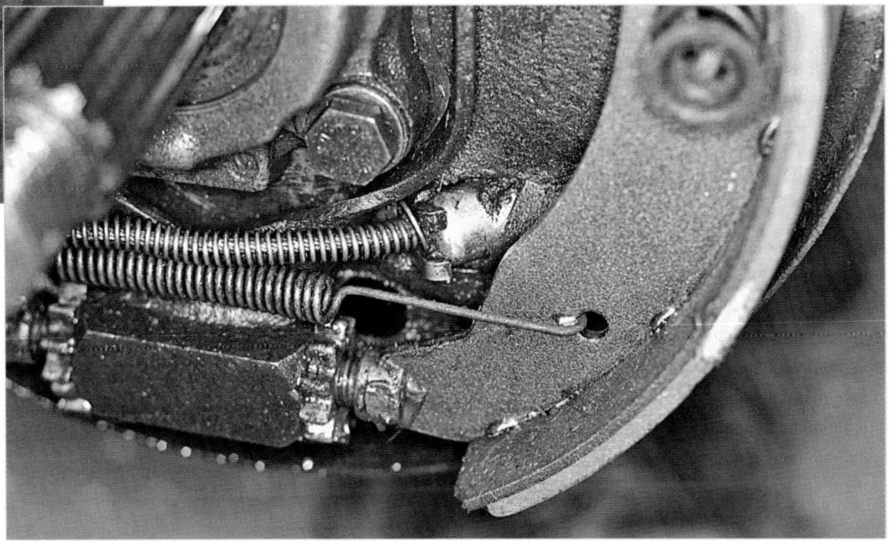

A touch of grease in the bifurcations of both the wheel cylinder pistons and the adjusters helps the shoes move easily, and keeps the mechanism working efficiently.

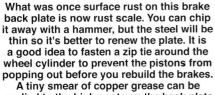

remove the shoe/spring assembly.

Examine the wheel cylinder boots and brake back plate for signs of brake fluid leakage; if this is suspected, then a wheel cylinder kit, comprising new piston (tappet) seals and boots, should be acquired and fitted. Clamp off the length of flexible brake hose before removing the wheel cylinder, and bleed the system afterwards. Check that both tappets are free to move and, if they are seized, try using a large screwdriver through the jaws to turn and free them - don't use too much force or you will spread the jaws. On really stubborn wheel cylinders which are completely seized, the last resort is to remove them from the car, drain ALL brake fluid from them, and then use heat to free the tappets. The heat destroys the tappet seals, which must be renewed. Examine the wheel cylinder bore for damage, and renew if necessary.

The hub oil seal can also leak with the result that the brake back plate becomes covered with fluid which, in this case, is obviously oil. Because you will normally discover a leaking hub oil seal when working on the brakes, a brief description of the necessary work is included here.

Either drain the transaxle of oil, or jack up the side of the car being worked on so that the hub is at a higher level than the transaxle. Unbolt the four hub cover bolts, then pull the cover from the back plate, having placed a suitable receptacle underneath to catch escaping oil. Remove the old oil seal, the spacer, the 'O' rings from the casing and axle, and the gaskets each side of the brake back plate; clean all components. Use a block of wood to drive the new oil seal into position, not forgetting to replace the washer first. Fit the axle 'O' ring, spacer and the 'O' ring in the cover. Pull the back plate gently forwards until the inner gasket can be gently fed through the hole in the centre of the back plate, and into position. Fit the front gasket, and carefully reassemble, taking care not to damage either of the gaskets as the bolts are passed back through. Torque the bolts to the recommended level, then, with the car back on its wheels or only slightly raised to allow access to the transaxle filler plug on the near side, top up the transaxle oil level.

On poorly maintained cars, the adjuster star wheels may be seized; if so, try soaking them in penetrating oil and then gently tapping them. If this fails, try gently heating them - avoid the use of too much force, because the adjusters are easily damaged. Apply plenty of copper grease when rebuilding the adjusters, to prevent them from seizing in the future. The adjuster tappet slots are tapered, and should be fitted with the wider end upwards.

Adjusting the front drum brakes. The bottom adjuster should be turned left to right in order to push the shoes.

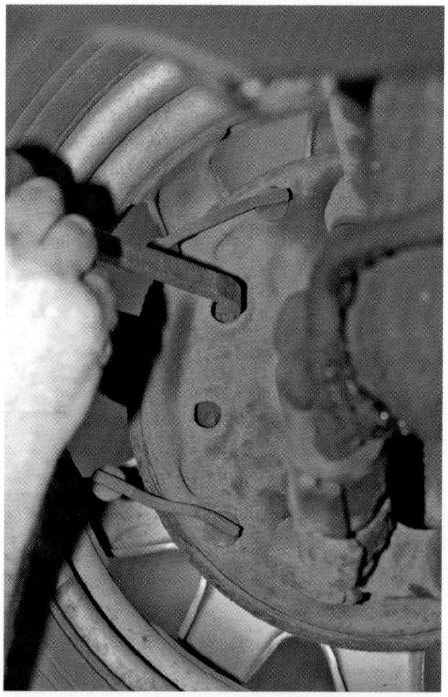

The top front drum brake adjuster should be turned right to left to push out the shoes, which means that the hand shown in this shot needs to move left to right.

During a bodyshell-off restoration, it's a good policy to renew the handbrake cables whilst access is good. Frayed handbrake cables should be renewed as a matter of course because, sooner or later, they will either jam in their sleeves or break. To dismantle the system, undo the nuts on the cable ends, remove one circlip from the handbrake pivot, drift this out and pull the handbrake assembly forwards. DO NOT touch the ratchet button until the handbrake has been refitted. To remove a cable, remove the drum, free the handbrake cable end from its lever, remove the return spring clip, undo the sleeve/back plate bolt, and pull the cable end through the back plate. Pull the cable from the spine.

To reassemble, feed the cable end through the back plate along with its return spring and washer, then replace its clip. Feed the other end of the cable through its tube in the spine, and ensure that the sleeve is correctly positioned in the end of the tube. The threaded cable end should now be visible under the handbrake aperture in the spine.

Feed the two cable ends through the holes in the lever base, then replace the lever assembly, its pivot and circlip. Replace the equaliser plate and nuts. Adjust the system.

FRONT BRAKES (DRUM)

The front drum brakes can, to all intents and purposes, be treated in the same manner as rear drum brakes.

FRONT BRAKES (DISC)

Disc brakes work by pressing two friction brake pads onto a steel disc, which is attached to, and rotating with, the road wheel. The friction caused slows the rotation of the disc and of the wheel. Disc brake pads are held within a casting called a caliper, within which two pistons are moved by brake fluid under pressure to push the pads against the disc.

Disc brakes are easy to service but are not so easy to repair, and most people seem to opt for exchange reconditioned units rather than tangle with the pistons and seals. If the pads have less than 0.08in of frictional material, they should be exchanged as a set.

Problems with disc brakes include excessive disc run-out and general wear and tear, piston seal failure, and piston corrosion. We shall deal with each in turn.

Disc run-out refers to a condition in which the disc is not rotating properly because it is out of balance, perhaps as a result of uneven wear or a knock. Disc run-out can be checked at home by rigging up a screwdriver, scribe, or similar, on a stand and placing it so that the tip is next to the disc, rotating the wheel and noting whether the disc surface remains a constant distance from the object, but it's far better to have this check carried out professionally at a service centre.

Disc wear and tear includes rusting and thinning of the steel disc through usage, scoring of the disc, and colouring of the disc because it has overheated (the disc will be soft and should be renewed). Scoring is obvious to the eye, but, in common with the other faults mentioned, if you suspect that the discs are defective, have them checked professionally.

Replacing brake pads is very quick and easy. Remove the spring clips from the retaining pins, then drift the retaining pins out using a long parallel punch. Lift away the spring retainer plate, then the pads.

Corroded caliper pistons must be replaced. As the frictional material on the pads wears down, so more and more of the piston emerges from the caliper to take up the 'slack' (disc brakes are therefore self-adjusting). If the pistons are left sticking out from the body of the caliper for any length of time, or in the wrong conditions - such as after driving in salty air - then the exposed portion becomes corroded. This condition is most commonly found on cars which have been standing idle for a long time. Obviously, when new, thicker pads are eventually fitted, the pistons must first be pressed back into the calipers; if the piston outer side is corroded this will negate the effectiveness of the rubber sealing rings - and the whole lot will have to be replaced.

It is possible to renew caliper pistons and seals using the hydraulic system to push out the pistons, although the job is much easier if the calipers are first disconnected from the brake hoses and removed from the car.

Remove the pads as already described, then place a clamp on the length of flexible brake hose to minimise fluid loss. Fold back the locking tabs and remove the two hexagon-headed bolts which hold the caliper assembly to the stub axle; remove the flexible hose.

The caliper pistons may be removed by hand, although normally some assistance will be required from a low-pressure compressed air source. A foot pump will suffice and, if a compressor is to be used, turn down the pressure if possible. Alternatively, release most of the air from the cylinder until the pressure is no more than 20psi. If you try to use higher pressure air, the pistons will fly out at great speed! Whether you use a foot pump or compressor to push out the pistons, always wear eye protection, just in case the compressed air sprays brake fluid into the air; for the same reason, don't work near a naked flame.

Fit a clamp (a small G-clamp is ideal) to retain one of the pistons, then use the air to move the other piston forwards but not out of the caliper. Open up the G-clamp to accommodate the freed piston, then use the air to drive the other out of the caliper.

Ideally, you need a parallel punch to drift out the pins, but a nail will do as long as the pins aren't rusted in.

If the car has not been recently laid up the pads might pull out easily.

The pins hold this spring clip, which holds the pads.

If worn pads are being renewed, the pistons must be pushed back into the calliper to accommodate them. To push the pistons back into the calliper, first check that the brake fluid reservoir is not full to the brim, otherwise, it will overflow. Take a strip of steel around ½in wide (photographed is a tool made up to remove the transaxle oil level plug), and an adjustable spanner, and use as shown in the photograph.

The first piston should now be removable by hand.

Examine the pistons and their bores for scoring and replace if necessary. Inspect the dust sealing ring and piston sealing ring for cuts or undue wear, and replace

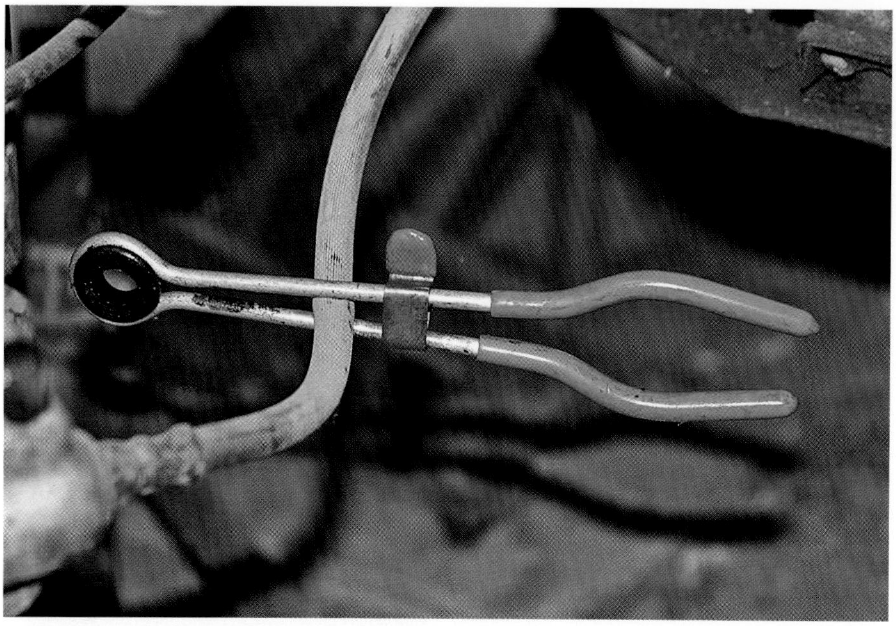

To minimise brake fluid loss, clamp the brake hose before removing the calliper. If the hose is to be reused it's imperative the hose end is held still as the calliper is rotated. If the hose is to be renewed, it's quicker to cut it and unscrew the calliper end afterward.

Calliper nuts MUST have shakeproof washers.

It's necessary to remove the McPherson strut complete in order to work on it. Unscrew the calliper brake line union with the flexible hose.

if necessary. Before reassembly, lubricate the cylinder bores and pistons with clean brake fluid. Fit the piston sealing ring, then the piston, ensuring that the piston does not tilt within the bore. Push the piston in until approximately 1/8in remains proud, then finally fit the dust sealing ring and its retaining ring.

Occasionally, a car which has been standing idle for a time will suffer sticking brake caliper pistons. This greatly reduces braking efficiency, and the extra load it places on the wheels with good brakes will manifest itself by those brakes locking-up under hard braking. Remove the pads, then examine the exposed portion of the pistons on the sticking calipers to ensure that they are not badly corroded and in need of replacement. If the pistons seem okay, try replacing one pad and using a small G-clamp or a proper piston pusher to move the other piston back into the caliper. If you don't possess either tool a length of 1in by 1/4in (approximately) steel bar can be inserted and the exposed end twisted with a self-locking wrench to push a piston home. Then fit the pad to the other piston, and repeat. When both pistons are fully home, fit worn (less than 0.08in of frictional material) brake pads and push the pistons back out by pressing on the brake pedal; repeat the process until the pistons are able to move properly. Check the brake reservoir fluid level frequently as you work.

One final point on this subject: when replacing the brake hoses on the front wheels following a restoration, check that they will not foul the tyres with the steering on full lock; in addition to being an MoT failure point, this causes high wear of the brake hose.

MASTER CYLINDER

Brake master cylinders use force from the brake pedal to move a piston which, in turn, forces brake fluid through the rest of the system. The main problems encountered with master cylinders concern the cylinder bores and pistons. The bores can be honed using small honing tools which fit into the chucks of electric drills, and kits containing new pistons, return springs, circlips, boots and seals are widely available.

Alternatively, new master cylinders are available. Single circuit master

A calliper bleed nipple. Callipers are handed and, when fitting them, ensure that the bleed nipple is at the top of the calliper, or you'll never bleed air out of the calliper.

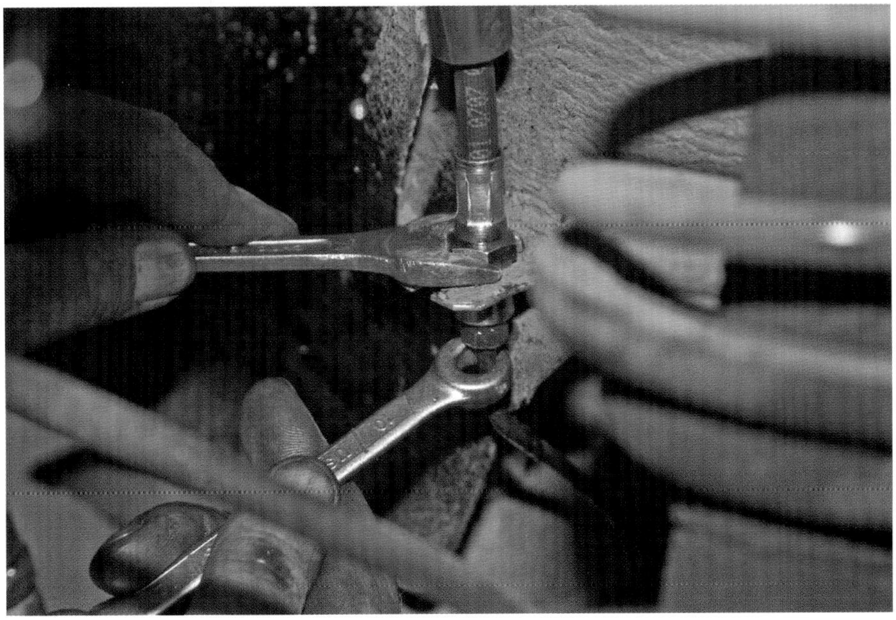

Top left: This brake calliper has two bleed nipples - top and bottom - so can therefore be fitted to either side of the car.

Middle: You can tighten union nuts using an open spanner, but a proper brake spanner - in effect a ring spanner with a hole to pass over the brake line - is best.

Bottom: After joining the brake line and hose, secure them in the bracket using the spring clip provided.

This is the very basic early master cylinder - later types are tandem.

A tandem brake master cylinder. Tandem cylinders are quite a bit more expensive than the earlier, single circuit cylinder so, if you have a honing attachment for your electric drill, get hold of a reconditioning kit and use it.

cylinders cost little more than the price of a reconditioning kit, so there seems little virtue in home reconditioning. Dual circuit master cylinders are more expensive, and the difference in price between a reconditioning kit and a new master cylinder is marked.

Bleeding the brakes

If the brake pedal feels soft and spongy, there is air within the system. Unlike brake fluid, air can be compressed, and the soft feel of the pedal is due to the fact that pushing it is compressing air rather than pushing non-compressible fluid to operate the brakes. In this case, the brakes have to be bled. The brakes also have to be bled

The brake master cylinder push rod is adjustable.

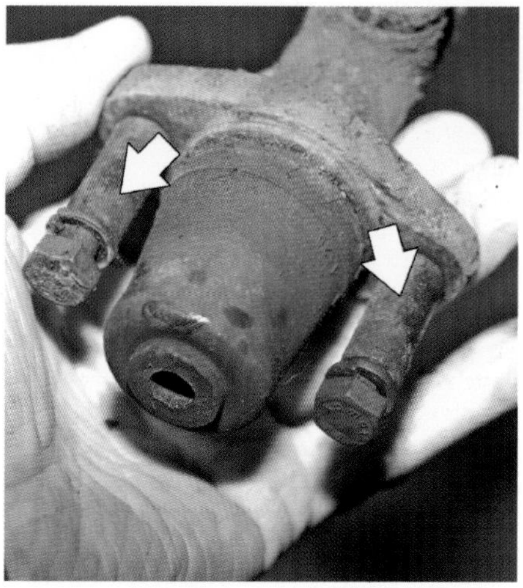

When removing the brake master cylinder, don't withdraw the bolts fully, or the two anti-crush spacers seen here will drop down into the front crossmember.

When reassembling the pedal assembly, ensure that the brake pedal return spring is on the correct way round, or you'll have to strip it again.

after any part of the hydraulic system has been disconnected.

Bleeding the brakes entails pumping fluid through the pipes until all air bubbles are removed from the system via one of the bleed valve nipples. The nipple is turned to allow fluid to escape as the pedal is pumped, then tightened before the pedal returns. To prevent air from re-entering the system via the bleed nipple, a short length of transparent plastic pipe is attached to the nipple and the other end immersed in a container of clean brake fluid.

If you have to bleed the whole system, begin with the wheel furthest from the master cylinder and work forwards (single circuit) or, in the case of dual circuit systems (in which you'll have a tandem master cylinder and front and rear brakes with individual circuits), bleed nearside front, offside front, nearside rear, and finally offside rear.

To bleed a brake you will require the help of an assistant to push the brake pedal for you. Attach the pipe to the brake nipple and immerse the other end of this in a small container of clean brake fluid. Open the nipple by turning it and call for the brake pedal to be depressed and held down. When your assistant has done this, tighten the nipple, and then ask your assistant to release the pedal. Repeat the exercise until clear fluid with no air bubbles can be seen coming from the nipple. Ensure throughout this operation that the level of the fluid in the master cylinder is correctly maintained.

Sometimes air can become lodged somewhere in the system and refuse to be bled in the normal manner. If this happens the pedal will feel spongy. The air can usually be dislodged by going through the motions of bleeding the brakes, but asking your assistant to let his or her foot slide off the brake pedal so that it returns sharply.

A good brake pedal is nice and solid, and has not too much void travel, so that if one circuit fails (tandem master cylinder), the other will still operate, though early cars do not have a tandem system, and if a brake hose leaks all braking is lost. If the pedal travel is too great, check first that the rear drum brakes are correctly adjusted, then adjust if necessary the master cylinder push rod. If the rear brakes are not correctly adjusted - and even one shoe out of adjustment will cause this - the pedal will travel some distance as the shoe(s) concerned is moved by the pedal. When this happens you will usually hear a muted thump as the shoe moves and contacts the brake drum.

You don't necessarily HAVE to jack up the rear of the car to adjust the handbrake; it is possible to reach the adjuster holes by lying on the ground at the rear of the car (watch out for the hot exhaust!).

If in doubt about which way to turn each adjuster, take a nut and bolt under the car with you. Place the nut next to the star adjuster, and turn it so that the bolt extends in the correct direction - turn the star adjuster in the same direction. It is very easy to become confused and to wind an adjuster fully in, but to believe that it is fully out! In addition to the extra brake pedal travel which will highlight the error, the handbrake lever will also possess far too much travel.

Brake bleeding is one of those activities which goes without a hitch nine times out of ten - on the tenth occasion, it can be very frustrating when you are unable to obtain a good solid feel to the pedal. This usually happens following a full restoration, when you're racing against time to get the car ready for the scheduled MoT test. Don't carry on feeding good brake fluid through the system; it's expensive and should never be reused. Try using a brake hose clamp (or two on front then rear, in the case of dual-circuit systems) on each flexible hose in turn, and feel whether this makes any difference to the pedal. The chances are that when one particular hose is clamped, the pedal suddenly behaves perfectly, showing you which wheel cylinder or caliper still has air inside, so bleed this one until all the air is removed.

If, after all your attempts to bleed the system, the pedal is still soft, leave the car alone for a while and then re-test;

occasionally - and for no apparent reason - air bubbles back out of the system into the reservoir. If this fails get a second opinion from an experienced mechanic. It's probably that the master cylinder requires attention in the form of new seals, although dirt in the system, persistent air bubbles, sticking caliper pistons, and other factors could be to blame.

One-man brake bleeding kits, which are fitted with a small, non-return valve to prevent air from being sucked back into the system, are available. The author has tried various types and found that, while some work satisfactorily, some of the cheaper kits gave problems with the non-return valve. As ever, the best advice is to buy the very best tools you can afford.

SUSPENSION/STEERING

When a moving car hits a bump or hole in the road, the tyre receives a heavy impact. Some of this impact is absorbed by the compressed air contained within the tyre, and is apparent as distortion of the tyre wall (the air in the tyre acting as a kind of spring), whllst the rest is conveyed to the suspension system. The object of suspension is to isolate as far as possible the car chassis and body from such forces and, to accomplish this, the suspension has two components; springs and dampers.

Like the walls of the tyres, suspension springs distort when subjected to forces and so absorb those forces - springs are actually 'shock absorbers.' Springs which are compressed (or twisted, in the case of torsion bars) contain energy, which they try to release when the force has gone by re-extending. If a spring is compressed and then allowed free movement - as happens when the car is driven over a bump - it will extend beyond its unstressed length to a certain point (at which it still contains energy), then re-compress under the force of the tension. The spring continues to extend and compress in this way until the initial energy is dissipated. This is called 'resonance.'

Resonance is controlled by damping. The effects of undamped resonance in the suspension springs of a road car would be disastrous, because every time a spring re-compressed, it would reduce the traction of its wheel, perhaps even lifting it from the road. Four wheels all shifting from full to light traction on an undamped car would severely reduce road-holding effectiveness. To control the resonance of the spring, dampers (often erroneously referred to as 'shock absorbers' or 'shockers') are fitted.

When a correctly damped wheel hits a bump in the road, the spring compresses to absorb the shock, but the damper limits the amount of its deflection and then limits resonance, so that the spring returns to its unstressed length very quickly. This keeps the tyres in the maximum possible contact with the road.

Essentially, Beetles have two types of suspension. The earlier system comprises torsion bars - bars of steel which work, in effect, as springs when they are twisted. Cars with this suspension are typically known as 'torsion bar' or 'swing axle' cars.

The later front suspension type, fitted to the 1302 and 1303 (and 'S') series cars, comprises McPherson struts (a coil spring with a concentric telescopic damper) suspension at the front and, although there are still torsion bars at the rear, the swing axles are replaced by double-jointed drive shafts, with diagonal arms to locate the hub. Cars fitted with this suspension are commonly referred to as 'McPherson strut,' 'double-jointed drive shaft,' or sometimes 'diagonal arm' cars.

FRONT SUSPENSION - TORSION BAR TYPE

This is a very simple suspension, comprising two torsion bars running across the car inside the tubes of the front axle, acting on sturdy torsion arms to which the hub assembly is bolted. The damper is attached to a special pressing which is a part of the axle assembly.

Later cars are fitted with an anti-roll bar. This simple device is, in effect, a 'U'-shaped spring which is attached to the lower torsion arms. When one side of the suspension is compressed during cornering, the anti-roll bar flexes and compresses the suspension on the other side to a lesser extent, evening out the forces at work and preventing the car from leaning over too far.

To strip the assembly, first chock the rear wheels, slacken the wheel nuts at the front, then raise the front of the car and support it on axle stands. Clamp the flexible brake hose as close to the brake end as possible to prevent fluid loss, then back off the adjusters and remove the brake drums, shoes, wheel bearings and brake back plates (drum brakes), or unbolt the caliper and tie it out of the way so that no strain is placed on the flexible hose (disc brakes).

On later cars, Use a ball joint splitter to part the tie rod end from the steering arm and split the ball joint in the lower suspension arm. Then remove the nut from the upper suspension arm ball joint, raise the arm using a jack, and free the eccentric bush. It should now, provided the upper suspension arm is raised high enough (you may have to press the lower arm downwards slightly), be possible to remove the stub axle.

Check the condition of the ball joints and renew if necessary. The upper ball joint is fitted using a high pressure press, and it may be better to replace the upper arm complete if one can be sourced. At the top of the ball joint there should be a plastic plug which, if removed, gives access to a threaded hole. Fit a grease nipple into this and inject grease using a grease gun, stopping to move the ball joint around to help the grease penetrate properly. Fit a new plastic plug. When replacing the eccentric bush, ensure that the notched face points directly forward.

Track rod ends are tightly held in the tapered hole or 'eye' in the steering arm, and are sometimes seized pretty well solid in the eye. They must be renewed if there is any play (have a helper turn the steering wheel - any play will be evident), or if the rubber boot is damaged. When restoring a Beetle it's worth renewing the track rod ends, because wear here results in asymmetrical play in the steering; one wheel will turn more or less than the other.

Remove the split pin from the castellated nut, then unscrew the nut (it might prove difficult to move). Replacement track rod ends should come complete with new nuts and split pins.

The best tool for removing the castellated nut is a ring spanner because the nut is shallow and a socket can easily slip off. However, on occasion, nothing less than a hexagonal socket and breaker bar will budge the nut.

An alternative method of moving a track rod end uses two hammers each side of the steering arm eye - one as a dolly and the other to strike. The idea is that the hole in the steering arm should distort just enough to free the track rod end - and it works.

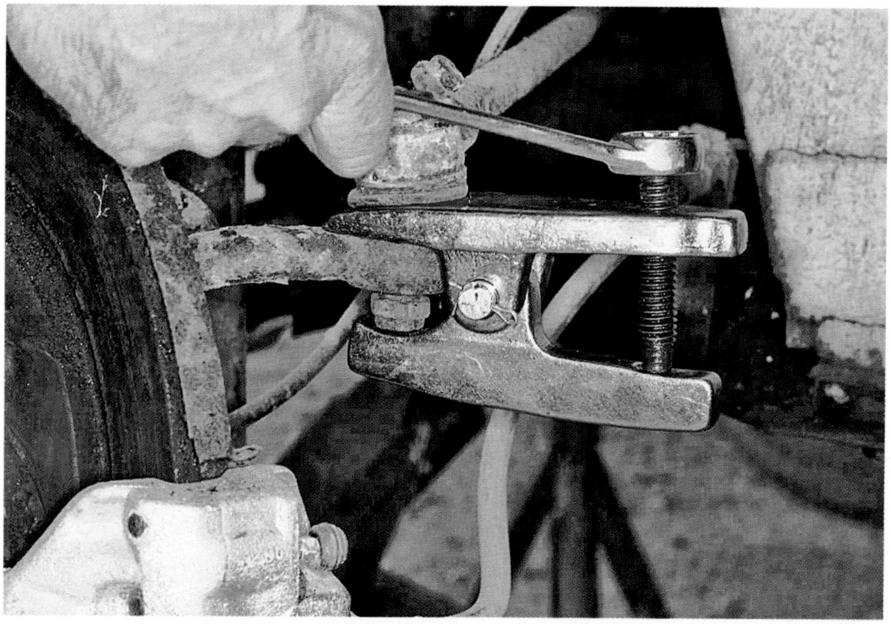

If a track rod end is to be reused, leave the castellated nut flush with the end of the thread to protect it while you use the ball joint splitter (a 'scissors'-type ball joint splitter). Be prepared for a loud 'crack' when the track rod end and steering arm part company! If the track rod end taper and steering arm won't budge, even under pressure from the splitter, try hitting the steering arm eye as described in the next caption.

This chisel-type ball joint splitter works well enough, but usually damages the rubber seal of the track rod end, so use it only if renewing the track rod end.

Early cars have a simple kingpin arrangement, and stripping involves taking the strain off the torsion bar by raising the arms and unbolting the nuts and bolts securing the kingpins. It may prove necessary (it often does) to have the stub axle reamed out before new bushes are fitted. See the section headed 'STEERING' for more details.

During a full restoration, it would be usual to renew the damper units. To remove the dampers, use a spanner on the flats of the damper shaft to hold it still whilst the top fixing nut is undone. The lower end simply unbolts. To test a damper, extend and compress it through its full range of movement: if stiff or weak points are found in the travel, or if there's any sign of fluid leakage, replace the unit.

Beam axle

The beam axle is a heavy assembly comprising two horizontal tubes, pressed steel assemblies for mounting the axle to the frame head, and pressed steel assemblies for the top damper mounts. If looked after, a beam axle should be one of the most long-lived parts in a car, although, in practice, rot is often found in the bottom of the end assemblies, after drain holes become blocked by mud. Welded repair of beam axles may be possible, though it will not necessarily be road legal, and renewal is the better option.

Renewing the beam axle is quite

a large job, easier if attempted while the bodyshell is off the chassis during a restoration, though I'll describe the process for a complete car.

Disconnect the battery. Remove the fuel tank. Slacken the front road wheel nuts, chock the rear wheels, raise the front of the car and support it on axle stands, then remove the front wheels. Clamp the brake hoses, remove the brake drums and back plate, and unscrew the wheel cylinder from the brake hose (drum brakes), or unbolt the calipers and tie them out of the way (disc brakes). Unbolt the steering damper mounting. Disconnect the speedometer drive.

Remove the bolts holding the steering box to the beam axle, and store them in a safe place, along with the two lower clamps

The steering box bolts have tab washers. They're awkward to get at but have to be folded back.

Access to the steering box bolts is good with the bodyshell off; less so with the shell in place. Use a socket and extension bar.

After disconnecting the track rod ends the steering box assembly can be removed. If the bodyshell is in place, disconnect the steering box link arm and remove the box alone - even then it's still a fiddle to get out.

(swing axle cars). On late McPherson cars unbolt the steering rack.

The beam axle can now be unbolted, or the torsion arms and bars removed first, if desired, which lightens the beam axle. This is held by four bolts at the frame head; be sure to take the weight of the beam axle on a trolley jack and have an assistant on hand to help steady it.

New beam axles are available but only in left hand drive form. This means that, for RHD cars, the locator for the steering box is on the 'wrong' side for RHD markets, in which case you can make and

continued on page 78

The brake hose and line are joined at this bracket. Unscrew the line fitting, but don't be surprised if the line twists and kinks and needs replacing.

The lower torsion arm nut might be difficult to start; leaving the wheel in place gives something to bear against. Note that Simon is pushing the spanner using the palm of his hand; if you grip it you'll smash your knuckles should the spanner slip.

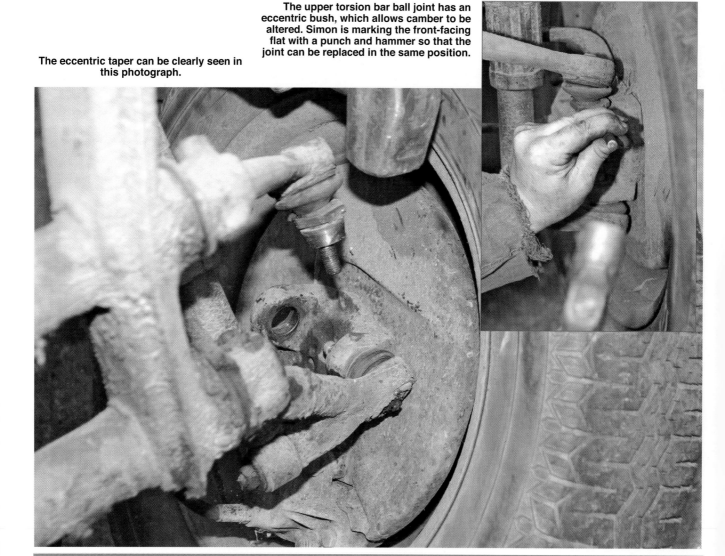

The upper torsion bar ball joint has an eccentric bush, which allows camber to be altered. Simon is marking the front-facing flat with a punch and hammer so that the joint can be replaced in the same position.

The eccentric taper can be clearly seen in this photograph.

The stub axle assembly ball joint holes should not wear because the ball joint pins don't move once the nuts are tightened.

Soak the exposed threads of the ball joints with penetrating oil (if they're covered in mud clean them first) before trying to turn the nuts.

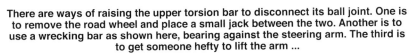

There are ways of raising the upper torsion bar to disconnect its ball joint. One is to remove the road wheel and place a small jack between the two. Another is to use a wrecking bar as shown here, bearing against the steering arm. The third is to get someone hefty to lift the arm ...

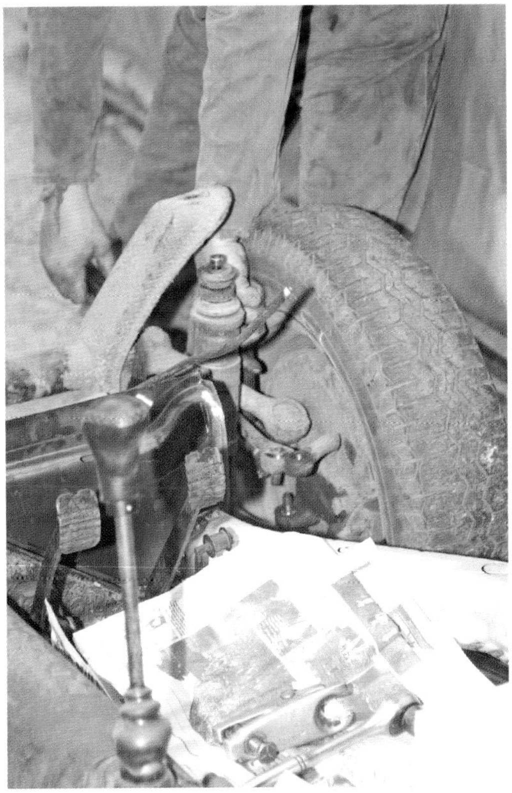

Even with the suspension at the bottom of its travel, there's still quite a lot of pressure in the top torsion bar - release it slowly.

By this stage, the torsion bars are at rest and can be removed.

The torsion arms are secured to the torsion bars by Allen-headed grub screws, which are locked by nuts. To remove an arm, first back off the locking nut ...

... then use an Allen key to remove the grub screw.

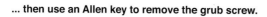

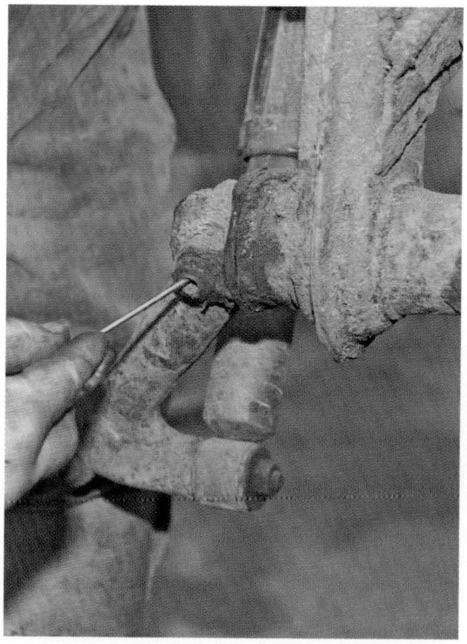

The internal Allen head of the grub screw will be filled with mud and rust - scrape this out before trying to move the grub screw.

The torsion arms can then be pulled out. It's a good idea to wrap each arm in a plastic carrier bag - the part that's exposed to the elements will be covered in mud and rust, the internal section in thick grease.

This shot clearly shows the grub screw hole and the dimple on the torsion bar into which the point of the grub screw fits. At one end of the torsion bar the dimple is machined into the sides of the torsion bar leaves; at the other it's machined into the flat. The torsion bar MUST be replaced in the original orientation.

The leaves MUST be reassembled correctly.

On the upper torsion bar a small piece of steel is spot welded on. This is the locator for the steering box. New beam axles are available in left-hand drive only, so the position of the steering box must be ascertained by measurement when a new beam axle is fitted to a right-hand drive car.

Also on new beam axles, the steering arm damper bracket is positioned for LHD cars, so, to use the axle on a RHD car, the support must be ground off and repositioned on the opposite side. Measure the old beam axle to find the position for the damper bracket.

The centres of the torsion bars are secured by the same arrangement as the ends: grub screw and lock nut.

Apply penetrating fluid, slacken the lock nut and remove the Allen grub screw. Don't remove the torsion bars until you've laid out a sheet of plastic to put them on.

Prise out the torsion bar end seals; they're often reusable.

tack one in the appropriate place for RHD cars, after taking careful measurements to get placement correct. If you have to do this, check that the front wheels turn by the same amount when full lock is applied.

When refitting the torsion bars, apply plenty of grease between the individual leaves, and lightly bind them with masking tape or zip ties. This keeps them correctly aligned so that they slide easily into position (sometimes - be prepared for several attempts before they locate properly).

FRONT SUSPENSION - MACPHERSON STRUT TYPE

Unlike torsion bar suspension, which feeds on-road stresses into the sturdy frame head, MacPherson strut suspension feeds

continued on page 84

Fit the seals into the new beam axle.

Apply fresh grease to the roller bearings. On the subject of grease, either transfer the grease nipples from the old beam axle to the new, or fit new ones.

Removing the torsion bars. First, Simon grips the leaves using a self-locking wrench (mole grips) so that they stay in the correct position.

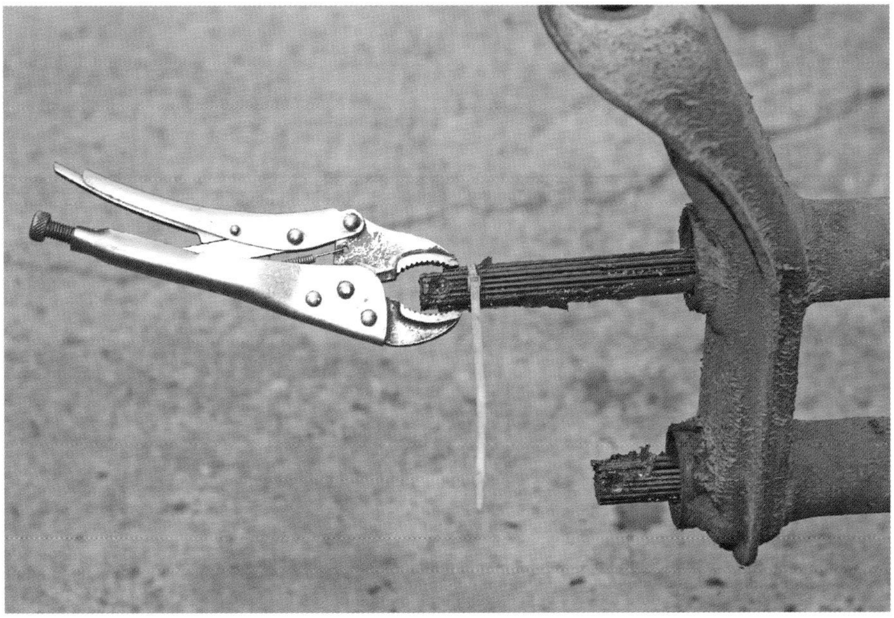

A zip tie is then fitted.

Partly pull out the torsion bar, then fit a second zip tie and pull out the bar completely. Have clean cloths ready to grip it - it's plastered in grease (or should be).

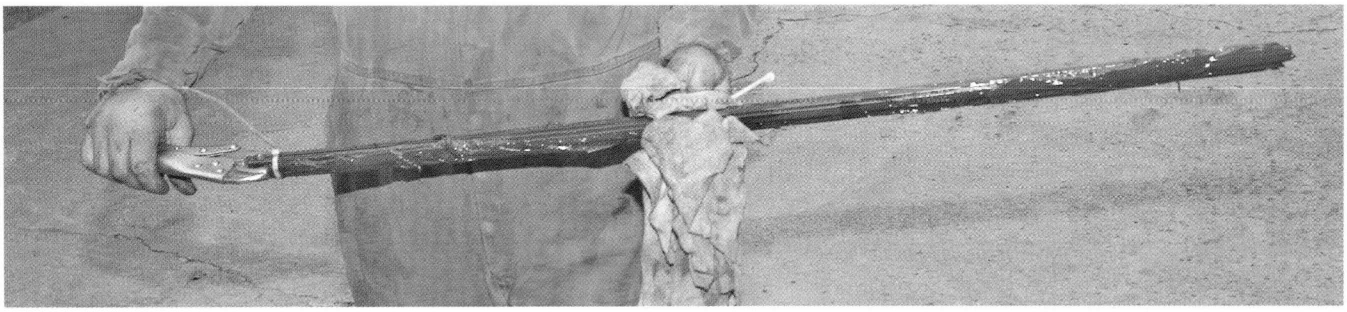

Fitting a torsion bar into the new beam axle. It's best to transfer the bars immediately they have been removed, because it's easy to fit them upside down or - as here - the wrong way round - my fault for distracting Simon.

The Beetle beam axle is not too heavy and can be removed single-handed. Start by slackening the four fixing bolts.

An air impact wrench makes life easy - these bolts have probably been in place since the car was manufactured, and they take some shifting!

When all the bolts are slack, take the weight of the beam axle and remove the bolts. If the body is on the car it's best to have some help to do this.

The old beam axle removed.

Fitting a new beam axle is fairly straightforward. If you're working alone and the bodyshell is on the car, try balancing the axle on a trolley jack while you hand-start the bolts, and be careful not to cross thread them.

The torsion bars pass through a machined block with a hole that's the same cross section as the leaves assembly, and it can be awkward to keep the leaves perfectly aligned and get them through the hole.

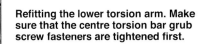

Refitting the lower torsion arm. Make sure that the centre torsion bar grub screw fasteners are tightened first.

Then the top torsion bar arm goes on. Check the ball joints for play first; they press in and that's not a DIY job.

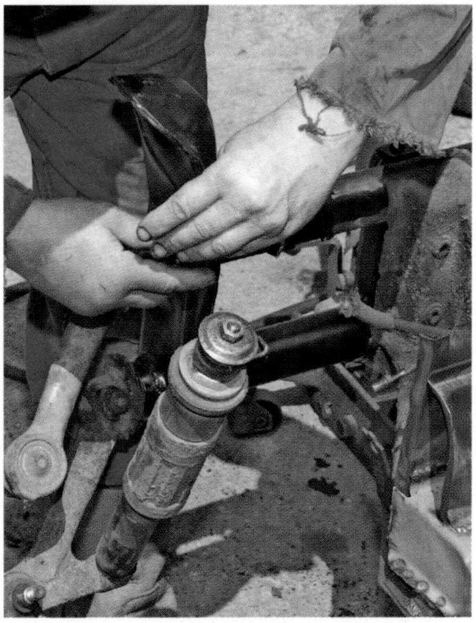

The upper torsion arm grub screw is easy to get at ...

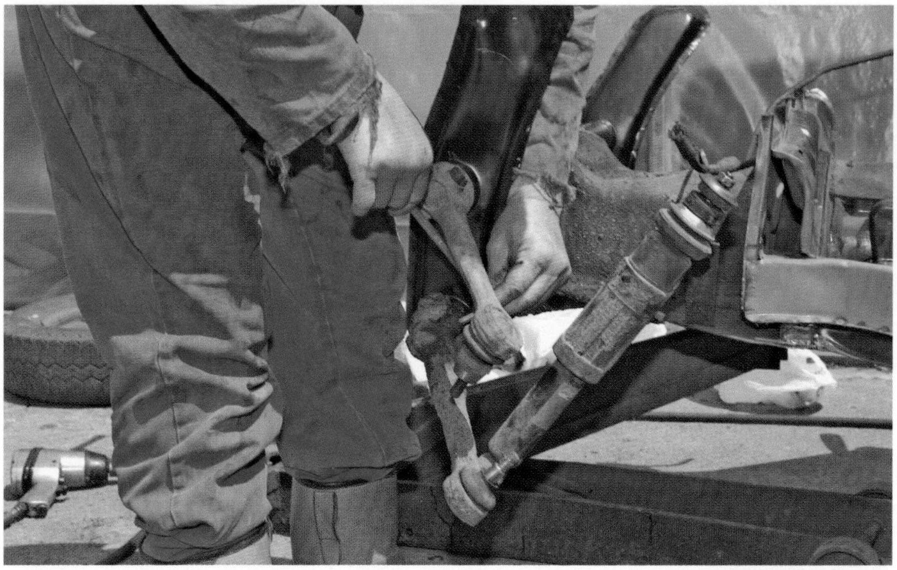

... the lower arm less so.

The correct way to fasten the torsion arm. Tighten the grub screw then hold it in that position while pinching up the nut.

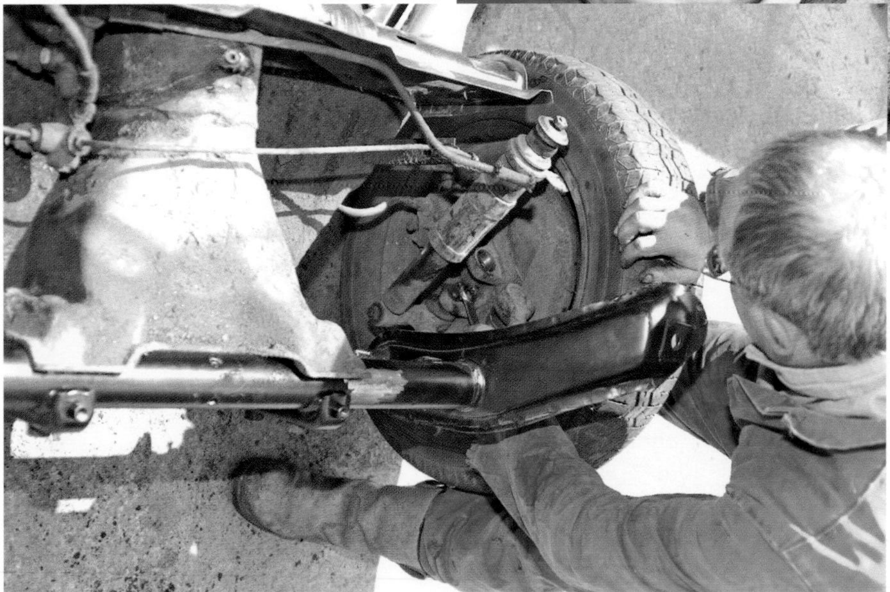

Offer up the stub axle assembly and fit the lower arm ball joint first.

Once the bottom of the tapered eccentric bush has located, it will find its own way in under pressure from the torsion bar.

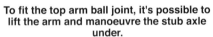

To fit the top arm ball joint, it's possible to lift the arm and manoeuvre the stub axle under.

Attaching the damper.

great stresses into the bodyshell - namely the flitch panel tops, where the top ends of the struts are located. On such cars, the panelwork around the strut top mounting must be very sound.

The MacPherson strut comprises a concentric coil spring and damper, combining both springing and damping roles in a simple unit, which is connected to the stub axle via a ball joint. The lower stub axle ball joint connects it to the track control arm which, in turn, is mounted on a bracket just aft of the frame head, the movement of which is controlled by the anti-roll (stabiliser) bar.

To remove the strut, chock the rear wheels, jack up the front of the car and support it on axle stands, then remove the road wheels. Undo the stabiliser bar end nut on the track control arm, remove the stabiliser bar mounting clamp nuts and detach the bar. Split the ball joint at the track control arm/stub axle, and the steering arm/stub axle. Clamp the brake hose and remove the brake pipe from the bracket on the strut.

The strut is held at the top in the flitch panel by three lock nuts; remove these - DON'T touch the large central nut, because this is keeping the spring compressed - and lower the strut downward.

DON'T even contemplate stripping a MacPherson strut unless you have spring clamps. The coil spring is under considerable pressure which can do great damage if not released slowly and safely. Broken or tired springs and ineffectual dampers may be replaced, but, unless you have a spring compressor, this work is best entrusted to a professional who, because he will not have to remove and refit the

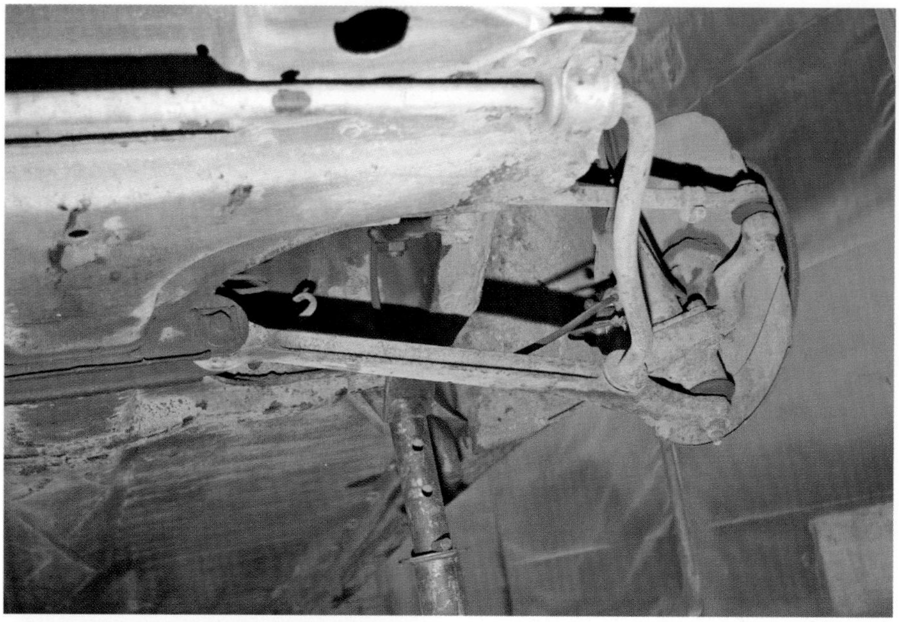

The MacPherson strut front suspension comprises a track control arm, which connects to the stub axle and the strut itself via a ball joint.

The strut is held at the top by these three bolts.

The anti-roll bar on MacPherson strut cars is secured in brackets fastened to the frame head.

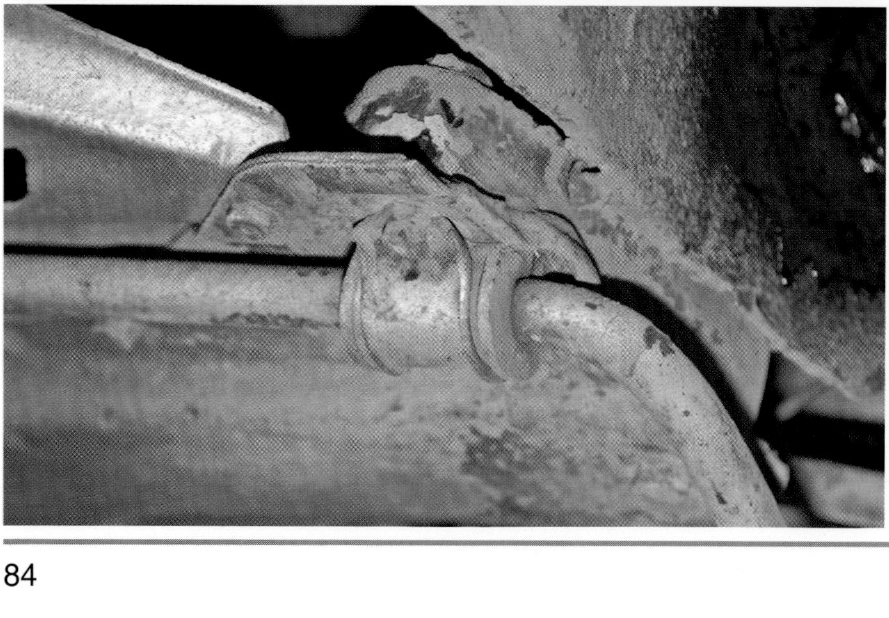

The MacPherson strut anti-roll bar has threaded ends secured in the track control arms by castellated nuts with split pins.

strut to the car, should not charge too much for labour.

REAR SUSPENSION

The two types of rear suspension fitted to Beetles are not vastly different - both have torsion bar springing - but their effect on the road-holding capabilities of the cars is!

Earlier swing axle cars can, when pushed to the limit, be very difficult for anyone other than the most accomplished competition driver to control. Later cars with diagonal arm suspension and joints at the inner ends of the drive shafts are far better behaved.

Swing arm suspension

Solid torsion bars with splined ends are attached to spring plates which in turn are connected to the axle hubs. A damper connects an extension of the torsion bar housing and the axle hub. The drive shafts have universal joints (UJs) only at their inboard ends, and their angle in relation to that of the road wheel is thus constant.

To strip the suspension, chock the front wheels, slacken the hub nuts (use a six foot long lever for this) and the rear wheel nuts, raise the rear of the car and support it on axle stands placed under the rear ends of the heater channels (with wood packing). Remove the rear wheels.

Slacken off the brake adjusters and remove the hub nut, then remove the brake drum. If it sticks, try tapping it with a leather-faced mallet to free off the brake shoes. Dismantle the brakes (see appropriate section of this chapter).

Use a sharp chisel to make a mark across the trailing arm and the axle housing flange so that they can be reassembled in the same positions. Disconnect the damper lower end, and either swing it out of the way or undo the top fastening.

The axle tube is secured to the swing plate by three bolts; undo these, and pull the axle tube away from the plate. Remove the torsion bar end cover plate bolts and the cover. Now for the interesting bit. The spring plate is under considerable tension when on its ledge and, when it comes free from the ledge, would fly with considerable force in a downward arc if tapped from behind. Alternatively, you could use a long lever with a cranked end to get the plate off the stop ledge and slowly release the pressure.

When the spring plate is off its ledge, note its position carefully, because you'll have to get it back in exactly the same spot if you don't fancy having a lopsided car! To raise the rear suspension ride height, incidentally, you refit the plate one spline lower, and vice-versa to lower the car. Refitting involves using a trolley jack under the plate to 'wind up' the torsion bar until the plate can be slipped onto its ledge. Replace the two large rubber bushes as a matter of course.

To remove the torsion bars, detach the rear wings and pull the torsion bars from their casing, noting their position so that they can be replaced accurately. The splines on each end of the torsion bars are of different size, so that by moving either the inner splines one notch, or the spring plate one notch, a wide variety of ride heights can be achieved.

When reassembling, coat the torsion bar rubber bushes with talcum powder before refitting. Raise the spring plate over its stop ledge with a trolley jack, then use long bolts to pull down the torsion bar cover plate and so force the spring plate fully home onto the torsion bar end.

Diagonal arm suspension

Raise and support the car as already described. Remove the road wheels and hub nut, remove the brake drum, clamp the flexible brake hose and disconnect it from the back plate. Dismantle the brakes, the handbrake cable end, and remove the back plate. Remove the six Allen-headed screws which fasten the outer end of the drive shaft to the hub assembly. Remove the damper.

Mark the spring plate and trailing arm for correct reassembly, then remove the three bolts securing the hub assembly to the spring plate. Lever the spring plate from its ledge stop as already described for swing axle suspension, and note the attitude of the spring plate at rest, so that it can be replaced in the same position.

Note the positions of the washers on the diagonal arm pivoting end; these must go back in exactly the same position, otherwise the suspension geometry will be altered. Remove the diagonal arm socket screw and washers. Undo the four bolts to release the torsion bar end cover plate, then pull the plate end from the torsion bar splines.

Use a lever as already described to take the tension of the torsion bar before levering the plate off its ledge.

WHEEL BEARINGS

To check the front wheel bearings simply raise the wheel concerned off the ground and spin the wheel - damaged or worn bearings can generate clearly audible noise. Grasp the tyre top and bottom and push/pull to rock the wheel - any movement, especially if accompanied by noise, indicates play somewhere in the suspension. To check whether the wheel bearing is to blame, have a helper apply the foot brake and repeat the test - if the movement disappears then the play is in the wheel bearing; if not, the fault lies with the suspension.

To adjust the wheel bearings, remove the speedometer drive and both bearing caps, slacken the lock screws and torque the clamp nuts to 15ft/lbs, then slacken them until the thrust washer can just be moved with the tip of a screwdriver. Tighten the lock screws. Refit the road wheel and check again for play as already described.

A wheel bearing comprises two

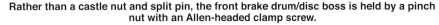

Rather than a castle nut and split pin, the front brake drum/disc boss is held by a pinch nut with an Allen-headed clamp screw.

The outer bearing is not gripped in position, so take care not to allow it to drop into the dirt when you remove the disc or drum.

On swing axle Beetles, the rear bearing can be removed by drifting the axle inward slightly and pulling it back out, which often pulls the bearing along with it. Alternatively, you might be able to hook it out, though that could damage the bearing."

components. The outer race is made from hard steel and has to be pressed out or in. The inner race - containing the rollers or balls - sits inside the outer race and can be lifted out.

To renew the front bearings, disconnect the battery, slacken the nuts of the wheels to be worked on, chock the other wheels, raise the car from the ground and support it on axle stands.

Remove the road wheels and the brake drum or disc and hub (see 'Brakes'). The outer bearing roller section should lift out of the drum or, in the case of disc brakes, the hub; remove the grease seal to free the same component in the inner bearing.

The outer races of both bearings have to be drifted - or preferably pressed - out. Any car service centre should have the facilities to carry out this minor job for you, as well as pressing in the new outer races.

The rear wheel bearings are fitted into the hub rather than the brake drum (which turns with the axle shaft). To renew the rear wheel bearing on swing axle cars, disconnect the battery, then slacken the hub nut - which takes some shifting. To prevent transmission oil loss, either drain some of the oil, or jack the rear of the car or the side of the car being worked on so that the hub is higher than the transmission oil level. Back off the brake adjusters and remove the road wheel and brake drum complete. Remove the brake back plate (see 'Brakes').

Remove the oil seal cover and the oil seal components. It is possible to remove the bearing without disturbing the hub or axle tube by drifting the axle inwards a little and then pulling it back out - which sometimes pulls the bearing partially out with it - or by finding something to hook inside the bearing to pull with. The alternative is to disconnect the spring plate and remove either the hub alone (it's held to the axle tube by a pin that can be drifted out from the top), or the hub and axle tube complete.

Swing axle car rear bearings are removed by disconnecting the drive shaft from the axle, then pressing out the axle. The bearings are located by circlips

STEERING

Earlier cars have a steering box mounted on the front axle, 1302 (and 1302S) have the box mounted on the bodywork, and the 1303 is fitted with rack and pinion steering, again, mounted on the bodywork.

During a restoration, check the condition of the steering damper (where fitted) by pulling and pushing the arm in and out; if increased or reduced resistance is felt at any point in the travel, replace the damper. Also, feel for lost steering

On RHD cars with steering boxes, adjustment is via a screw and nut situated under a removable panel.

It is possible to get at the steering damper bolt with the fuel tank in place, but it's much easier if the tank is removed.

wheel movement; that is, movement of the perimeter of the steering wheel in excess of 1in which does not also turn the front wheels. If this is discovered, check whether there's play in any of the joints, including the track rod ends, before turning your attention to the steering box or rack.

In the case of the steering box, play between the worm and spindle axle can be dealt with by adjusting the screw (turn the steering to full lock and slacken the lock nut first) on the front of the unit whilst the spindle is moved from side-to-side. If this fails to reduce void movement to the recommended level, the roller/worm play will have to be reduced.

Steering boxes can be adjusted to take up this void movement by slackening off the lock nut on the top of the unit, adjusting the screw (don't tighten it completely, but screw it in until slight resistance is felt), then hold it in that position and tighten the lock nut. Check that the steering is not tight before using the car on the road; if it is, readjust the screw. If there's still too much void steering wheel travel, it's best to exchange the steering box.

With steering racks, adjust the bolt situated under the rubber bung in the spare wheel well until it can just be felt to contact the thrust bearing, slackening and re-tightening the lock nut accordingly.

Cars up to August 1965 have kingpins and stub axles between the upper and lower torsion arms, and later cars have steering knuckles attached to the torsion arms by ball joints.

Kingpin suspension usually develops too much play because it's not greased often enough and the bushes consequently wear. If greasing is omitted completely the pin can become pitted and has to be renewed. If the pins are good, reconditioning entails pressing the old bushes out and the new ones in (leave them in a sealed plastic bag in the fridge for a few hours first - they contract and might be easier to fit), then using a reamer to resize and align their holes before reassembly. While reconditioning the kingpins, fit a new link pin set. If the king pin is corroded due to lack of regular greasing, it is worth checking that the grease nipples are not seized and renewing them if they are.

For details of how to remove the kingpin and steering knuckle assemblies from the torsion bars, see the section headed 'Suspension.'

As a matter of course you should renew all tie rod ends (ball joints) and set the tracking by eye until you can have it set professionally at the earliest opportunity.

STEERING WHEEL & COLUMN

To remove the steering wheel, disconnect

The kingpin-based front suspension of the earlier Beetle was superseded by the ball joint set-up. The kingpin system is usually long-lived and trouble-free, provided it is kept well lubricated, so grease the kingpins every three months or so; more frequently in wet driving conditions.

The stub axle/kingpin assembly of early cars, complete with everything necessary - except a reamer - to rejuvenate it.

This is the reamer with which to size the bearings.

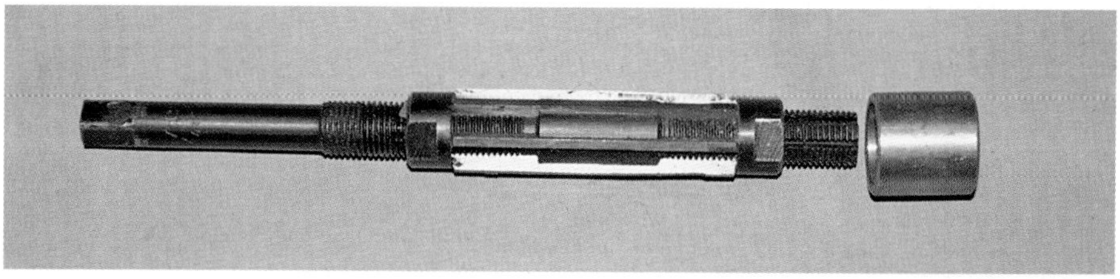

the battery, pull the horn push from the centre of the steering wheel, and disconnect the horn wire. Hold the steering wheel while unscrewing the 27mm retaining nut. The steering wheel can now be pulled from the column, though, if it sticks, try striking both sides of the steering wheel simultaneously from behind using the heel of your hand, which usually does the trick.

To gain access to the indicator mechanism, steering column bearing or ignition switch/steering lock inside the steering column shroud, first disconnect the battery and remove the steering wheel. Remove the external circlip from its locating ring just below the column splines on which the steering wheel locates. Remove the four small set screws that secure the indicator switch. To remove the indicator switch it is necessary to pull some of the wiring up into the shroud, though the individual wires are held in a sleeve, and are often twisted inside, so that the sleeve cannot be pulled

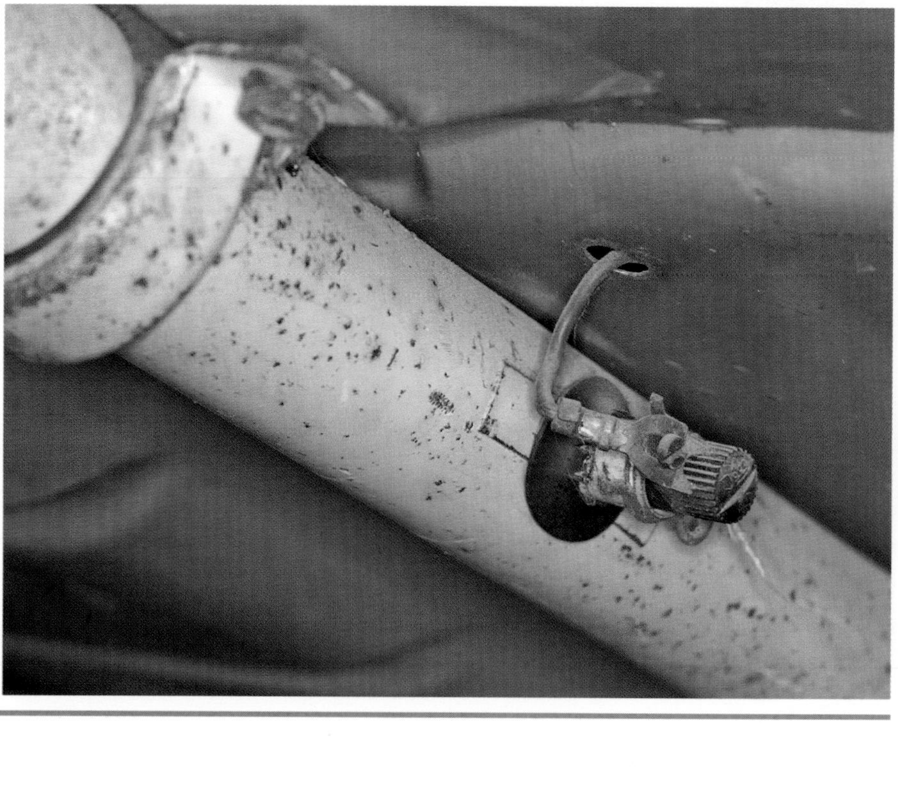

The early Beetle steering column had the horn contact here, just below the steering wheel, rather than the wire travelling all the way up the tube, as on later cars. The wire, incidentally, is live (the horn button completes a path to earth), so ensure that insulation is in good condition.

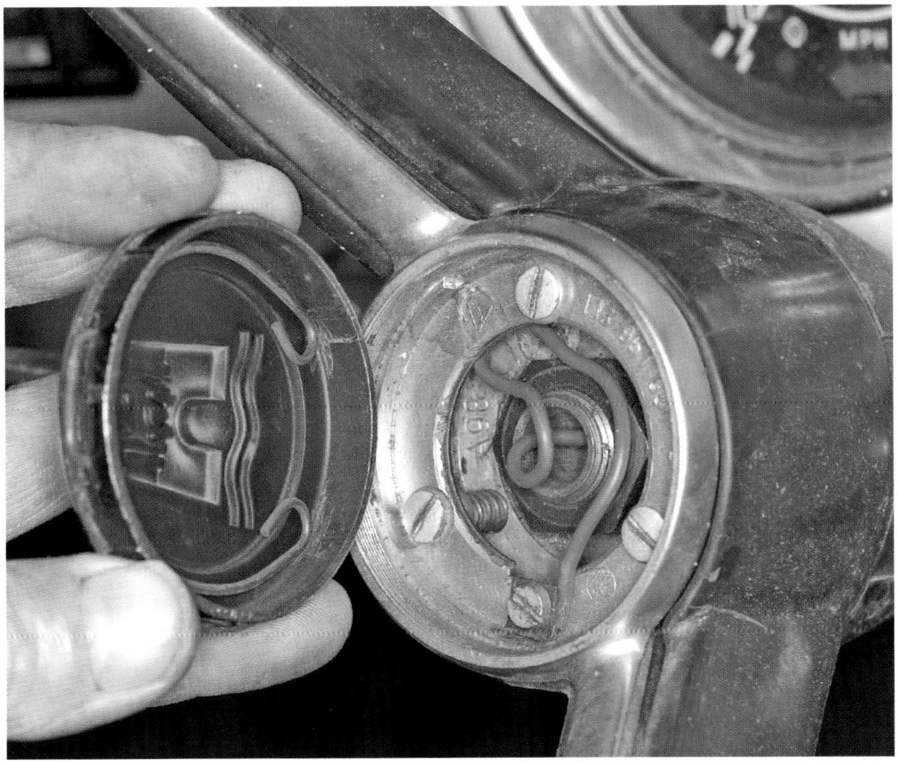

The horn push on earlier Beetles can be prised off, giving access to the steering wheel/column nut.

into the shroud through the narrow slit. You can cut the sleeve using side cutters (leave enough to push back into the shroud to prevent the wires chafing), which should free enough wire to be able to pull the switch clear of the shroud. If the switch is to be renewed, remove whatever plastic tape binds the wires together and pull them out of the luggage bay. New indicator switches come complete with their own loom.

The ignition switch is held by a small casting, held in turn by two set screws. Turn the ignition key to the 'on' position to disengage the steering lock, remove the screws, then the internal circlip above the bearing, whereupon the ignition switch can be removed.

The bearing can be drifted out from the underside. Wear can develop in the bearing and affect steering, so it's worth renewing the bearing as a matter of course during a restoration.

When replacing the indicator switch, be sure to secure the wires under the clips provided. This will prevent them from becoming trapped when the shroud

To remove the steering wheel, disconnect the battery, remove the horn button, and disconnect the horn wire. Horn button removal varies according to model; most simply lever off.

The steering wheel nut is usually very tight and requires a lot of force to start it.

Remove the external circlip at the lower end of the steering column splines, taking care not to allow it to fly off and become lost.

You can remove the circlip using circlip pliers, though mine kept slipping off the ends of the circlip. I resorted to using two screwdrivers to bear against the ends of the circlip which - miraculously - I did not lose.

After removing the steering wheel, remove the Allen-headed clamp bolt (arrowed on the right of this photograph), and the two longer examples arrowed on the left, then lower the column end.

Turn the ignition key to release the steering lock, and the top shroud of the column can be lifted away.

Below: The ignition lock is held by a small casting, in turn held by two set screws (positions arrowed on the left), only one of which is on my car, and the internal circlip (arrowed, right), which also locates the bearing.

Above: The indicator mechanism is fixed by four small set screws, three of which have already been removed in this photograph.

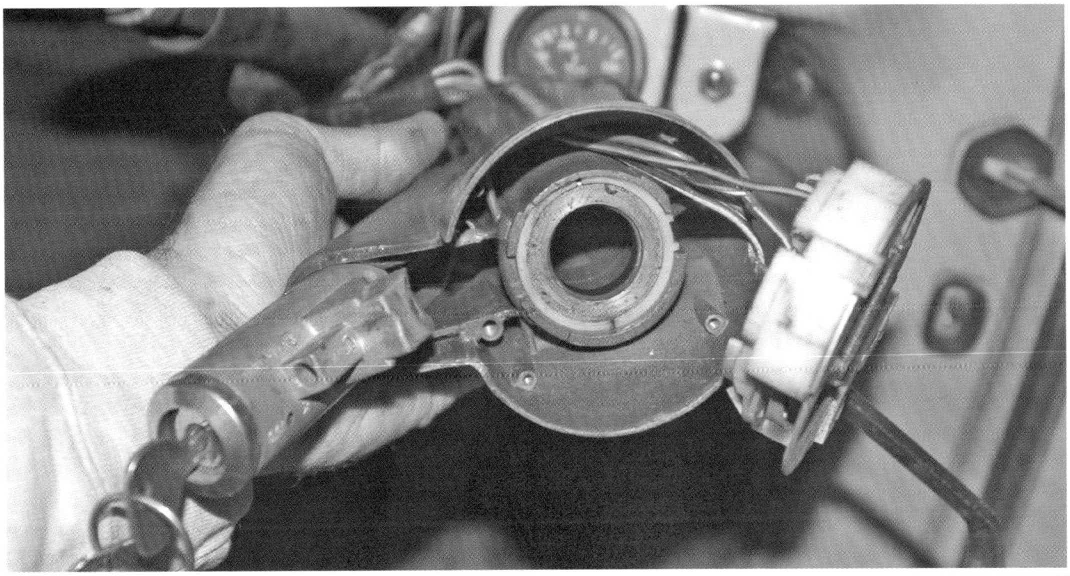

In order to remove the indicator or ignition lock you'll probably have to unwind insulation tape and separate the wires. Then trace them back into the luggage bay area and try to pull them into the cab - or cut them.

The wires from the indicator and ignition switches pass through a grommet into the luggage bay area. ALWAYS disconnect the battery before carrying out any work in the vicinity - there are lots of non-insulated spade connectors. After finishing work in the area, make sure you have not accidentally knocked any connectors from their terminals.

assembly is replaced on the steering column tube.

GENERAL ELECTRICAL SYSTEM - OVERVIEW

When the car is being driven, electricity is generated by either a dynamo (early cars), or an alternator driven by the crank pulley belt (later models). This is used to provide energy to create a spark at the sparkplugs, to operate the electrical equipment such as lights and wipers, and to keep the battery fully charged.

The battery provides a source of electricity to operate the starter motor, and to make up the shortfall in generated electricity when the car is on the move if demand exceeds available supply.

The battery can provide a great deal of power, despite being 'only' 6 volt (early cars) or 12 volt, because it can provide a high amperage, or current. To help visualise just how much power a battery can generate, remember that it is possible to move the car by putting it in gear and turning the engine over using the starter motor, but don't try this except in an emergency. In doing this, the battery is supplying not only the energy needed to turn over the engine, but also to actually move the car!

One terminal of the battery is connected to earth; that is, to the bodyshell/chassis of the car. This allows every electrical device on the car to also be earthed, so that just one feed wire is needed to complete a circuit to the battery and provide power for the device concerned. Most electrical faults - incidentally - are caused by poor earthing, so always check the earth connection first when tracing faults.

If a wire which is live (connected to the live terminal of the battery) touches any part of the car which is earthed, current will flow through the wire to earth. When the battery is connected to a circuit which has very little resistance (i.e. when it is shorted to earth through a wire rather than passing through an electrical component such as a light), current passes through the wire at the battery's maximum amperage. Not even the meaty wire which connects the battery to the starter motor is capable of passing this current, and, as a result, the wire which shorts gets hot very quickly, burns off its insulation, and an electrical fire ensues.

The ability of a wire to safely carry electricity is determined chiefly by its cross-sectional area, so wires which have to carry more current (starter motor feed, high-tension (sparkplug) wires and, to a much lesser extent, the headlights) are thicker in section than wires which have only a small current to carry. The smaller the diameter of a wire, the more easily it catches fire if too great a current is passed through it.

To prevent wires carrying dangerously high currents through shorting to earth or some other electrical fault, most car circuit are fitted with fuses. A fuse is a short piece of non-insulated wire of a thickness designed to melt if the current passing through it exceeds a certain level. In the interest of safety, the lights and ignition are not normally fused - though Beetle lighting systems usually are. Whenever a fuse blows, this is not a fault in itself but a symptom of a problem elsewhere in the circuit. Most people simply replace blown fuses - sometimes with fuses of a higher rating - but this is a dangerous practice, as it allows too high a current to pass through the wiring which the fuse is intended to protect; that wire could overheat and start an electrical fire because a fuse that is too highly rated has been fitted.

If a fuse blows, always trace the fault before fitting a new fuse. NEVER replace the fuse with one of a higher rating or, worse, with bits of tin foil, unless you enjoy being inside a burning car.

For the same reason, never add extra electrical devices to a fused circuit. Either the demand will outstrip the fuse's safety level, causing it to blow or, if a higher rated fuse is fitted, it can cause a fire in the existing wiring if a fault develops.

What is an electrical fire like? The author can answer this one - a minor incident, thankfully - from firsthand experience. Within a few seconds of a wire shorting to earth on a non-fused circuit, the insulation melts and begins to give off choking fumes, which could fill the interior of a Beetle to the extent that you literally cannot see your hand in front of your face within, maybe, thirty seconds. If there are combustible materials in the vicinity of the fire, these, too, will ignite from the heat and, within a minute or two of the short to earth occurring, the car could be full of flames as well as smoke. If the fire includes brake fluid or fuel lines, the car will be a burnt-out shell in minutes.

Unless you are a qualified and experienced electrician, leave electrical problems and the fitting of extra electrical devices to a qualified auto-electrician.

RESTORATION & ELECTRICS

Car wires are carried tightly bound in the loom. In order that you can, with the aid of a wiring diagram, trace which wires go where, the wires are colour-coded. Many elderly cars have at some time been fitted with extra lengths of wire, either to replace damaged lengths or to power an extra device. Sometimes, the wires are of an appropriate colour and rating, but often they are not. For this reason, it is well worth taking colour photographs of wiring under the front scuttle (behind the dashboard), under the end of the rear seat (where the regulator is situated), and in the engine

The fuse box is situated under the dashboard. The colours of the fuses denote their rating. Never replace a fuse with one of a higher rating.

bay, to remind you which wires go where at a later date.

A damaged loom (frequently caused by welding too close to the loom and melting off the insulation, but also often caused by a wire shorting to earth, which also burns off the insulation) is best replaced, even though looms are far from cheap to buy and anything but easy to install. Damaged individual lengths of wire outside the loom may be replaced with others of the same colour and diameter, except in cases where the damage is melted insulation and the wire runs into the loom, because the wire (and adjacent wires) in the loom could also have melted insulation.

The Beetle has many non-insulated spade terminals, and if any of them drops or is knocked off they can short to earth. If the circuit is fused the fuse blows but, if the circuit has no fuse an electrical fire can result. Replace non-insulated spare connectors with insulated ones. Kits containing a crimping tool and a selection of end terminals, and terminals for joining two lengths of wire, are not too expensive and very useful. An alternative to renewing non-insulated spade terminals is to acquire 'heat shrink' tube, available from automotive electrical suppliers. Cut a suitable length of tube, slip it over the spade terminal, and apply gentle heat (a hair dryer is sufficient). The tube shrinks to fit the terminal tightly.

The alternative to using crimped connectors is to solder them on. Soldered joints should not - unlike crimped joints - suffer from internal corrosion, which acts as an insulator and is a common cause of electrical faults. A drawback of soldering is that the heat needed to melt solder makes the wire more prone to work hardening, though using heat shrink tube as already described offers the end of the wire enough support to prevent it from flexing, and so prevents work hardening.

It's a good policy to place in-line fuses in any unfused circuits.

The black polythene item seen here is cut from an old oil container, and sits on top of the underseat electrics so that nothing can drop on the non-insulated terminals and short circuit them.

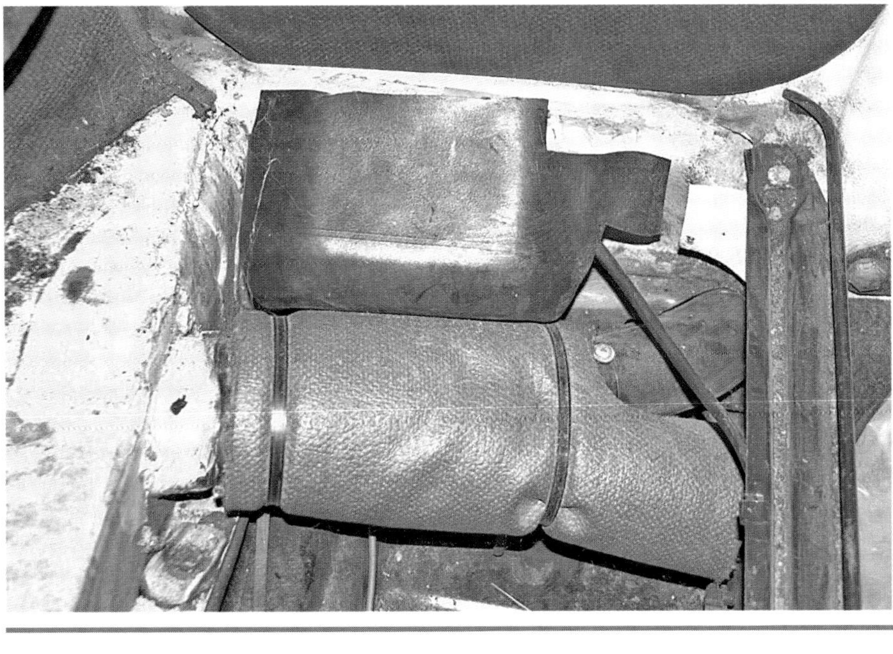

BATTERY

The battery must be securely held to prevent it tipping (and possibly spilling electrolyte, or the positive terminal touching an earth), so must be of a design with a lip suitable for locating under the battery clamp.

It is good practice to make or buy an insulating cover for the live battery terminal and the live feed clamp.

To check a battery's condition, remove the filler caps (no smoking or sources of ignition nearby, because the battery can give off explosive fumes) and check the electrolyte levels; the electrolyte should just cover the plates. After checking the electrolyte, check the ability of the battery to take and hold a charge. Fully charged, a 12V battery should produce 13.2 volts, and this is easily checked using a multimeter. If the battery measures under 12 volts, charge it and re-test and, if it still shows under 12 volts, one or more cells have failed and the battery will have to be renewed.

On an original Beetle, the battery terminals should have one live wire and an earth strap only; any additional wires connected to the clamps are there to power after-market electrical accessories, and bypass both the ignition switch and fuse box, so check out the associated circuits very carefully and, if you discover an non-fused circuit, fit an in-line fuse.

LIGHTS

Never be in too much of a hurry to fit wing-mounted lights after spraying the wings. Allow the paint to harden properly, preferably for two weeks.

It is tempting to fit higher wattage headlights, but if you do this then be sure to obtain a light dipping relay that can handle the extra wattage, because the standard relay is prone to arcing across its points if it is asked to handle more power than it was designed for. The arcing causes carbon to build up on the contact points and the unit fails.

Beetle headlights have varied over the years but all are similar in principle. To remove a headlight, first remove the rim

The headlight bowl. The bottom screw passes through the rim; the top two are for beam angle adjustment.

fixing set screw, located at the bottom of the rim (the other two are adjusting screws, so leave them alone). It should be possible to prise off the rim with your fingers. Pull the headlight out just far enough to enable you to pull the feed plug off, and the light unit can then be removed. When refitting the rim don't over-tighten the screw, because old rims are liable to crack if you do. During a restoration, it's as well to renew the cable sleeve, all grommets, and the headlight-to-wing seal.

Use new seals when fitting the rear light clusters, and be careful not to over-tighten the lens fitting screws, because the lenses can be very brittle and crack. The rear light clusters can exhibit a range of apparently strange faults, usually caused by a bad earth connection, such as the stop lights flashing weakly instead of the indicators. The earth connection is usually a metal tab in the engine bay, so cleaning it and applying a smear of petroleum jelly can remedy a range of faults.

The light feed wires pass through panels, and the original loom had moulded grommets to locate in the holes and prevent the wires from chafing. If the grommets are in very poor condition, obtain new examples.

FUSES

A fuse blowing is not a fault in itself but a symptom of a fault in its associated circuit. When a fuse blows, don't simply replace it but trace and rectify the fault that caused it to blow (usually a short circuit to earth). Some short circuits can be located visually if wire insulation is damaged, though it's best to trace them using a multimeter set to show resistance.

Disconnect the battery. Attach one multimeter terminal to earth and the other to the fuse connector. If the meter shows no resistance there is a direct short to earth, which you can locate by tracing the wire from the fuse block to the associated

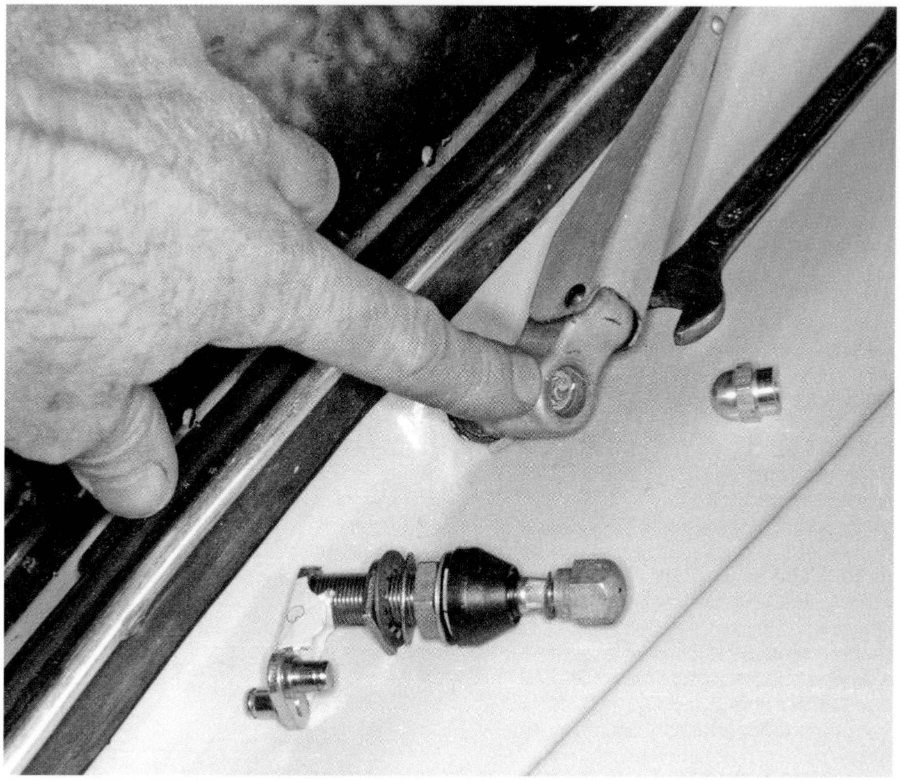

The threaded stud on this windscreen wiper rocker has snapped, and there's not enough thread left to properly attach the domed nut. This is a fairly common problem, and the solution is to fit a new rocker.

Removing the domed nut, wiper blade and shroud/washer/nut reveals that there is little more than one complete turn left on this damaged thread - not enough to rely on.

electrical component and repeating the test just outlined. When you get a reading other than no resistance, the fault lies in the length of cable preceding that point.

Any non-original wiring for accessories should be fused; if you find any wires that draw power directly from the battery and don't appear to be fused (such as feeds for after-market accessories), fit an in-line fuse.

WINDSCREEN WIPER ROCKER REPLACEMENT

It's not uncommon to discover that the windscreen wiper rocker assembly threaded studs (which secure the wiper blade) have been broken, leaving only a short length of thread to secure the capped nut that holds the wiper blade in position. This is not satisfactory, because the slightest bit too much pressure when refitting the domed nut will strip the remaining thread, there will be no way to secure a wiper arm, and the car cannot be used on the road with a missing wiper arm. The fact that replacement wiper rockers are widely available suggests that stripped threads due to over-enthusiastic nut tightening are common, though fitting them is far from easy.

Take a look behind the dashboard of your Beetle and you'll discover that, not only is it crowded in there, but there are loads of non-insulated spade connectors to knock off their terminals, plus a host of sharp objects to cut your hands. The first job is therefore to improve access - after, that is, you've disconnected the battery just in case you accidentally tangle with the wiring!

Rocker removal

Remove the centre air ducting assembly. This is secured by three self-tapping screws on top and a nut on the drain. Remove the riser pipe that feeds the demister, then the demister mouldings. To remove a demister moulding, push against the sides of the lower moulding just under the lip (which disengages a grip mechanism) as you not-too-vigorously tug at the moulding, and it should come apart. Press against the side of the demister slot moulding and push uphill, and the moulding should come partially free of the dashboard, so that you can pull it out from inside the car. Pull the head lamp dipper assembly from its mounting. There is now (just) room to get a spanner on the rocker fastenings.

Remove the wiper arm, the moulding from the nut, and the 17mm nut. Working under the luggage bay lid, carefully remove the circlip from the stud on the rocker arm, taking care not to allow it to shoot off and fall down the inside of the A post.

You now need a thin, 17mm spanner to undo the nut that fastens the rocker to the frame; many 17mm spanners will be too thick to fit into the narrow gap, but a 11/16in spanner may be thin enough. When this nut is removed, the rocker simply pushes backwards out of the frame.

Refit

Before fitting the new rocker you might care to modify it. Rockers were originally 'handed;' made specifically for either the nearside or offside, and the difference was that the drive stud was to the front on the offside and to the rear on the nearside. Replacement rockers usually have both studs *in situ* and so could be used either

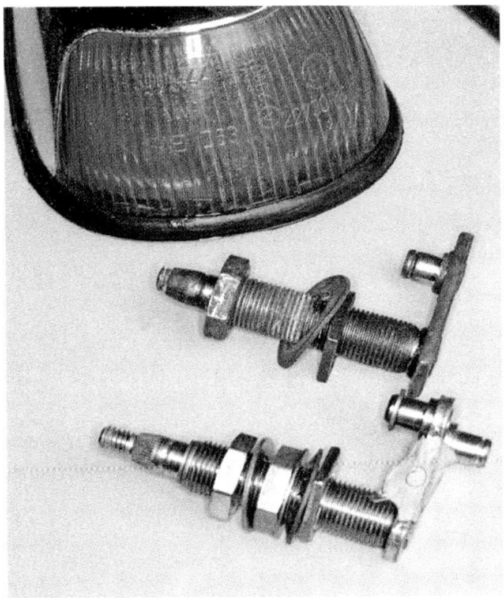

Comparing old and new windscreen wiper washers reveals that replacement rockers come with both studs attached. There's such a tangle of wiring under the scuttle of a Beetle that the spare rocker, if left, might snag a wire, so it's best to cut off the surplus one.

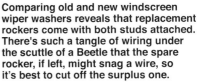

It is easiest to drill out the (riveted in) spare rocker stud (arrowed in red). The rocker attaches to its arm via the remaining stud, and is fastened by a circlip (arrowed in blue).

When refitting the wiper rocker mechanism, try not to accidentally hook the stud through the demister slot!

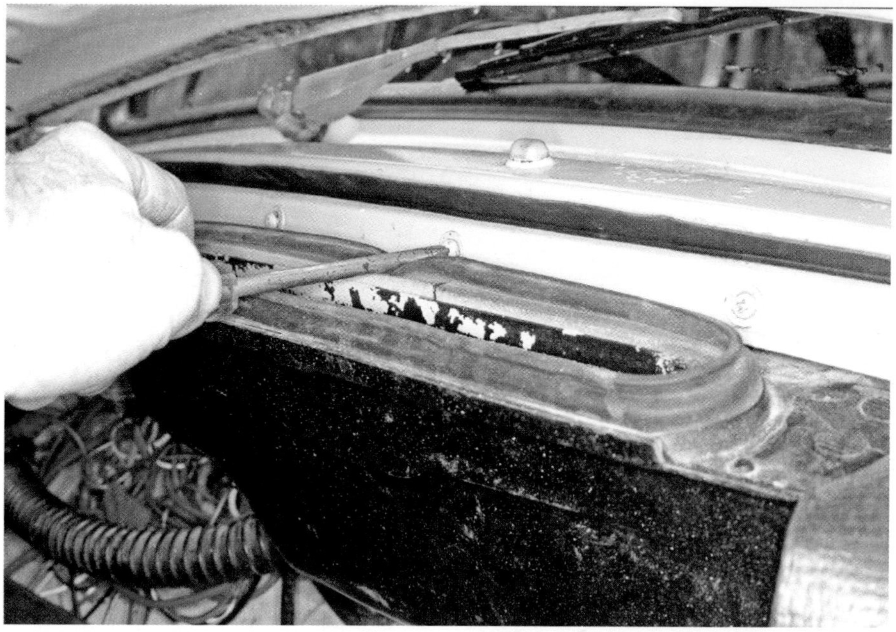

The fresh air intake is secured by three screws. The elbow at the lower end is secured by a nut.

To remove the rocker, use a thin, 17mm spanner to undo the nut (arrowed). Whenever you work near either end of the area under the scuttle, always begin by stuffing rags down the 'A' posts - anything dropped down there can be gone for good!

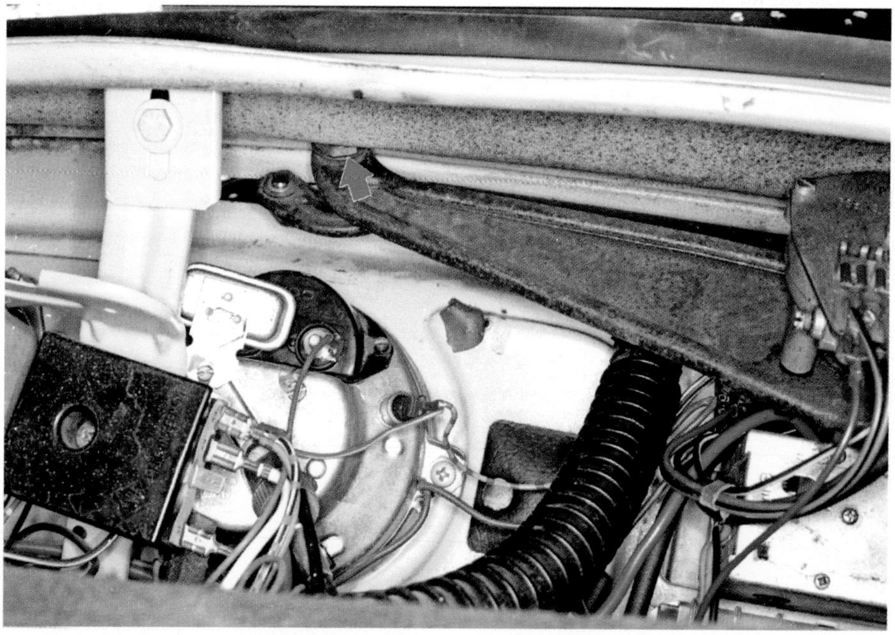

side of the car, though there's a risk that the unused stud might foul the demister. Rather than rebuild everything and risk having to take it apart again, centre punch and drill out the riveted-over end.

Refitting is the opposite of removal, only easier. Push the rocker into position, threading it through the securing nut and washers, and start to turn the nut, which should be easier to turn than the old one, because the threads are all clean.

It's a good idea to test the wiper mechanism before fitting the blade and refitting all the behind-the-dashboard bits and pieces.

Wire damage includes anything which bares the copper core, or anything which reduces its effective internal cross-sectional area, such as being pinched so that some of the strands of wire break, but others don't. Check all visible wiring in the car for damage, and also check that spade and bullet connectors are insulated - it's not unknown for a non-insulated connector to drop off its terminal and start an electrical fire.

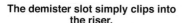

The demister slot simply clips into the riser.

STARTER MOTOR

The starter motor needs a huge current because of the amount of energy required to turn over the engine. In the interest of safety, the ignition key does not have to handle this high power, but instead actuates a small current which operates the starter solenoid. A solenoid is simply a switch which is operated by a small electrical current, but which controls a circuit capable of carrying much higher currents.

The starter motor is a powerful electric motor that drives a gear which meshes with the teeth on the flywheel, turning the flywheel and hence the crankshaft. Competent electricians can carry out repairs to the motor (fitting new carbon brushes) although exchange reconditioned units are recommended for the rest of us. If the drive pinion teeth are damaged then

The starter motor and solenoid in position (car bodyshell obviously removed!).

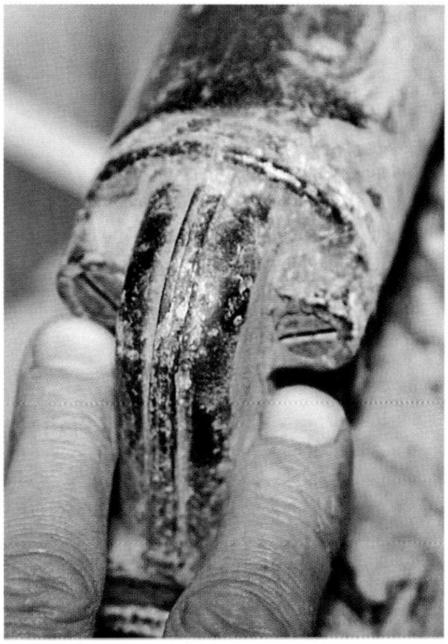

These two screws are the solenoid to starter motor fastenings. On the solenoid from the project car, they refused to turn, no matter how much force was applied, and even when removed from the car. If the solenoid is faulty the best option is to remove both the solenoid and starter from the car and get an exchange reconditioned unit.

Below: Check the teeth on the starter dog for damage - if you find any then renew, and also check the flywheel, because damaged starter dog teeth usually damage the flywheel ring gear.

Above: Starter solenoid damage inflicted by the author when trying to remove the nut from the terminal (the solenoid was scrap, anyway). If the nut on the post is seized solid, it might be cheaper in the long run to cut and renew the lead, remove the solenoid and starter, and try to repair the damaged thread in order to remove the nut without wrecking the solenoid.

The replacement starter motor bush and the bits of the original.

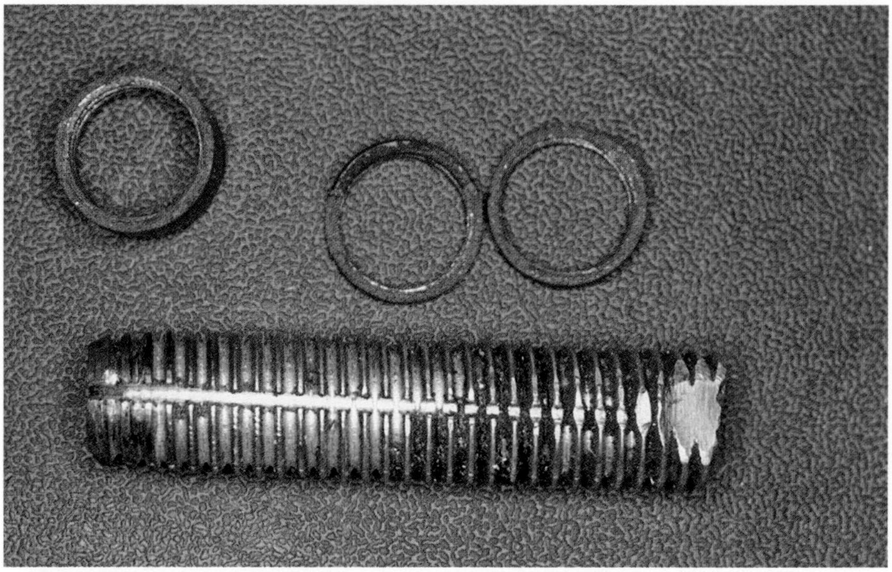

There are several possible ways to remove the old starter motor bush. 1) Fill it with grease, insert a close-fitting steel rod and give it a tap with a hammer - the theory is that hydraulic pressure will push out the bush, but this is very unlikely to work. 2) Fit an expanding bolt and try to grip the bush with it and pull it out; this, too, is an uncertain solution. Simon at BSW suggested running a bottom tap into the bush, the theory being that when the tap does bottom, turning it further screws out the bush. Good idea IF you've got a suitable-sized tap. This is the alternative.

Two home-made taps. The lower one is a 'lead' tap, which starts to cut the thread: it's a sawn-off section from a bolt with the front end ground into a taper and the threads re-cut using a hacksaw, followed by a triangular section file. It also has longitudinal saw cuts, to form reservoirs for the material it cuts from the bush. The top tap is much the same but with only a slight taper, and is a bottom tap.

the unit is also best replaced (in which case, the flywheel teeth will also be damaged and in need of attention).

The solenoid is mounted on the starter motor. The solenoid is an electrically-operated switch that uses a small current to energise an electromagnet when the ignition key is turned, which closes a pair of contacts that carry the huge current needed to operate the starter motor.

Most problems with the solenoid occur because it sticks (which can often be cured with a sharp tap from the handle of a screwdriver, or by putting the car in gear and rocking it backward and forward), although other faults can occur. If the starter motor does not operate when the ignition key is turned, listen for the 'click' to ascertain whether the solenoid is operating - if it is, check the battery terminals and the battery. If both are okay, chances are that the starter motor brushes need replacing. During the course of a full restoration it would be advisable to replace the starter motor and solenoid complete with professionally reconditioned alternatives.

If the original starter motor and solenoid are reused, clean the terminals and apply petroleum jelly to prevent future corrosion.

In theory it's possible to remove the solenoid independently of the starter motor, but, in practice, the two fixing screws are fairly inaccessible and likely to be seized, so it's necessary to remove the two as a unit. After disconnecting the battery, remove the thin wire from the solenoid terminal and the thick wire from the starter motor. Note that the nut securing the starter motor wire connector might be seized solid, so try to clean the thread of the stud first and give it a dousing with a lubricant. The starter motor will be secured by two bolts/nuts; according to the year, one of the bolts may be captive at the starter motor end.

Whenever you renew the starter motor you should also replace the associated bush - reconditioned starter motors should be supplied complete with one. The easiest method for removing the old bush is to run a thread-cutting tap into it which, with a bit of luck, will cut a thread inside the bush and wind the bush out after it has bottomed in the blind hole. If you

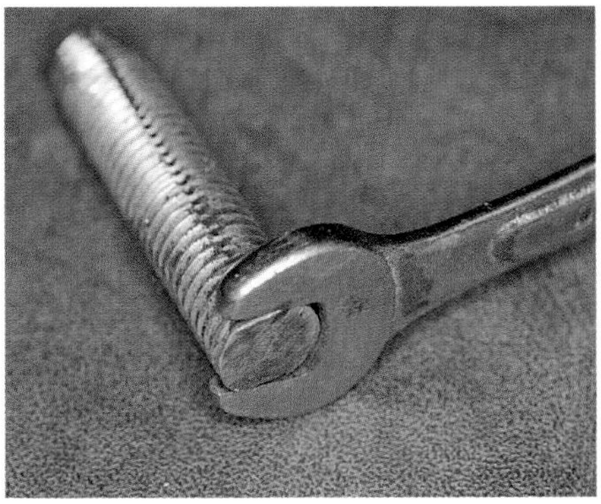

With two flats ground onto the rear of the DIY lead tap, a 10mm spanner can be fitted to turn it. An alternative would have been to weld on a handle.

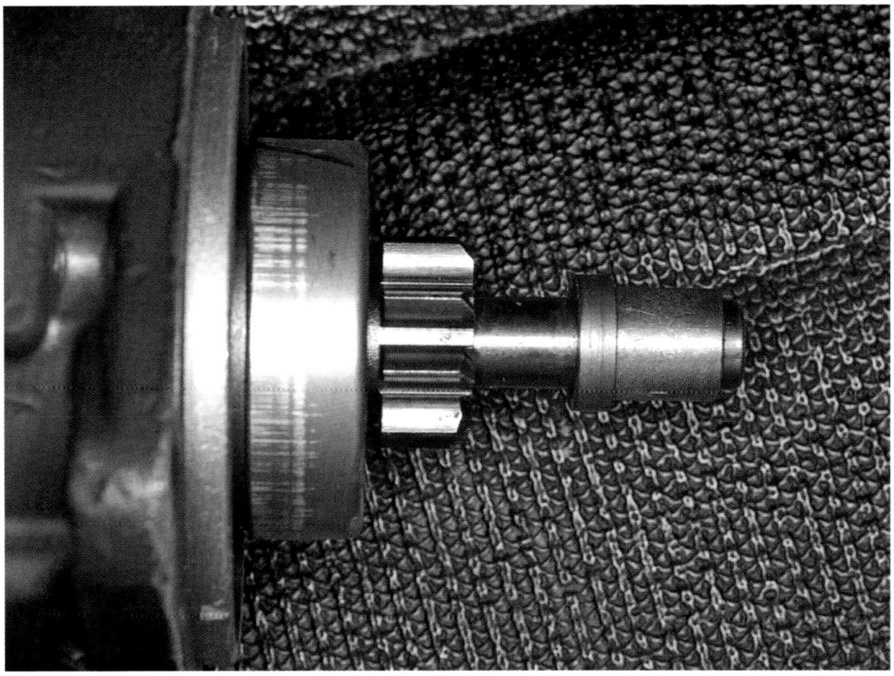

The new bush can be fitted along with the starter motor if you're careful. Make sure the motor is lined up correctly, and push the bush into position by tightening each of the starter motor bolts a fraction in turn. The problem with this method of fitting the bush is aligning it correctly - there is a better way.

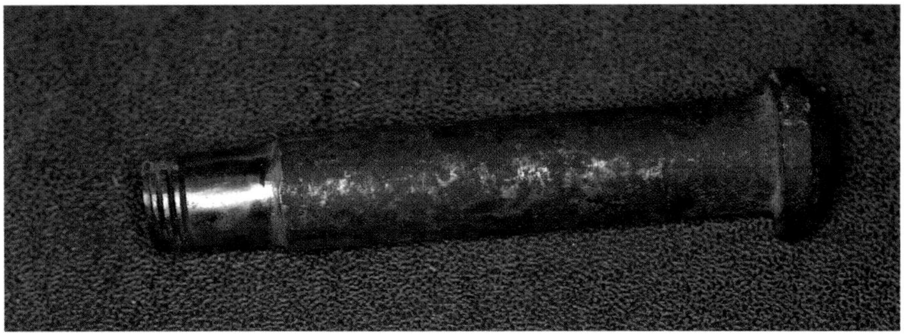

The bush is a fraction too large to seat in its hole, but you can make it smaller by freezing it. However, the bush is very thin-walled, so will warm and expand almost as soon as you touch it. I ground down the end of a bolt to the internal diameter of the bush, placed the bush on the bolt and put both in a freezer for a few hours, sealed in a plastic bag. The thermal inertia of the bolt meant that the bush stayed very cold whilst being started in the hole, and it drifted in easily.

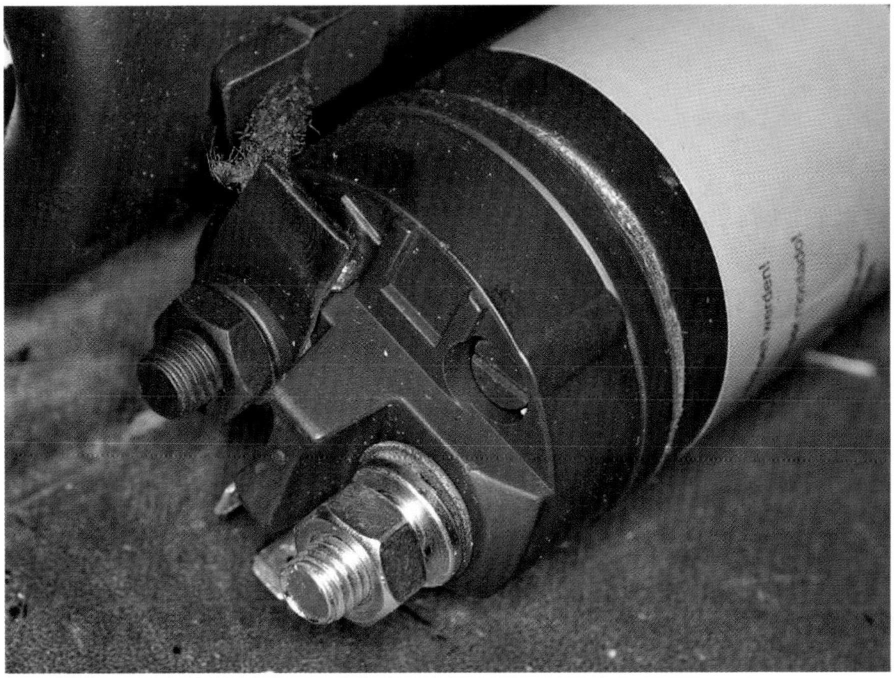

don't have taps, you can grind a taper into the end of a suitably-sized bolt, re-cut the thread using a hacksaw and/or Swiss file, and make cuts along the thread - in effect, making your own tap (see photographs).

The new bush will be slightly too large to fit into the hole. Some people fit the bush onto the starter spiggot and use the starter mounting bolts to push the bush into position, but it's better to shrink the bush by freezing it, so that it slips easily into place.

The starter bush is thin-walled, which means that it heats up in seconds and won't stay cold for long enough to fit it. The solution is to make a drift from mild steel, onto which the bush is a fairly close fit (see photograph). Place the drift with the bush *in situ* in a plastic bag and leave in the deep freeze for a couple of hours; you should then find it possible to seat the bush by hand and drift it home with a minimum of force.

When fitting a new starter and solenoid, always apply grease to the starter cable post thread.

It is far easier to fit a new starter bearing with the engine off the transaxle.

The voltage regulator prevents the generator from overcharging the battery. It lives under the rear seat. Some alternators have voltage regulation built-in; other alternators and all dynamos need a separate voltage regulator.

GENERATOR

A dynamo is far less efficient and generates less electricity than an alternator - perhaps by as much as 60 per cent. If either is faulty, the author recommends that the unit is taken to a specialist for renovation or exchanged for a reconditioned one, and that one of these courses of action is taken during a restoration irrespective of the condition of the unit, because removing and refitting either is not the easiest of tasks.

The only DIY repair that can be done to a dynamo is replacing the brushes, but on most Beetles still fitted with their original generator, the bearings will be fairly worn. Rather than simply renew the brushes it's far better to obtain an exchange unit, which will have new brushes, new bearings and, if necessary, have been rewound.

When fitting a new generator, it's a good idea to also fit a new drive belt.

The generator drive belt should not deflect more than half-an-inch under firm thumb pressure. To alter the tension, lock the generator by inserting a thin screwdriver through the hole in the front pulley half into the screw in the generator, then remove the pulley nut. There should be a number of shims between the two halves of the pulley, and removing some of these will increase the belt tension (and vice versa). Keep the spare shims under the pulley nut on the outside of the pulley. If you do not save the shims and decide to fit a new belt (if the existing one becomes frayed or cut), you will have to acquire and fit shims, otherwise the belt would be too highly tensioned and would place unacceptably high strain on the generator bearings.

VOLTAGE REGULATOR

The voltage regulator prevents the generator from overcharging the battery (which can cause the electrolyte to boil off - wrecking the battery) by disconnecting the generator when the battery voltage reaches a predetermined level - around 7 volts for 6V systems and 14 volts for 12V batteries. Beetle voltage regulators rarely give any problems because they are situated in the dry under the rear seat, rather than in the engine bay as with most cars.

To check the voltage regulator, check the voltage at the battery terminals with the engine running at a fast idle - a 6V system should show around 7V at the terminals, and a 12V system should show slightly over 14V. If the voltage is much more than the figures quoted, change the voltage regulator; if it's much less, either the generator or voltage regulator is faulty.

Don't confuse the voltage regulator with the fuel gauge voltage regulator (or 'trembler,' as it is widely known). The latter component reduces voltage (to typically 7V on a 12V system) so that the fuel gauge sender receives a constant voltage rather than fluctuating battery voltage.

HEAT EXCHANGERS & EXHAUST

Heat exchangers comprise a finned core which is contained within the body. Hot exhaust gasses passing through the core heat the fins which, in turn, heat the air that is forced through by the engine cooling fan. The heated air then passes through the heater channels to the interior of the car.

When replacing heat exchangers, as usual, you have a choice between expensive, original equipment components and spurious versions. Some of the latter components may not have the same fin surface area, which considerably reduces their efficiency at heating air, so do bear this in mind when considering making economies.

The exhaust is a low-cost item which is not really worth welded repair once it begins to blow (exhaust gasses escaping through a hole in the exhaust), because patches will be welded onto adjacent metal which will have thinned through rusting, and severe corrosion of these areas will usually occur very rapidly. A holed Beetle exhaust will make its presence felt by popping and banging.

On the overrun, some unburnt air/fuel mixture passes into the exhaust system. If air from a leak mixes with this, the chances are that the hot gasses released into the system following the next exhaust valve opening will ignite it. The resultant burn is quite rapid and, because the resultant expansion occurs in a confined space, you get the bang. The air induction can be due to faulty gaskets on the exhaust manifolds but, most usually, it comes from rusted holes in the silencer box, or inside one of the heat exchangers.

Expect to find rust holes just ahead of the flange at the bottom of the box. Don't look so much for an actual hole (which might be quite small and not easily spotted on the rust and dirt-covered box), but for the black carbon deposits surrounding the hole, which show up well.

It might be tempting to apply one of the many exhaust repair pastes over the hole or, if you possess a MIG welder, to slap on a cover plate, but such repairs will usually prove very shortlived. If a silencer box has rusted right through - even in one small area - you can bet your bottom dollar that the rot is pretty extensive and it won't be long before other holes appear. Best to renew the silencer; happily, they don't cost an awful lot.

Don't be in too much of a rush to rip the old silencer off - you might do terminal damage to repairable but weak heat exchangers. Cut the connector pipes gently rather than wrestle them away.

Renew the gaskets and all fittings - available in 'silencer fitting kits.'

At over £100 a pair even for pattern parts, rotten heat exchangers are worth repairing if at all possible. You don't need to search for the rot - I'll tell you exactly where you'll find it; in the short length of pipe at the back of each exchanger where it connects up to the silencer pipes. These are invariably covered with rust scale and mud, so you might not see a hole, nor carbon deposits; the gentlest of prods with a screwdriver will usually be sufficient to reveal a gaping hole.

Getting heat exchangers off a Beetle can be so awkward that - if you've the facility - it can be less traumatic to remove the engine complete!

When removing heat exchanger nuts, take great care not to shear the threaded rods - if they're reluctant to start, clean the thread as best you can and leave it soaking in penetrating fluid for as long as possible before trying again.

Hot spots suffer two common problems - internal blockage and corrosion. At some point, someone has tried to cure the latter problem using what looks like exhaust repair paste.

When removing the nuts at the exhaust flange during exhaust renewal, be ultra careful not to snap the exhaust port threaded studs, or you'll have to take the head off to remove the remnants of the stud.

You can cut the damaged pipe off and weld in shouldered repair sections to save the heat exchangers, or fabricate and weld in new steel.

If the hole is quite small, it may be possible to simply turn the MIG right down and weld onto the edges of the hole until it is fully closed off. If the holes are larger then fit backing material. After cleaning all the rust from the pipes, cut repair sections and put a curve into these so that, when inserted into the pipes, they touch the edges of the holes. Next, tack weld them into position using the MIG. It should then be fairly simple to seam weld them into position, after which, you can build up the thickness with weld. Finally, grind down the proud weld so that the outside of the pipe is round.

Before refitting the heat exchangers, run a die up each manifold stud to clean off dirt and surface rust. What's that? You don't have a die? Okay; take one old manifold nut and make a hacksaw cut through one flat, run it onto a bolt to clean up the cut, and you've made yourself a paint/rust removing die. Run this up and down each manifold stud a couple of times, and the stud should be so clean that you'll be able to run the nuts on using finger pressure alone, rather than having to turn a spanner one flat at a time - saves time.

HEATING SYSTEM

The cab heating system - and especially the demisting system - of the Beetle is not very good, even when new, and in old examples it can be terrible. Fitting new heater channels is a big help in restoring performance, and gains can be had from renewing the flexible heater pipes that connect the heat exchangers to the cab and their gaskets, as well as any damaged ducting in the system. Fitting the demister down pipes into the 'A'posts, and especially locating them over the stubs on the heater channels, is not easy. There should be a small access hole in the bottom of the 'A' post which allows you to see the heater channel stub - you can use a screwdriver through the hole to help locate the pipe, though it might be necessary to back off the door hinge bolts first, because they can touch the stub.

Further improvements in the demisting can be made by blanking off the air feed to the rear footwell, because heat is lost even with the flap closed. If the temperature of your front seat passenger's feet is not a worry, removing the footwell vent cover will allow you to place a sheet of steel behind it to blank this off, too.

FINAL SETTING UP

After the bodywork restoration is complete, and the mechanical, electrical and hydraulic components have all been fitted, some components will require setting up, or at least checking. In practice, many of these checks and adjustments will have been made whilst components were renovated, so ignore any that you've already covered.

Check the tension of the generator drive belt and, if it deflects more than half-an-inch under firm thumb pressure, tighten it. To do this, lock the generator by inserting a thin screwdriver through the hole in the front pulley half into the screw in the generator, then remove the pulley nut. There should be a number of shims between the two halves of the pulley, and removing some of these will increase the belt tension (and vice versa). Keep the spare shims under the pulley nut on the outside of the pulley. If you don't save the shims and decide to fit a new belt (if the existing one becomes frayed or cut), you will have to obtain and fit shims, otherwise the belt would be too highly tensioned and would place unacceptably high strain on the generator bearings.

The valve clearances should be checked. The engine should be cold. Disconnect the HT leads (mark them if appropriate with the relevant cylinder number to aid correct replacement), and remove the sparkplugs. The rocker covers are held by spring clips; prise these away and lift out the covers - there will be some engine oil leakage so have something on the floor ready to mop it up. Take the car out of gear. Remove the sparkplugs so that the engine turns over easily by hand.

Valve clearances should be set with the piston of each cylinder at the top of its travel - called Top Dead Center (TDC). Remove the distributor cap, then turn the engine until the rotor arm is pointing where the number one cylinder HT lead terminates in the distributor cap. Do this by either pulling the generator drive belt, or with a spanner on the generator pulley bolt (if the engine will not turn over then the drive belt is slipping, and should be tightened before carrying on). The rotor arm should be pointing at a notch in the distributor body rim. The notch in the crankshaft pulley should be pointing upwards, in line with the crankcase centre join or, if there are two notches, they should be slightly to the right of this line. The piston of cylinder number one is now at TDC.

Check the valve clearances for number one cylinder. Try to gently place a feeler gauge of 0.006in (0.15mm) in-between the rocker arm and the top of the valve stem; if it won't go in, or is very slack, the clearance has to be adjusted. Undo the lock nut on the adjuster screw, then place the feeler gauge in position and tighten the adjuster screw until very slight drag can be felt on the gauge when it is moved. Remove the gauge, hold the adjuster in position with a screwdriver, and tighten the lock nut using a ring spanner. Recheck and readjust if necessary.

Turn the engine anti-clockwise until the crankshaft has gone through 180 degrees (the rotor arm will have travelled through 90 degrees and be pointing at the position of number two HT lead within the distributor cap). Check and, if necessary, adjust the clearance for number two cylinder. Repeat the anti-clockwise movement as before (rotor arm 90 degrees, crankshaft 180 degrees) and check and adjust the clearance for cylinder number three, then repeat the process for cylinder four.

Refit the rocker box covers, using new gaskets.

Carburation

The problem with attempting to adjust the air/fuel mixture at home is that there is no accurate method of accurately testing the results of your efforts, unless you have one of the small exhaust gas analysers which are available to the DIY motorist. Now that exhaust gas is measured as part of many roadworthiness tests, it may be as well to ask that the mixture is set by the tester before your car is tested. Even accurately setting the tickover (750rpm for most models and 850rpm for cars with semi-automatic gearboxes) requires the use of specialised equipment.

However, if you wish to do the work at home, here are the basic principles. Begin by warming the engine and adjust the throttle adjusting screw (which bears against the throttle lever) until the revolutions rise to just under 1000rpm (fast idle). Turn the mixture control screw slowly clockwise until the point at which the engine begins to run erratically (the mixture is weak); turn back by 60 degrees (one third of a complete turn). Reset the tickover. As stated, it is best to have this work carried out by a professional with the aid of an exhaust gas analyser, and you would normally only carry out this adjustment following an engine or carburettor rebuild, in any case, in order to get the engine running well enough to make it to your local garage, where the mixture would be set properly.

In addition to the home exhaust gas analyser machine now available, a number of devices are advertised to make setting mixture easier. Chief amongst these is the Colourtune system, which uses a special sparkplug that allows you to see the combustion colour and adjust the mixture to obtain the correct colour, and hence, appropriate mixture.

Still on the subject of fuel, check the fuel tank and lines for leakage, and that the fuel filter is fitted the correct way around (an arrow on the casing indicates flow).

Setting the valve gaps. Slacken the locking nut, then adjust with a screwdriver until the feeler gauge is lightly held.

Whenever the rocker box cover is removed it's as well to renew the seal to avoid oil leaks.

Fitting twin carburettors on separate stub inlet manifolds is a popular modification, and setting up these is rather more complicated. Basically, the process involves disconnecting the linkage between the two carburettors and adjusting the tickover speed on each (holding one end of a tube to the carburettor inlet and the other to your ear allows you to judge and balance the airflow). Stop the engine, connect the linkage, and check that both carburettors open fully and in unison.

Restart the engine, then adjust the tickover speed via the linkage. Finally, take the car to a company with a rolling road to have the correct jets fitted, and for final set-up.

Transmission

Check the transaxle oil level. Park the car on level ground and remove the 17mm hexagonal transaxle filler plug. If you don't have the correct tool for this, try making your own by bolting - or preferably welding - a 17mm bolt to a length of steel. If this is the first time you've tried to remove the plug, you may find that it is very tight, in which case a hexagonal key will probably be needed to start it. The oil should be level with this but, if not, top up. In the case of Stickshift models, a dipstick is provided to show the oil level: if this is low, top up using the correct fluid - Dexron 1 or Dexron 2.

The clutch travel should be checked and adjusted if necessary. There should be half-an-inch of free play. To adjust pedal travel, turn the large wing nut on the clutch operating lever, which can be found in front of the engine on the left side of the car.

Grease the nipples on the front suspension (beam axle). Using a pumping oil can, lubricate the door, luggage bay lid, and engine lid hinges and locks.

Check the condition of the drive shaft joint gaiters and renew if necessary. Split gaiters will allow water and dirt into the joints, where it will cause accelerated wear.

Brakes

Check the fluid level in the brake master cylinder; if this is a little low, top up with new brake fluid. If the level is very low fluid has been lost and the car should not be used until the cause has been identified and dealt with.

Check the thickness of the lining of the pads/shoes. The minimum acceptable thickness is 1/8in (3mm) for pads, and 1/10in (2.5mm) for shoes. If the pads or shoes are approaching this thickness, it's as well to renew them. There are inspection holes in the brake back plate for checking shoe thickness,

If the brake pedal travel is too great and the handbrake is inefficient, the rear drum brakes will have to be adjusted. Note that later cars have self-adjusting rear drum brakes, and poor braking performance usually means that either the pads and shoes are contaminated or worn, or that some part of the mechanism is sticking.

Drum brake shoes are supported at one end by the wheel cylinder pistons; these are pushed outwards so that the shoe presses against the drum when the brake pedal is pressed. At the other end the shoes are located in the adjusting screws. Adjustment is carried out by removing the two blanking plugs in each back plate, and using a straight-bladed screwdriver (an old screwdriver with a cranked end is better) to turn the star adjuster wheel for each shoe in turn. Adjust each shoe until the wheel is locked, then back it off until the wheel will turn freely.

Operate both the handbrake and foot brake to centralise the shoes, then readjust the brakes if necessary; sometimes this process will have to be repeated several times before the shoes are correctly adjusted.

Check the handbrake travel and adjust if necessary. When the handbrake is pulled up onto the fourth notch, the rear wheels should be locked. If not, adjust as follows.

Chock the front wheels, raise the rear of the car and support it on axle stands. If you have just adjusted the brakes, pump the pedal to centralise the shoes. Pull the handbrake onto the second notch and remove the rubber gaiter from the bottom of the handbrake lever. Slacken off the lock nuts on the cable ends, then insert a screwdriver into each cable end slot in turn to prevent it from turning whilst you tighten the nut. Adjust the cable end nuts so that equal pressure is felt on both, then test the handbrake by pulling it up to notch four and seeing whether the wheels are locked. Repeat if necessary and finish by tightening the lock nuts and refitting the gaiter.

If, in common with the author, you have difficulty remembering which way to turn the adjusters in order to spread the shoes, try holding a nut and bolt by the adjuster so that the bolt head takes the place of the shoe end, and the nut imitates the adjuster. By turning the nut you will see (there are no left-hand threads) which way the bolt head moves and can deduce whether to turn the adjuster up or down. The front adjusters are the more difficult to get at, and a cranked screwdriver will be a positive aid.

To test the handbrake, on private land off the public highway (such as a driveway) drive slowly - 5mph is adequate - on a loose surface like gravel, and apply the handbrake. After stopping, check to see whether either wheel locked up during braking by examining the tyre marks - a locked wheel will scuff the surface. If either wheel locked up then the other is not operating properly - it might just need adjusting, or it could be seized.

Chapter 3
Bodywork & trim restoration

Let me begin this chapter by saying that a full DIY car restoration is incredibly hard work. Very few people really appreciate just how much work is involved until they've either finished one, or - more commonly - given up partway through. Obviously, the amount of work needed in a restoration will depend on the original condition of the car, and on the desired end result; concours cars can take much, much longer, and require more work, than 'everyday' cars. The amount of work is also dependent on the quality of the restoration; cut corners and you can reduce the time it takes, but you'll have to be prepared for second-class workmanship and the certain knowledge that the bodywork repair panels will soon be rusting ...

The best restorations can take thousands of hours; many run into years of part-time work. Many are never completed at all. Before embarking on a full restoration, therefore, consider very carefully whether your motivation (and funds) will be sufficient to last the project.

On the financial side, make as comprehensive a list as possible of necessary panels, mechanical components, and consumables (paint, MIG wire, etc.,), and see whether the total is so high that you could get a better deal by simply selling your own car and buying one in good condition. Chances are you could, because the cost of both professional and DIY restorations can exceed the end value of the car.

You can cut costs by repairing expensive pressings rather than replacing them; i.e. building up a floor edge from sheet steel rather than spending a lot of money on a proper repair panel or a full floor. The drawback with repairing panels in this way is that, as they normally rust through first along the edges of welded seams, a car which is extensively repaired with part-panels will require body repair work sooner than one which is largely re-panelled, if for no other reason than that the former has more seams.

You also need to consider honestly whether your own skills are sufficient for the job. If you have to pay a professional

Simon and Terry reunite a Beetle bodyshell with its chassis, which has new floor pans and heater channels.

restorer to put right your mistakes, his bill will probably be greater than it would have been to do the restoration in the first place. Many people seem to prefer to have the bodywork and painting carried out by a professional, and to undertake the mechanical build-up themselves, which can greatly reduce the cost of a restoration.

An alternative to doing the complete job yourself is to project manage the restoration, bringing in a skilled mobile welder and, perhaps, a competent mechanic, as and when required. This means you will do all the donkey work, such as the strip down, cutting out rotten metal, cleaning, and so on, and using professionals as and when required, so that you can have confidence in the quality of the welding and the mechanical build-up.

Maintaining motivation can be a real problem. The author finds that decorating the workplace with photographs of the car being restored, and of really nice examples of the same model, can often provide that little extra inspiration needed to carry on working when every fibre of his body is screaming to get out of the workshop! Whilst on the subject of photographs, it's worth keeping the fullest photographic record possible of a restoration as, not only does this prove that the car has been properly restored should you ever wish to sell it, it also shows the full extent of the restoration.

In the many available books and magazines on the subject, classic car restoration is often portrayed as largely consisting of cutting away old, rotten panels and grafting in new, like a brilliant surgeon performing lifesaving surgery. Whilst this work is important, it's actually a relatively small part of car restoration. In fact, the bulk of the work of restoration is concerned with the far more humdrum business of cleaning. For every minute spent welding, there will usually be an hour or more of cleaning, ranging from scraping away old underseal, accumulated mud and rust from the underside of the car, to removing burnt oil deposits and sundry dirt and gunge from engine and transmission components.

A large part of the restorer's time will also be spent trying to establish and maintain a coherent and workable 'filing system' for the various components of the car. This is essential if you are not to later waste countless hours during the build-up trying to find the right nut, bracket or set screw for a particular component.

If the foregoing has not completely put you off the idea of restoring your Beetle, take heart in the fact that the Beetle is probably the easiest (no, that's not true; the Beetle is the least difficult) of cars to restore. Spares availability and pricing has, if anything, improved over the years, the chassis construction is easier to restore than the monocoque bodyshells of the vast majority of cars, and the lack of sophistication of the Beetle makes mechanical work straightforward. In fact, if someone was contemplating having their first attempt at restoring a car, the Beetle would be the obvious choice!

PREMISES, TOOLS, SKILLS & EQUIPMENT

Even more important than when doing mechanical repair work is a good workshop. Ideally, the workplace should allow you a bare minimum of one metre working area all around the car and, if you intend to separate the chassis and bodyshell (which is likely), you'll need three metres, plus twice the width of the car as a minimum. If you have to carry out a full mechanical and trim strip down, do not underestimate the amount of dry storage that will be required for the components which, in a full restoration, can pretty well fill a room in your house (which is where many people store them, because it's dry and secure).

A damp workplace will be a constant source of frustration, because new steel panels will begin to rust as soon as (if not before) they are fitted, tools will quickly become rusty, and new paintwork will suffer bloom. So, in addition to a sound and leak-proof roof, this means full guttering on the outside and a dampproof membrane in the walls, because rain blowing against the walls, or moisture rising through them, will eventually get into the atmosphere in the workshop and condense on your car's bodywork, causing rust.

Good, all-round lighting which illuminates the sides and underside of the car is essential, and a solid, level, crumble-proof concrete floor is absolutely vital. An inspection pit is very nice to have for some mechanical work, but a liability in certain circumstances. If petrol vapour emanates from the car it falls into the pit (being heavier than air) and can fill it, which means that your car is, in effect, sitting on a firebomb that could be ignited by welding, grinding, or any cutting operation: even a tiny electrical spark could ignite the mixture. So a pit is great for spannering, but a liability for most other work.

Some specialised tools and equipment are essential for restoration. Some form of welding equipment, if only a cheap MIG, is recommended, even if you intend to bring in an outside welder to carry out the bulk of the work, in order to allow you to tack panels into position for final welding by the professional.

WELDING EQUIPMENT

There are four types of welding equipment which the DIY restorer might consider: arc (often called 'Stick'), MIG, gas, and spot. Arc welding equipment is relatively cheap to buy, but has severe limitations regarding the thickness of metal it can be successfully used on. If the metal is less than 1/8in thick (i.e. all body panels), the fierce arc welder will quickly burn right through the metal which it is supposed to be joining! Arc welders are most suited to use on heavy section agricultural vehicle metal, and are useless for most car restoration work.

The MIG (Metal Inert Gas) welder is

Having the best tools always makes the job easier, though few DIY restorers will have access to car lifts.

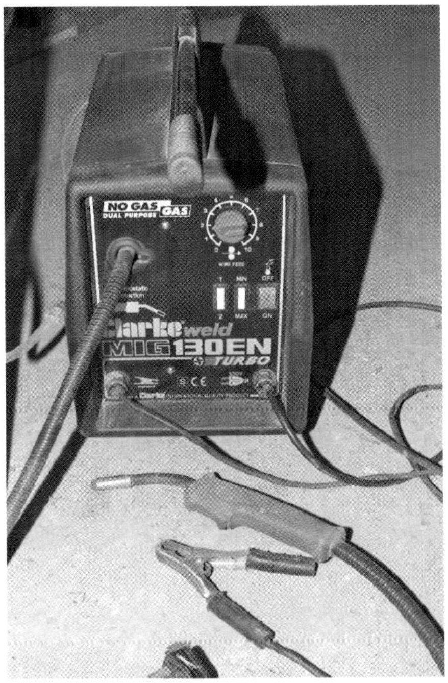

The MIG (Metal Inert Gas) welder is the most common choice for the DIY restorer. This 130 amp example has proven quite capable of handling all Beetle bodywork.

the type normally used by the DIY restorer, and the majority of professionals, as well. It surrounds its electrode (in wire form) in an inert gas, so preventing the metal from burning through. It may, therefore, be used on the thin metal of car body panels. Two types are available. The more traditional MIG welder uses gas from either a small cylinder strapped to the unit, or a larger, remote cylinder, and different gasses are required for welding different metals. The newer type of MIG (the 'gasless' MIG which can only be used on steel) uses instead a substance contained as a core within the wire for the gas. Because large gas cylinders are expensive to buy, hire and fill, and because small gas cylinders have to be replaced frequently at relatively high cost, this newer type of welder appears to offer advantages, the main one being that it has only one consumable (the cored wire) to run out of! The MIG welder is probably the best type for a newcomer to the art. The author uses a Clark MIG welder; a unit which needs a gas cylinder and which has proved quite easy to use and capable of first-class results. The gas cylinder was supplied by a friendly hotel owner, and is refilled with CO_2, used by the licensing trade in beer cellars.

The cored wire needed for gasless welders is often (erroneously, the author believes) referred to as 'flux cored.' It's essential you're not inadvertently supplied with standard, non-cored MIG wire for use with a gasless MIG, because without shielding gas, this will burn through body panels.

Gas welding is arguably the most versatile of all, and can provide excellent results in the hands of a skilled person. Arc, MIG and spot welders all use electricity to heat a very small area, whereas in gas welding a torch is used to heat both metal and welding rod, and a larger area of metal tends to become very hot as a result. The greatest drawback is that the required heat tends to warp body panels, and can easily give a new panel a corrugated finish. Gas welding equipment can also be used for brazing, and for heating stubborn nuts and bolts which refuse to otherwise move.

Spot welders are the easiest to use, although limited insofar as they can only be used for joining together the edges of two metal 'lips' (unless a range of quite expensive special arms is available). For joins such as these, spot welders offer an unbeatable combination of ease of use, strength, and neatness. Neither wire or welding rod is required, because the spot welder uses electricity to heat and fuse two panels together. Few DIY restorers would go to the expense of buying a spot welder because of its limited applications, and most opt to hire them, as and when required, from a DIY store or tool hire business.

When using a spot welder two conditions are necessary for good results. Firstly, the two pieces of steel being joined must be tightly held together. Secondly, the surfaces must be spotlessly clean. It is nowadays normal practice to spray special zinc-based paints onto the metal before performing the weld, in order to reduce the chances of corrosion occurring.

An accessory which has been available for the arc welder for some time is claimed to allow users to spot weld two sheets of steel with access from one side alone, whereas the spot welder requires that an electrode is placed each side of the join. The arc welder accessory has not been tested by the author, so whilst he cannot personally vouch for them, he cannot see any reason why they should not work. It would be vital that the panels being joined were firmly clamped together in some way immediately each side of the single electrode, because the top layer would expand more rapidly due to heat than would the underlying layer, so the two would tend to move apart.

Still on the subject of arc welder accessories, kits are available which allow the welder to be used for brazing. The author has heard nothing detrimental about any of these arc welder accessories, but has yet to find an experienced professional restorer who champions them ...

A new type of welder has appeared in recent years which, although initially sold at far too high a price for most DIY restorers, has now come down in price to the point where it's a viable alternative to MIG welding. The TIG welder (more about which later) is, perhaps, halfway between MIG and gas welding, because it generates intense heat between two electrodes in order to heat the steel to be welded, and a filler is fed into this in the form of a rod.

Most welding equipment can only produce neat, strong results if the operator has the appropriate skill. The quickest way to acquire this skill is to enrol on a short welding course, perhaps at an evening class at a college? Whilst it's possible to teach yourself to weld, it's not recommended that you do so (especially using your own car as a guinea pig).

Because the MIG seems to be the type of welding equipment most commonly owned by the DIY restorer, an introduction to its use follows. If you wish to find out more there are several excellent books available on the subject, check out your local bookshop.

Using a MIG welder

Apart from the spot welder the MIG is, arguably, the easiest of welding devices for the beginner to use for general bodywork repairs. This does not, however, mean that it is an easy matter to produce clean and strong welds on typically thin body panels because, unless conditions and the user's skills are both excellent, there are many obstacles to good welding.

The worst problem to beset the novice is that of 'burning through,' when the electric current melts straight through the metal it is supposed to be joining. This can occur if the wire feed speed is too slow (or intermittent, which indicates a fault in the welder - usually either the wire jamming in the liner, or the driving wheels slipping); if the gun is moved across the metal too slowly; if the current is set too high, or if the shielding gas/core fails to do its job.

When the metal to be welded has become thin through rusting, the chances of burning through greatly increase, hence the advice to always cut back to clean, strong, thick metal before attempting to weld.

The correct preparation of the metal to be welded is vital. All traces of rust, paint, oil, grease, and any other contaminant must be cleaned from the surface to avoid poor penetration and spitting. ANY impurities which find their way into the welded joint will substantially weaken it.

When a joint is being welded, both surfaces should be thoroughly cleaned; if paint or other contaminant is present on the underside of the pane, it will mix with the molten weld/steel and weaken the joint. Recently, special paints have become available which can be used on surfaces to be spot or MIG welded. The use of these products, such as Autoline weldable zinc primer, will ensure that the welded joint does not - as is usual - become the first part of the repair to rust through again. The metal panels must, in some way, be clamped so firmly that the heat of the welding process does not distort either and allow them to move apart. Small sections may be clamped using mole grips, although longer runs are usually fixed using self-tapping screws or ,alternatively, pop rivets at regular intervals.

In recent years the TIG (Tungsten Inert Gas) welder has appeared, a cross between MIG and gas welding, in that an intensely hot electric arc is generated (like a MIG), which heats a small area of steel onto which a welding rod is fed, as in gas welding. The advantage over gas welding is that the TIG heats a smaller area of steel, reducing the potential for bucking. TIG welding equipment is very versatile but, at the time of writing, the most expensive option.

First steps with a MIG

Always practice on scrap metal and do not attempt any welding to the bodywork of your car until you are capable of producing consistently good results.

Safety is the most important consideration. If your workshop does not already possess one, buy a fire extinguisher. Never weld in the vicinity of a petrol tank, or any container which holds or has held combustible fluids, especially if the container is now empty or near-empty (an empty petrol tank contains more explosive fumes than a full one). Remember that paint, underseal, and certain other materials found in a car (such as some sound-deadening material) can be flammable, and many can be ignited by heat moving along a panel which is being welded. Keep a fire extinguisher handy for putting out small welding fires.

Always use a proper welding mask. If you view the electric arc with the naked eye you will later suffer an immensely painful phenomenon called arc eye, which is painful enough to drive most sufferers to seek hospital attention. Wraparound face masks, particularly those which attach to the user's head, are recommended, because the alternative lollipop-type flat mask can allow in extraneous light from the top and sides, which contracts the pupils and makes the viewed image of the welding process appear very dim. The wraparound mask will also allow you to use your 'spare' (and heavily gloved) hand to help guide the MIG. Basically, the visor is tilted upwards so that the wearer can place the pistol grip onto the metal and support it using both hands (do not allow your hand too close to the 'business' end), then a flick of the head moves the visor downwards over the eyes, and welding can begin. (Don't blame the author if you crick your neck trying this, though!) The alternative is to wear MIG-proof goggles, but the author does not like these because the radiation given off during a MIG welding session is not only harmful to eyes, but also to skin, so always ensure you are well protected.

Always wear protective clothing, especially strong leather gloves, and a hat (to prevent your hair from catching fire as the sparks shower) is a good idea. It is as well to wear old, thick items of clothing and stout leather shoes (red-hot weld splatter will burn through flimsy shoes and your socks - and when it reaches your foot it hurts like hell).

Never take liberties with the electric current; though of a low voltage, it's still powerful enough to kill you. Ensure that you weld only in dry conditions, and keep trailing leads off damp floors.

In MIG welding, an electric current passes down the MIG wire, melting both the end of the wire and the metal underneath it, so that the two fuse together. If the surface of the metal has any contaminants on it, including paint, rust or oil, these will mix with the molten metal and weaken the joint. When welding typically thin car body steel, the steel panels become molten right through, and paint or other contaminants on the underside can be drawn up into the molten metal, again weakening the joint.

When first starting to weld, try to run a bead onto a flat sheet of 18g - and preferably 20g - steel rather than attempting a joint between two pieces. Begin by cleaning the metal top and bottom thoroughly of all rust, paint, and grease. Trim the wire protruding from the MIG nozzle to around 10mm. Place the earth clamp on the steel, put on all protective clothing, and switch on the machine. Place the wire against the steel, pull the face visor in front of your eyes. Press the trigger and begin to push or drag the gun along the surface of the steel, keeping the gun at an angle of around 70 degrees from the horizontal. Do not allow your mask to get too close to the weld, because sparks will quickly ruin it.

When you first attempt to weld it will seem that everything happens at once - sometimes too quickly for you to establish gun movement before burning through begins. The solution is to keep on practising and adjusting the settings on the MIG to suit the steel you are welding until you master the art. The author is not possessed of particularly steady hands, and has never found achieving good welds with the MIG an easy matter. The greatest problem is that of running the weld away from the intended join. This problem can be overcome to a large extent by resting the side of the MIG pistol grip against a solid object, such as a length of scrap box section steel, arranged so that it is in line with the intended join. MIG 'plug' welding is an easy method of producing neat and strong joints. This simulates a spot weld, and is achieved by drilling holes in the uppermost of two panels which are to be joined, then clamping the panels tightly together and filling the holes with weld. The weld fuses to the bottom panel and to the side of the hole in the top panel. After surplus weld has been ground down, the result can be very neat and strong. However, do not use plug welds if you envisage ever having to remove the panel thus welded because, unlike spot welds, plug welds can turn out to be irregularly shaped, and cannot simply be drilled or cut out like spot welds. If you do elect to plug weld, the welds should be as frequent as the original spot welds they are replacing.

Please check with your local vehicle testing authorities that plug welds are still acceptable for roadworthiness test purposes (MoT in the UK) before rebuilding your car using this technique. Although plug welds were perfectly acceptable at the time of writing, legislation does change and the author and publisher cannot be held accountable for future laws!

There are various types of joint that you will have to deal with. The butt joint is, as the name suggests, a join between two sheets of metal which butt against each other. A small gap should be left in-between the two so that the weld can properly penetrate the joint, and the ideal tool for achieving this is the 'Inter-Grip.' This small device (sold in packs of five) can hold flat or curved panels tightly together for butt welding equally well. The author always tacks the two pieces of metal before continuously welding them, because if you start continuous welding at one end of the join and weld the whole lot in one go, distortion is very likely to occur.

Other joints include right angles (which can be difficult), and stepped joints (detailed in the following paragraph). Practice all types of joint because they'll all be needed during a typical restoration.

A joddler (variously referred to as a 'joggler,' 'jodder' and, more properly, an edge setter) is a great aid. This tool places a step into the edge of a panel to allow it to overlap, yet remain at the same level as the panel to which it is to be joined. The better joddlers incorporate a 1/8in punch, for punching holes in steel through which you can produce neat plug welds.

Two types of commercially manufactured joddler are commonly available. The less expensive is the

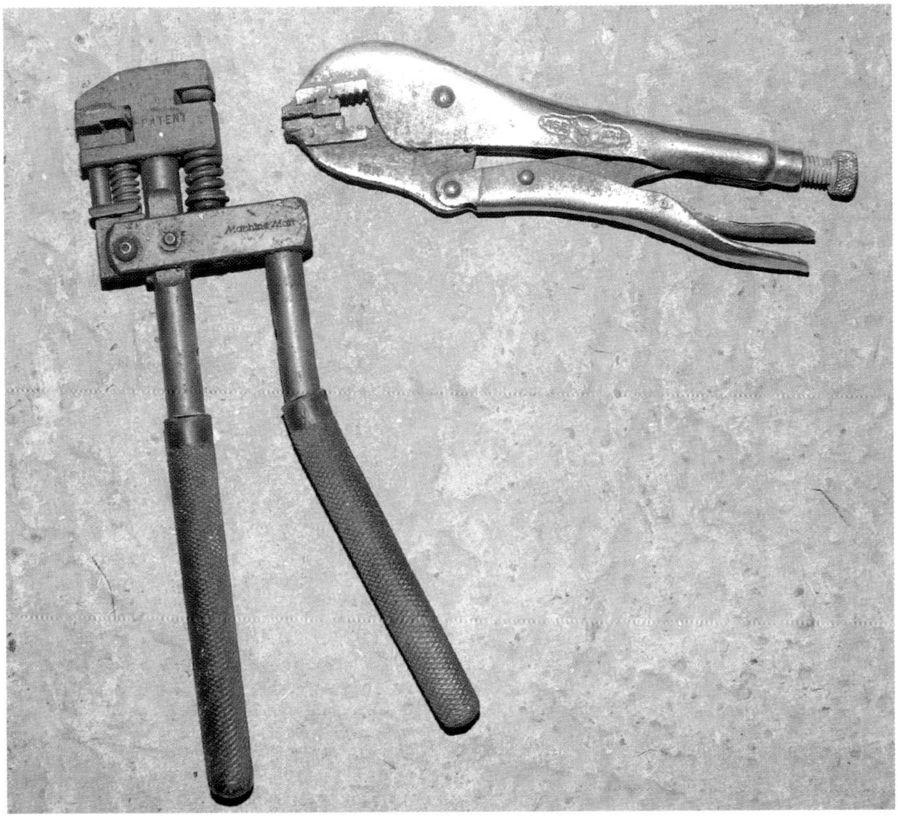

When two flat panels are to be edge welded together, it's easiest if they overlap, and one panel has a stepped edge pressed into it, because this allows the faces of the panels to lie flush, whilst reducing the chances of spoiling the job by burning away the edge of one panel; all too easily done when butt welding. On the left is a commercially made joddler (as the tool is known), and on the right a home-made alternative comprising two hand-filed steel blocks welded into the jaws of a mole wrench. The head of the commercial joddler can be rotated, turning it into a hole punch, which creates holes for plug welding.

scissor type, which can incorporate a plug weld hole punch. The more expensive alternative works rather like a can opener, and uses two stepped wheels which are pressed each side of the steel, and then turned using a 1/2in ratchet drive as a winder. The author uses the scissor type, but found that the effort needed to step an edge into steel of greater thickness than 20g was too high. He made up a cheap alternative using a large mole wrench, with two stepped blocks welded to the jaws (see photograph). The adjustable mole wrench allows pressure to be progressively built up as two or more passes with the tool are made over thick steel.

The joddled joint has a great advantage over the butt joint. Because the two halves of a joddled joint can be pulled tightly together, and because the stepped edge of the joddled panel is parallel with the rest of the panel, the two panels naturally tend to lie flat when welded together. With the butt joint, it's easy to inadvertently weld the panels so they're not quite in line with each other. This becomes important when one of the two panels being joined is under any stress. One instance which springs readily to mind is when a lower side repair panel is being welded into position. The cutting process which removed the unwanted metal can easily have distorted the remaining metal. A joddled repair panel pulls this back into correct alignment when the panels are temporarily clamped with pop rivets or self-tapping screws prior to welding.

If you have access to a spot welder, you can use a handy alternative to joddled joints. By spot welding a strip of steel behind one edge so that it overlaps the other, you have a nice, flush joint to weld.

The alternative to doing the welding yourself is to bring in a skilled welder as and when required. There are many self-employed and mobile MIG and gas welders who may be hired by the hour, and they can usually be found in any commercial telephone directory.

When hiring a skilled welder it's as well to prepare as much of the work as you can, otherwise the travelling expenses could eclipse the actual welding charges! For most DIY restorers who will only ever restore the one car, hiring a skilled welder is probably a better solution than learning to weld, because you'll get better results, and be able to drive your car safe in the knowledge that the welds will not spring open the first time you drive over a pothole!

OTHER TOOLS AND EQUIPMENT

If you intend to carry out a full body-off strip down prior to welding, a means of holding the chassis/floor pan at a comfortable working height is very useful. Strong steel trestles can easily be made by welding (good practice for the novice welder) and, if two steel box sections are laid across these, you'll have a solid and level platform, onto which a few strong adults should easily be able to manhandle the floor pan assembly after it has been stripped of heavy fittings such as the transaxle and front suspension beam.

An angle grinder with cutting and grinding wheels, plus a sanding/linishing wheel and, perhaps, a cup brush, will save hours of very hard work when you have to clean old paint, underseal or rust from metal. It is well worth spending extra to buy an angle grinder with a rheostat trigger, allowing variable speed, because this gives enough control to allow the use of coarse abrasive discs with which to clean off old paint and rust without ripping right through the steel.

You will need a selection of tools for cutting sheet metal, such as tin snips, aviation shears (straight and curved), a Monodex cutter, hacksaw, sharp bolster chisel, and lump hammer. Pneumatic chisels and air hacksaws which are powered by compressors are marvellous if your pocket runs to a large enough compressor, because they allow you to cut body panels without the distortion that a bolster chisel produces. The twin problems with the air chisel are its noise level (guaranteed to annoy neighbours), and its appetite for air, which can easily outstrip the capacity of smaller compressors.

Powered shears and nibblers are also very useful, and offer the considerable benefit of leaving a 'safe' edge that won't lacerate your hands. Some fit into the chuck of an electric drill, and others are powered by an air compressor.

Another very useful - but incredibly noisy - air tool is the descaler. This tool uses air power to hammer a number of pins onto a rusted surface, and can quickly remove all traces of rust and leave a surface ready for degreasing prior to welding or spraying. The noise level generated when working on a large, resonant panel with either this tool or the air chisel, however, is so great that the user must wear some form of hearing protection. In some countries, laws allow neighbours the legal means of curtailling such noisy activities. In the UK, noise is now regarded as pollution, and neighbours can involve the authorities if you make too much noise.

Speaking of compressors, these are incredibly useful, not only for spraying, but for blowing rust and dust out of nooks and crannies. They are also useful to have to hand for blowing out minor welding fires which can start when paint, underseal or trim in the vicinity of the area being welded catches fire. Buy the largest compressor you can afford, because very small units are quickly drained of air by certain attachments, and the motors have a short 'duty cycle' which causes them to shut off automatically to prevent overheating. This sometimes happens at a crucial moment ...

The author has found an old, cylinder-type vacuum cleaner to be one of the most useful tools in his workshop. Cleaning off an old bodyshell generates a tremendous amount of dust which, if you try to clear it with a broom, will mainly rise into the atmosphere only to resettle elsewhere. If you're intending to spray paint in the near future then this dust will ruin the finish and, if you're rebuilding a mechanical component, the dust will enter the 'works' and cause accelerated wear. The vacuum cleaner deals with this problem, is useful for cleaning loose paint and rust flakes from the bodyshell, and for clearing filler dust from nooks and crannies before painting.

A pop riveter is essential for fixing some items of trim, and also very useful for positioning some panels prior to welding. Hand-powered pop rivet pliers are cheap to buy, and you should always look for a set which has long handles, because using them for any length of time can really make your hand ache! Air-powered alternatives are available, but it's up to the individual to decide whether the amount of pop riveting to be done justifies the extra cost of these.

The more ambitious restorer who wishes to fabricate some of the repair panels will benefit from a good set of panel beater tools, although these can be very expensive. A rubber-faced mallet, plus a small selection of hammers and dollies, can be substituted with some success.

Lead loading. First, a 'tinning' paint is applied to the surface, heated and wiped with a cloth. This covers the steel with a very thin layer of solder that adheres well. Then, lead is softened and applied to the tin, after which the lead is softened again and shaped using a wooden paddle dipped in tallow (candle wax can be used). Finally, the lead is shaped using a body file

Cutting out scuttles and dashboards often results in minor dents, and lead loading is the very best method of filling shallow dents in car bodywork, though most people nowadays use body filler. The real beauty of lead is that it seals the steel underneath.

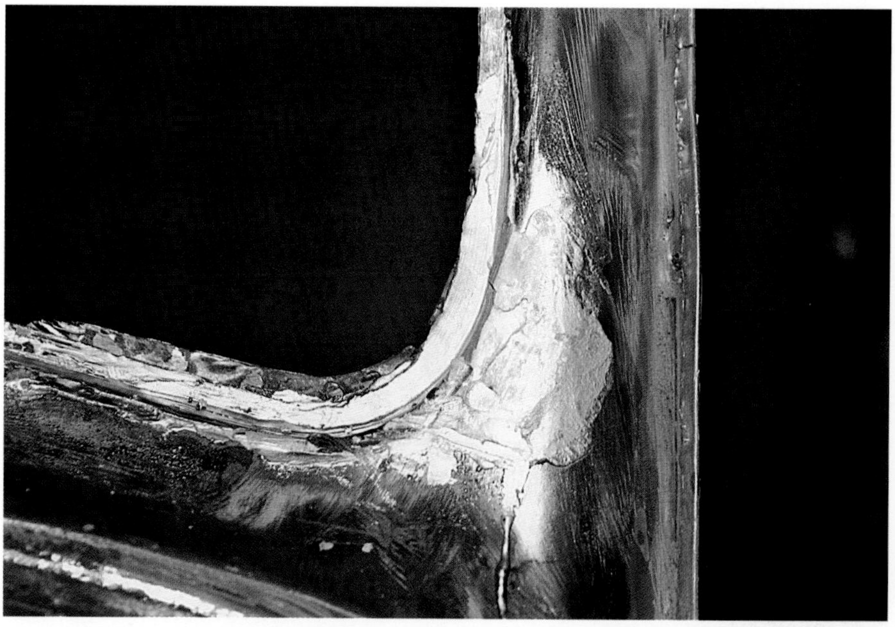

USE & ABUSE OF BODY FILLER

Whilst the appearance of panels which will ultimately be concealed underneath carpets or underseal is not important, it is obviously vital that external panels are not only strongly fitted, but also look good. Unfortunately, some of the operations during a restoration create welded seams which will be visible through paintwork, so will need to be hidden before painting. Shallow dents in external panels, which can easily be accidentally caused during the mechanical build-up, also have to be hidden. The materials for achieving a smooth surface and the correct lines in such cases are either body filler, or lead (or a combination of these).

Many classic car enthusiasts abhor body filler, despite the fact that, if properly used, this material can give perfectly acceptable results. Unfortunately, body filler has suffered from a 'bad press' because the number of cases of filler misuse easily outnumber instances of proper use.

Body filler is intended - and is perfectly acceptable for - filling shallow dents in external and non-structural car body panels. It is not intended to be used to bridge holes, nor to fill deep dents, or cover up areas of body rot. Yet those viewing Beetles with a view to purchase will doubtless encounter many cars in which quite large holes and deep dents have been filled with a lump of body filler, or a mixture of GRP and body filler.

Body filler should only be used to achieve a smooth surface on metal which has shallow dents, such as might result from heat distortion during welding operations, from minor parking bumps, or on a seam produced following the fitting of a repair part-panel. Deep dents should be beaten out so that a minimum of filler is needed. Body filler is the modern equivalent of lead, because, for many years, body shops and car manufacturers rectified small undulations in external car body panels by firstly painting on a lead 'paint,' melting this to 'tin' (coat) the area in question and to form a strongly-bonded layer to which the lead can adhere, then melting on and spreading with a spatula more lead to build up to the required height. This process is known as 'lead loading' or 'body soldering.' Body filler is far easier to use than near-molten lead, as well as being inherently safer. Lead loading kits and associated equipment are available and are widely advertised.

Lead loading offers one big advantage over body filler in that the lead actually seals the surface over which it is applied. In doing this it prevents future rusting (as long as the metal underneath is bright when coated with lead). In the author's experience, many professional restorers use lead loading for this reason, although achieving a final smooth finish with lead is not an easy process, and you could use a very thin layer of body filler on top of the lead to have the best of both worlds!

A combination of lead loading and the use of body filler is especially useful when dealing with welded seams. Clean, then degrease, all of the area in question (the metal must be perfectly clean), and paint on solder paint. Apply heat to the solder paint until it melts and wipe it so that it coats the metal, then wipe away any flux from the surface using a damp rag. The metal is now sealed, and may be built up using either lead or body filler.

It should be pointed out that lead is highly toxic, so if you do decide to work with it, treat it with the same caution you would when dealing with any other toxic chemical. Don't attack a leaded joint with a power sander, because this will fill the air with lead particles you will breathe in; always use a body file to profile lead, and wear a fine dust mask.

Using body filler

In order to use body filler successfully, it is vital that all traces of rusting, paint (including primers), oil, and other contaminants are removed from the surface to be treated. Filler cannot adhere properly to painted metal, because the join can only be as strong as that between the paint and the metal. If you apply filler over the slightest amount of rust, you can expect it to literally drop out at a later date when the rusting spreads sufficiently underneath. If you apply filler over contaminants you may find that poor adhesion is the result, or the filler could chemically react with certain contaminants.

If cleaning the metal makes it very thin you should not use body filler, as it will offer little or no strength. Furthermore, most types of filler are quite rigid and will be very inclined to lose adhesion to a thin, and hence very flexible, panel, or even to break up as the panel flexes. The only safe option in this situation is to weld in new metal.

Before using body filler, check the surface carefully for high spots. Whilst you can fill and smooth down low areas, high spots cannot be linished out and must be beaten out before the filling process begins. If there are deep holes, beat these out as much as possible, where access permits. Equipment is available for pulling out dents, and consists of a sliding hammer rod to which a number of attachments may be fixed. The attachments can fit through a small hole in the surface of the metal, and the sliding hammer is then used to knock out the dent. If the surface can be made clean and yet remain sound, 'key' the surface with a 36 grit disc, then use spirit wipe to remove any grease or oil contaminants.

Most fillers consist of a thick paste and a separate hardener; a chemical catalyst which accelerates the hardening of the filler. The filler itself usually comprises a polyester resin with a mineral-based powder, which forms a thick paste. Alternatives which have tiny metal particles instead of mineral powder can be obtained today. These offer the advantage of not being porous but might not give as good adhesion as the mineral products, which have far smaller particles. Mineral body fillers are porous.

Mix up the smallest quantity of body filler that you feel you can get away with, and always follow the manufacturer's instructions regarding the relative amounts of filler and hardener. Ensure that the filler and hardener are properly mixed and of a uniform colour. Cleanliness is vital, because any foreign bodies in the filler will simply 'drag' as you try to smooth the surface.

Apply body filler in very thin layers, allowing each to fully harden before adding the next, and gradually build up the repair to the required level. Do not be tempted to apply one thick layer of filler, because this may have small air bubbles trapped within it, which will only become apparent when you begin to sand the surface. Also, some resins and hardeners generate heat as they cure, and, if you apply too thick a layer, the extra heat generated by the greater mass might over-accelerate the curing process.

Build up the surface until it is slightly proud of the required level and leave it to

When applying body filler it pays to put on a greater depth than appears necessary - with any luck, you'll be able to get the final surface straight away rather than having to apply further thin layers to fill shallow troughs.

Nothing removes body filler quite as well as a D/A sander. It is strongly recommended that you wear a dust mask when using it.

Initial flatting can be done with 80 grit abrasive paper, but change to something finer as you get down to the final surface, otherwise the finished surface will be full of 80 grit-sized scratches.

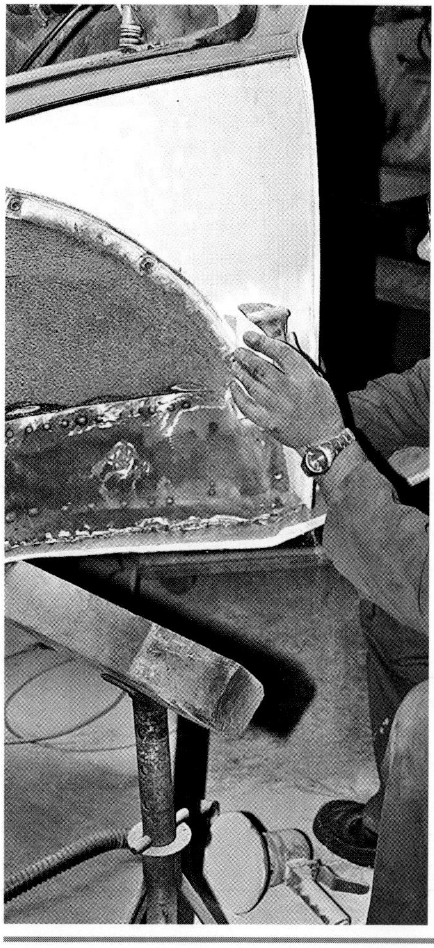

When flatting body filler by hand, always use a sanding block or you'll sand grooves into the surface. If you don't have a block, use a planed piece of wood.

fully cure before sanding it. If sanding by hand, use a sanding block. Electric random orbital sanders and air-powered dual action sanders really come into their own when working with body filler, and can save much hard work and help to achieve better results. The author has found that the random orbital electric sander, which takes 1/3rd of a sheet of paper, gives the best results, because it offers a large contact area and helps avoid sanding the filler into a concave section. The best tool for the job - if you can afford to buy one, or can hire it - is the long bed sander, which is powered by a compressor. However you sand down the filler, always wear a dust mask, because the tiny particles of filler in the air can cause respiratory problems.

Before you begin sanding body filler, ensure that no engine or transmission components are lying out in the open workshop, as the filler dust really does manage to get everywhere! Always finish off the sanding process by hand, using a block.

Most body filler is porous; that is, it can absorb moisture. If the filler is allowed to become wet before it is primed, the moisture can remain in contact with the surface of the metal underneath, and all of your hard work will have been to no avail. Therefore, it pays to spray primer over a filled area as soon as the sanding is completed. For the same reason, never use wet and dry paper wet when sanding filler.

PANEL BEATING

A set of panel beater hammers and dollies is near-essential for the serious restorer, for both truing up existing body panels and carrying out final shaping of bought-in repair panels; imperative if you buy cheaper, after-market panels rather than OEM. With some practice you should become capable of fabricating certain repair panels yourself, which saves money, and also means that there are no delays whilst repair panels are ordered or collected.

Two basic skills have to be learnt; how to stretch metal and how to shrink it. This is because whilst it's easy to form a folded lip on a straight edge, to do the same to a curved edge means that either the lip must be stretched (concave curve) or shrunk (convex curve). To shrink metal, you have to make it 'bunch up' by striking it repeatedly with hammer blows at an angle of 45 degrees, alternating left to right then right to left. In order to stretch metal, you thin it by beating. Heating the metal makes both stretching and shrinking easier.

Never use panel beating hammers for anything other than shaping sheet steel, because using them to hammer home nails and suchlike puts dents into the striking surfaces, and the dents mark sheet steel.

The author has a short log of around 9in diameter, into the ends of which he sanded hollows, shallow at one end, deeper at the other. Used in conjunction with a hard rubber mallet, this is excellent for producing compound curves in very small repair sections, often allowing a large panel to be repaired instead of renewed. Another useful DIY tool is a fence post with one end rounded, which serves as a simple anvil for panel beating.

Panel beating is a very skilled job that takes years to learn, even if taught by a master. Although it's unlikely the self-taught panel beater will ever aspire to fabricating something as complicated as a wing, most people will be capable of shaping small repair sections with complex curvature.

REPAIR PANELS

When you are using a repair panel, as opposed to a full replacement panel (for instance during a simple MoT bodywork repair rather than during a full restoration), take time to consider whether it's wise to fit the whole panel as supplied, or if you could usefully cut it down.

If you are able to cut down a repair panel (and still find strong metal to weld it to), then should you ever have to renew that panel - perhaps in five or ten year's time - you can fit the full repair panel. Alternatively, if you use the full repair panel as supplied and subsequently have to replace it, you will discover when you have cut out the old panel that the resultant hole is too large for the intended replacement panlel.

Repair panels can vary greatly in quality and fit. Original Equipment Manufacturer (OEM) panels cost more than copies, but are usually far easier to fit, longer-lasting, and often stronger. If an OEM panel won't fit, either it's the wrong one, it has been damaged in transit - or your car is bent! With copies, the more complex the panel, the more likely the user is to have to shape them.

Panels as bought have some sort of paint covering; many repair and full panels are often finished in a matt black paint (probably cellulose). I acquired four new wings for RVH 403J at the excellent Stanford Hall show in 1993 and, before fitting these, decided to remove the existing paint and apply Tractol anticorrosion primer in its place.

I began by using 80 grit wet and dry (used wet) to remove the bulk of the paint and, after slashing my hand for the second time on the sharp edges of the wheelarch, decided to wear strong welding gauntlets! The areas around the head lamp bowls (one of the usual rot spots) needed another paint removal method, and I used cellulose thinners and an old toothbrush to first soften, then remove, the paint. Because this did not - unlike rubbing down with wet and dry - also rub down the metal surface along with the paint, I was able to see exactly what state the surface of the metal was in - and I found light rusting! Surface rusting was also discovered at the wheelarch top, which is the other usual rot-spot on Beetle wings.

When rubbing down the rest of the panel I also discovered quite large areas of contamination - spots where (probably) oil lay on the steel before it was dipped and the paint had no adhesion. Had the wings been fitted as supplied and merely painted over, rusting would probably have broken through within three years or so. Stripping the paint and de-rusting the wings took ages but, ten years on, the wings are still sound.

It's a real pain to clean paint from new panelwork (it took three full days to clean and prime four wings), and the question of whether or not the effort is worthwhile must rest with the individual. Acid dipping would remove the hard work from the process, but add cost to the restoration and also thin and weaken the panels.

RUST PROOFING

As you fit new/repair panels into position, it pays to give them some rust protection at the earliest opportunity. The author has tried many lotions and potions which are supposed to arrest and/or prevent rusting. Of these, just two primer paints and one rust killer are recommended here. Bonda Glass Bonda Prima can be sprayed as well as brush-painted onto lightly rusted steel, and the author has achieved good long-term results with this product. The second rust-resistant primer recommended is for use on clean steel and is called Tractol, which, as the name suggests, is an agricultural product available from most agricultural engineer supply companies/ agricultural merchants. Tractol is an excellent product and economical as well. It should never be used as a primer for two-pack paints, but works well with other top coats, including cellulose.

The author has never felt able to recommend any of the commercially available products which are claimed to neutralise rust because, of those he has tried, none has proven as satisfactory as the two named. However, in 1993, *Practical Classics* magazine ran a test of these products, in which Dinitrol RC800 scooped first place by beating all other products, whether used alone, with primer, or with both primer and topcoat.

Following his own tests, Dinitrol RC800 Rustkiller is the only product of its ilk which the author has ever found to work to his satisfaction - literally, penetrating and converting the rust into a passive organic compound which bonds to the underlying steel. After waiting fifteen minutes for RC 800 to become touch-dry, simply prime as normal.

It is arguable whether using products like this over rust is as good a solution as eradication of the rust through sanding and wire brushing, or metal replacement. Any panels which are structurally important must retain their original thickness and, hence, full strength. If you wish to extend the life of a non-structural panel, however, correct use of some of the products mentioned here can help.

A combination of rust-resistant primer, weld-through paints, and seam sealant should prevent rust from re-occurring. Don't forget to give the insides of box sections plenty of protection before they are welded.

Further protection against rust can be achieved after welding has been completed by applying various wax products, grease, or old sump oil.

RESTORATION - ASSESSING THE CONDITION OF THE CAR

There are, essentially, two ways to tackle bodywork restoration: carry out the work on a piecemeal basis - in effect, treating the restoration as a series of separate bodywork repairs - or begin by stripping the car and rebuilding the entire body and chassis.

Before embarking on bodywork repair or a full restoration, it's necessary to properly establish the full extent of rusted or rotted metal on the car. If you don't do this you could discover partway through the job that some of your freshly welded repair panels have to be cut off again in order to allow you access to a newly evident area of rot.

The easiest way to locate all of the rot in a car is to strip it to a bare chassis/ bodyshell and send or take it away for dipping in an acid bath. This process strips all paint, underseal, and rotten metal from the shell, leaving some surfaces ready for immediately priming, and others clean enough to begin welding to. The problems with acid dipping are that the process can thin some panels slightly and might make some otherwise salvageable panels unusable, and the shell will be left unprotected against rust until you can get some paint onto it.

Begin by vigorously probing every panel of the car with a sharp metal implement (an old screwdriver is useful and a pointed panel beater's hammer is ideal) to find all rust and rot. As well as probing for rot, use a magnet to find thick layers of body filler and GRP, which are invariably there to cover up serious rot or holes in the metal. What you discover in this way will have much bearing on how work on the car can subsequently proceed, so make a list of panels that need attention. Ultimately, this list may persuade you that it would be better to entrust the job to a professional, or even to consider re-shelling the car or replacing the chassis/ floor assembly. Better to make that decision now, rather than partway through a body restoration ...

As you check out the car, draw up a list of the full and part-repair panels you will need, which you can later price to see just how much the restoration of the chassis and body of your car is going to cost. Bear in mind that, if your car turns out to have been bodge-repaired with welded-on cover plates, the restoration will be both more difficult and more expensive than it would be if the panels - however rotten - were original.

The most serious rot is that found anywhere in the chassis and frame head, so this is the place to start probing. Inside the car, remove the front seats, lift the carpet and examine the lower edges of the spine - if you find rot here it may be repairable depending on extent, though the spine is the backbone of the car and finding a better chassis assembly might be worth considering. Remember that the rot you find is not the complete extent of the problem, because areas that have rotted right through from inside will be surrounded by slightly less rotted weak steel, which will also have to be cut out and replaced. If you find that steel plates have already been welded over holes in the spine, a new chassis assembly will probably turn out to be your only option.

The strength of the frame head is paramount because it contains the front suspension mounting points. Rot is not common here but is far from unknown. To examine the entire frame head it's necessary to remove the fuel tank, though rot usually strikes the base plate and lower portion of the upper pressing, which you can see by removing the front road wheels and raising the front of the car. The frame head is made from heavy steel and should not be patch-repaired, but repaired using professionally-made, full repair pressings, and preferably an original equipment full frame head assembly. Bear in mind that a frame head weakened through rot might have distorted, which throws the front suspension out of alignment and makes the car dangerous to drive.

At the rear of the spine, the transmission mounting arms are very strong and problems, although rare, do occur, sometimes in the form of the arms fracturing. Examine the arms carefully from under the car. If you see any sign of previous repair (usually a line of MIG weld across the top of the arm), the arm is of no use. Replacement transmission arms do not seem to be available: a new chassis is the only safe option.

On McPherson strut Beetles, an area that can be considered near-terminal if it is rotten is the assembly of pressings associated with the top mounting for the McPherson strut because, at the time of writing, full replacement panels are very expensive and not all repair sections appear to be available. If you find rot in any of the heavy pressings in the assembly then the rest of the flitch is likely to either be completely rotten or already repaired and the repair camouflaged. Any attempts at patch repair will be short-lived and compromise the road holding of the car.

Next, turn your attention to the heater channels, which will usually need renewal. If you find that the heater channels have been welded to the floor pans, or signs of patch repair, the car has been bodged - badly. Expect to find similar bodges elsewhere. You will probably have to remove carpet and the rear seat to see the portion inside the car, and will have to judge the condition of the rest by this, plus the condition of the floor pan edges and the small part of the heater channels visible after the running boards have been removed. To be honest, even if the heater channels are in fair condition it's probably best to renew them while you have the opportunity when the bodyshell comes off the chassis for other repairs.

Check the edges of the floor pans, especially around the jacking point. Floor pan halves and edge repair pressings are available, though, in most cases, fitting half floor pan sections will be the best option - it's not much more work than fitting edge repair sections.

Remove the rear seat base and check out the rear crossmember (heel board) - rot is likely at the outer ends - and check the section of the floor pan where the battery sits, because spilt battery acid can cause rusting here. The large pressing that runs from the top of the heel board, forms the luggage or boot floor, and ends up under the rear window, is available as an OE repair section - though fitting it is a big job; strictly localised rot is best dealt with by cutting out the rot and welding in new steel. The boot floor tends to rot from underneath, so probe it vigorously if you check it from the top to see whether the steel is sound or weakened by rusting from the underside.

Raise the luggage bay lid. Remove the spare wheel and any trim. The rot spots here are the sealing strip lip, the area around the brake fluid reservoir, the spare wheel well, the flitch panels, and the top scuttle edges. In terms of difficulty, the flitch panels and spare wheel well (including the front panel) top the list, because advanced rot here points to a front-end rebuild. With the exception of the flitch panels for very early cars, the panels are all available (McPherson at a price!), and the difficulty comes from getting everything lined up for welding. Briefly, this entails trial fitting the panels, refitting the luggage bay lid and doors, and checking all the shut lines. You also need to check that the front bumper mounts when fitted are in the same plane. Also, from under the car, probe the framework that lies under the luggage bay

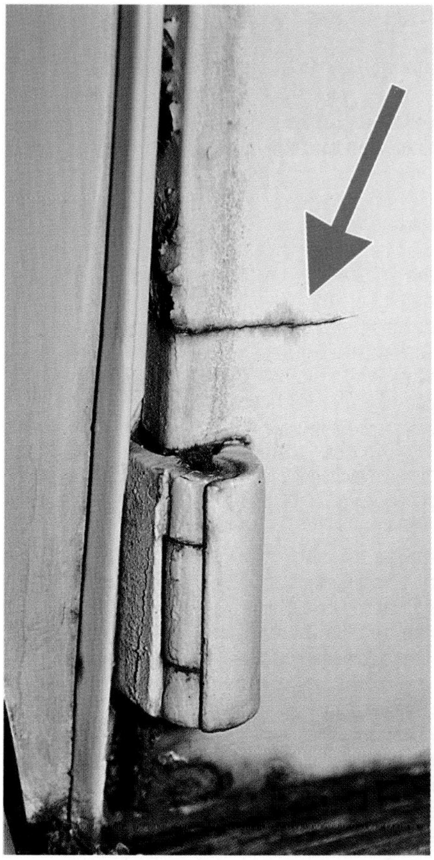

A line of rust across a door panel indicates that the lower portion is a repair panel and that it has rusted from inside. A new skin is the best option here.

pressings – rot here is more difficult to deal with and, even if the above mentioned panels have been replaced, they might have to be cut off and renewed at the same time as the framing underneath.

Also visible from under the front of the car, the front cross panel (toe board) is prone to rot, especially at its ends. This double-skinned assembly is available as both OE and after-market versions.

Raise the rear of the car and remove the road wheels. The rot spots to look for here are the rear bumper mounting reinforcing pressing, the rear body mount pressing, and the area to which the wheelarch is bolted. The first two of these are not too difficult to repair, but the same cannot be said for the section of the quarter panel where the rear wing fits. Full quarter panels are available, but fitting them entails unfolding and re-folding the edge seams, which is a difficult job.

Inside the engine bay, remove the side sound-deadening material and check the engine compartment side plates - a fairly straightforward repair provided you take the time to get them lined up - and the rear valance, which is not so easy.

Positioning is the problem; the engine bay rubber seal retaining strips must line up and the tinware fit properly afterwards.

Expect to find the bases of the 'A' posts rusting or rotting, and some rot in the door skin and lower edge of the door frame - this is entirely normal.

By this stage, you ought to have a fairly comprehensive list of what body and repair panels you will need to make the shell and chassis sound, though don't be surprised if you find one or two other panels that need attention after you've started the body/chassis restoration. Now is the time to add up the cost of the panelwork and decide whether to restore this car, or find one in better condition!

PAINT AND UNDERSEAL

Underseal makes it difficult to judge the condition of the steel it is covering. No matter how unblemished the surface of underseal, it can hide serious and spreading rot. It has to come off, and this can be accomplished in a variety of ways.

Underseal clogs abrasive papers and cloths very quickly, rendering them useless. Ordinary wire brushes will have no effect on underseal, and high-speed cup brushes used in angle grinders merely rip away filaments of underseal which stick to whatever they hit. Large, flat areas of underseal can be dealt with initially using a blowtorch to soften the material, and a wallpaper scraper to remove the bulk of it. Have a fire extinguisher handy before trying this! Alternatively, underseal can be scraped away using an old wood chisel - wear some form of eye protection against flying chips of underseal. Both of these methods will remove much of the underseal, but leave enough of it on the surface to still clog abrasive papers. Use paraffin to soften the remaining traces of underseal, then wipe it clean with a rag. Again, beware the fire hazard; have a fire extinguisher handy, and do not smoke or work near a naked flame.

It is not necessary to strip back all of the paintwork at this early stage; if you do, the exposed steel will soon develop surface rusting. Do use a magnet to locate patches of filler or GRP, and vigorously probe the usual trouble spots with a sharp metal object to check for rot.

When you examine the car to determine what work needs to be carried out, bear in mind that mature rot in heater channels almost invariably points to rotten floor edges. It is common practice to replace heater channels but not floor edges, because to replace the latter the bodyshell must be lifted away from the chassis. This is not good practice as, sooner or later (usually sooner), the floor edges will rot to the point at which the job has to be carried out in full, and the bodyshell and chassis parted. Replacing a heater channel without lifting the bodyshell off the chassis is also bad practice because the final welding of the heater channels (particularly the ends) does the belly pan gasket no good at all.

RESTORATION

The actual method of working and order of work will depend on the extent of the job. A single task, such as replacing the rear bodyshell/damper arm mount, may be carried out with the body on the chassis; for a thorough restoration (which will usually entail floor pan repair or replacement), it's as well to strip down the car to the point of separating the bodyshell from the chassis assembly.

The following text describes a complete bodyshell-off restoration, detailing how the individual task can be carried out in isolation, where applicable. It also includes coverage of which components (such as interior trim) have to be removed before welded repair can start, how to remove them, and how to restore them.

Seat removal

I's advisable to remove the front seats if you intend to later lift the bodyshell off the chassis, so you won't have to lift the bodyshell quite so high. Have an assistant operate the seat forwards/backwards adjustment lever whilst you sit on the rear seat, and push the front seat off the rails with your feet. If the seat won't move far enough forward, look at the side of the outside runner; you may find a small catch which, if pressed, will allow the seat to come free.

The rear seat base simply lifts out. To remove the seat back, remove the bolt from the hinge at each end, and remove the screws that retain the webbing strip at the rear of the seat back.

Seat repair

Watching a skilled, professional car upholsterer at work gives the impression that upholstery is a simple business, when, in fact, it's an art that takes years to master. Happily, high quality, accurately tailored Beetle seat covers make the task a lot easier, giving us the opportunity to renovate our own seats and achieve, if we're careful, good-looking results.

Cleanliness is paramount when working on upholstery, and the typical restoration workshop is just about the worst place to re-cover seats; far better to do the work in your house.

If the frames of the seats are badly rusted you'll need to find replacements from a breaker's yard as they do not appear to be available new, though the front seat runners and fill cover sets are.

Before looking at seat re-covering, note that seat covers which are merely scuffed can be treated with a number of proprietary products not unlike vinyl 'paint,' and small tears can be stitched. However, whilst repairs will be fine for an everyday car, they are not as long-lasting a remedy as seat re-covering, which is the recommended option for a restored Beetle.

Re-covering seats using good quality covers (that fit!) is not too difficult, and allows you to renew or modify the padding which, on restoration project cars, is usually sagging.

Although the seats fitted to Beetles appear similar at first glance, there were actually seven designs, varying in shape and size. It's vital that you use the correct seat covers for your car; check with owners of similar aged Beetles that the seats fitted to your car are the originals - it's far from unknown for Beetles to be fitted with later seats. Seat recovering kits usually include a complete set of covers - both front seats,

Before consigning your seat covers to the bin, take the time to see whether they'll clean up using proprietary vinyl cleaner and a paintbrush to work it in.

and the rear bench seat, making a total of six covers - and they are very reasonably priced in comparison with seat covers for many contemporary cars. If any of the seats sag, consider ordering new padding along with the covers.

The first job is to make doubly sure that the seat covers as delivered are indeed the correct ones for your car (an old Beetle might not have the original seats) by comparing them with the original covers.

Rear seat

The rear seat covers are held by pointed folding tabs located on the frame, and to remove the covers simply bend the tabs back and pull off the cover. Bear in mind that the tabs quite quickly work-harden; if bent too many times or too much the metal will fracture, so bend them just enough to get the cover off, and take care not to stab yourself with them. When free of all the tabs, the old cover should pull off easily.

There should be a steel rod inside a pocket in the seat backrest which has to be retrieved, so make a cut and pull it out or, if it won't budge, cut along the length of the pocket. The rod will usually be rusted, so take time to clean it. before fitting it in the replacement cover.

The seat backrest support is in the form of a spring with padding, and is usually serviceable. If any part of the frame is rotten, either obtain a replacement from a breaker's or carry out a welded repair; it doesn't have to be anything fancy, because the rear seat frames are hidden from view.

It's easier to fit the cover if you place a thin sheet of plastic over the backrest and hold it with adhesive tape (masking tape will do), which helps to slide on the cover. The backrest cover should be a fairly snug fit but not so tight that the seams stretch as you fit it. If the seams appear under pressure then the cover is not the correct one for the seat and the seams would probably tear open when the seat is used, so go back to your supplier and find a cover that does fit.

If the cover seems okay at this stage, pull the front lower edge down so that the front top seam is in the correct position and, provided the steel rod is in the correct place relative to the tabs, pull the cover onto the tabs. If the steel rod does not align with the tabs when you pull the cover then you've got the wrong cover! When the front lower edge is secured by the tabs, tension the material at the back of the backrest and locate it on the tabs. Getting the tension just right is, unfortunately, something that comes only with experience, but when it is the cover will look right with no sagging or folds.

The seat base cover will have a steel wire running through its lower seam. Untwist the ends of the wire to de-tension

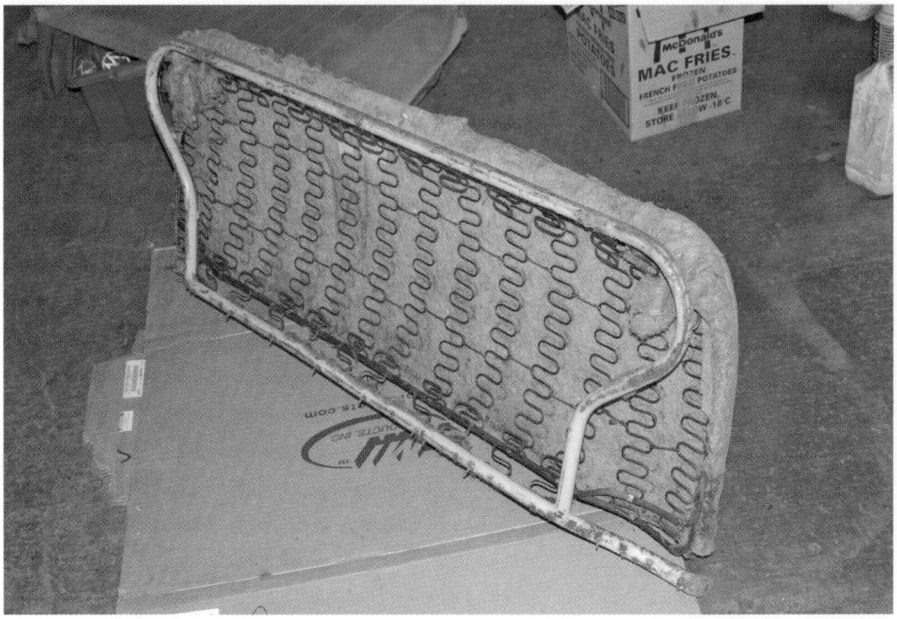

The rear seat back is very basic and fitting a new cover is not terribly difficult. It would be worth sanding the surface rust from the frame and repainting it.

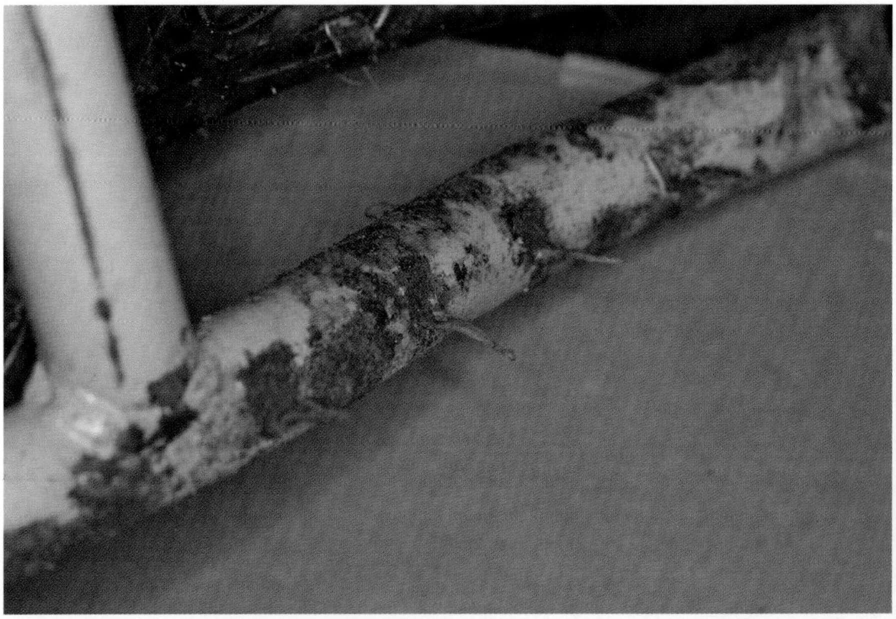

The cover is secured by only these pointed tabs on early models. Bend them back in order to remove the old cover, but don't bend them more than absolutely necessary, because they quite quickly work-harden and snap.

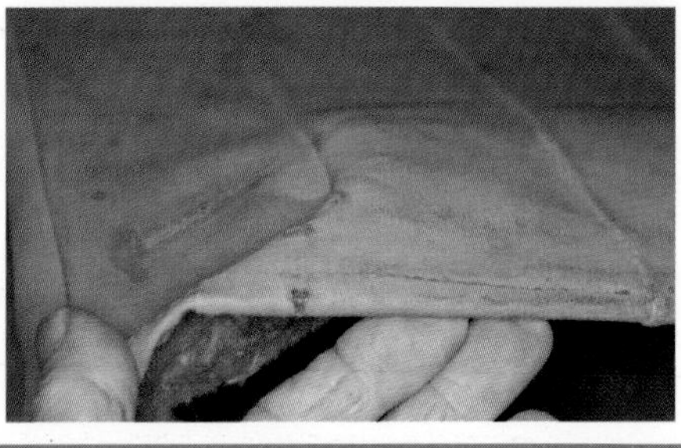

In the front of the old cover is a steel rod, which needs to be retrieved.

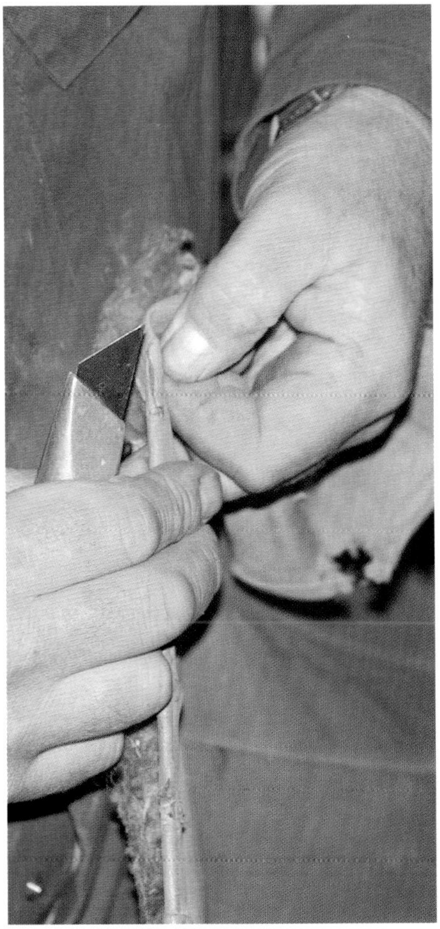

A craft knife is the best tool for cutting out the steel rod, but it is better to place the cover on a sheet of wood rather than hold it in your hand and risk cutting yourself.

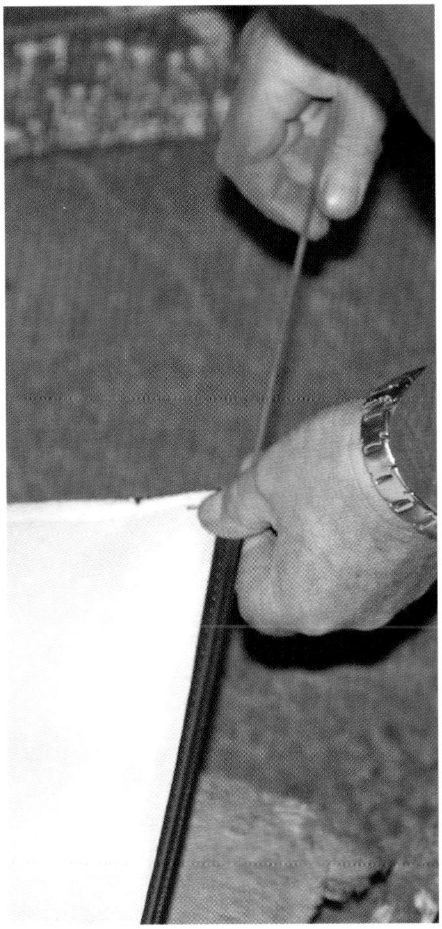

Slide the rod inside the leading lower edge of the new cover. The rod is usually rusty, and cleaning off the surface rust first makes it easier to fit.

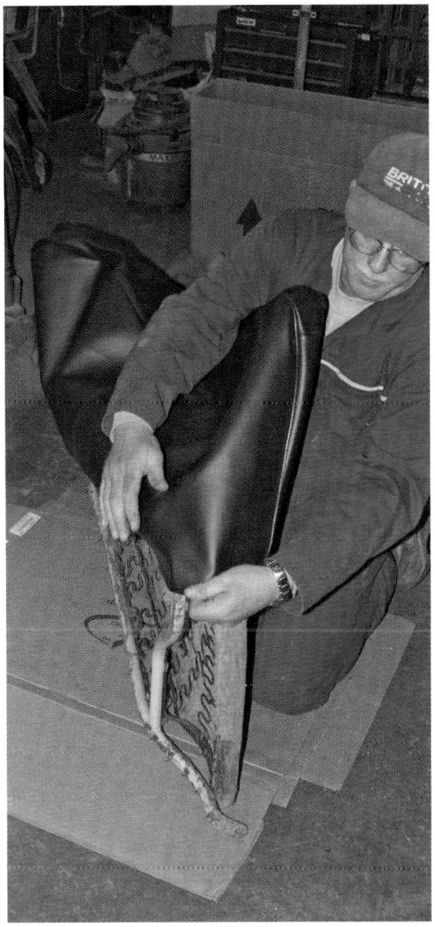

A cover should be a fairly tight fit, and putting a plastic bag over the frame assembly helps the cover slide on more easily. If it's very tight, double-check that it is the right cover for your seat - it probably won't be. If you fit a cover that's really tight, the seams might burst the first time anyone sits in it.

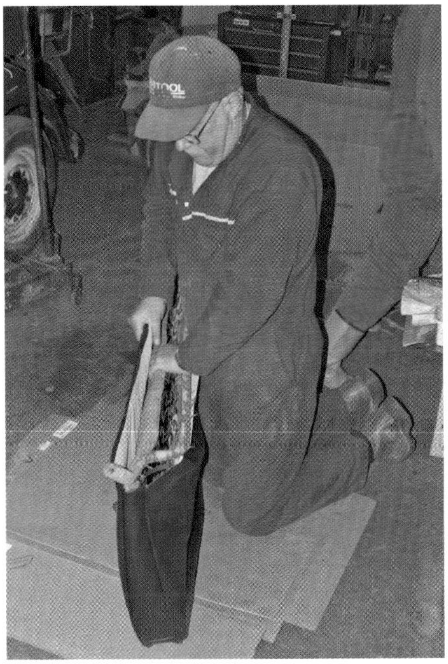

it, then fold back the tabs and pull off the cover. The replacement cover will have a nylon cord in place of the wire.

When fitting the new cover the important point is that the front seam is in the correct position, so pull the cover roughly into position and begin fitting the front lower edge on the tabs, starting in the middle and working your way to each side, ensuring that the seam is at the correct height, is level, and that the top side seams of the cover are also level. Only when the front and side seams are right should you tension and fit the back of the cover.

Front seats

The front seats usually receive far higher usage than the rear seat, especially the driver's seat, and, in time, the seat base padding sags, meaning that shorter drivers might have difficulty seeing over the steering wheel! Another problem is that new covers are made to fit full padding, and tend to sag when fitted to tired old padding; all things considered, it's good policy to renew the padding along with the seat covers.

Pull the cover into position, ensure it's central, and fix the front tabs. The position of the front face of the cover is determined by the steel rod.

In fact, you might like to consider improving the comfort of the front seats by adding a little extra padding in the form of thin foam rubber glued to the seat back padding, to give lumber support (the small of your back), which makes a big difference during a long journey.

Because the front seats receive much more wear than the rear bench, it's worth positioning the covers and attaching the fastenings but not tensioning the covers immediately. If a little time is spent sitting in them, this pre-stretches the material as it will be when the seats are in use, and

Tension the material at the rear of the seat back and locate it on the tabs, ensuring that the side panels lie correctly.

Fold the tabs using a light hammer.

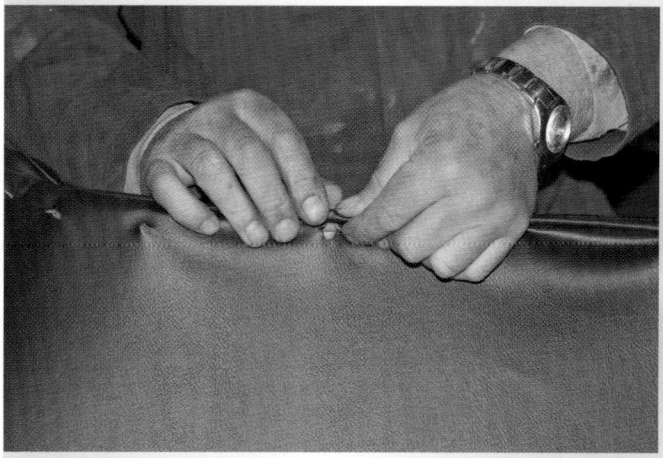

The tabs will tear the fabric if you tension it too much, so be careful.

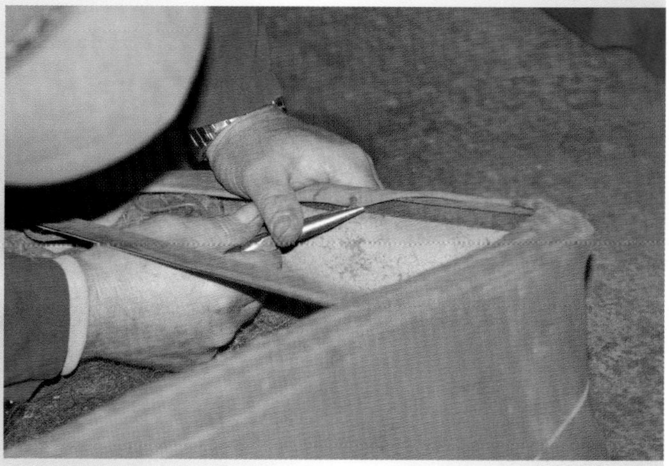

The seat base cover is also held by folding tabs.

This wire runs inside a sewn pocket and is used to tension the cover. Untwist the ends.

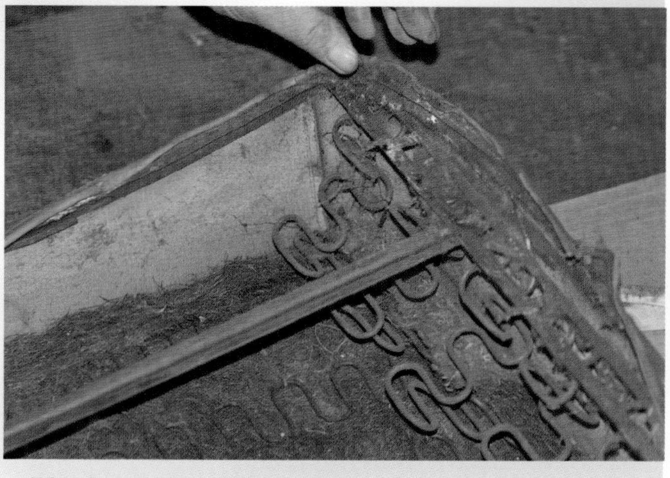

With the tabs freed, the seat base cover edges should be free.

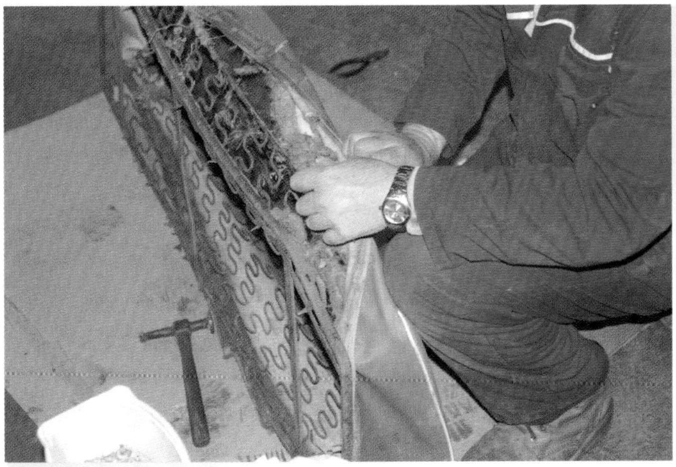

The seat base cover might be glued to the padding. Gently prise it away.

After carrying out necessary repairs to the seat frame and padding, pull on the new cover and make sure it's central. A plastic bag over the top of the seat back will help the cover to slip on.

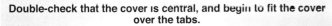

Double-check that the cover is central, and begin to fit the cover over the tabs.

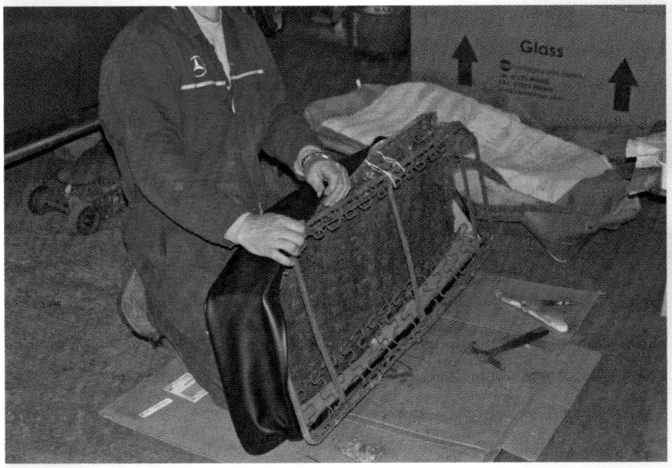

The material may need to be stretched slightly to persuade it over the front corners - if it needs a lot of stretching you probably have the wrong cover.

Get the front seam in exactly the right place, and then begin fitting it onto the tabs.

Modern replacement covers substitute cord for the tensioning wire originally used: pull it tight and tie the two ends.

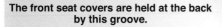

The front seat covers are held at the back by this groove.

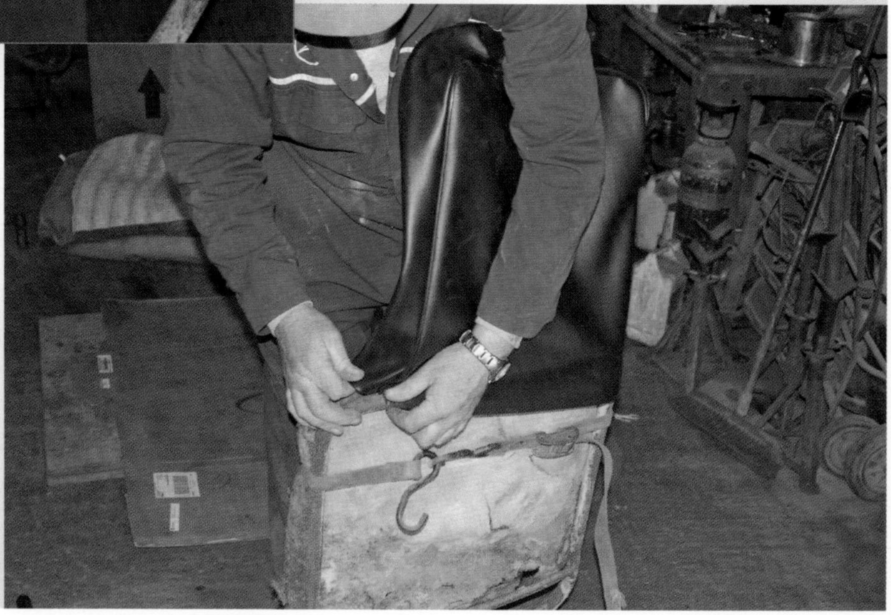

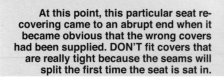

At this point, this particular seat re-covering came to an abrupt end when it became obvious that the wrong covers had been supplied. DON'T fit covers that are really tight because the seams will split the first time the seat is sat in.

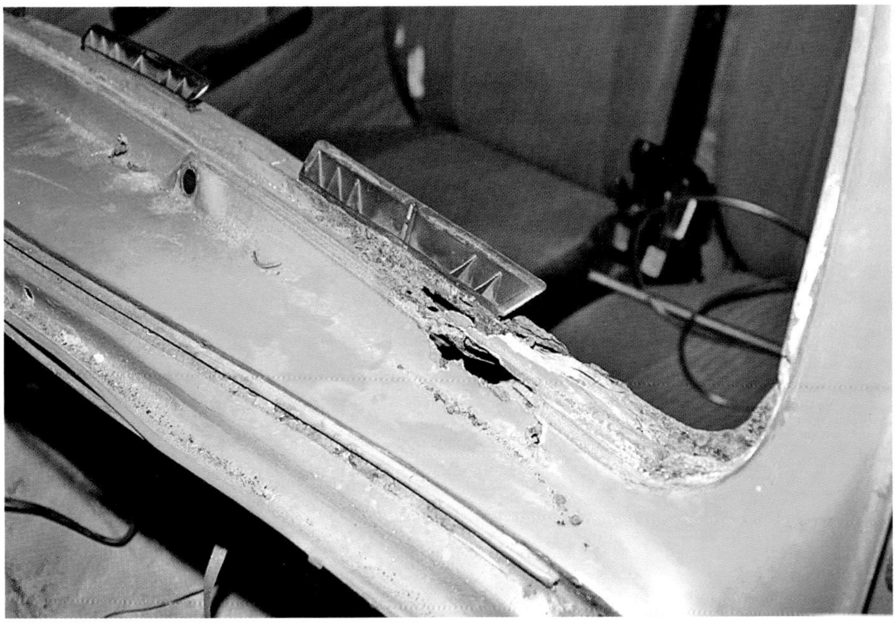

Left: The window aperture and adjacent portion of the top scuttle panel are very prone to rot, along with the steel section of the side demister ducting. Rot here is most commonly covered up with body filler.

Below left: When rot is found in the windscreen surround, it's not uncommon to discover that someone else has already attempted a 'repair' using body filler. Both rot and body filler often extend into the roof pillar.

Whenever you find a lump of body filler you can bet there will be a lot of rot around and under it. This is a major repair, and your best bet is to cut steel from a scrap Beetle - if you can find one with good roof pillars, windscreen surround, and demister ducting.

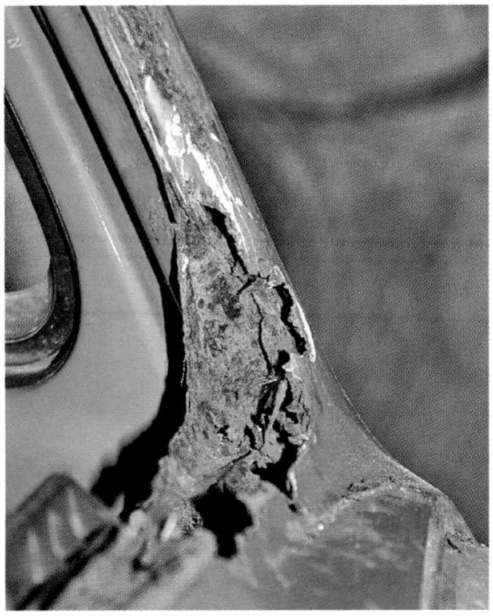

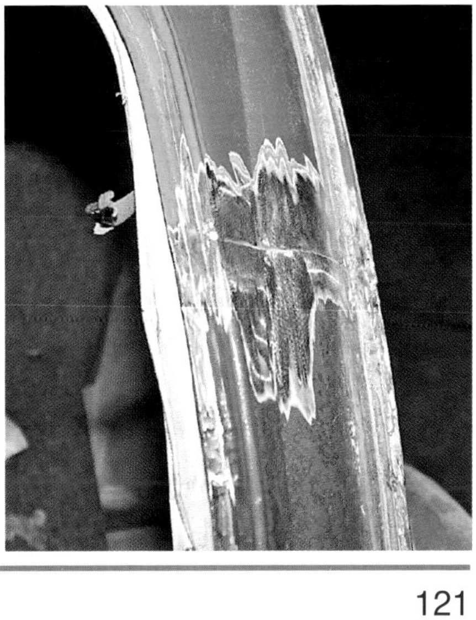

should help prevent sagging when you tension and finally fasten the covers. In addition to using the fastening clips (which vary according to the year), apply a contact adhesive where the covers wraparound the seat frame - but only after the covers have been pre-stretched as described.

FIXED GLASS REMOVAL

Although a cheap and cheerful respray can be carried out without removing the windows (provided they are well masked off), most restorers will opt to remove them. This becomes necessary if the headlining - which is gripped under some or all of the window surround rubbers depending on the model - is to be removed. Leaking window rubbers can result in rot developing in the surrounding steel, and surface rusting, or even minor paint bubbling adjacent to the rubber, is a strong indication of this.

If all the rubbers are to be replaced (obtain new rubbers before doing this just in case you have trouble finding new ones), the old ones could simply be cut away from the edge of the glass using a sharp craft

The best way to tackle windscreen aperture repair is to use sections cut from a scrap car.

knife. If the rubbers are to be retained, the easiest method is to simply push windows and rubbers out together. In either case it's always a good idea to place some padding on the luggage bay lid just in case you drop the screen. On the subject of safety, always wear leather gloves and safety glasses when working with glass.

Remove the windscreen wipers and arms and disconnect the rear windscreen heater wire (where fitted). Working around each window, lift the edge of the rubber from inside the car in order to break the seal, then, with an assistant to catch the window as it comes out, push out one top corner using both feet. It should then be easy to work out the rest of the window.

WINDOW APERTURE REPAIRS

Underneath the window rubbers, the metal lips can rust away. In the case of the front screen this rust can spread to the top scuttle. The top scuttle also rusts if the drain holes are allowed to become blocked so that water cannot escape.

To deal with rusted window lips, simply grind out the rot and butt weld in two thicknesses of steel, giving the insides plenty of protection with weldable zinc paint beforehand. Top scuttle repair panels do not, at the time of writing, appear to be available, leaving the options of fashioning a repair panel (which can be done with a few basic panel beater's tools), or cutting the section out of a scrap shell. In either case, butt weld the new steel in very carefully to avoid distorting the scuttle.

FIXED GLASS REFIT

You will need; sealing compound, strong twine or, preferably, plastic-covered wire which is long enough to fit around the screens, some lubricant, and an assistant.

The chrome filler/trim strip can be difficult to fit and is easily damaged during refitting. Re-used or damaged strip often refuses to sit correctly, so consider fitting 'Cal' rubbers, which have no chrome strip. Fit the rubber to the glass, using sealing compound to prevent leaks. Fit the chrome trim into the rubber, then work plenty of lubricant (some people use washing up liquid, which works well, but may contain industrial salts that rot the window aperture lips; hand soap is better) into the groove in the rubber. Feed the twine or covered wire into this groove, so that the centre of the wire is at the top of the screen and the two ends cross at the bottom.

With your assistant holding the window in position from outside the car and applying pressure to it, pull on one end of the wire to pull the rubber lip over the steel window aperture lip. Work from the centre bottom (taking care that the window does not ride up), each lower corner in turn, up the front pillars, around each top

Fitting a windscreen is one of the most awkward jobs to do, but can be accomplished single-handed (though it's easier with help).

Below: The rear screen ready for fitting. The chrome insert is placed, and wire has been worked into the groove in the rubber, and the two ends crossed over in the middle.

Bottom: The side windows ready to go in. Note that the chrome insert is a bit damaged; new trim is available but, if you do opt to fit new trim, buy the best quality you can. Some poor quality trim is so weak that it may well end up more damaged than this after fitting.

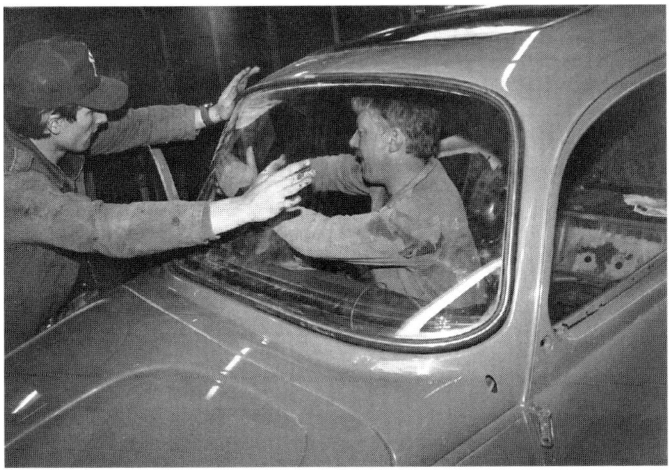

Ask your helper to bear against the section of screen you're trying to fit, and ensure that the screen does not ride up as you fit the rubber along the lower aperture lip.

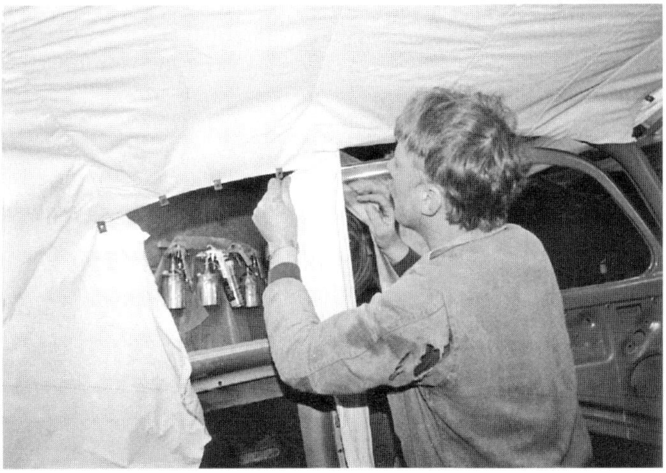

Threading the rods through the headlining and fitting them in position is straightforward, though take care to get the headlining central to the car. The headlining will be glued to the aperture surrounds, but first rough fit it with clips or clothes pegs, and attend to the door pillar lining.

corner in turn and, finally, along the top. It's then usually necessary to knock the window edges finally home, using the palm of your hand. If this thought (or the thought of a window popping out the first time you slam the door) worries you, bring in a mobile windscreen fitter, who should be able to glaze a Beetle in about 30 minutes and who should not, therefore, charge too much.

Removing and refitting the side windows is essentially the same as fitting a front of rear screen, though the author has found the small side windows to be more difficult.

HEADLINING REMOVAL

Remove the front, rear, and two fixed side windows as already described. To remove the rear view mirror, turn and then pull it. Remove the sun visors; the swivelling end is retained by a stud and a screw. Remove the screw, then turn the fixing until it comes free - don't use too much force, because the stud breaks easily.

The passenger side grab handle is affixed by one large and one small Philips-headed screw at each end. To expose the screw heads, use a small, flat-bladed screwdriver to unclip the end trim, and work this away from the edge. The grab straps on the B posts are fixed with screws; prise up the cover to reveal these.

Take care when removing the interior light because it's brittle and easily damaged. At each end there's a spring clip; push these inwards and the lamp unit should come out.

The headlining will probably be glued to the window surrounds; if you want to re-use the lining, be very careful when easing it away from the lips. Within the front and rear window apertures, the lining may also be held in place by spring grips. Remove these.

The headlining is held aloft by either sprung steel rods (there could be four or six depending on year) which run through loops sewn into the material, or is glued to hardboard which is sprung into position. According to the type of headlining fitted, the year and model of Beetle, there may or may not be separate pieces glued or clipped to the pillars. The sequences described here relate to a McPherson strut car, which has everything!

To remove the rods, spring them upwards until one end can be eased from its plastic endpiece, then pull the other end free.

At the top of the door aperture, ther's a row of clips, under which the headlining edge is tucked. Gently prise these down, and the headlining should pull free.

Work from the front window backwards to the B post, then from the rear window forwards to the B post. Where the headlining joins the B post, remove it by pulling it downward to free the edge trim from its retaining clips.

HEADLINING REPLACEMENT

Fitting a headlining is not too difficult, but fitting it so that it looks good can be another matter. It should not take a professional vehicle upholster long to do the job, so the cost of having it done professionally should not be too great. Good professional upholsterers make the job look so easy that you end up wondering why you're paying someone to do such an apparently simple job; remember, though, that the reason for this is because they're so damn good at it!

If you decide to fit your own headlining you will need glue (it is best not to use a contact adhesive, but something which allows you to slightly adjust the position of the material before it sets), a Stanley or art knife, and a selection of screwdrivers. Also of great help are scissors and (especially) clips to hold the headlining on the window aperture lips whilst the glue sets.

Begin by fitting the rods through the loops in the headlining top, then fit the centre rod into position inside the car, and adjust until the headlining reaches both the front and rear screens. Check that the lining is not skewed, then fit the other rod ends and check positioning again. Bear in mind that you're more likely to run out of material at the rear end, so check there's enough there to reach down the C posts before you begin fixing it permanently.

Fit the material back into the clips at the top of the door aperture, pulling and smoothing it out as you go. If you are fitting a new headlining it will probably be necessary to trim this and other edges.

Spread glue around the front windscreen aperture lip, and attach the headlining to this, using clips to hold it whilst the glue sets, and smoothing it out as you go. At the top of the front windscreen pillar and B post, the material folds under to give a neat edge. Glue the headlining to the rear, then the side window aperture lips, and stretch it down the C post and glue in place.

The B post covering is separate to the headlining and, if you are fitting a new headlining kit, you will probably have to trim the material. Open up one of the lower B post retaining clips enough to be able to feed in the edge moulding, and slide this into place. Glue the material to the B post and side window aperture lip. The last two pieces of the headlining kit go underneath the side windows. Glue them

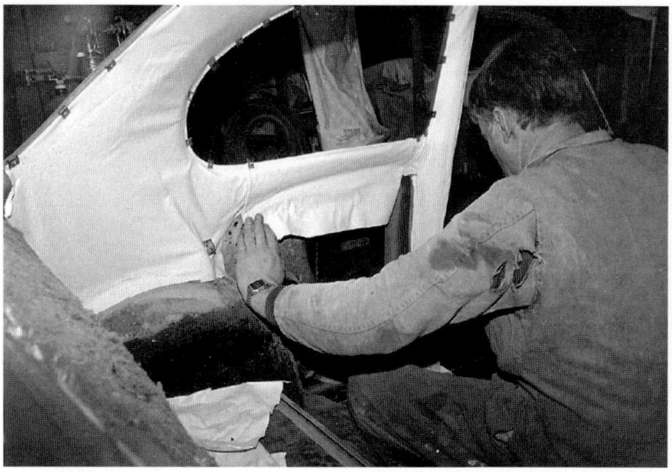

As you work, try to smooth out wrinkles from the headlining.

Watch out for the various fittings that pass through it when making holes in the headlining.

to the aperture, then stretch and smooth them down and glue the lower edges.

Fit the rear view mirror, sun visors, grab straps, and other furniture. You can usually feel their fixing holes through the material. Finally, gentle heat from a hairdryer can be used to help smooth out the (hopefully few) wrinkles in the headlining.

DOOR REMOVAL

The door check strap can be disconnected by driving the pin upwards. There are two ways of removing the doors. The simplest (though you'll have to first remove the running board) is to remove the check strap pin and drift out the hinge pins from below. This method has the advantage that, if the same doors are to later be replaced, the hinges will be correctly aligned. During a full restoration, in which the doors are probably repaired or replaced, the answer is to remove the door complete with hinges.

Each hinge is held by three large set screws with a Philips-type crosshead, best tackled using a large Philips screwdriver or similar. The author uses the bit and 1/2in square drive adapter from an impact wrench, in combination with the speed wrench from a socket set, which gives good purchase on the set screwhead. Have an assistant handy to help manoeuvre the door, because a Beetle door with full furniture is rather heavy.

Before you re-hang the door it's as well to remove the striker plate first (ignore this if you only removed the hinge pins). Having an assistant or two to take the weight of the door while you refit it is a good idea. Fasten the hinge set screws lightly, with just one screw per hinge tightened sufficiently to take the weight of the door. Adjust the position of the door until its lines match that of adjacent bodywork, then tighten all hinge screws and refit the striker plate.

The door check strap can be disconnected by driving out the pin (arrowed).

DOOR STRIP DOWN

Door furniture varies from year-to-year, though the majority of remaining Beetles will have furniture very similar to that fitted to my 1970 car. If your own car differs, stop and think before attacking anything that does not want to come off.

Begin by looking for screw heads and bolt heads, which can be hidden under plastic trim caps. If fixings haven't been used on an item of furniture then the chances are that it simply clips in and out.

Begin by prising out the inside door pull cover to reveal the fixing screw, and undo this. The window winder fixing screw is situated under either a plastic plug or, on some models, the one-piece trim cover. Prise out the plug or lift the cover and remove the screw and handle. On early models, the door pull and winder handle are fixed by a pin, which should be drifted out.

Remove the armrest (where fitted) by undoing the two fixing screws. These screws are angled on some models, in which case better purchase will be obtained by angling the screwdriver.

The door trim panel can now be removed. This is secured by spring clips which can quite easily be broken, so work carefully, starting at the bottom of the door and using a flat implement to prise

The weight of a furnished door is quite sufficient to slightly distort bodyshell pressings, so don't open the door and leave it unsupported.

To remove the door mirror, simply unscrew it. Apply a little grease to the thread before refitting, and take care not to cross-thread it.

Adjust the door striker in the horizontal plane if the door skin does not align with the 'B' post, but don't adjust the striker plate up or down in an effort to pull the door into position whenever the door is shut. Get the door position right, then adjust the striker plate to align with the lock.

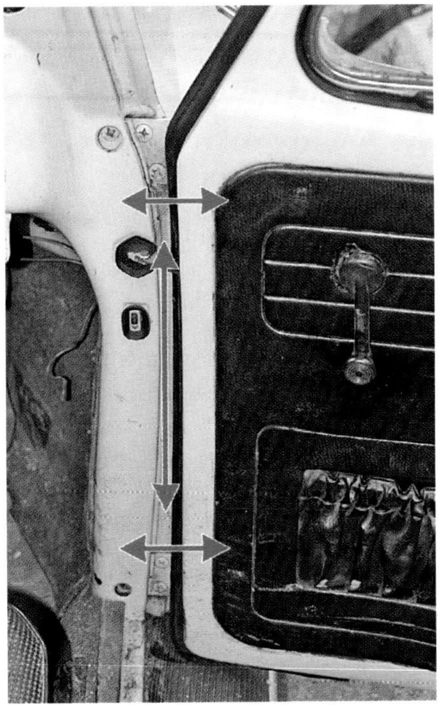

The door hinges allow the door to be raised and lowered, and the top and bottom to be moved in and out.

out the spring clips. On later models, a spring situated behind the window winder mechanism will come free, so try and catch it before it disappears into the dark recesses of your workshop!

Wind down the window, and take out the quarter-light assembly by removing the bolt at its base, then the small set screw at the top. Wind up the window.

Before progressing further, support the window by taping it to the top of the door frame using wide masking tape. Remove the winder mechanism fixing bolts, and pull the mechanism from the door. The glass may now be lowered and removed through the lower door aperture.

Gently ease out the window channel inner, then surrounding trim - both are held by spring clips and the trim is very fragile - use a small, flat-bladed screwdriver for this. Undo the screw at the top rear of the quarter-light pillar and remove the quarter-light assembly. The chrome door trim can now be removed.

The external door handle is held by a single crosshead screw in the door rear edge. Remove this, then tap free the handle assembly. The internal locking mechanism is held by one screw in the door frame and two in the edge. Remove these, then the bolts which hold the remote pull and turn the lock plate in to the 'locked' position. The assembly can now be removed - with some difficulty - from the door.

continued on page 133

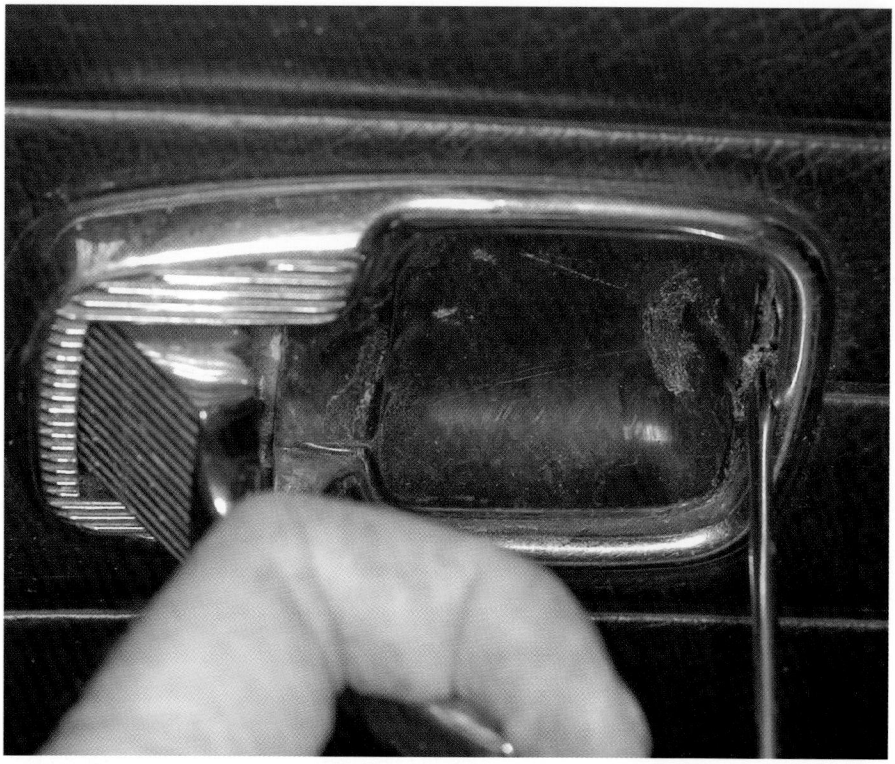

The door lever surround is secured by a single screw hidden by this trim panel. Use a small, flat-bladed screwdriver to lever out the trim.

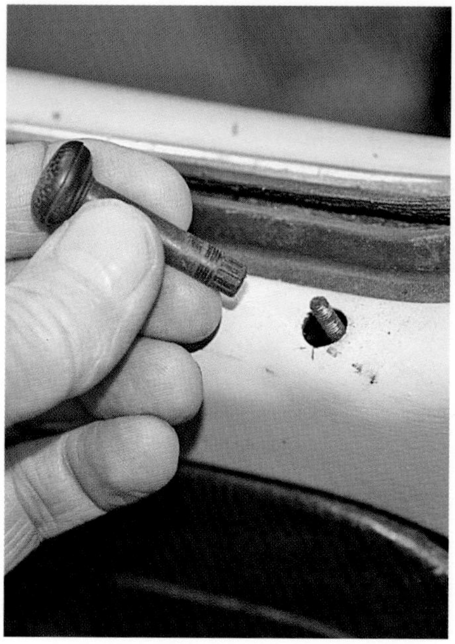

Door furniture strip. The interior door lock knob simply unscrews.

Remove the crosshead screw and the lever surround can be lifted away.

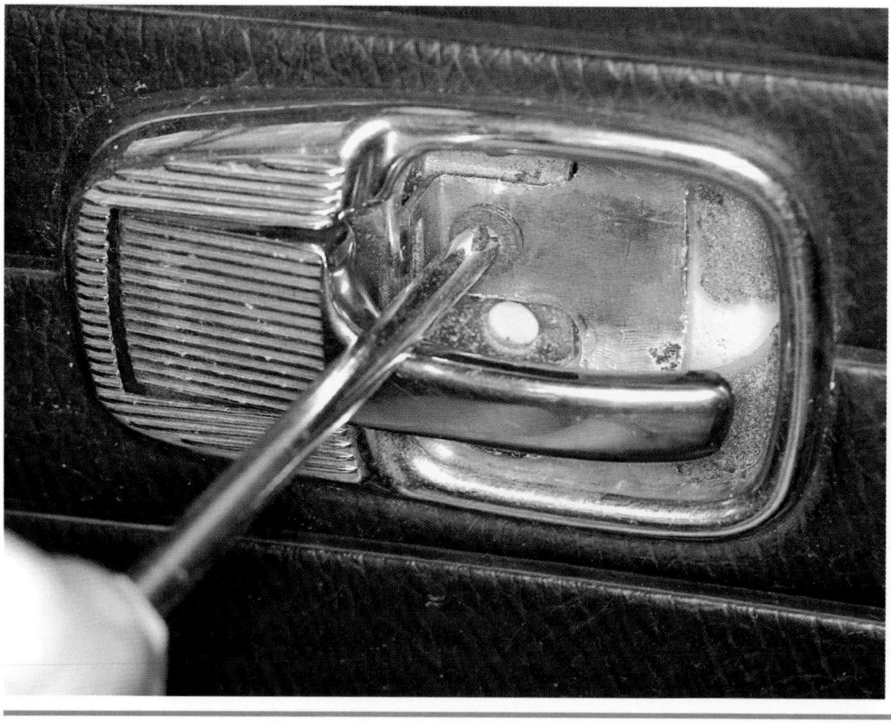

Prise the plastic cover from the door window winder, remove the set screw, and pull off the winder.

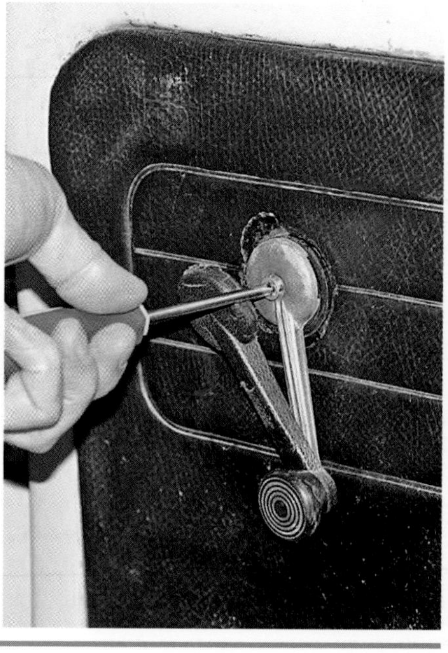

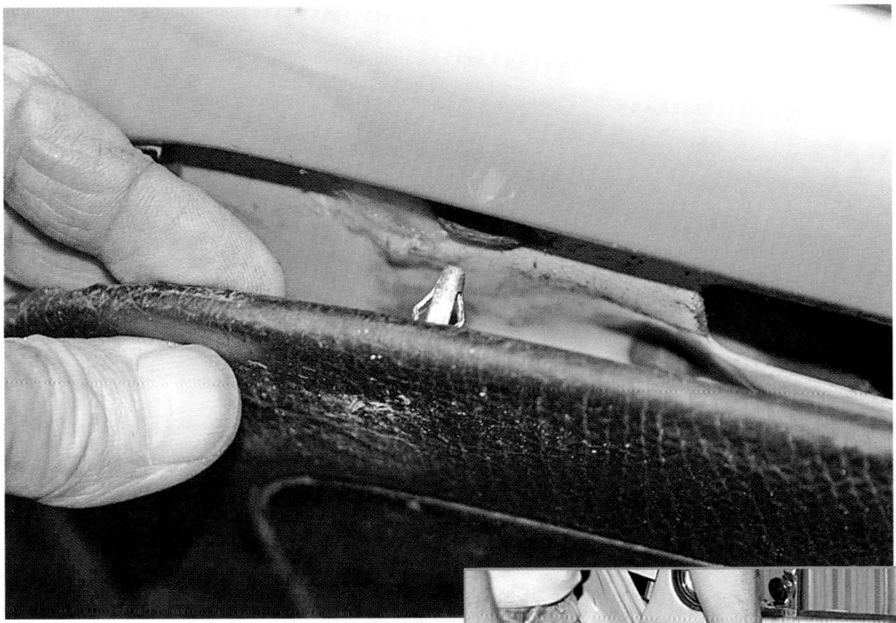

Above: The door interior trim is held by these spring clips. They can be pulled or levered out, though take care not to chip the door paint. Work your way around the trim panel, trying to pull the trim away with your fingers until you find a section that lifts. Then use a lever, bearing against steel which will be covered when the panel is refitted, to free the clips each side.

Below: On most Beetles, the door interior trim has a bracket that slides over a lip, so the panel has to be lifted to remove it.

Before removing the window winder mechanism, use masking tape to hold the window shut.

Above: These are the bolts that secure the window winder mechanism. Remove these, then remove the quarter-light.

Below: The window mechanism won't want to come out if - like me - you don't remove the quarter-light first! After the mechanism is removed, try not to drop the window glass as you remove that.

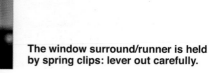

The window surround/runner is held by spring clips: lever out carefully.

Above: The quarter-light top is secured by a set screw which, on my car, refused point-blank to move under pressure from a screwdriver. I resorted to a crosshead bit and a small ratchet drive, which enabled me to get enough pressure on the screw head to prevent the bit from riding out as it turned.

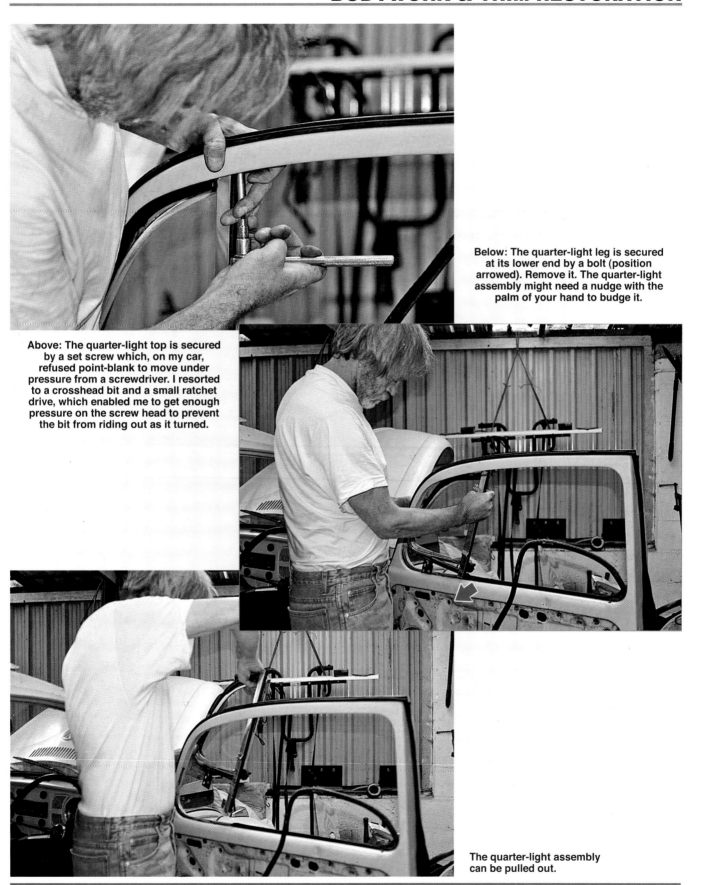

Below: The quarter-light leg is secured at its lower end by a bolt (position arrowed). Remove it. The quarter-light assembly might need a nudge with the palm of your hand to budge it.

The quarter-light assembly can be pulled out.

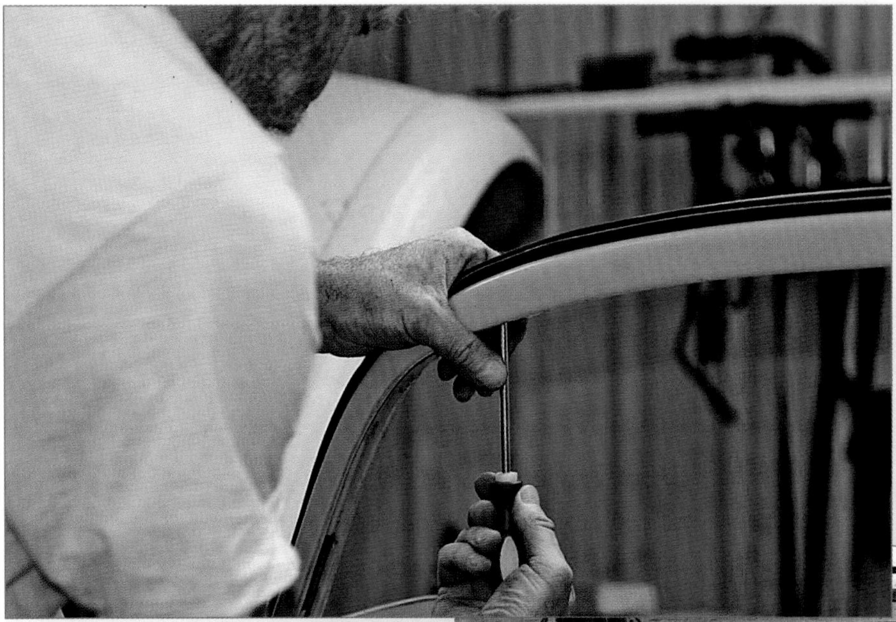

Above: The chrome trim should be held by a small set screw: remove this.

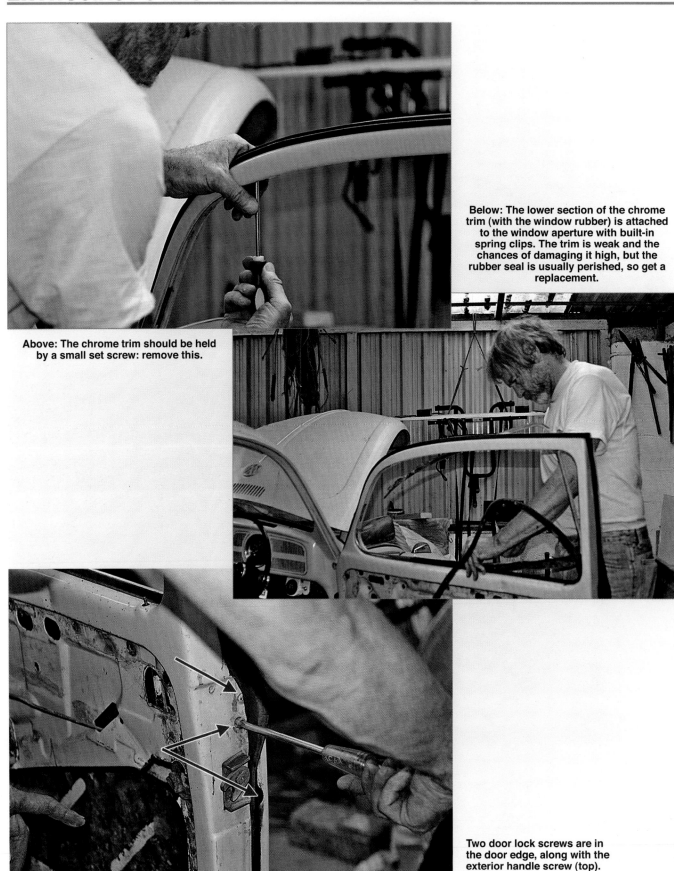

Below: The lower section of the chrome trim (with the window rubber) is attached to the window aperture with built-in spring clips. The trim is weak and the chances of damaging it high, but the rubber seal is usually perished, so get a replacement.

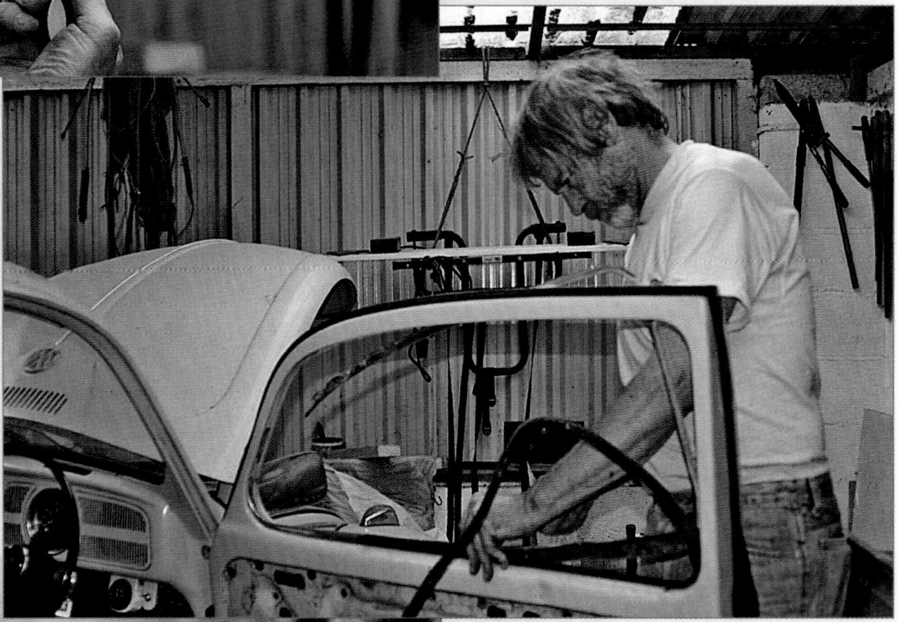

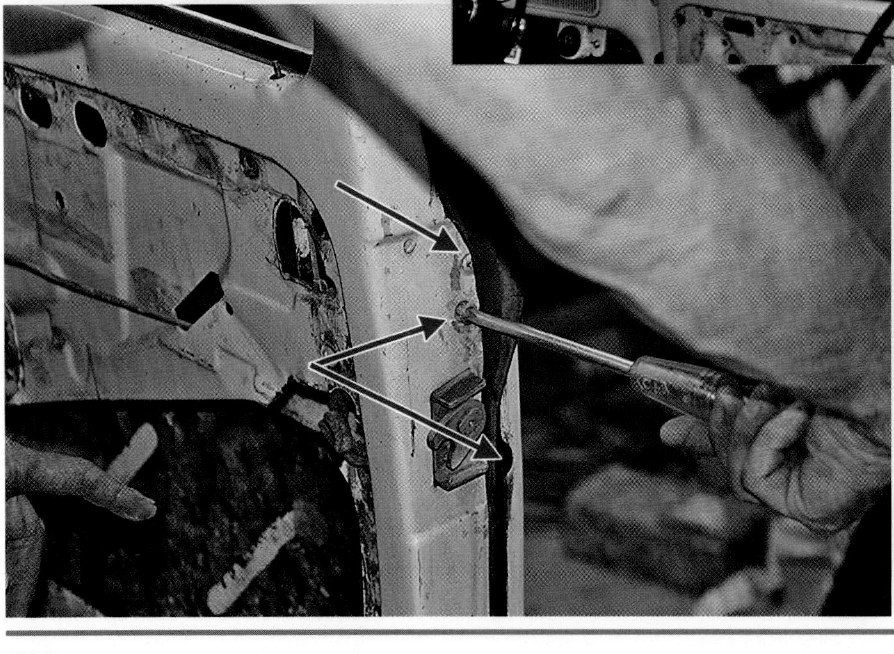

Two door lock screws are in the door edge, along with the exterior handle screw (top).

Above: Even after removing the door exterior handle screw, the handle stays put ...

Below: ... a gentle tap with a rubber mallet in the direction shown shifts it - it is clipped in.

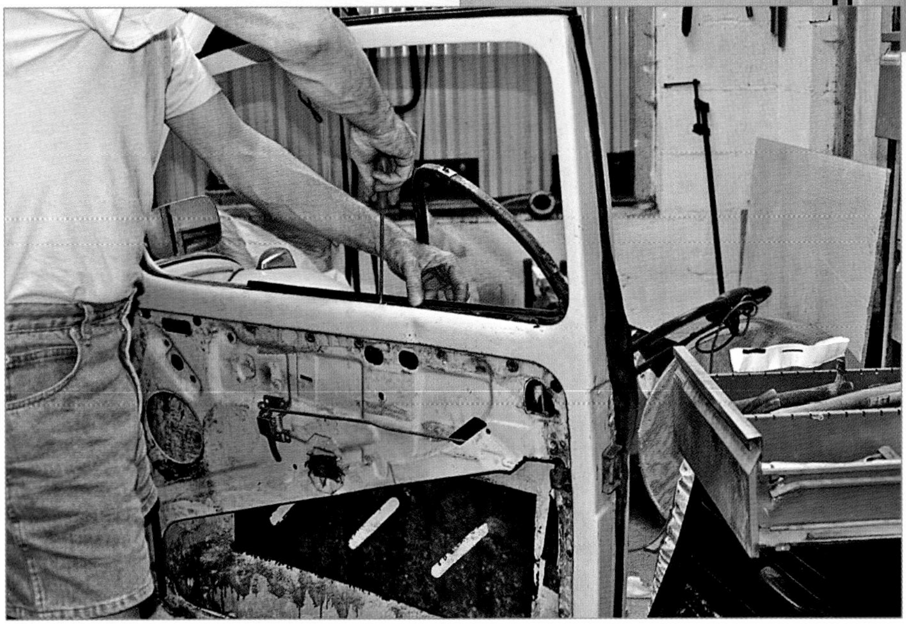

The door glass interior seal clips into place and can be levered out.

Unclip the interior handle from the operating rod.

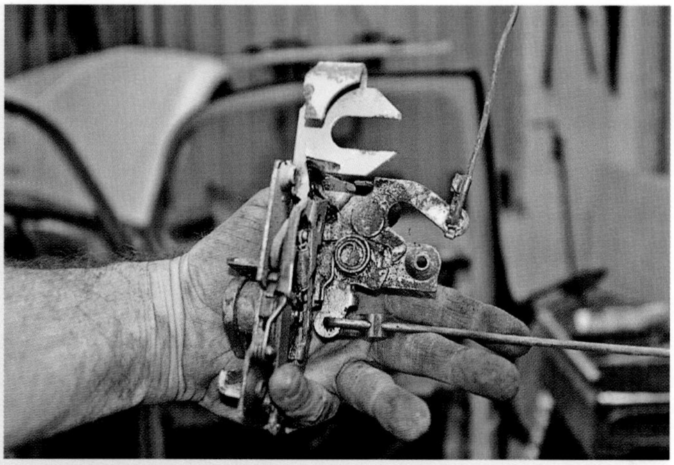

Removing the door lock is simple, provided it's the last item removed from the door.

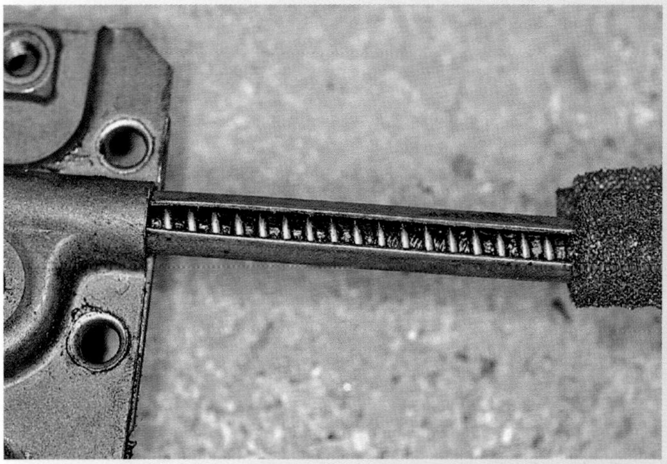

The spiral-wound wire that engages with the winder cog wears, usually causing the winder mechanism to jam with the window when part or fully wound down. Removing the cable and reversing it moves the worn spiral to an area that does not come into contact with the winder cog.

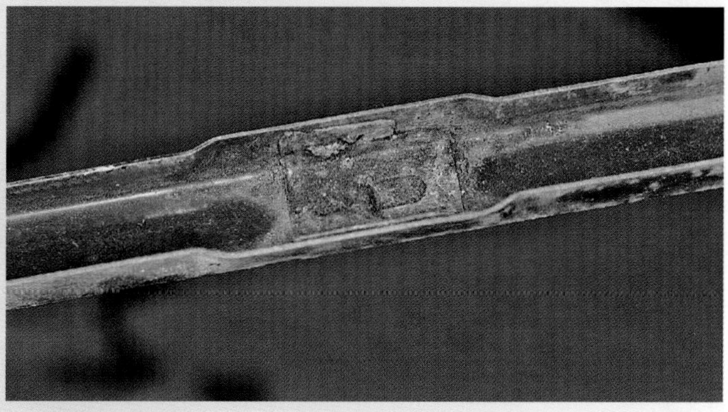

This window runner clip is hopelessly seized into its channel. Attempts to remove it will probably destroy it and replacements do not seem to be available. This one will be left where it is; it should grip the runner well enough.

The door interior trim of most Beetles uses spring clips to fasten into these rubber cups. Replacements are available and it's advisable to renew the spring clips along with the cups.

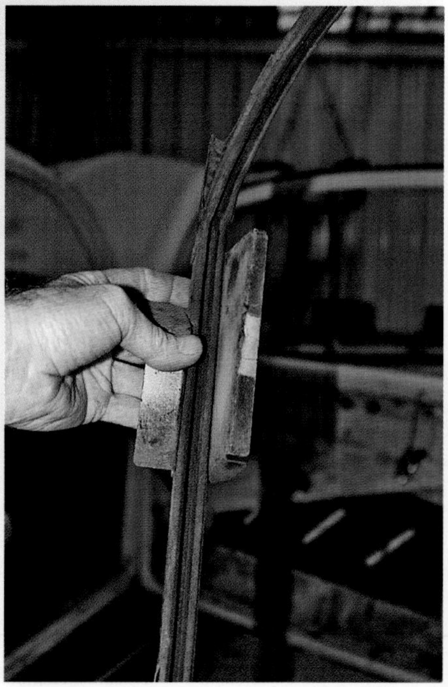

The window channel is anything but easy to fit. Fit the metal component first, then feed the channel into position.

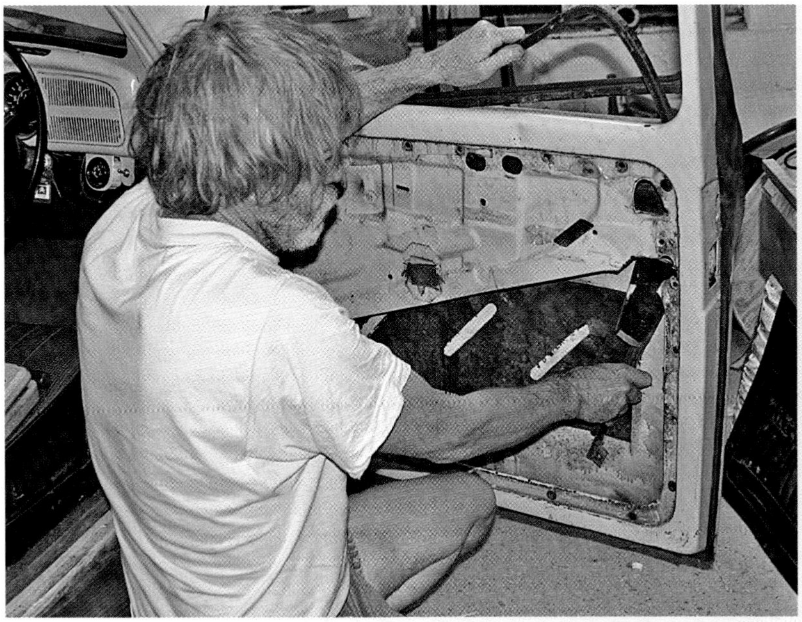

We all make mistakes! Don't fit the window channel until the lock mechanism is in place.

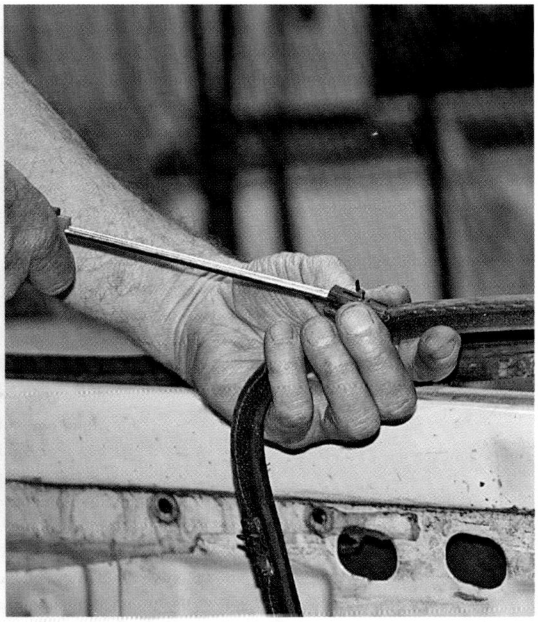

Lever off the spring clips from the window channel.

Finally, the window channel lower leg can be unbolted and pulled from the door.

Make a note of any components which need replacing, and be sure to obtain the necessary spares before you begin the rebuild. The spring clips which hold the window channel are especially prone to breakage when you try to refit them, so it's a good idea to have a few spares.

Door trim panels are available for most Beetles and come ready to fit. Re-covering your own is not usually practical because the board is either broken or de-laminating.

As workshop manuals so often say, door furniture replacement is the opposite of removal. Only joking - instructions follow the section on door repair.

DOOR PANEL REPAIR

The economics of repairing Beetle doors are influenced by the availability and attractive prices of second-hand doors - go to any major Beetle show or autojumble and you should be able to acquire a pair of doors in good condition at a reasonably low price. By comparison, door skins and repair panels are far from cheap, and far from easy to fit.

Furthermore, the main part of the door panel is large and susceptible to denting when being manhandled and fitted, plus, if a door skin is badly rusted, it would be very unusual for the base to be good enough to weld to, so the repair would consist of replacing the base, removing the old skin and fitting the new. The cost of the

The leading lower corner of the door. Frame and skin have rotted and, although it's possible to get repair panels, or cut good sections from other doors, very localised rot is most easily dealt with by fabricating small repair sections.

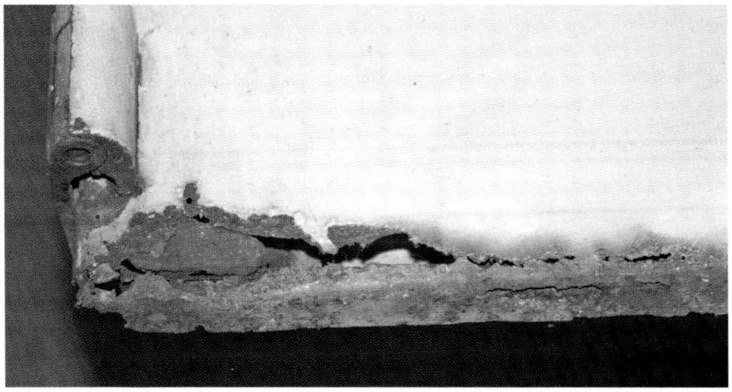

Fitting a lower door skin repair panel. Step one is to make sure it fits!

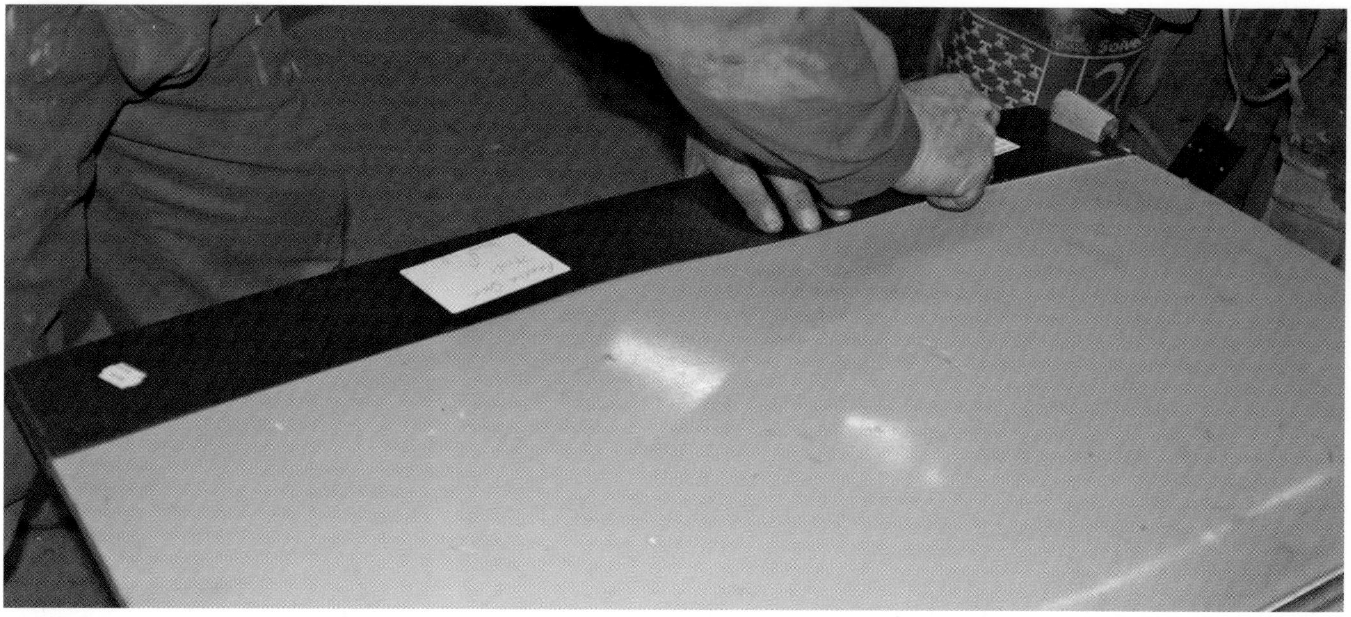

With the panel in position, scribe a line on the existing skin, then remove the repair panel and scribe a parallel line the same depth as whatever tool you use to create a stepped edge - this will be your cutting line.

Here's a very good tip, courtesy of Terry Ball. Run masking tape along the cutting line - it's much easier to see than a drawn or scribed line.

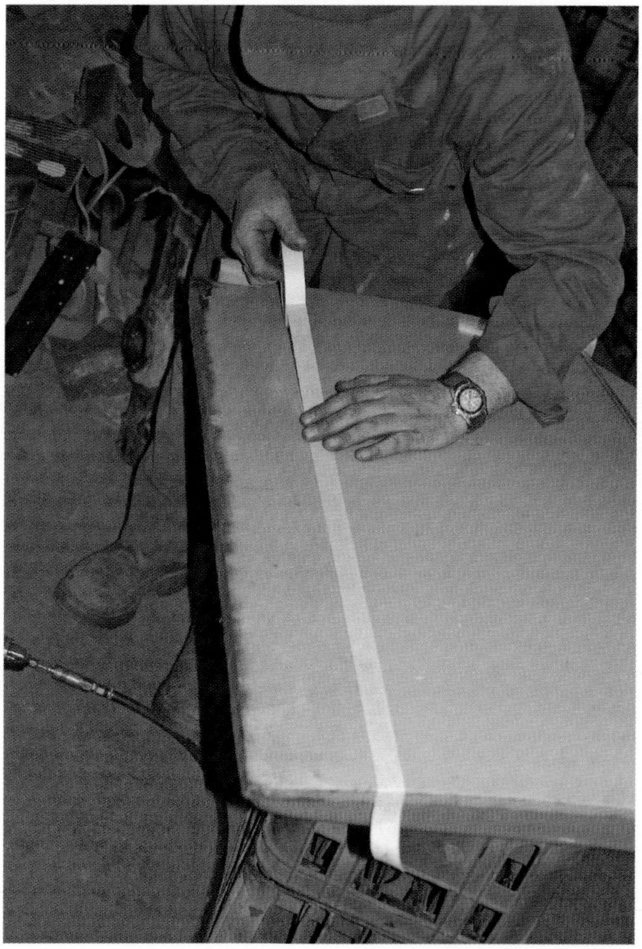

It is possible to cut the door skin using other tools, but nothing does the job as easily and quickly as an air hacksaw.

If you cut right along the lower edge (which will be weak and should cut easily), it makes it easier to pull apart the spot welded flange.

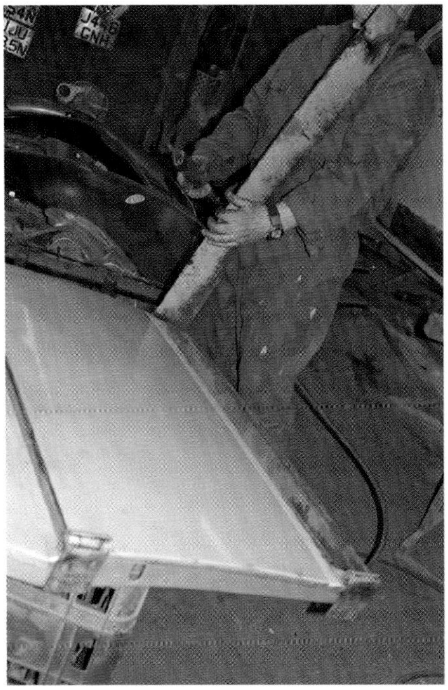

When the bulk of a panel has been cut away and is free, moving the cut section backward and forward through an arc can work-harden the remaining joints.

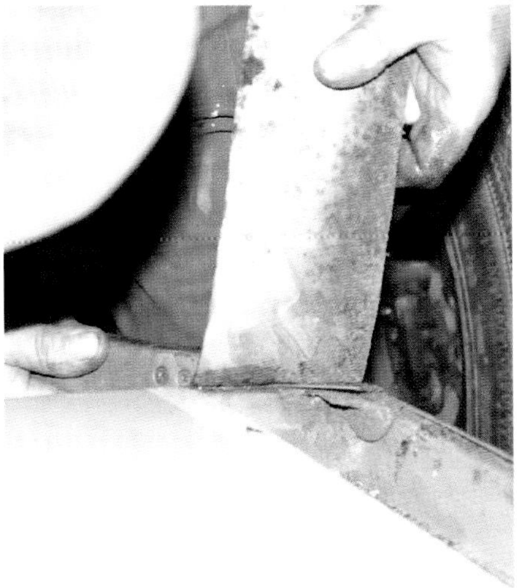

At the edges, cut away the main skin from the welded flange.

It's then possible to get at the thin area of door skin next to the flange.

panels would represent over 60 per cent of the price of a new door and could never be as good; sooner or later new rust would start to bubble through.

However, doors mostly rust first at the base, and in the lower portion of the door skin, for which repair panels are available at reasonable cost. The repair sequence is to cut away and replace the base first, leaving the existing skin bottom in place to help correctly position the repair panel.

In cutting away the door bottom edge, you will also have to partially cut the skin panel; this will still leave the skin attached sufficiently strongly to allow it to be used as a guide for fitting the bottom repair panel, which is best MIG butt-jointed.

Because the main outer door panel is so large, it is very prone to buckle if you attempt to gas or MIG weld it, no matter how careful you are. The best method of carrying out the lower door skin repair is to cut away the rotten metal, clean it, and then spot weld a strip of steel on the

Finally, the bottom lip can be cut away.

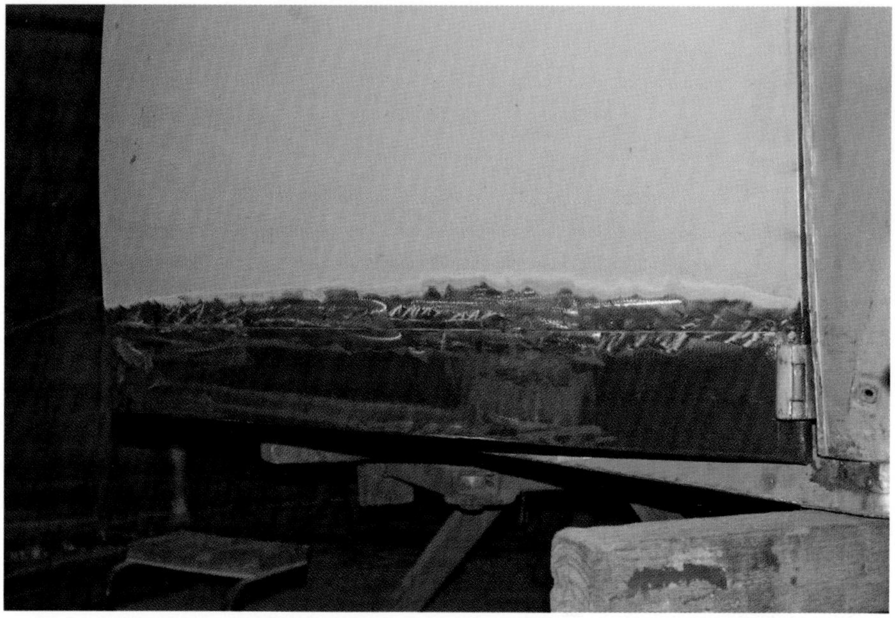

The lower door skin repair panel looks great, but even careful stitch welding will have caused some minor buckling that will show up once shiny gloss paint has been applied. Carefully tap down any high spots and use body filler on low points.

Note the stepped joint and plug welds. Apply lots of rust-proofing (paint/grease) and make sure that there are drain holes in the door frame base, or all your hard work will have been in vain.

back. The repair panel can, in turn, be spot welded to this, to give a neat butt joint ready for body filler.

The door panel is also prone to rot out in the centre, because water which gets past perished window seals can lie trapped underneath the patch of material stuck to the inside of the skin. Very few people will have access to the long spot welder arms necessary to let in a repair patch and, from personal experience, the author can vouch that even the most careful attempts at MIG seam welding in a patch will buckle the panel. If a door skin is rotted in the centre, GRP and body filler repair might be a short-term solution - better to obtain a good second-hand door.

DOOR REBUILD

Refitting door furniture is one of the most exasperating jobs in car restoration. The chrome trim is flimsy and bends or breaks at the slightest provocation, and components have a tendency not to want to fit. All-in-all, this is not a job for the short-tempered. Whatever they pay professional restorers to re-furnish doors, it's not enough!

Start by fitting the lock mechanism. Place the lock in the 'locked' position (vertical). Feed the small rod upwards through the aperture in the door top, and screw the interior lock onto its rod, which will hold the unit while you secure it with screws. Then, try to fit the channel leg by easing it past the lock mechanism. The window trim has a number of spring clips which locate into holes in the door; at the top it is held by a small screw, and the side and top are partially held in by the spring clips. Fit the clips.

Fit the glass and tape it in the uppermost position with masking tape.

Then fit the winder mechanism, ensuring it locates under the door top lip. Use the handle to wind down the mechanism, and carefully slide the window back into the door before fitting the window aperture trim.

It may prove difficult to get the quarter-light assembly back into position. Offer it at an angle to begin with, then simultaneously push it downward and forward into position. If it won't go use a

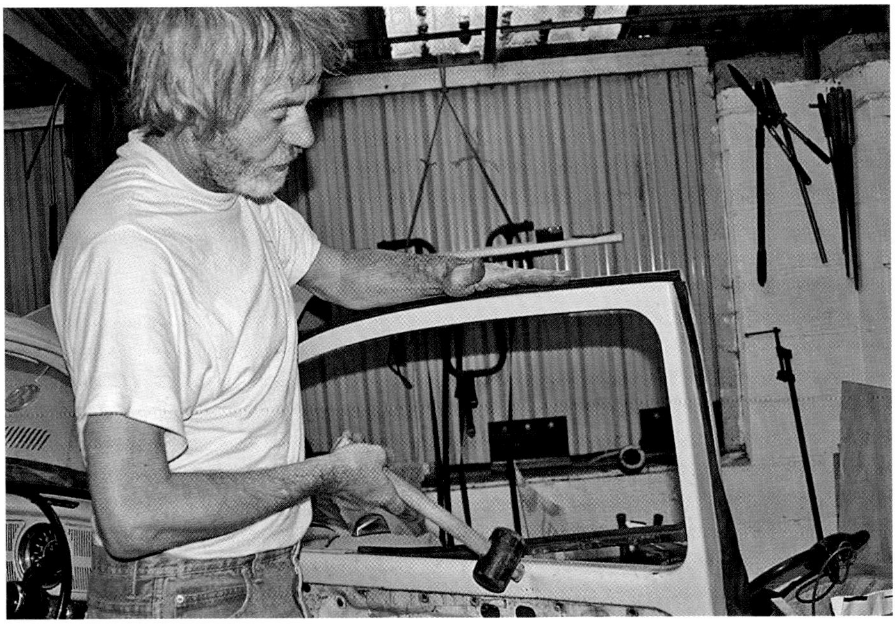

A few taps with a rubber mallet help bed the window channel in place.

piece of softwood to slightly spring open the window aperture. Take care not to damage the flimsy chrome trim.

Bolt the window to the winder mechanism. Before replacing the door trim check that all fastenings are tight, the window opens and closes, and the quarter-light opens and closes without sticking.
Tip: If the winder mechanism jams, or doesn't raise or lower the window, the culprit is usually wear in a section of the wire spiral that the winder cog engages. Try taking out the cable and reversing it; this places the worn section where it isn't going to contact the winder cog and usually does the job.

WING REMOVAL

Disconnect the battery. If the existing wing is to be scrapped, then you can make

The window channel spring clips help hold the window trim in place.

In order to fit the quarter-light, it's best to spread the sides of the window aperture - don't overdo it, though.

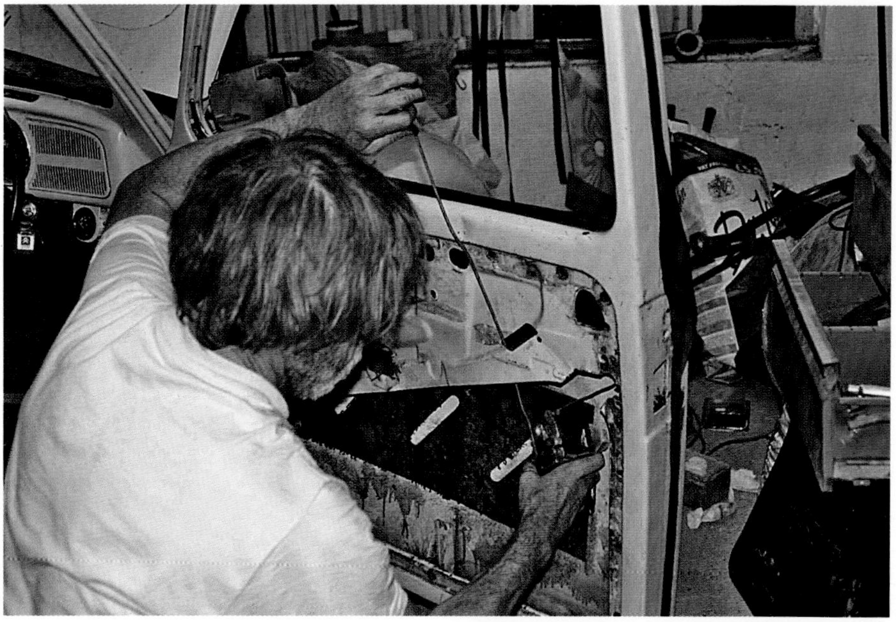

The correct first stage in a door rebuild is to fit the locking mechanism.

After fitting the lock, fit the window channel, but don't try fitting it complete with the insert - fit the metal part and then feed the insert down through the window aperture.

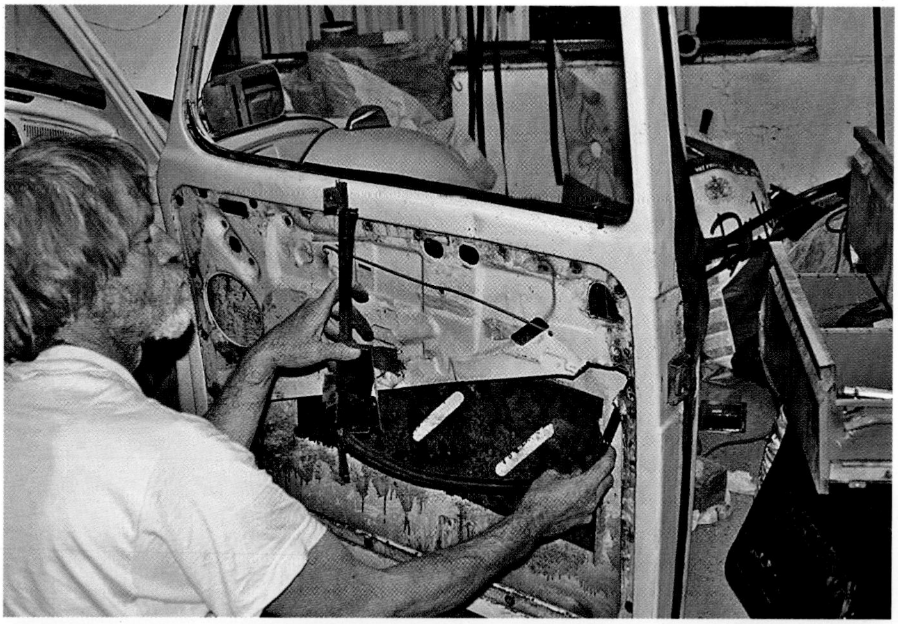

Getting the window channel leg into position past the door locking mechanism is a matter of juggling, swearing, and brute force. If you lose your temper, walk away and come back only when your mood has improved!

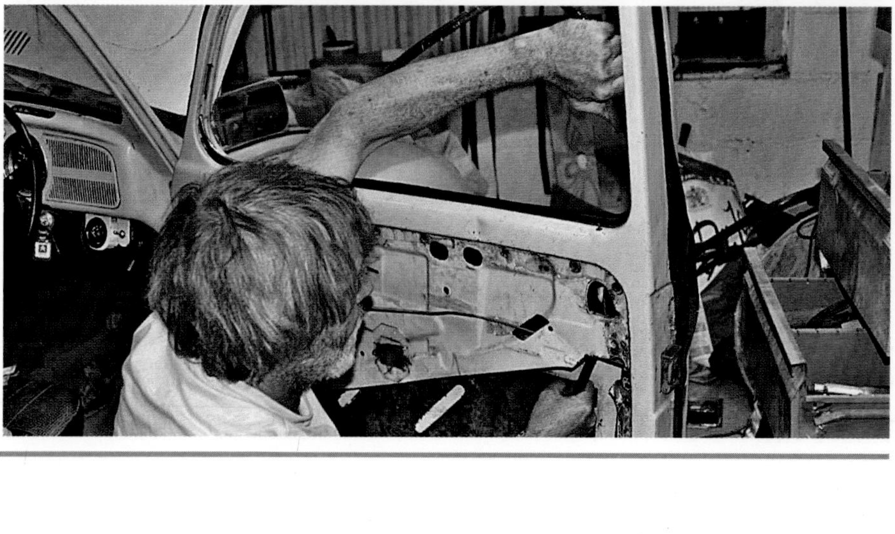

Getting the inner window channel through the window aperture is a two-handed business.

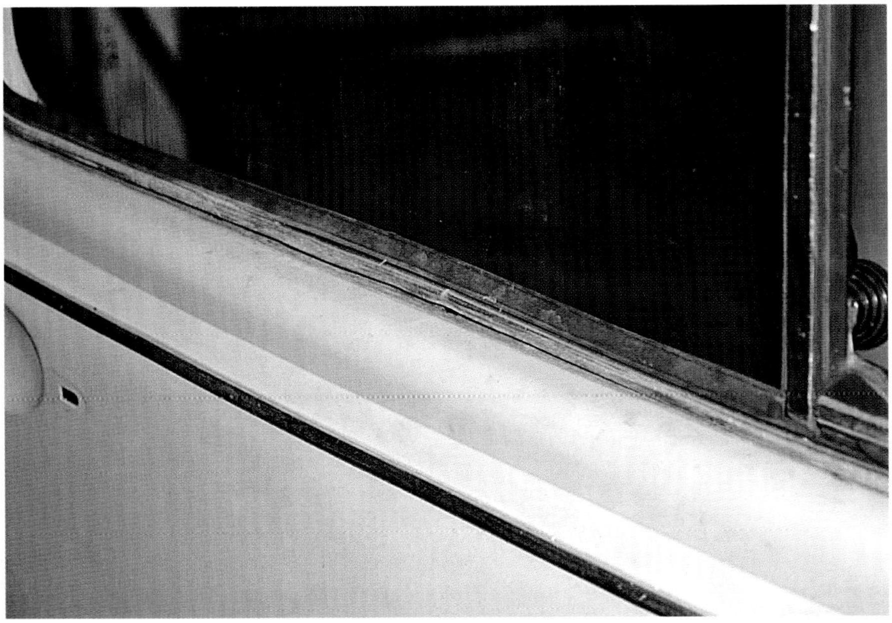

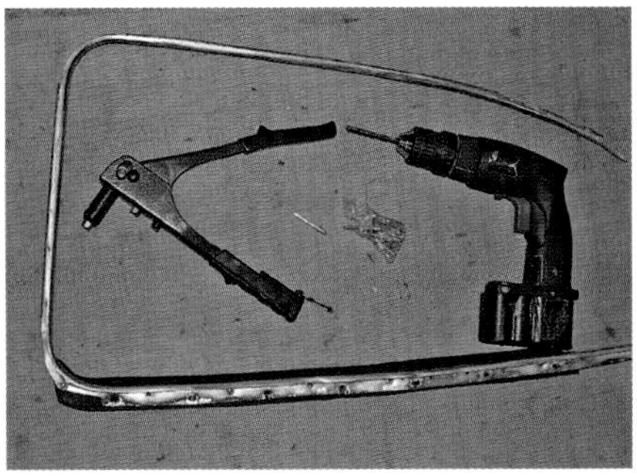

I had previously bought some new reproduction chrome window trim, which proved only slightly thicker than tin foil and which buckled when I attempted to fit it. The only solution was to drill out the rivets holding the rubber seal to the scrap new chrome, and pop-rivet it, along with the backing strip, to the original chrome.

It is quite difficult to position the spring clips that hold the chrome window trim, and they break very easily during fitting, with the result that the chrome rides up as the window is raised, as shown here. In which case, there's no alternative but to start again.

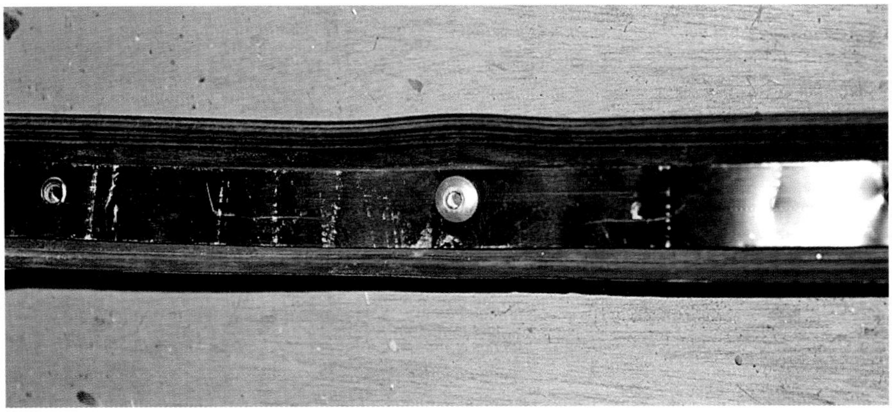

The only pop rivets I had were slightly larger diameter than the originals, so the holes had to be enlarged. Not a problem, but the thicker rivet needed more squeezing force to break its stem, which over-pinched and distorted the rubber. Maybe I'll fit Cal-look, one-piece windows ...

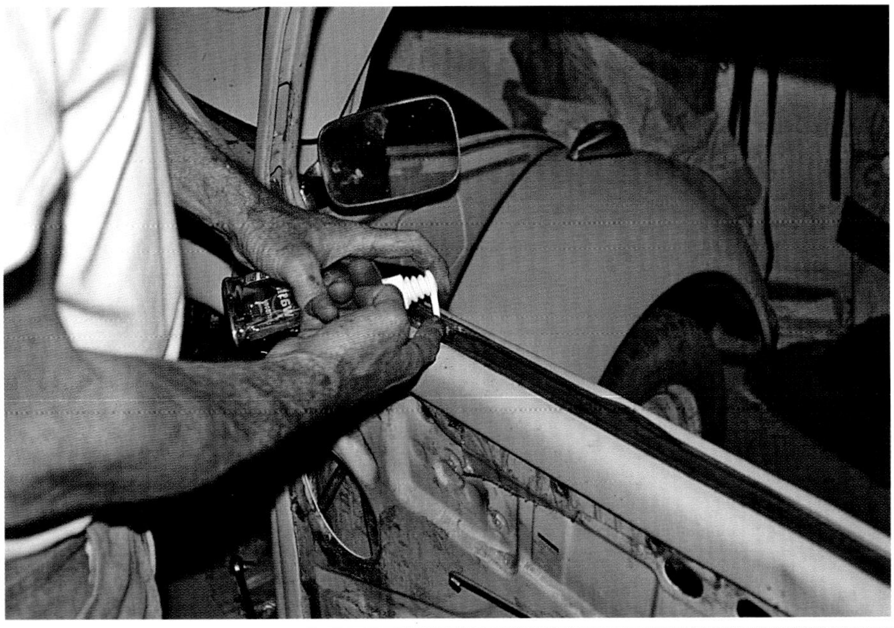

Before trying to fit the quarter-light, smear a little hand cream or hand soap on the rubber against which the quarter-light will have to slide, to stop it pulling the rubber with it.

removal rather easier by cutting away the bulk of the wing with an air chisel, air hacksaw or, preferably, a nibbler (which gives safe cut edges) so that you can get a socket onto the bolt heads.

All four wings are bolted in place (yippee!) but the bolts are often seized to the extent that they will shear, or the captive nuts break free (boo!). Begin by cleaning away the dirt from the bolt heads, then apply penetrating oil and leave it to do its work for as long as possible before attacking the bolts. Also apply oil to the bumper bolts, because these, too, will have to come out.

While the wing bolts are soaking up

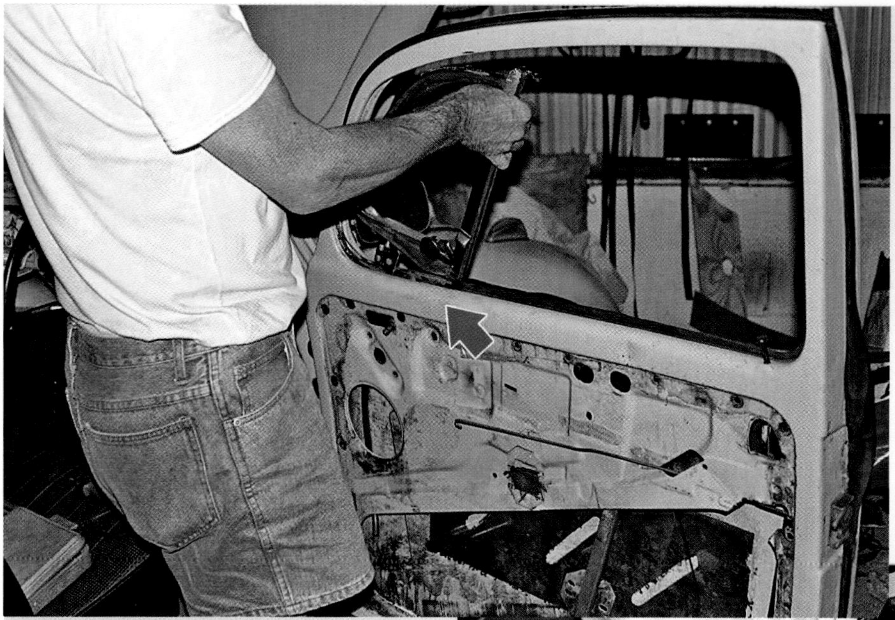

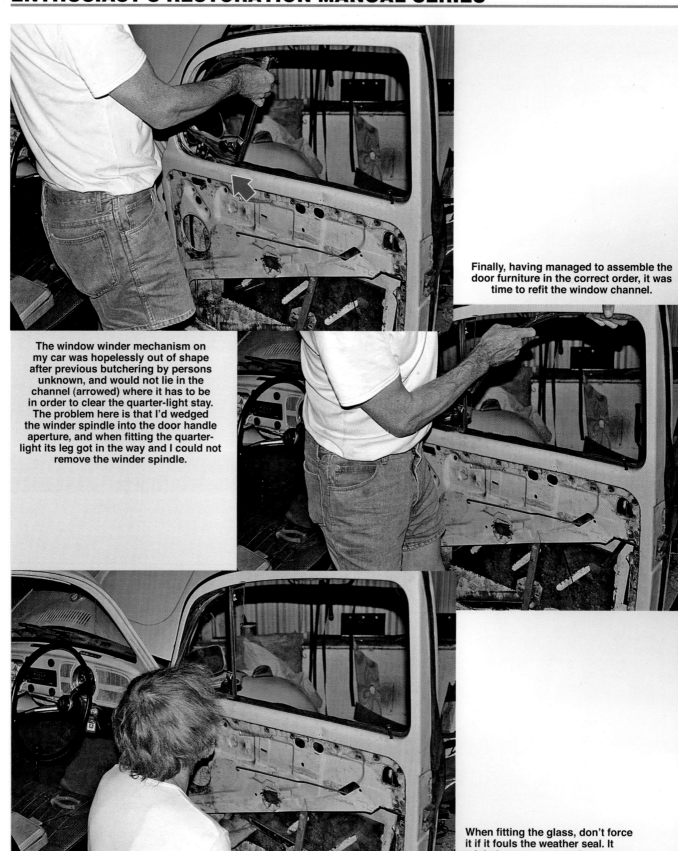

Finally, having managed to assemble the door furniture in the correct order, it was time to refit the window channel.

The window winder mechanism on my car was hopelessly out of shape after previous butchering by persons unknown, and would not lie in the channel (arrowed) where it has to be in order to clear the quarter-light stay. The problem here is that I'd wedged the winder spindle into the door handle aperture, and when fitting the quarter-light its leg got in the way and I could not remove the winder spindle.

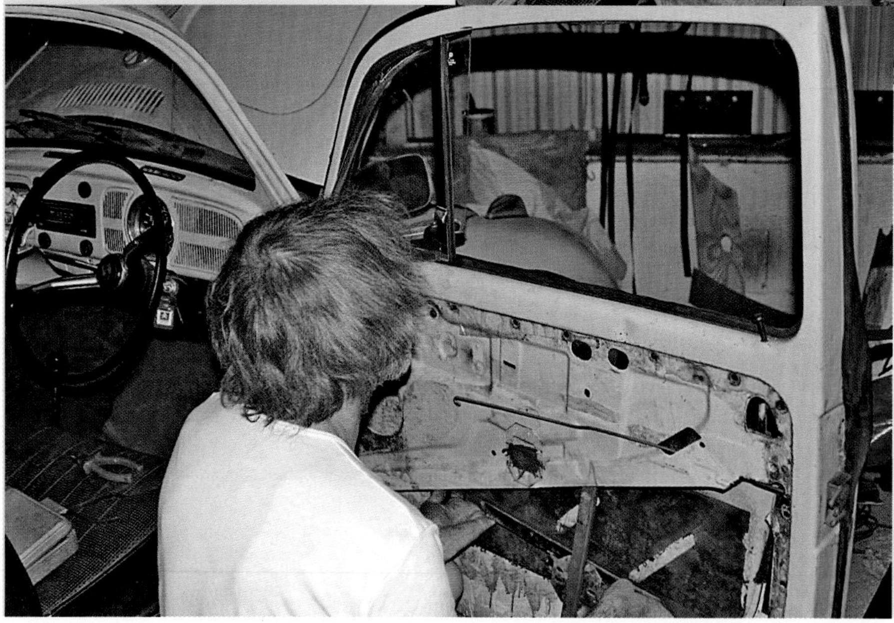

When fitting the glass, don't force it if it fouls the weather seal. It might be necessary to force open the window aperture slightly.

Because the glass is a tight fit and reluctant to rise through the aperture, I fastened it loosely so that I can use the window winder handle to raise it. Don't tighten the bolts until the window has been raised and has 'centred' itself.

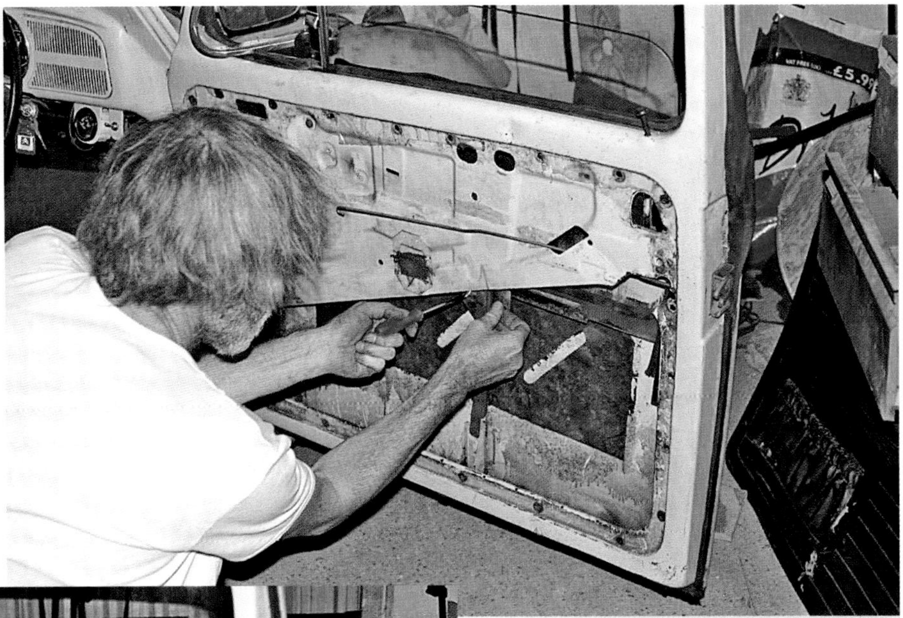

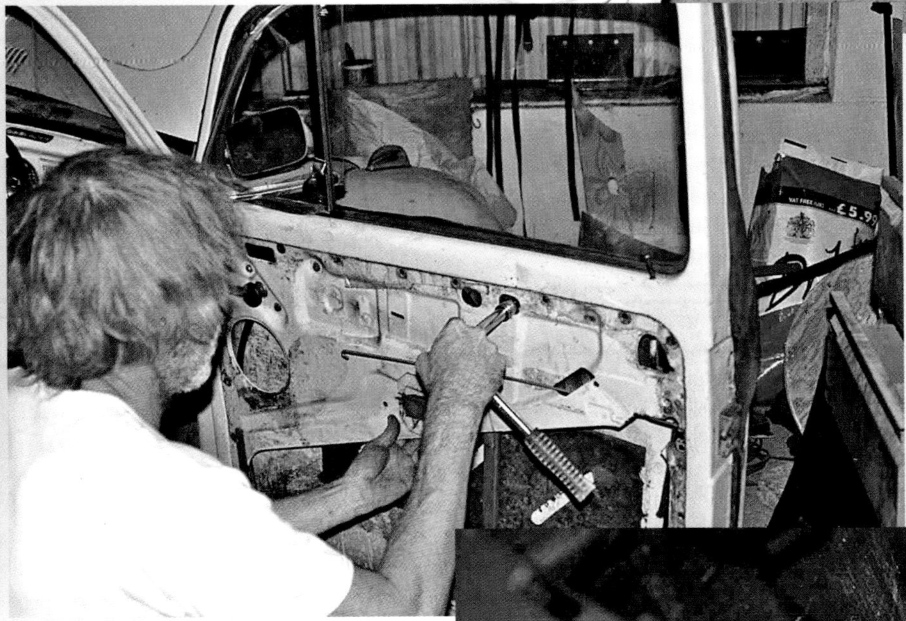

Above: Wind up the window fully, and tighten the bolts through the two holes provided for this purpose.

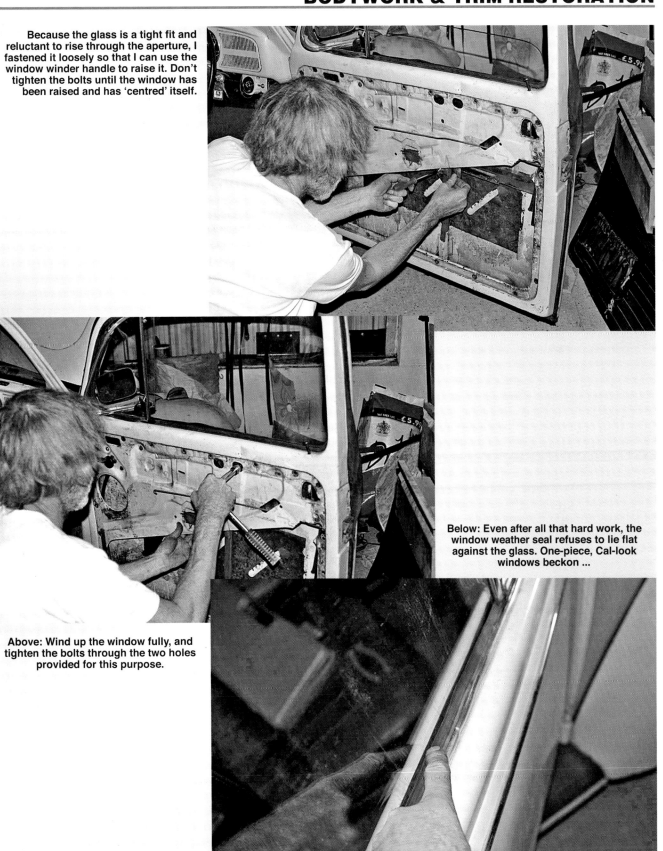

Below: Even after all that hard work, the window weather seal refuses to lie flat against the glass. One-piece, Cal-look windows beckon ...

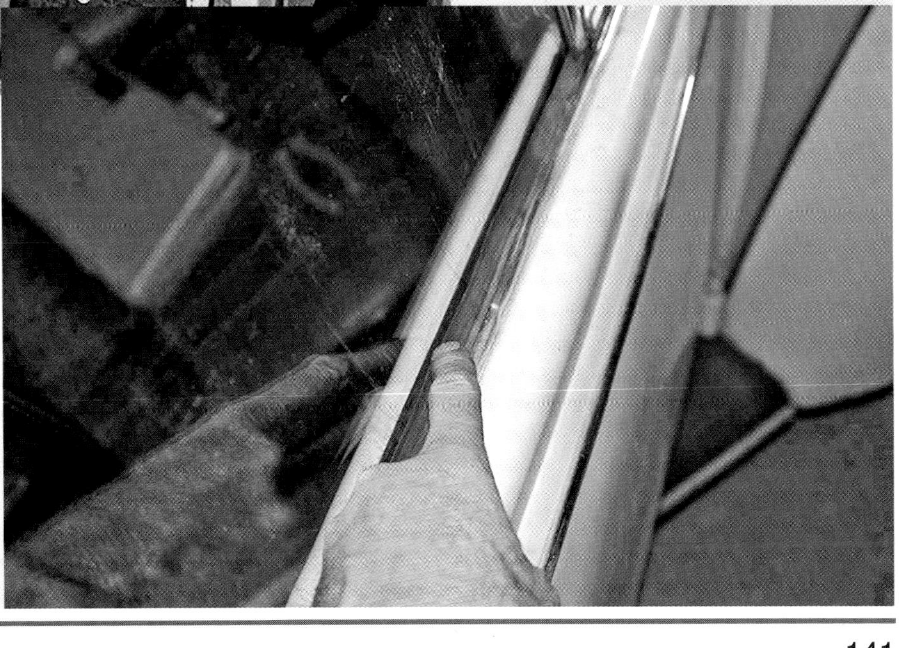

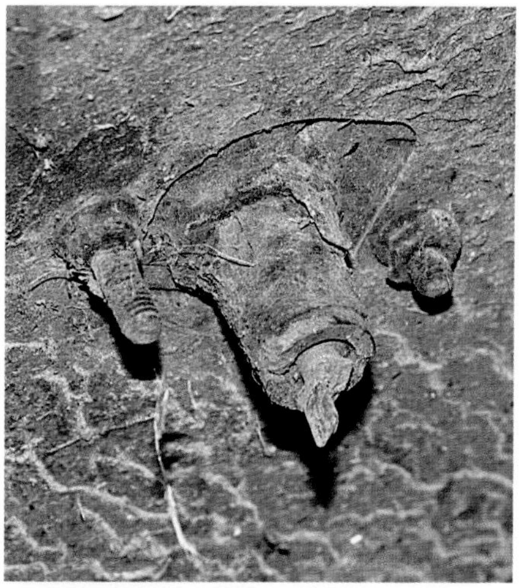

Wing-mounted indicator threads are rarely in good condition. To save them, use penetrating fluid and spend time cleaning the threads with a wire brush before attempting to turn them.

Right: If the wing is to be renewed, make life easier by cutting away the bulk of the wing before dealing with the wing bolts.

It's now possible to get a 13mm socket onto the wing bolts, though a ring spanner is less likely to slip off,

With the retaing bolts removed or ground off it is possible to lift away the wing.

the oil, remove the light clusters, taking great care not to break the plastic rear lenses, which become brittle with age. The rear lamp reflectors (which hold the bulbs - remove these now to avoid breakage) can be fastened in a variety of ways: remove the screws and lift off the lips according to type. Disconnect the wiring from the terminals, and feed the wires back through the wing. Put tabs on the wires to remind you where each goes.

Remove the wing fixing bolts, starting with the nut and bolt to the running board and the bolt at the rear, then work your way upward to the centre top bolt. Use brute force sparingly; not only can you shear bolt heads, you also run the risk of losing the captive nuts. If you do shear any of the bolts you can either drill them out afterwards and re-tap the captive nuts, or try using a proprietary screw extractor. *Tip: If you can obtain longer bolts with the same thread as the original wing bolts, use them with spacers to hold the wing away from the bodyshell during the respray.*

Following a respray, the first job is to bolt the wings back on - black wing beading against new paint looks so sharp that it motivates you to get on with the rest of the rebuild.

WING REPAIR

When a wing rots it is invariably in an area that's difficult to fabricate: around the headlight bowl, the rounded outer edge, or the flange where the wing bolts live. Wings are also fairly low cost items and, taking into account the difficulty of repair, it's usual to renew the wings rather than try and repair them.

Dents in wings are another matter, and can sometimes be repaired by beating out the dent until it's as shallow as possible, and finishing off with a thin layer of filler. Some dents, when beaten out, cause secondary undulations which, when they're beaten out, cause yet more rivelling. By all means try beating out a dent but, if the wing starts to lose its shape, considering renewing it.

WING REPLACEMENT

If the old beading is in reasonable condition it can be re-used. If it has been painted during a general respray, use thinners to remove the paint; Beetles look so much sharper with nice, black wing beading! If it's damaged, renew the beading and, if possible, use new wing fixing bolts, with plenty of copper grease or similar on the threads to make subsequent removal easier. If using new wings, be aware that some cheaper varieties will be difficult to fit and the holes might not align perfectly. Fitting a new wing can quickly degenerate into a wrestling match between you and the wing, in which case remember that the wing almost certainly has sharp edges, so wear gloves!

Begin by fixing the top centre bolt, but fit this - and all other bolts - loosely until all are in position and you're satisfied that the wing will mate well with the shape of the car. Then begin to tighten the bolt which is adjacent to the 'corner' to ensure that the wing pulls properly into shape. Work down each side of the wing, then fit the beading and tighten the bolts. Watch the wing while you apply force to the bolts to make sure you don't pull it out of shape, and be prepared to remove the wing and enlarge the bolt holes, if necessary.

Having ensured that the wing will fit, slacken the bolts and pull the wing a little way from the body for spraying, so that paint goes on the lip of the wing and the section of the quarter panel it will eventually cover.

RUNNING BOARDS

The running boards are secured to the sills by four 10mm bolts, and to the wings by nuts and bolts. To remove the running boards simply undo these; if they're rusted solid, they will need grinding off.

Brazilian-made or other third-party running boards are usually of much lighter gauge steel than the more expensive German-made ones, and it is worth paying extra for the German items if you can. Also in the interest of longevity, the author recommends using a good, corrosion-resistant paint.

As supplied, the running board rubber covers are not always fitted, so start by stretching the rubber over the steel and fastening the other edge. Then, slide the chrome trim clips into place in the trim strip, and push these through the run of fixing holes in the running board. Grab each tag from the other side with a pair of pliers, pull and twist to secure.

BODYSHELL WELDED REPAIR

The panelwork welded repairs described so far have concerned detachable panels. Before cutting, grinding or welding panels that are part of the shell or chassis, disconnect and remove the battery, disconnect the electrical connections at the generator and - if the welding is at the front of the car - remove the petrol tank. All of these jobs are described in Chapter Two.

REAR INNER WING (BODYWORK MOUNT REINFORCING PANEL) REPAIR

Within the rear wheelarches, the prime rust spot is the reinforcing panel which contains the rear body mount and (on some cars) the 'Z' or anti jacking bar. It's the same old story: mud (sometimes salt-laden) is kicked up from the wheels and settles in every nook and cranny, such as the folded pressed steel body mounting. If this area is not well protected, it will succumb to rust quite quickly and, in the UK, fail its roadworthiness test (MoT).

The first step is to raise the rear of the car and rest it on axle stands, then remove the road wheel and clean the area so that you can establish the extent of the rust. Also clean the bumper bracket bolts, the wing bolts, the damper bolts, and the body mounting bolt, and apply penetrating oil to them in order to make removal easier.

The 10mm running board bolts run into captive nuts in the heater channel. They rarely come out easily and are apt to shear, which means drilling them out and re-tapping the thread in the running board.

Expect the nuts and bolts front and rear of the running board to be hopelessly seized.

Drill out the spot welds after cleaning the panel so that you can see them. Check that there's nothing on the other side of the panel that might be damaged.

Disconnect the battery and the wires leading to the generator, then remove the tail lamp lens, remove the wires from their terminals (use masking tape tags to remind you which is which) and pull the wires back into the wheelarch. Remove the bumper bracket bolts and pull the bumper assembly away from the car.

When welding the nearside rear bodyshell mount repair panel, do remember that the wiring loom runs very close to the line of your weld. It's advisable to move the rear half of the loom before undertaking this task - new looms are quite expensive.

Remove the rear wing bolts and place the wing and filler strip to one side. This improves access, and it may be wise to double-check the inner wing condition at this stage, including the bumper mounting areas.

Using a hexagonal socket if possible, undo the 17mm body mounting bolt. This might prove very reluctant to start and, if you resort to brute force, you can easily shear off the bolt head, so clean out the recess, apply more penetrating oil, and leave until later. If you do manage to shear the bolt try putting a blob of weld on what remains of it; this can break the seal (by the heat from the welding process) and give you something to grip with a mole wrench. If this fails you have no alternative but to

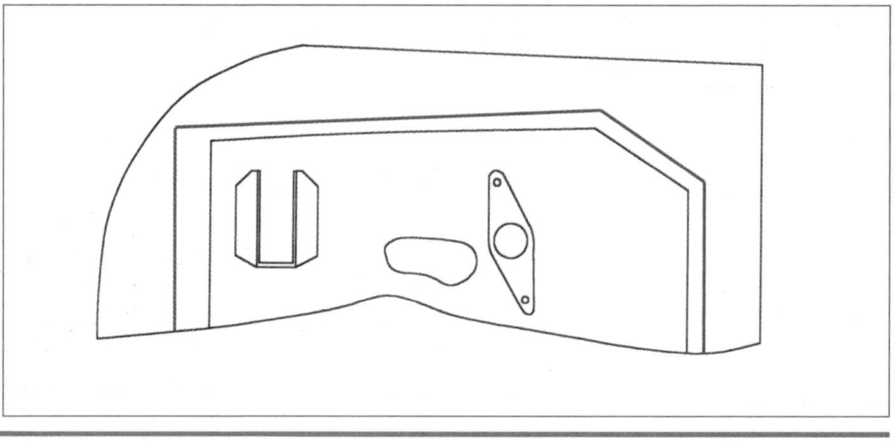

The reinforcing panel comes with a section of the inner wing. If you can, cut down the panel (as suggested by the red lines). If the repair ever has to be repeated, a larger section of the same panel can be fitted.

With the reinforcing panel off, clean the area back to bare steel.

Offer the repair panel into position and bolt it to the damper mounting bracket. Tack weld in place, beating down the edge as necessary.

drill out the bolt.

Remove the rear damper; again, if the fittings are too tight, apply penetrating oil and leave this to soak in. Locate and drill out the spot welds which hold the reinforcing panel in place. Using, if possible, a 'chisel' fashioned from a 1in hacksaw blade, part the welds. You may discover that the lower trailing edge is MIG or gas welded if this panel has (as is likely) been replaced at an earlier date: a proud weld should be ground down.

Clean the newly-exposed and surrounding metal bright. As ever, it's not necessary to fit the entire repair panel and it may, in fact, be preferable to cut down the panel, provided you can find sound metal to weld to. Future rusting is likely to occur around the area of the welded joint, so by fitting what is, in effect, a smaller panel, you have the option of fitting the full repair panel if rusting occurs. Trimming the repair panel also gives you less welding to do!

Inside the car, remove the rear seat and adjacent trim panel, plus any combustible material on or near the inner rear wing. If you have a fire extinguisher, place it inside the car, and if you have an assistant ask him or her to assume the role of fire-fighter should this be required! If you're working alone check for (and possibly deal with) minor fires inside the car every few seconds, which will make the welding process a protracted one. Small welding fires are usually burning paint, and can usually be beaten out using a piece of sheet steel, or blown out using compressed air, though it's essential to keep a fire extinguisher to hand just in case a fire really takes hold.

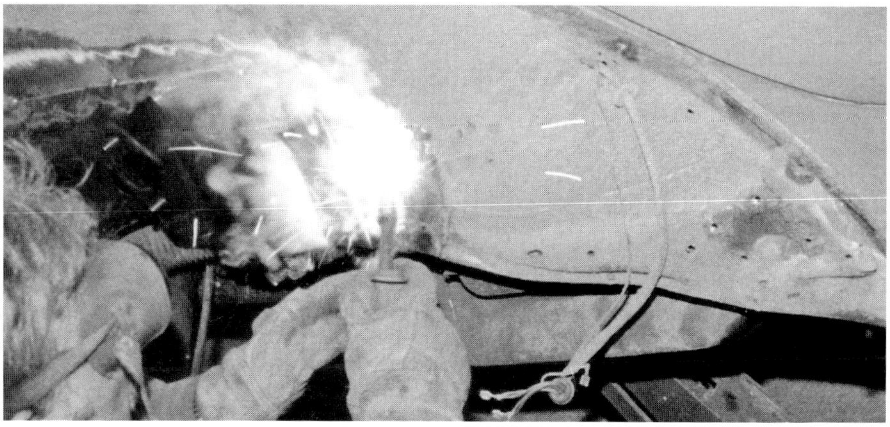

Finally, seam weld the edges.

This is the panel seen from underneath the car. Clean the surrounding steel and weld the edge on the inside to keep out water.

The rear body mount and reinforcing panel job completed. The body has been temporarily bolted to the chassis without a spacer. This is because the heater channels are not yet welded to the body, as the heat from doing this would melt the belly pan gasket. No gasket and no rear body mount spacer means that the shell sits square, while panels, such as the flitches, are welded on.

Clean the edges of the panel which are to be welded, then apply weld-through paint to all the newly exposed bright metal if you want the repair to last. Bolt the panel onto the damper top mounting bracket. Use a self-tapping screw to pull it roughly into the shape of the inner wing, then push it further inwards, tack it, and beat it until the panel edges touch the inner wing. It is as well to tack weld the repair panel edges perhaps as often as one inch intervals, and to check during the welding that the repair panel is not bucking away, which would increase the chances of burning through. Continuously seam weld the repair panel edges, grind down surplus weld, and apply plenty of paint to slow the rusting process.

On the inside, the panel has to be welded to the parcel shelf panel. All too often it will be discovered that this has rusted away at the edges; if it has, make up an 'L'-shaped repair panel and continuously seam weld it into place.

Don't forget to use copper-based grease on all bolt threads when you come to reassembly. Remember to test your rear lights before taking the car out onto the road; if there are any problems with the wires connected to the correct terminals, clean all of the spade connectors and retest. Any remaining faults will either be due to bulb failure or, more commonly, poor earthing.

REAR BUMPER MOUNTS

Like the rear body mounts within the rear wheelarch, the rear bumper mounts tend to catch lots of mud and water thrown up by the road wheel and rust out, resulting in a loose bumper (and roadworthiness test failure even if the bumper doesn't move).

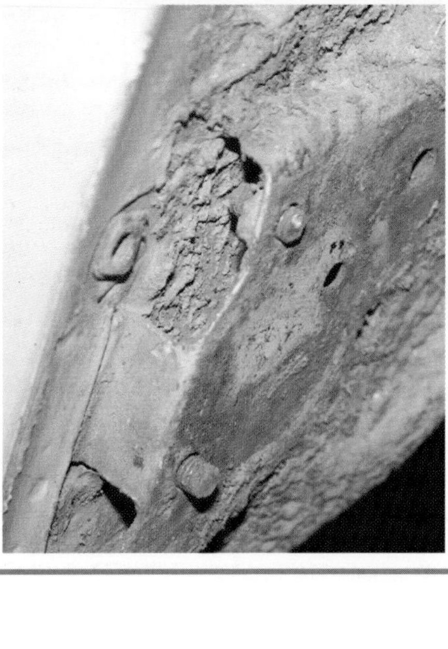

Repair patches for this panel are widely available, though rather difficult to fit.

Begin by removing the bumper, then the rear wing, and scrape away the accumulated mud from the vicinity of the mounting points so that you can see clearly enough to judge the extent of the rot. Fold back the retaining tabs and remove the sound-deadening material from the side of the engine bay, taking care not to spear yourself on stray lengths of wire protruding from the material. Also remove the engine bay seal.

Very often, bumper mounting bolts will be so seized that they shear as you try to remove them. If the bumper mount panel is to be retained, get a set of stud extractors, or drill them out and run a bottom tap through the captive nuts.

The bumper mounting panels must have been 'attended to' at some point in the past because, outwardly, they appear sound. The inside, however, reveals that the rotten original panels were simply covered with a repair panel.

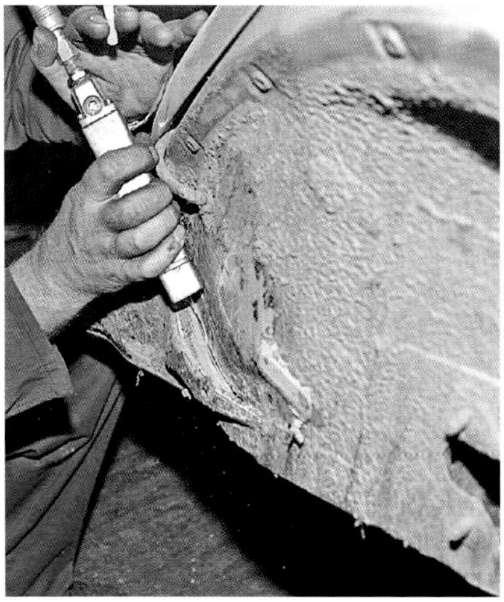

The rear bumper mounting brackets and adjacent bodywork is apt to rot, and the extent of it will vary from car to car. Cut away the old steel a bit at a time until you reach sound metal.

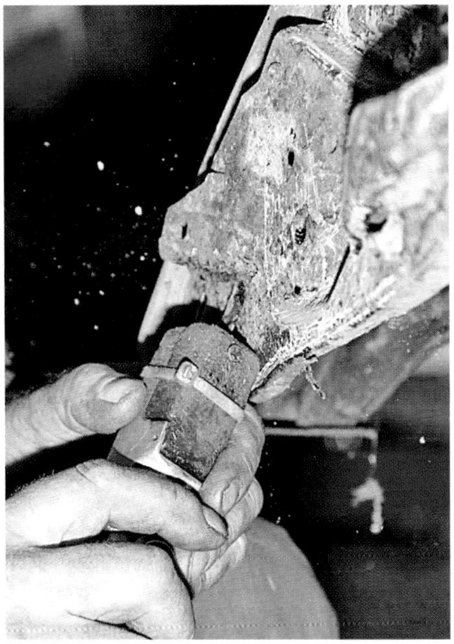

When cutting out the old rear bumper mount, try to cut well away from the edge of the rear valance, if it's sound and to be retained.

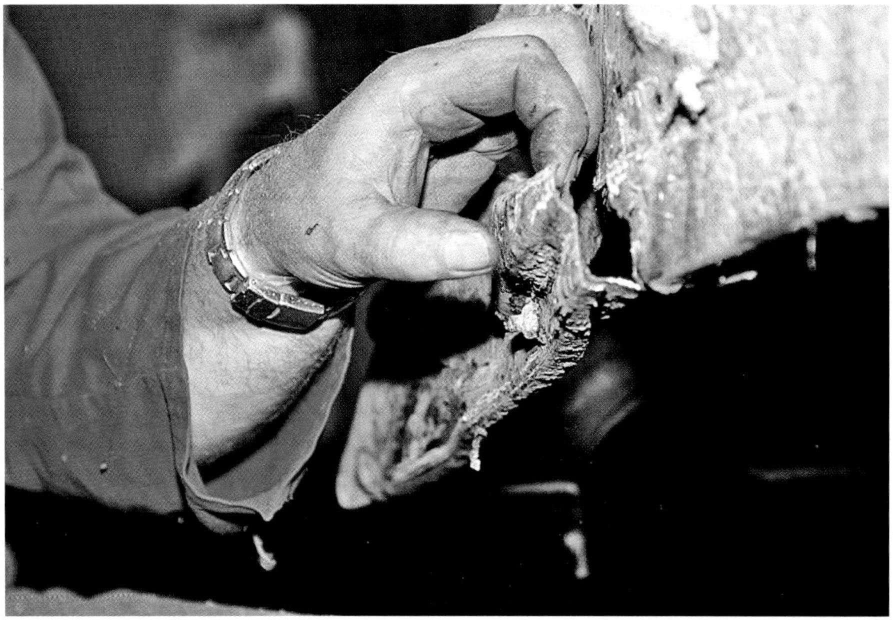

The small, horizontal panel each side of the engine bay often rots, along with the bumper mounting panels. However, if it is sound, carefully cut the bumper mount panel or you'll slice into it.

If you're not sure how strong the steel in the vicinity of the bumper mounting is, clean it well and any rust will become all too apparent. Cut down the repair panel to the smallest practicable size, so that, if you ever have to do this job again, you will be able to cut back to sound metal without exceeding the area of the repair panel.

Drill out the spot welds which hold the bumper bracket, and part the seams. Then offer up the repair panel and scribe around its edges before cutting out the rot. The author recommends that the bumper is temporarily refitted to the fixed bracket on the other side of the car, and to the repair panel, to ensure that the new bracket is positioned so that the bumper sits level to the rest of the car.

Clean those edges of the new panel which are to be welded, check that the rear lighting wires are well out of harm's way, and weld the new panel (keep the fire extinguisher handy), using a continuous seam weld or plug welds.

With the bulk of the old steel cut away, offer the repair pressing into position to find your cutting lines.

Drill out the spot welds holding the remains of the old panel to the lip of the valance.

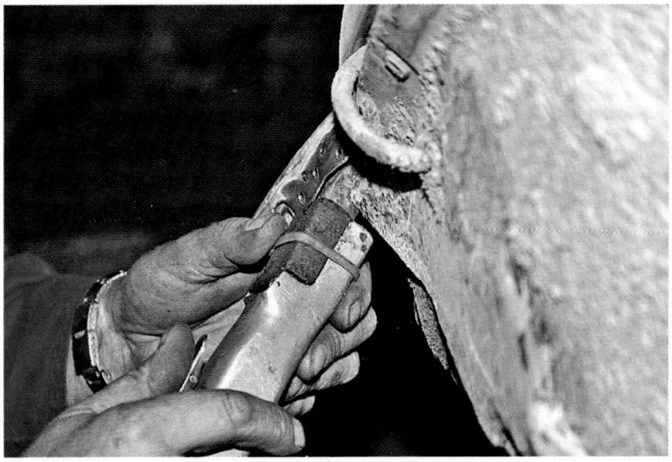

Cutting underneath the valance lip without damaging it is difficult, so it's reassuring to know that, if you do slice into it, the cut can be welded.

Cut the valance lip as far as possible, then move it backwards and forwards until it work hardens and comes away.

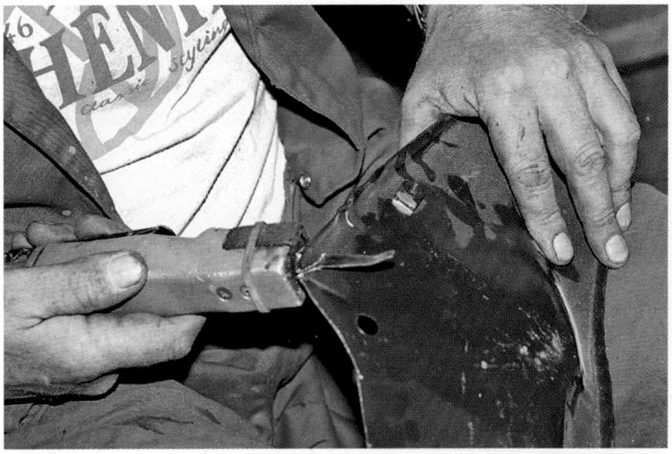

The repair panel will have to be trimmed unless you butt joint it.

Check the panel fit and trim off more if necessary.

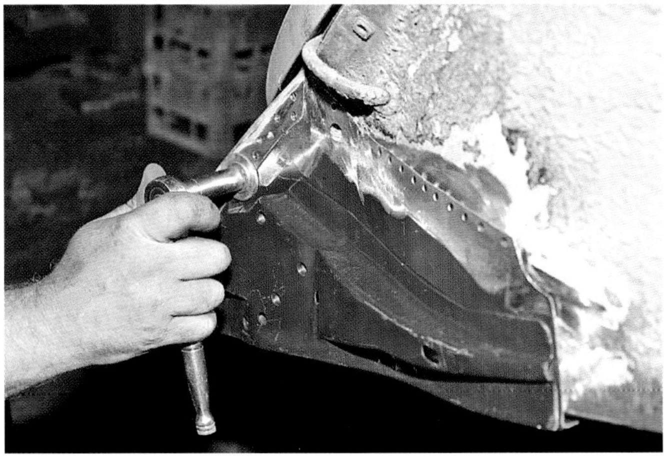

The panel can be bolted in position using the wing captive nut.

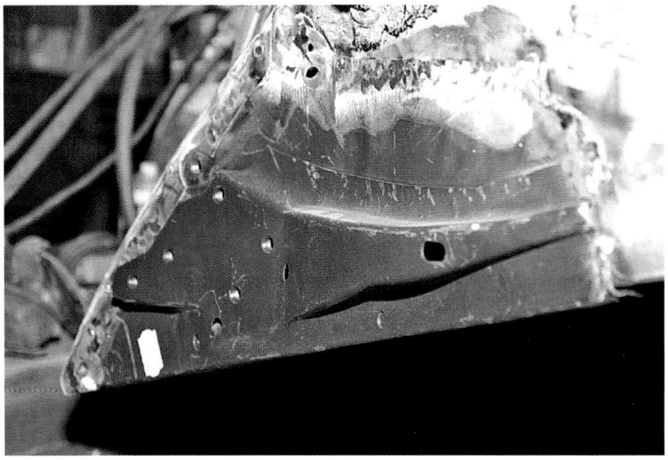

The panel can be plug welded to the rear valance, and plug or seam welded elsewhere.

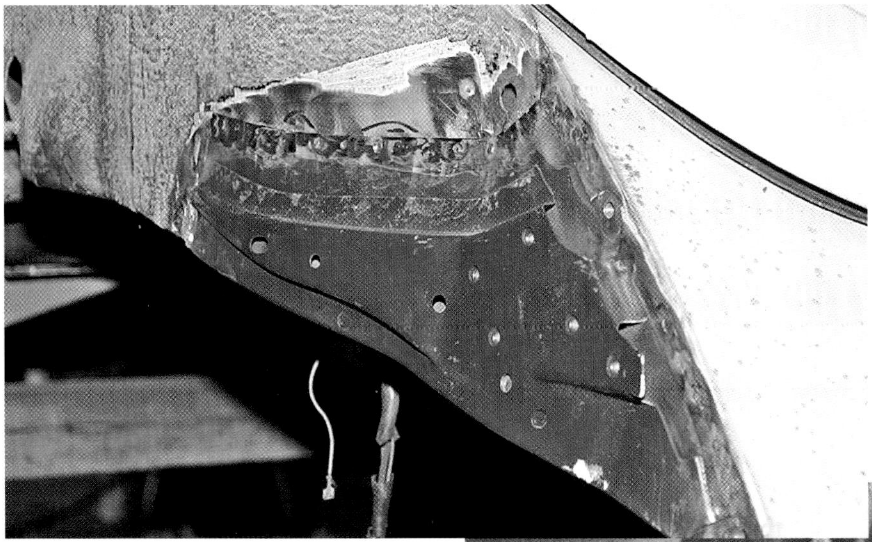

If you plug weld the repair panel, be sure to use seam sealer around the edges afterward.

If necessary, drill a hole for the rearmost wing fixing bolt, then fasten a bolt and nut through the hole and tack weld the nut (on the inside) to provide a new captive nut for the wing bolt.

FRONT END - OVERVIEW

The pressings which make up the Beetle front end differ to some extent between the torsion bar and McPherson Strut versions; in principle the two are quite similar, consisting of the dashboard/'A' post/roof pillar assembly, flitch panels, luggage bay floor, spare wheel well and valance, though, of course, on McPherson strut cars, the flitch is designed to hold the top of the suspension strut and is subjected to great stresses. New McPherson strut flitch assemblies will, at the time of writing, be prohibitively expensive for many people, so both flitch replacement and some repairs are covered here.

To completely rebuild a front end on a piecemeal basis - flitches, luggage compartment floor, spare wheel well and valance - is approaching the limits of economic and practical DIY restoration. Not only is the chance of ending up with a lopsided car disturbingly high, but there's a strong possibility that more serious rot will be discovered in various adjacent and underlying panels. When this happens, you should give serious consideration to using a better, or new, bodyshell.

If you do decide to undertake front-end repairs, don't weld any panel finally into position until you have offered up the wings and luggage compartment lid, to check that the shut lines are all correct. Even after taking this precaution, you could still discover that panels are not correctly positioned, only after fitting the bumper and getting the car back on its wheels.

LUGGAGE BAY LID REMOVAL/REPLACEMENT

Rather than removing the luggage bay lid complete with hinges, it is easier to remove the luggage bay lid and leave the hinge mechanisms in place. This involves marking the precise locations of the hinges relative to the lid, and having a helper - or preferably two - take the weight of the lid whilst you remove the two bolts that hold each hinge to the lid, then lifting away the lid.

To remove the hinges, remove the circlip from the lower end of the spring, then the single pivot bolt holding each hinge - take great care not to drop any of

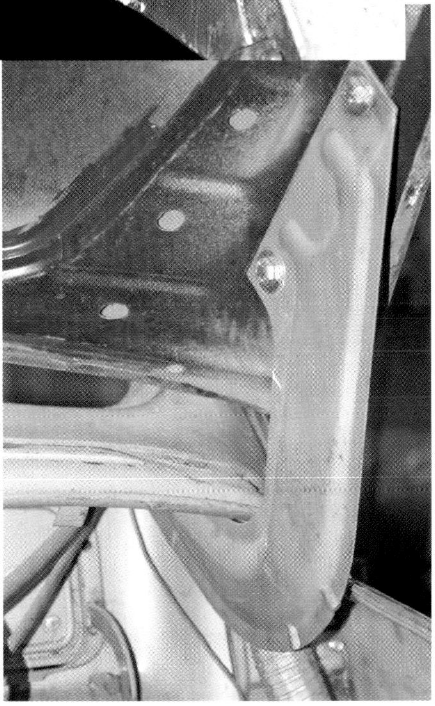

Luggage bay lid brackets are available for all Beetles. A helper should support the weight of the lid while you bolt the brackets; be prepared to spend some time adjusting them to get the shut lines right.

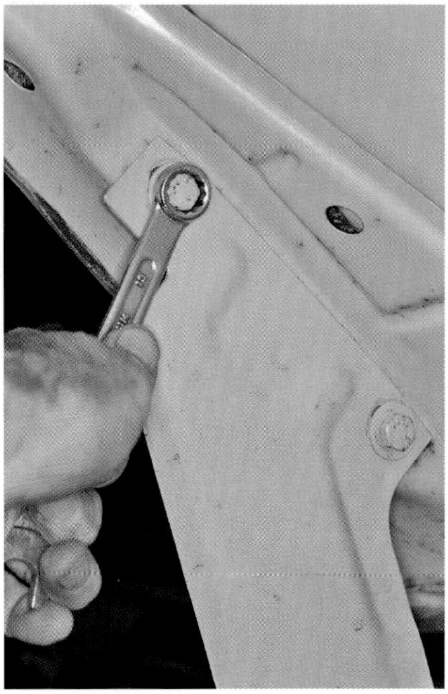

To remove the luggage bay lid, remove the 13mm bolts holding the lid to the hinges, rather than remove the lid and hinges together. Mark the lid and hinge bracket to help realign the two when you come to refit the lid.

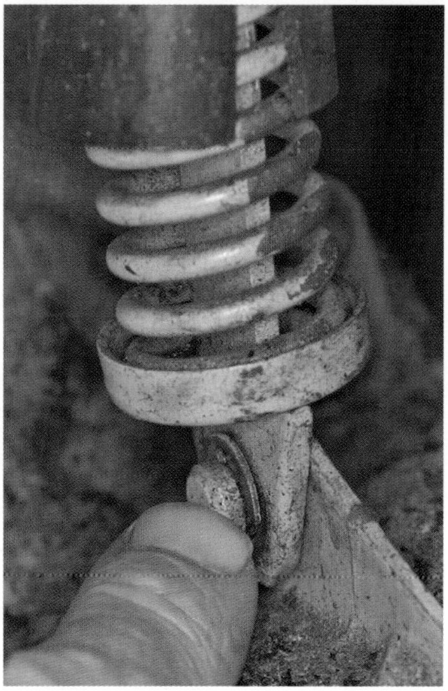

The spring assembly lower end is secured by this circlip. Before attempting to remove it, stuff rags into the 'A' post because, when the circlip flies off, this is where it usually drops into.

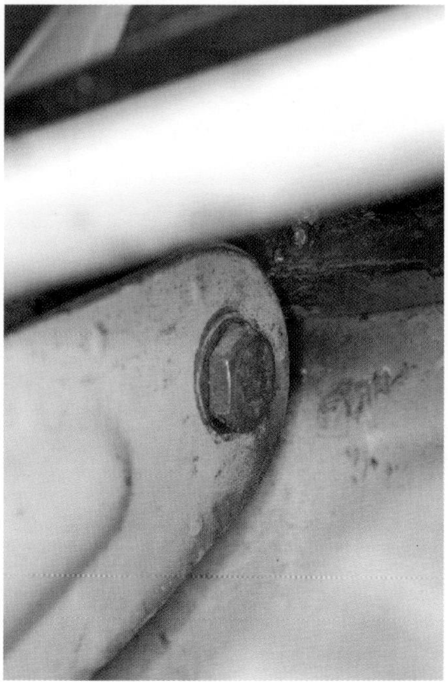

The hinge bolt is tucked away under the scuttle panel, but you can get a ratchet and socket onto it.

The luggage bay lid lower locking mechanism contains a moving segment that secures and releases the upper lock striker. Check that this moves fully to the side when the lever is operated before closing the luggage bay lid.

When the operating lever is pushed back, the moving segment of the lower lock should have more than enough travel to engage with the striker. Adjustment is made by altering the cable position; not easy, because it's on the underside of the panel.

The upper lock striker prevents the lid from coming loose should the upper lock fail or anyone try to break in. To adjust the striker simply turn it. If you wish to remove the handle assembly, unscrew the striker completely to gain access to the lower handle mounting bolt ...

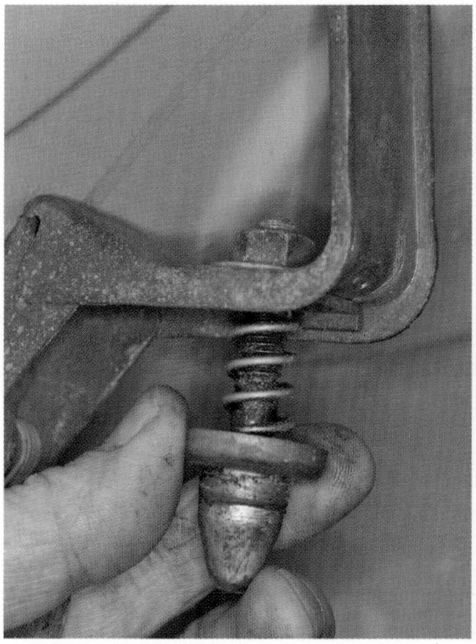

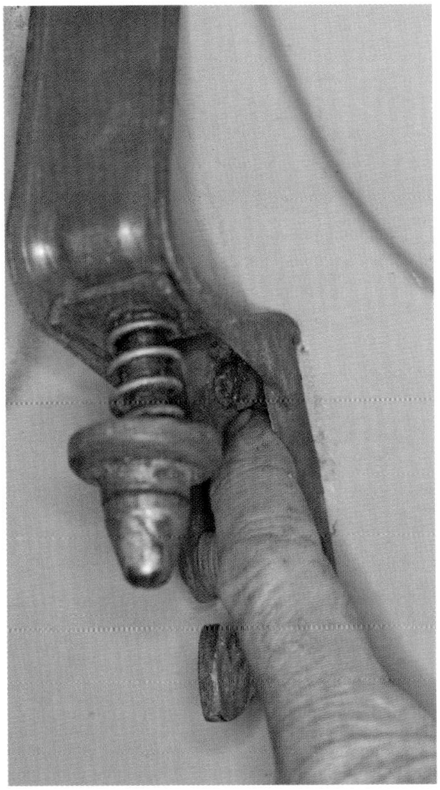

... which is directly behind it.

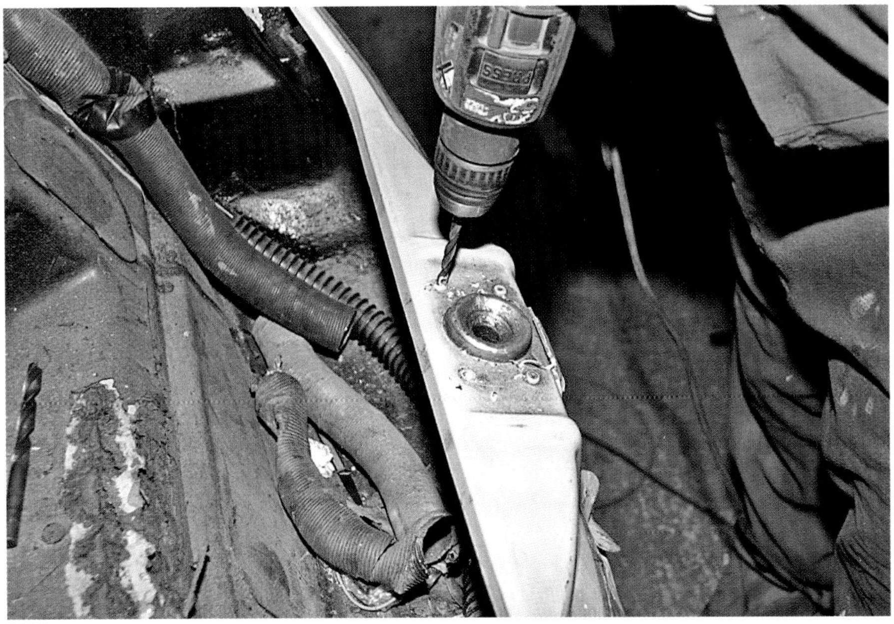

To remove the bonnet catch, drill out the pop rivets.

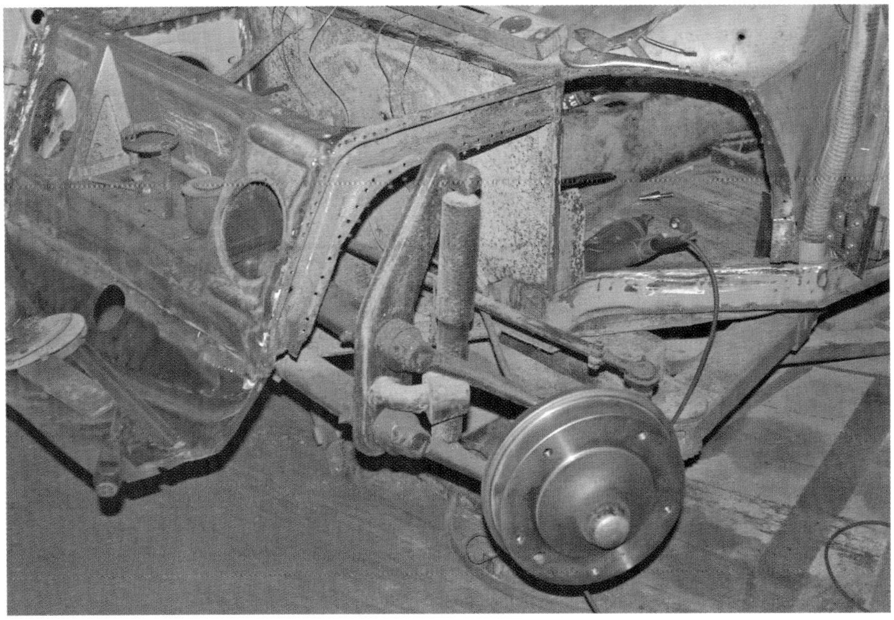

Flitch replacement is one of the most demanding and difficult restoration jobs, and there's plenty of scope for things to go wrong. Consider having the job done professionally.

the fittings down into the 'A' post, because it's almost impossible to retrieve anything from inside it (it's not uncommon to find deutschmarks dropped by VW workers inside Beetle 'A' posts).

When reassembling, fit the hinge mechanisms to the car, and then fit the luggage bay lid to the hinges. If there are no alignment marks to tell you where the hinges should fit on the luggage bay lid, it's safest to remove the luggage bay lid lock while you get the bonnet correctly aligned (by trial and error) because, if the lock engages and the luggage bay lid is sufficiently out of alignment, it might not be possible to release the lock, leaving you with no other alternative than to grind off the lock handle! For the same reason, have an assistant operate the luggage bay lid release lever in the glove compartment while visually checking that the lower lock mechanism moves far enough to disengage from the striker, and adjust the cable if necessary. Finally, adjust the height of the lock striker, if necessary.

FLITCH REPLACEMENT

This is not a job for the faint-hearted; even on a Beetle which has not previously suffered welded 'repairs' to the footwell side panel area, the heater channel, front panel or, in fact, any of the panels in the vicinity, the job can still be very tricky. On a Beetle which has been bodged in these areas, the job can be soul-destroying. It's recommended that all but the most experienced (and hardened) DIY enthusiasts hand this particular job to a professional Beetle restorer.

If you do decide to have a crack, you will need an air hacksaw, although you might get away with a pad saw if you have several days to spare for cutting out the old flitch panel. The use of air chisels or other brutal devices is ruled out because they'll damage the lips of adjacent panels.

Disconnect the battery. Remove the front bumper. Remove the fuel tank and push the fuel line well out of the way. Disconnect the lower ends of the luggage compartment lid springs, which are held by circlips (take care not to drop them down into the 'A' posts). Use a prop to hold up the luggage compartment lid (remove the luggage compartment lid if you prefer, although, if you do, it will have

Torry cuts out as much as possible of the old flitches so that he can get a drill onto the spot welds.

The first section cut away. Note that Terry has avoided the spare wheel well lip by a fair margin, and is now cutting the rear top of the flitch, avoiding the heavy section steel in the MacPherson strut top housing.

Having cut around the wheelarch until he met up with a hidden welded lip, Terry now cuts down the front of the 'A' post.

With the rear of the flitch cut away, access is greatly improved to the spot welds which will have to be drilled out.

to be refitted to check flitch alignment at a later stage), remove the front wing(s), and remove the spare wheel. According to the model being worked on, and which side of the car is being attended to, remove any wiring, piping and components from the vicinity.

Strip the front suspension and brakes. On MacPherson strut cars, support the frame head from under the car and remove the strut complete. Remove the three large bolts which hold the steering box. Before starting to hack away at the offending flitch panel, make up a measuring device with which you can fix the distance between two suspension strut holes (MacPherson strut models), or two fixed points on the flitches, to help later with correct alignment of the new panel. The ideal measuring device is a length of box section steel with holes drilled to correspond with the MacPherson strut holes in the flitch or, alternatively, for torsion bar cars, holes which you drill (accurately measuring for the hole placement in the new flitch) and which can later be filled with weld. You can run nuts and bolts through these holes, which not only positively locate the flitch, but also hold it firmly in position whilst welding is carried out. Alternatively, a series of measurements could be taken.

The flitch panel should be cut away in stages, starting at the top and working slowly downward, at all times taking care not to hack through the various lips of adjoining panels. The photographs illustrate this process. As sections of the old flitch are removed, compare them with the replacement sections, and salvage any brackets or other fittings which may be absent from the new panels.

The flitch is generally joined to adjacent steel by spot welds, which have to be partially drilled and then split. Try to avoid drilling holes right through any lip which is visible from within the luggage compartment, because the holes will later

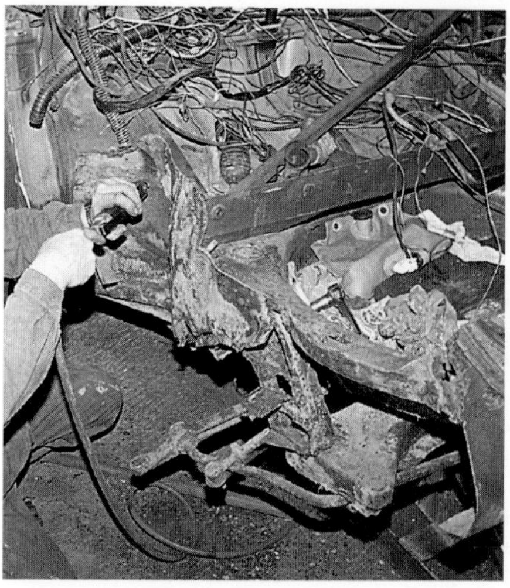

Now a cut is made underneath the welded lip. This part of the flitch forms the footwell side panel.

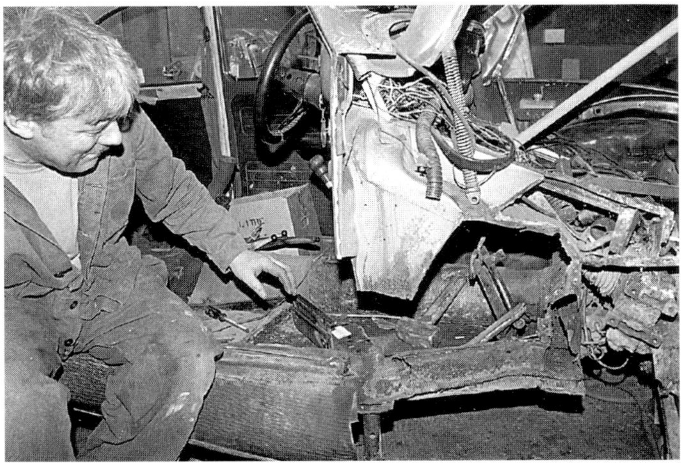

With the flitch fully removed, Terry is left wondering what he has let himself in for - rot as far as the eye can see!

The new flitch being spot welded into position. Note the cross brace, which has been refitted to precisely locate the flitch. Failure to do this could result in the suspension strut being fitted at an angle, ruining the suspension geometry

The flitch removal process is broadly similar on a non-MacPherson strut Beetle. Here, Terry is cutting down the top of the internal reinforcing bracket.

Having cut alongside the bracket lip, Terry moves on to the rear of the panel. The folded seam at the rear of the flitch isn't easy to deal with, but start by cutting as close to it as you can.

Then cut the join between the flitch and the scuttle.

have to be filled with weld and ground down. Prise open the 'A' post folded seam to remove the flitch rear lip.

When the panel has been removed, examine all newly-exposed metal, particularly enclosed box sections, the 'A' post base, heater channel, and front panel. If these show signs of severe rusting they should be replaced, otherwise take the opportunity to apply rust-preventative measures and clean the edges to which the flitch will be welded.

Offer the flitch into place and check that it is accurately positioned, using both the measuring device you made earlier and by lowering the luggage compartment lid to check for any gaps or misalignment. Be prepared to spend some time getting the flitch in the correct position, because even the best repair panels can be problematic.

Also fit the bumper irons and check they're in alignment. If the bodyshell has been removed from the car for heater channel renewal, also fit the doors and check the gaps; if the gaps are uneven or the door fouls its aperture, this might have to be corrected by moving the 'A' post bottom end relative to the heater channel (if the two have not already been welded). Clamp the flitch tightly into position, lower the luggage compartment lid, and check that the two align correctly.

When you're satisfied that the flitch is in the correct position, clean the areas which are to be welded and apply weldable zinc paint. Fold the 'A' post seam back over the flitch rear lip with a hammer and dolly, and check that the curvature of the flitch is correct. Then begin welding the flitch panel

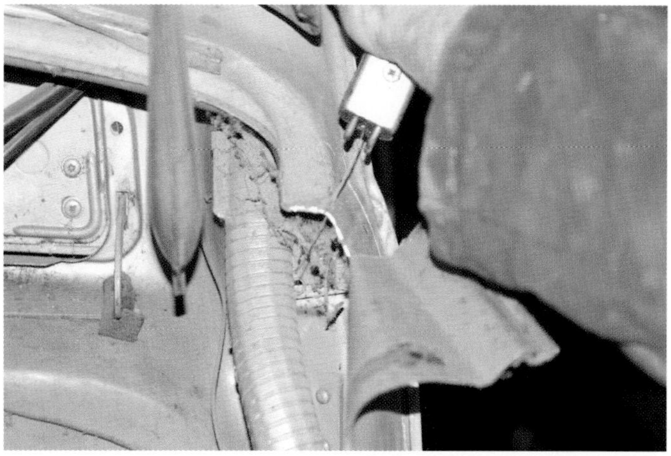

With the flitch panel top folded out of the way, cut alongside the scuttle outer edge.

Cutting the section of the flitch that forms the footwell side panel. Take care not to cut the seam on the 'A' post.

With the bulk of the flitch panel cut away, you can get a spot weld cutter to all the spot welds.

There are different ways of dealing with spot welds, one of which is to use normal twist bits to drill them out. This is the method to use when you need holes on the remaining steel through which to plug weld. Use a pilot bit, followed by a larger one.

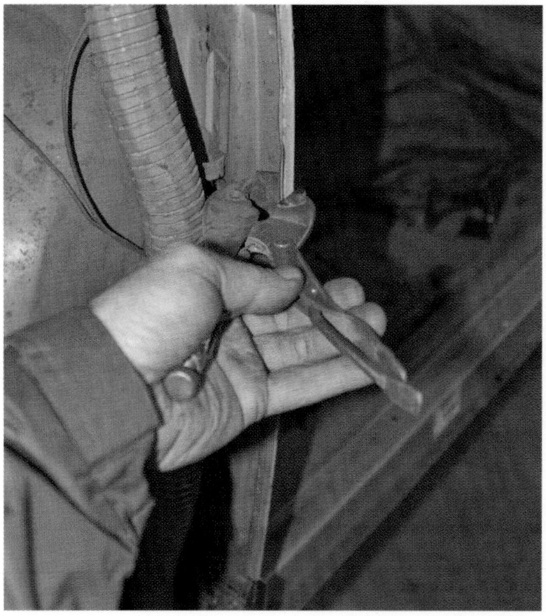

Terry made up a tool for unfolding the seam at the rear of the flitch panel. It's a simple blade, welded to one jaw of a self-locking wrench.

It can be very difficult to find spot weld marks in rusted steel. Giving the surface a vigorous wire brushing can help.

Some of the spot welds are very close together - a technique known as 'stitch' welding - which makes drilling out the spot welds impractical. This is the bulkhead edge, and the only practical way of dealing with the welds is to grind away the remnants of the flitch. Start by cleaning the area so that you can see the welds.

Flitch panels for early Beetles can be hard to come by but, in the UK, companies like VW Heritage - which supplied this panel - can sometimes come to the rescue. The 'L'-shaped fuel tank support bracket will not be needed, and will have to be removed.

Grinding down the stitch spot welded steel. Note that the angle grinder is being held so that the sparks fly downward; always a good idea.

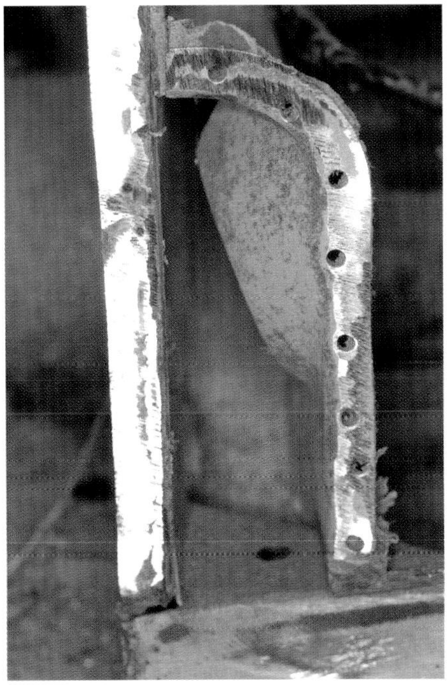

The result of all that hard work. A toe board and bulkhead virtually ready to weld to.

When you have to true-up edges to make them lie flat, always use a dolly, or you'll distort the steel.

There are many commercially available anti-rust preparations, but none is really better than grease!

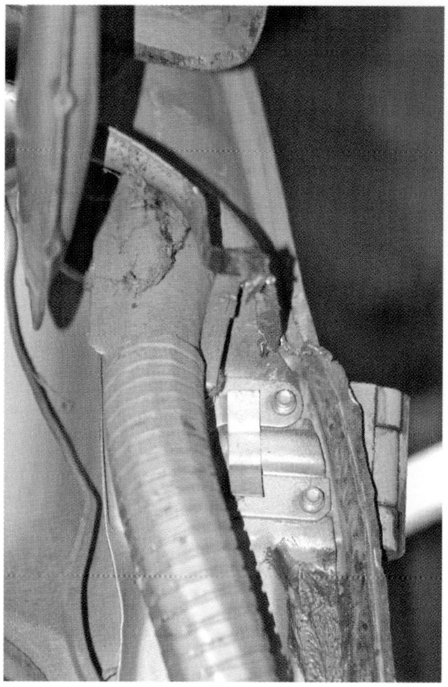

With a little bit more grinding, the scuttle will be ready to weld to the new flitch.

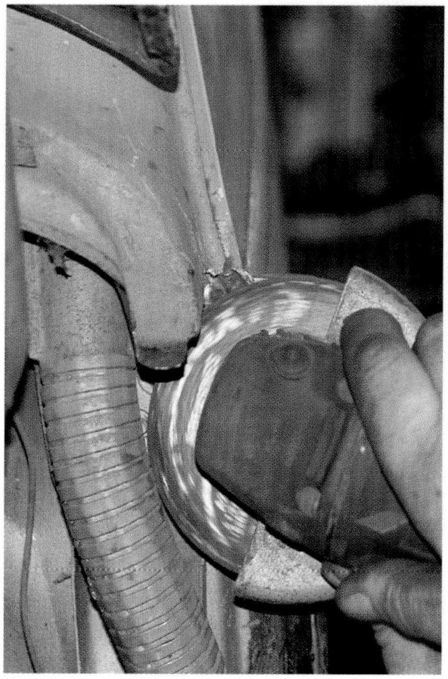

It is difficult to grind away the last vestiges of flitch where it is welded to the scuttle. Wear gloves to protect your hands.

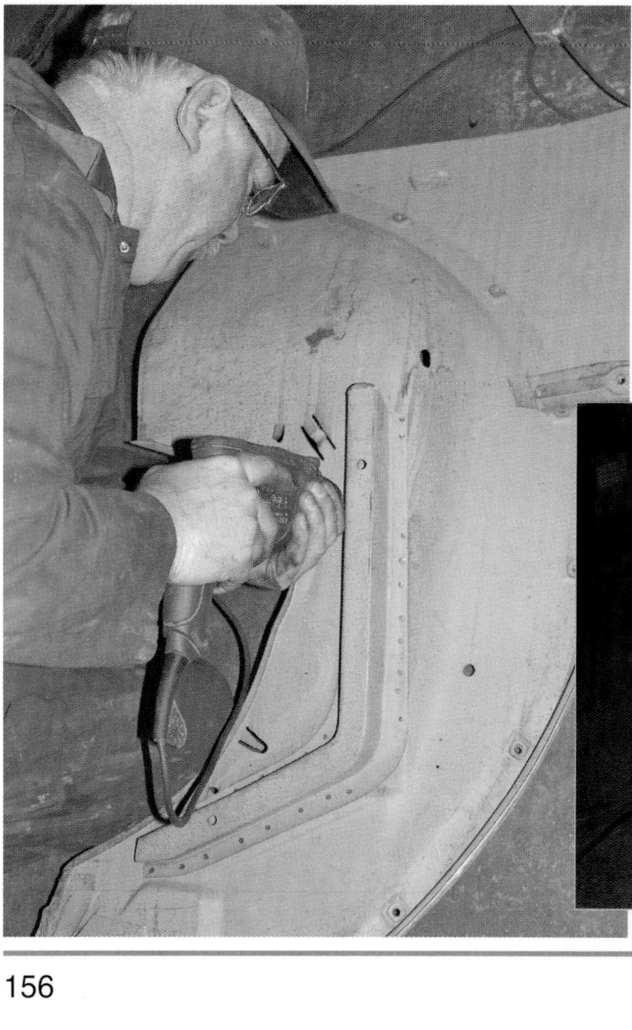

The replacement flitch panel fuel tank support bracket is superfluous in this instance, and has to be removed. Rather than drill right through both layers of steel, Terry is using a spot weld drill bit, which has a tiny pilot section at the end to keep it from wandering, and a hard shoulder that acts like a milling bit, removing just the top layer of the spot welded joint.

The right-hand flitch has been cut away and its replacement offered into position, and the leading edge of the left-hand flitch has been cut away to improve access for fitting the spare wheel well floor. It's important to leave one flitch in position while the other is fitted, as a datum point.

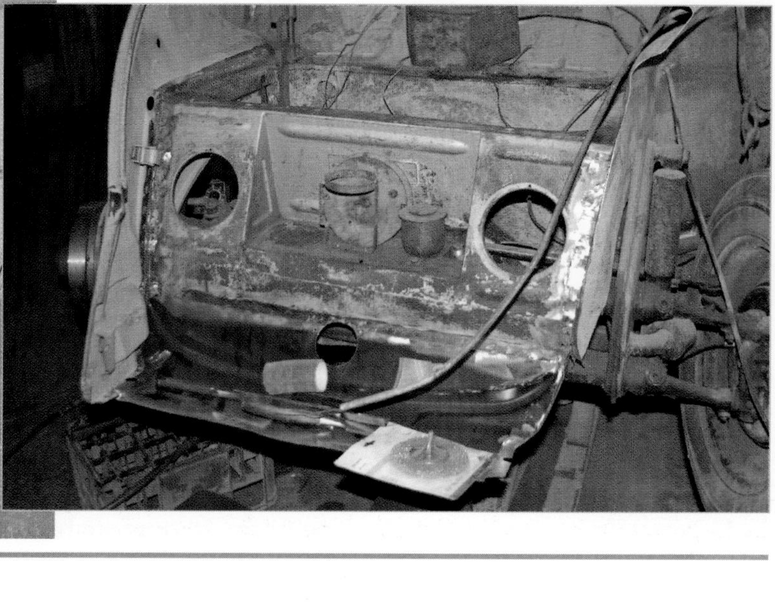

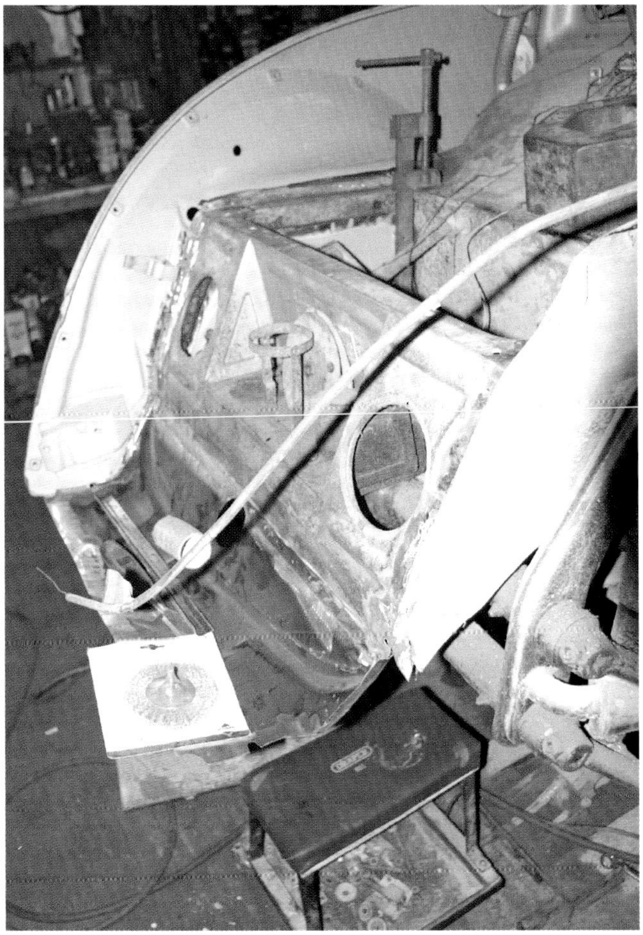

Above: This car had suffered a minor front end collision, the upshot of which was stress in the various pressings which caused the front, right-hand side to want to lift - hence the sash cramp to tether the framing to the chassis while the flitch goes on. Failure to spot something like this means the rebuilt car will have a front end that resembles a broken nose!

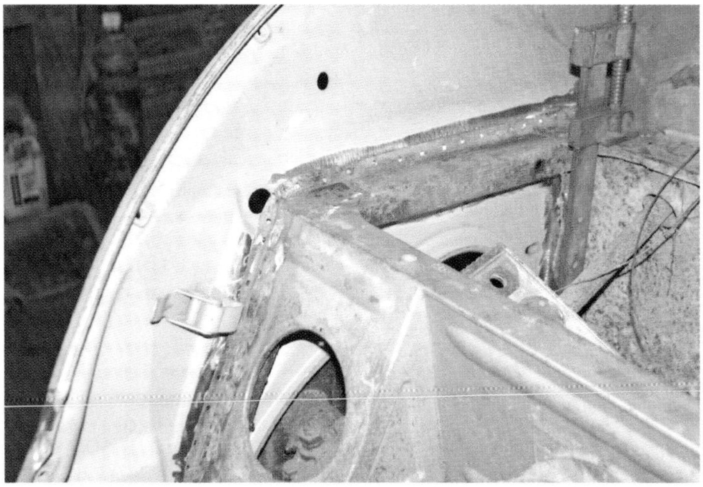

Inside, the flitch is not welded at all until alignment has been checked.

Inside the right-hand footwell, the flitch is a good fit against the lips to which it will finally be welded.

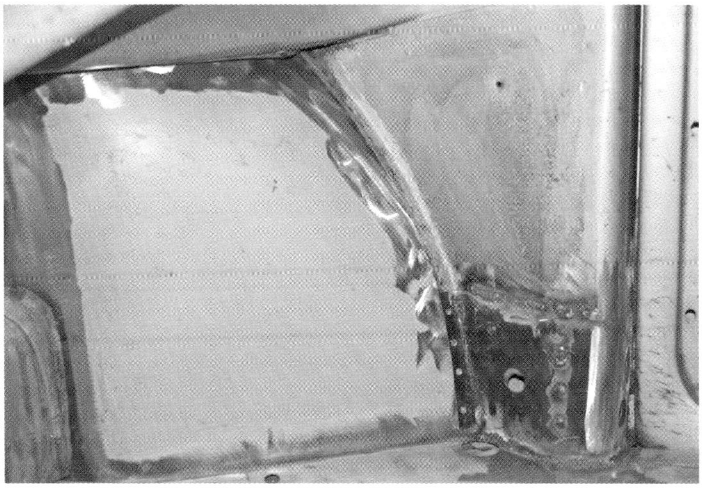

Left: Seasoned welders are usually fairly inventive when it comes to pulling panels tightly together for welding. Here, Terry is using a lever to pull the flitch tight against the luggage bay side bracket lip; if this isn't done before welding, chances are you'll burn holes in one of them.

The joint between the flitch rear top and the scuttle is best brazed; braze is soft and easily shaped to restore the sharp edge, whereas weld is too hard.

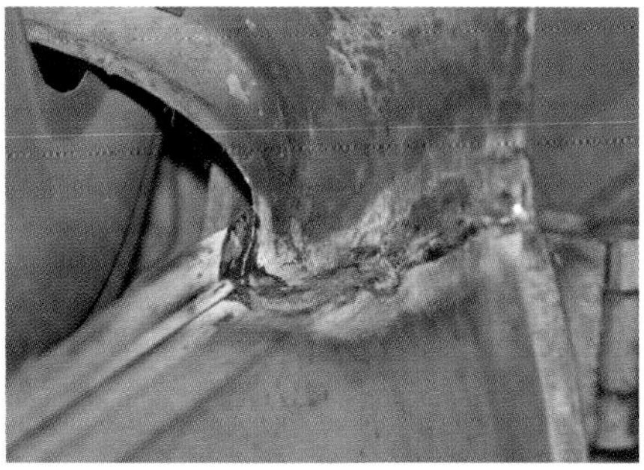

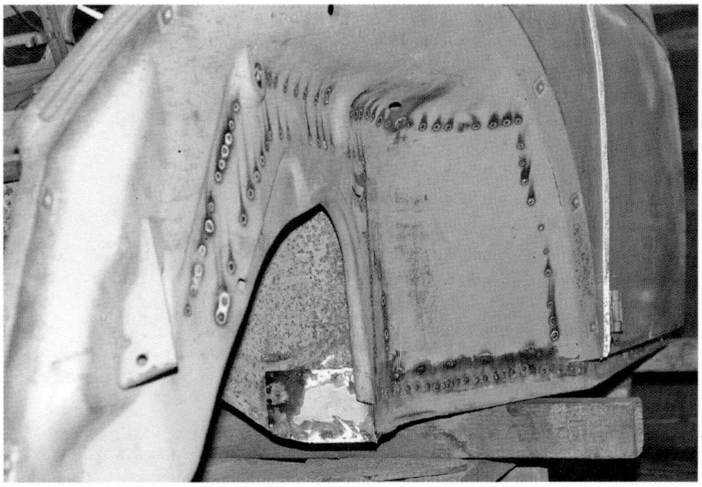

The plug welds on the flitch panel even resemble spot welds. Painted, they will be almost indistinguishable from the originals.

Before welding the new flitch, build up the front end of the car to check that all panels will fit. It's good policy to fit the bumper irons and check they point in the same direction, as well.

The right-hand edge lip of the bulkhead had been weakened through rusting, so a length of folded steel has been used to replace it. Make sure that the welds are good and strong, or you'll find the flitch will flap around, and eventually the other seams will start to work-harden and weaken.

Before welding on the flitch, fit the bumper brackets and bumpers: it's easy to get the flitch slightly askew otherwise, which makes fitting the bumpers a nightmare.

in place. If you don't have access to a spot welder and the appropriate arms, you could use plug welds instead; as many and as close together as the originals.

FLITCH REPAIR PANELS

The flitch panels (inner front wings) often rot out at the lower front ends, and repair panels are available for this.

Remove the front wings, fuel tank, and any wiring in the vicinity. As ever, first clean the affected area so that you can determine the extent of the rot in the existing panels before deciding whether to fit the full repair panel or to tailor it. Gently drill out the spot welds holding the luggage lid seal retaining strip and remove this; the chances are that the flitch steel underneath will show some sign of rusting, so clean and later treat this area with weldable zinc paint before fitting a new seal retainer strip.

Drill and part the spot welds to the valance and spare wheel well - the flitch end should now be free and can be cut away. Most people favour an overlapped

Bolt the flitch repair panel into position to mark the cutting line. If possible, cut down this repair panel (if you can still find clean steel to weld to) so that, if you ever have to repeat the exercise, you can use the same sized repair panel and fit it full height.

Seen from inside the cab, a cutting line for the lower flitch repair panel can be found by scribing along the bottom of the existing flitch, then allowing some extra to create a stepped edge.

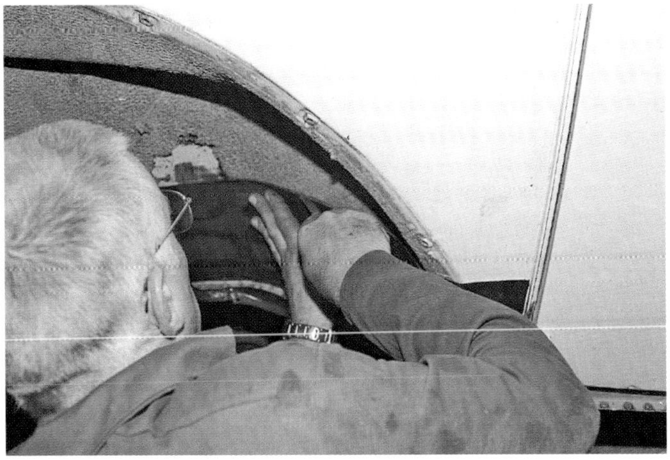

First, Terry scribes a line to mark the height of the repair panel on what's left of the existing panel.

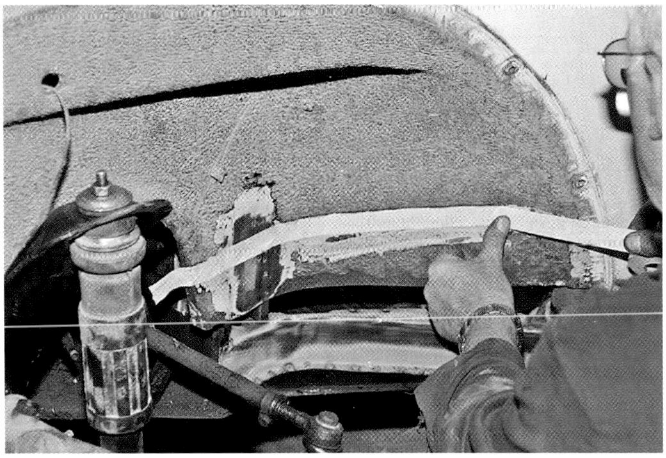

Scribed lines are difficult to see when you try to cut along them, so Terry makes the line more easily visible with masking tape.

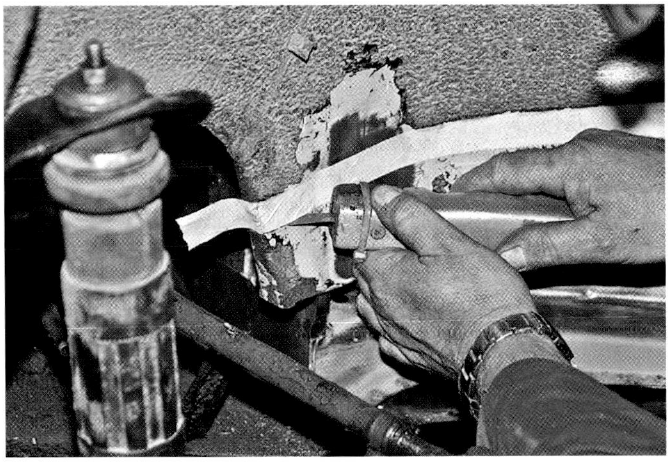

Cutting along the bottom edge of the masking tape leaves a gap between the cut and the scribed line, which will form an overlapping section.

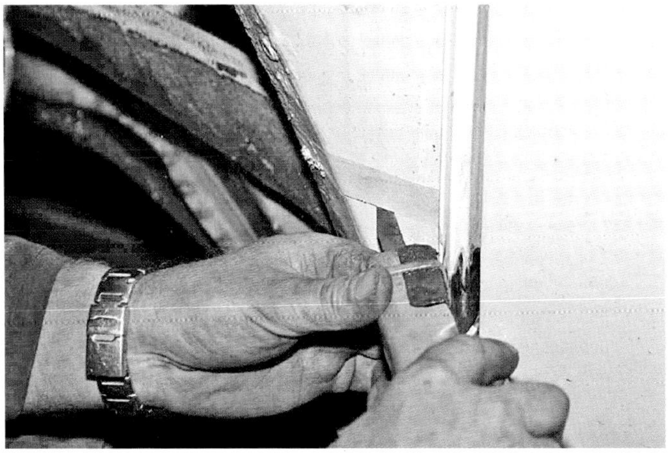

Be careful when cutting around the 'A' post - you don't want to cut into the steel underneath. Have a helper hold the wiring loom out of harm's way, as well.

Rather than cut straight up the flange, Terry prefers to cut away from it, as shown.

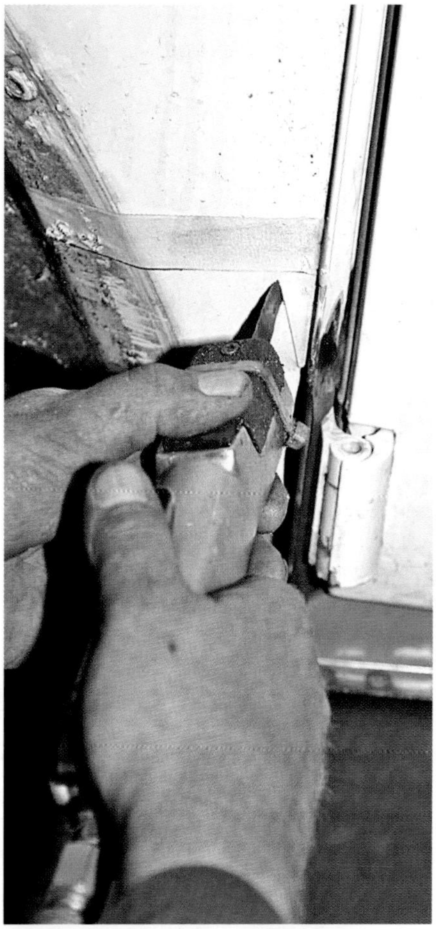

Having cleaned paint from the areas to be welded, Terry begins the (tiresome) task of punching out holes in the repair panel for plug welding.

Terry then punches a line of holes in the lower edge of the existing steel, so that there will be two parallel lines of plug welds joining the two, and increasing the stiffness of the flitch.

Drill out the spot welds.

joint between the flitch and the repair panel: it could be butt welded, but the extra strength of an overlapped joint favours this method.

Tack the repair panel into position and check the wing and luggage compartment lid fit (adjust the position of the repair panel if necessary), before welding the flitch, using continuous seam MIG welds.

SPARE WHEEL WELL

The spare wheel well will often be found to be rotten, due to water being allowed to lie in the base for long periods. Small areas of rot in the base may be patch repaired (remove all wiring from the vicinity, plus the fuel tank and line), and a full repair panel is also available for cars with more widespread rot.

However, if a full spare wheel well

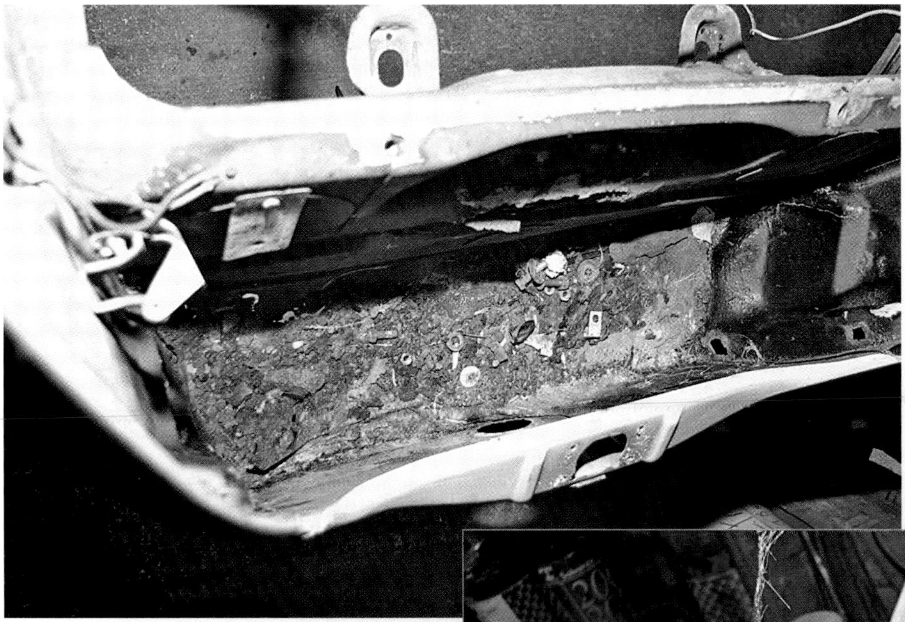

This spare wheel well has been very poorly repaired on more than one occasion, as will be evident when panels are cut away.

panel is required, the chances are that one or both flitch panels also require repair or replacement. It's recommended that these are attended to first, and the existing spare wheel well/front valance left *in situ* throughout to help locate the flitch or the flitch lower front repair panel. There is a temptation to cut away everything to improve access, and then try to reconstruct the front end using the luggage compartment lid and wings to locate panels. The author has seen more than one lopsided Beetle as a result of this technique: you have been warned ...

Remove the fuel tank, and all wiring from the vicinity. Drill out the spot welds

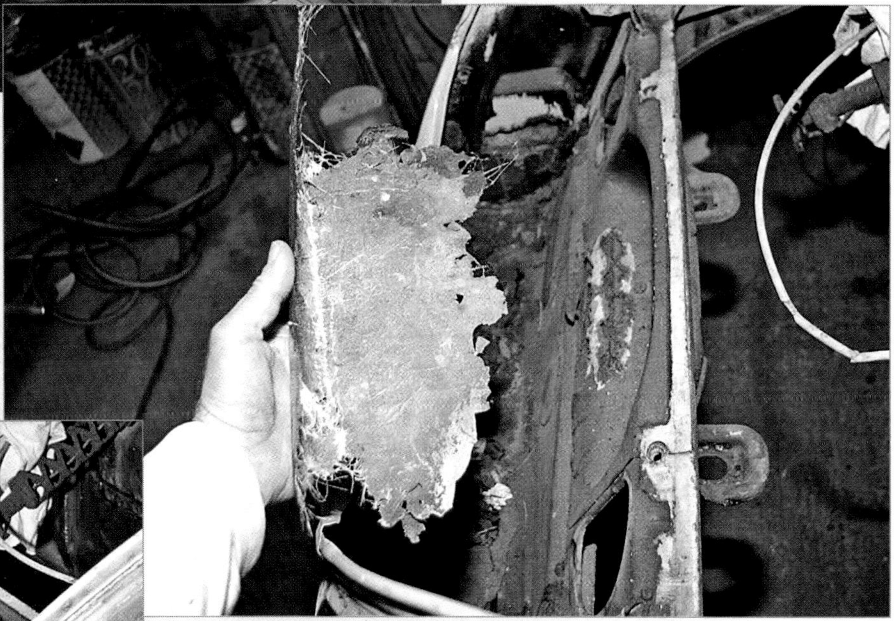

The most recent repair involved laying up chopped strand mat and resin along the disintegrating front lower edge. The panel it was attached to was not the original, but the result of an earlier shoddy repair.

The front valance is to be replaced, along with the sections of the flitch panels attached to it, so Terry first cuts out the old valance to gain access.

from the original spare wheel well panel edge flanges, then part the joints as gently as possible to avoid distorting the metal to which the new flanges will be welded. Because the original seam spot weld lines are easily visible, locating the new panel should pose no problem. Seam or plug weld the new panel into position, working a short length at a time, and allowing the steel to cool to avoid buckling.

continued on page 168

As the valance is pulled away, more GRP repair is revealed, along with the fact that there are two layers of steel (or the remains thereof) at the bottom of the well, and that there's a non-standard ridge in the back wall of the well.

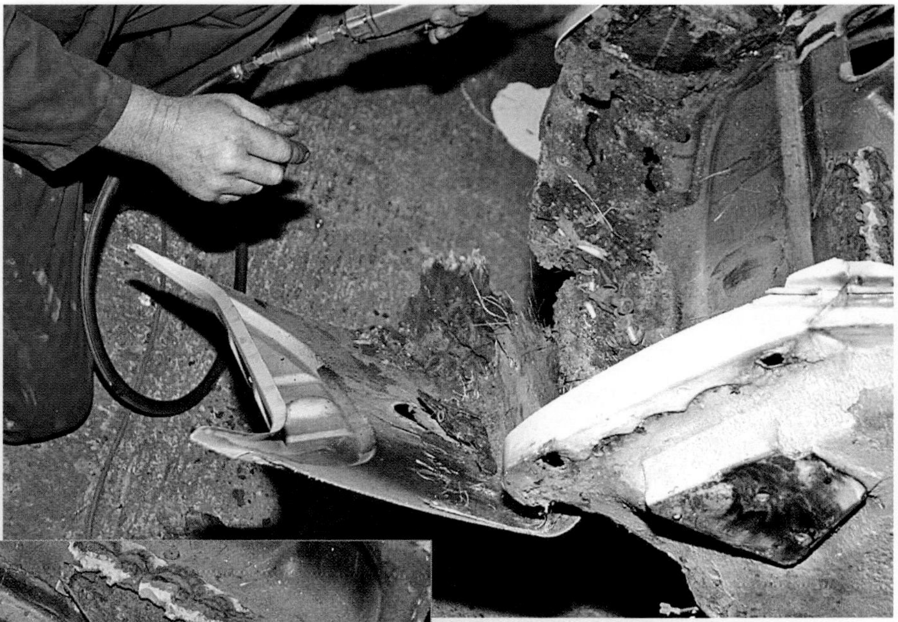

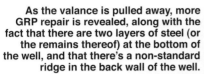

Again, in the interest of improving access, Terry cut away the steel at the bottom of the well ...

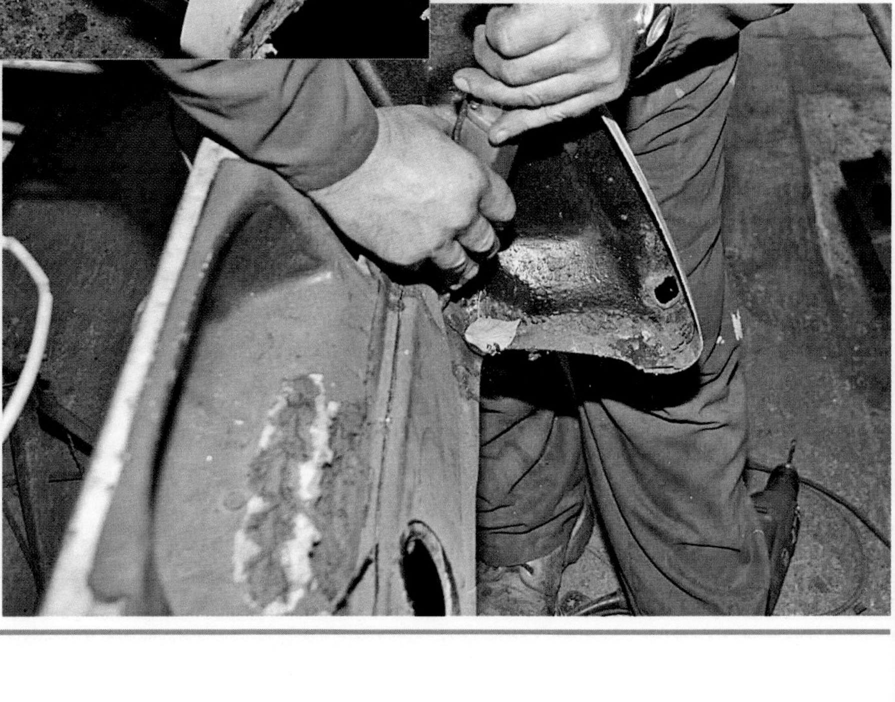

... then across the top of the unconventionally placed panel, and down the sides.

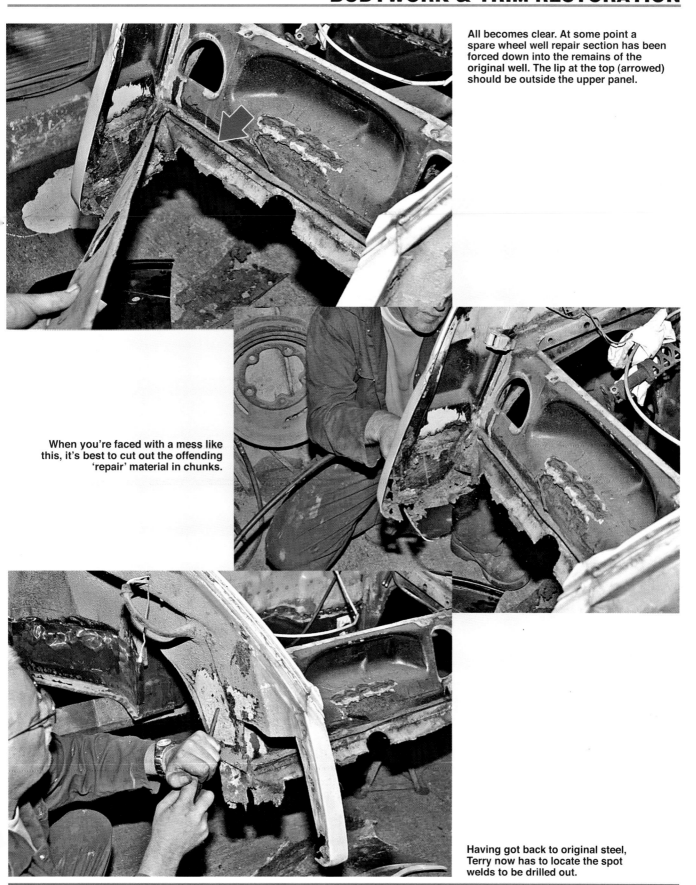

All becomes clear. At some point a spare wheel well repair section has been forced down into the remains of the original well. The lip at the top (arrowed) should be outside the upper panel.

When you're faced with a mess like this, it's best to cut out the offending 'repair' material in chunks.

Having got back to original steel, Terry now has to locate the spot welds to be drilled out.

The misplaced spare wheel well repair panel has been welded to the remains of the original with three seam welds - one each side and one length in the middle. Terry grinds away the weld.

This won't be the actual join line. It's a preliminary cut line that will allow the repair section to be offered up (bolted on by one wing bolt) to show where the best cutting line will be for both original steel and repair section.

The washer bottle recess panel is thoroughly rotten and will be renewed, so the spot welds are carefully drilled out

There are also 4 spot welds in the centre of the washer bottle recess. Terry drills right through these, and the fuel tank support pressing underneath, allowing the new washer bottle recess panel to be spot welded from underneath. Result: invisible welds.

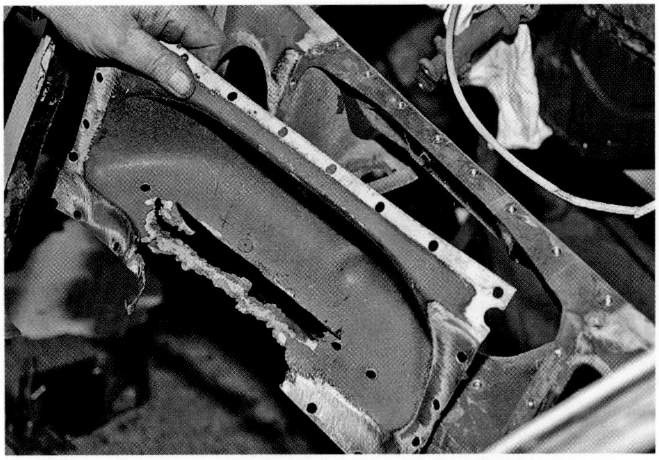

The washer bottle recess panel is scrap, but, when removing it, Terry took great care not to distort the panels that the new one will be welded to.

You can buy complete front reinforcing repair panels, which include the washer bottle recess and spare wheel well floor. If you do opt for a complete panel, ensure it has the two 'D'-shaped holes, which give access to the steering box and idler.

However much care you take when parting spot welded panels, there's still a little work to be done with the hammer and dolly to true-up the edge of the remaining steel.

Before the new valance is welded in, take the opportunity to drill holes for self-tapping screws - it's too tight to get a drill in after the valance has been welded on.

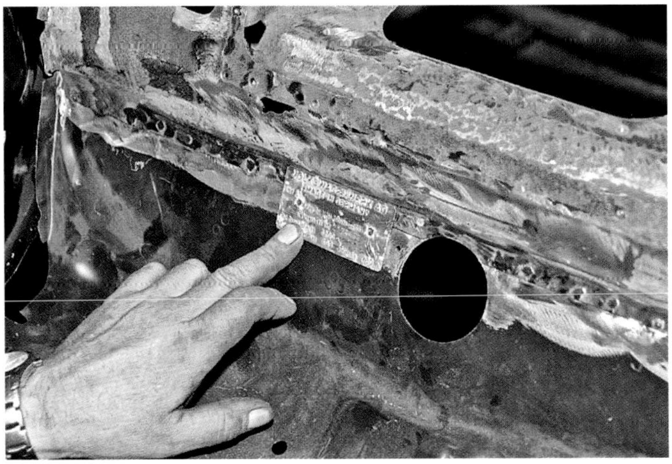

Also drill holes to mount the VIN plate. Many forget to do this, and have to mount the plate on the sloping section above, because it's the only place they can get a drill to.

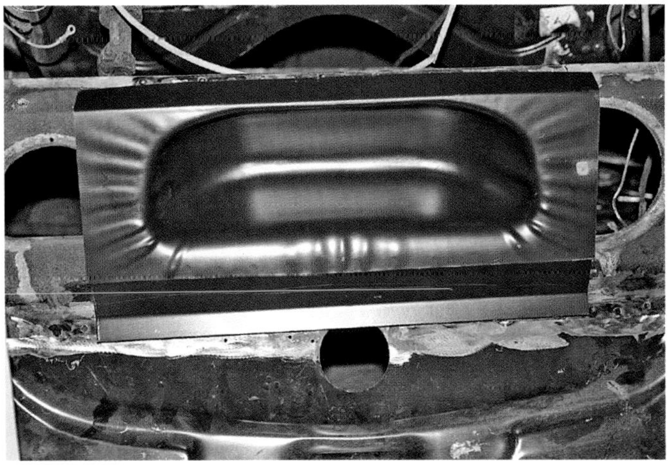

In the UK, VW Heritage offers an oversized repair panel for the windscreen washer bottle recess. It is best to cut down the panel to the size of the original, if rot extent in the surrounding panel allows it.

First, Terry scribes lines to show the width of the original panel (which will be covered up when the repair panel is offered up for sizing).

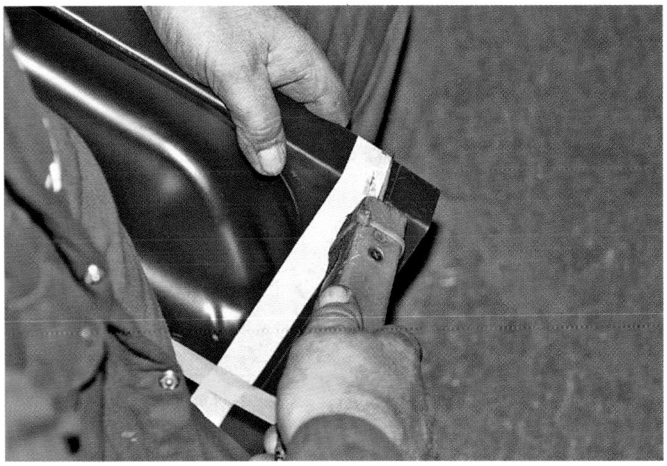

Having marked the repair panel, Terry, as usual, enhances the marks with masking tape, which is a lot easier to see than scratched lines.

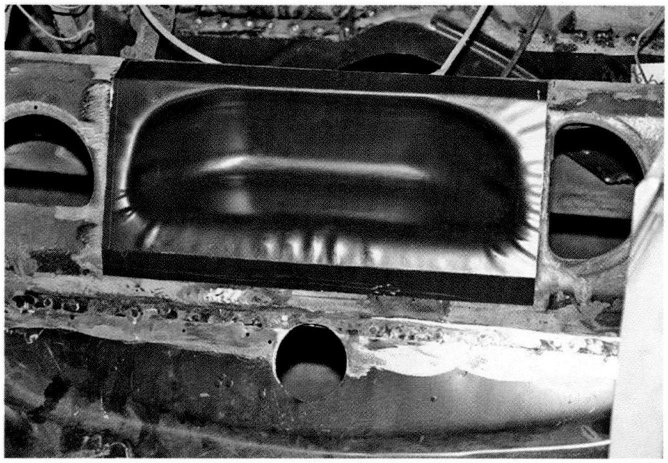

The panel has been cut to the original width, but is deeper because there's some rot immediately underneath which has to be cut out. The finished job will look much better if the creases in the panel are gently beaten out.

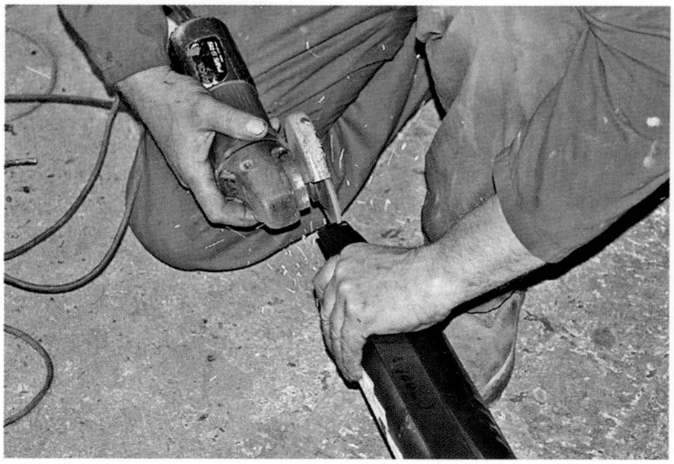

The panel overlaps two threaded holes for fuel tank clamp bolts, and so small semi-circles are ground out.

It was not possible to beat out all of the creases without risking buckling the panel, though the most visible areas are nicely flat. The alternative is to fit a complete 'front reinforcement panel' - also available via VW Heritage - albeit at high cost and far more work!

The washer bottle recess panel repair complete. It might be possible to reduce the remaining creases further with a hammer and dolly.

All that remains is to grind level the plug welds.

The lower front flitch repair panel part welded in. Note that the top joint is a butt joint, so that the part visible inside the luggage bay lid is perfectly flush.

To ensure that the flitches are at the same height, bolt up the bumpers and brackets and place a spirit level across the brackets - check that the shell is level first!

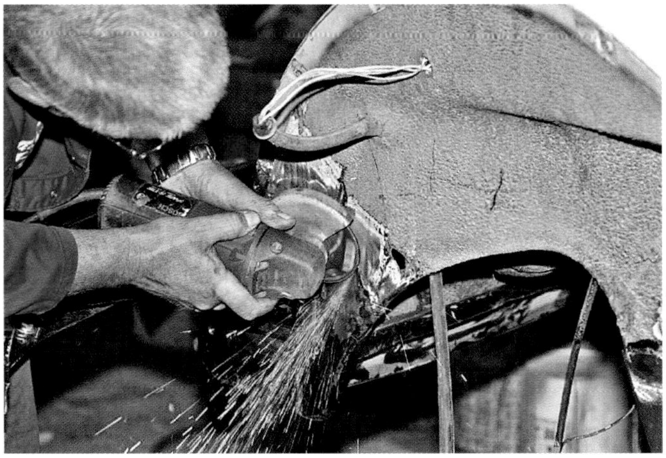

The secret of making invisible butt joints is to leave a tiny gap between the two panels, which fills with weld. Surplus weld can then be ground off both sides.

The repair panel overlaps the original steel, so when Terry cuts through both simultaneously, he creates a gap the width of a hacksaw blade that will fill with weld and allow both sides to be ground level.

When cutting off the last of the surplus from the repair panel, take care not to cut into the framework underneath.

Before welding the second flitch repair panel, take time to measure the distance from the bumper to the panel at the rear of the spare wheel well - it must be equal each side.

A replacement front panel offered up looked good until Terry noticed that the hole in the front was too large and lacked the step necessary to fit the blanking plate levelly. Many replacement front panels appear to be the same so, if you want an authentic Beetle and, more importantly, if you ever want to get out the gear linkage rod, make sure you use a good quality repair panel.

In the event, none of the regular suppliers had front panels with the aperture as it should be, so a section was cut out of the original and spot welded on.

The flitch front end repair panel, and the front panel joints, should be treated with seam sealer.

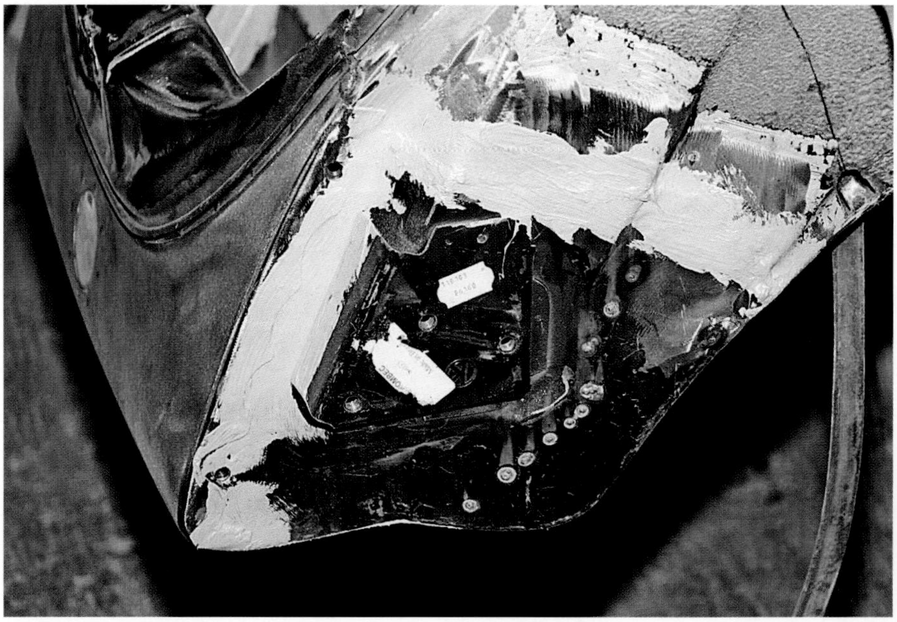

REMOVAL OF BODYSHELL FROM CHASSIS

This task can be accomplished single-handed, but it's recommended that four strong adults are on hand to do the lifting, plus an observer to shout out if you forget to remove or disconnect anything during the preparation.

The most common reason for parting the body and chassis is floor pan repair or replacement. If the floor pan has rotted sufficiently to require this, the heater channel/sill assembly is certain to have rotted also, and vice-versa. It's vital that the heater channels are replaced ONLY with the bodyshell *in situ* on the chassis, so that the bolt holes of the two can be correctly aligned.

If the heater channels are in poor condition, bolt or weld stiffening braces across the door apertures and between the 'A' posts to prevent the shell from distorting as it is lifted. BSW has made up a simple rectangular jig that bolts to the lower 'A' and 'B' posts to keep the shell in shape. Leave the rear seat support in position throughout.

Remove the seats, battery, fuel tank, and wings, then bleed dry the entire braking system before removing the flexible brake hoses. On McPherson strut models, support the frame head and remove the strut assembly from the wheelarch. Disconnect the wiring in the engine bay, including the oil light, ignition, and reversing light wire, if fitted, and disconnect the speedometer cable.

Underneath the fuel tank there are two holes in which you'll find 17mm-headed bolts which are the front body work mounts; remove them and also disconnect the brake master cylinder pipes. Remove the nuts and bolts from the steering column bottom flange (early torsion bar cars), or the clamp bolt on later cars.

Remove the 17mm-headed rear body mounting bolts from within the rear wheelarch, the two from the front of the heater channels and the 8mm-headed bolts which run along the heater channels. It's likely that some of the captive threaded plates into which the 8mm bolts run will break free from their position inside the heater channels; grind off the heads of the bolts concerned. Some bolts will shear; leave these until later, when the bodyshell is off. Even if you are replacing the floor pan and heater channels, be sure to keep the rectangular-shaped outer washers from the heater channel/floor pan fixing bolts.

From inside the car, first remove the rear seat (leave the support in place to help brace the body), then the four bolts from the spine. Disconnect the heat exchanger ducts. Disconnect the starter solenoid wires and the red/white wire running from the battery to the regulator. Disconnect the earth strap. Remove the front seats.

On the 1302/3 series cars, remove the steering stabiliser bolt under the spare

Having the right tool makes any job easier. With this car hoist, one person can easily lift a bodyshell but, if you're doing it manually, it's best to have four people to do the lifting.

At the front, the bodyshell position is dictated by the two front mounting bolts, which run into threaded holes in the beam axle.

wheel, and also the two adjacent 17mm-headed bolts which run into the frame head and, from inside the car, the two bolts at the top front of the tunnel. Split the track rod end ball joints and tie the track rod ends out of harm's way.

It is a good idea, if you've not already done so, to internally brace the bodyshell before lifting it, by welding lengths of box section steel across the door apertures and between the two 'A' post bases.

As a matter of course, it pays to renew all brake pipes and the fuel pipe with copper/nickel alternatives while the body is off the car. The steel originals do rust and burst brake pipes or a leaking fuel line represent obvious dangers.

The less you have to lift the bodyshell skyward the better, so always remove

Remove the heater ducting. If the crossmember is really rotten, the bolts running into the captive nuts (arrowed here) may well be seized and need drilling out.

This framework bolted to the bodyshell is keeping the bodyshell true while the heater channels are cut away.

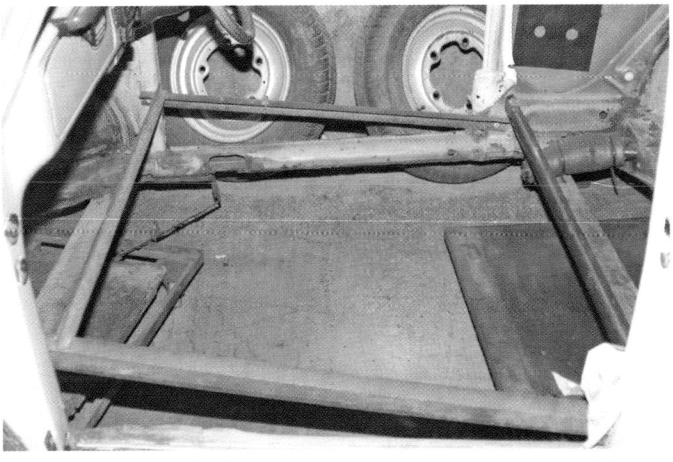

Floor edge repair panels are available, and are not only cheaper but also easier to fit than complete panels, though the latter are still infinitely preferable.

Although this floor pan and rear crossmember appeared reasonably sound, both are rusted and fairly thin. If you want to keep your restored Beetle, seriously consider renewing panelwork like this.

After the driver's side floor pan has been renewed, it will be necessary to weld on the pedal assembly strengthener, cut from the old floor pan.

the front seats. Also seriously consider removing the engine as this reduces the chance of damaging it when the body is lifted away. Rather than moving the bodyshell away from the chassis, you can make up supports (trestles are ideal) so that one end of the body can be lifted at a time and beams fitted between the supports. The chassis can then be wheeled out from underneath the bodyshell.

FLOOR PAN REPAIR/REPLACEMENT

Determine the extent of rot by thoroughly cleaning the floor pan/chassis assembly top and bottom. Be quite brutal when probing for rot (use a pointed panel beaters' hammer), because a sound-looking spine can, in fact, be very weak if it has rotted from within, and floor pans covered with sound-looking underseal can be heavily rotted underneath. Terry Ball found an apparently perfect pair of floor pans which turned out, on closer inspection, to be mainly beautifully-finished GRP, so don't go by looks alone - probe. If rot is found to extend up into the chassis spine, it may be best to scrap the chassis and either use a new one (if still available), or take one from another Beetle.

Whether to patch repair or replace the floor pans should be decided according to the extent of the rot and, more importantly, to whether you want to have to repeat the repair at some point in the future! If you patch it, sooner or later more patching will be required. Bear in mind that repaired panels usually rot first along welded seams so, if you choose to turn the floor pans into a kind of welded patchwork quilt, they will rot all over in double-quick time! Replace the lot, properly rustproof it, and the floor should last as long as the car.

Floor pan repair

If the engine has been stripped from the chassis (as it should), it's a small matter to turn the chassis on its side so that you can get at the underside of the floor pans. If money is very tight and repair is the only option, begin by cleaning both floor pans back to bare metal so that you can find every trace of rot. If possible, make use of proper repair panels and, for the sake of strength, use an overlapped joint continuously seam welded both top and bottom. Rot most frequently occurs at the floor pan outer edges, for which complete, front and rear half repair panels are available.

Combined floor pan halves/heater channel replacement

If the floor pan has rotted, it follows that the heater channels will have, too, and will need to be replaced. It's essential that this work is carried out in the correct sequence, which is as follows:

1. Internally brace the bodyshell.
2. Lift the shell off the chassis assembly, and clean off all traces of old belly pan gasket.
3. Cut out and replace the floor pans.
4. Bolt the new heater channels onto the floor pans.
5. Cut away old heater channels from shell.

Top right: The lip of the spine chassis should be cleaned bright before the floor pans are welded in. Check there are no remnants of spot weld on the lips (grind them flat), and that the lips are straight. True-up the lips with a hammer and dolly if not.

Middle right: The two large holes in the central chassis support are for the bolts that fit into the captive nuts within the heater channel. It's worth bolting the heater channel into place before welding on the floor pan, to ensure that the floor pan holes align with the other captive nuts in the heater channel.

Bottom right: The outer ends of the rear chassis support legs (arrowed) might need patch repairing. Alternatively, you may be able to find floor pans with this pressing already attached.

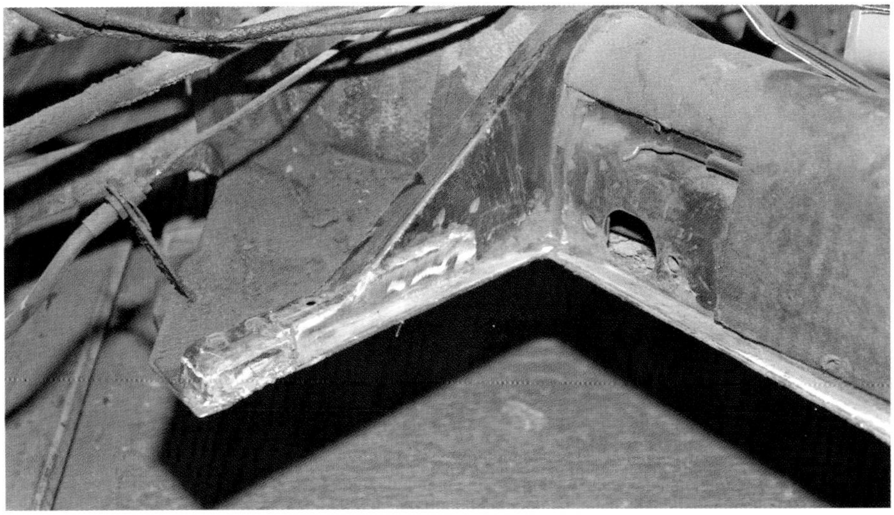

6. Lift shell back onto chassis.
7. Weld shell to heater channels.
8. Remove shell, fit gasket, refit shell.

If the front and rear crossmembers (toe board and heel board) are to be renewed, add an extra step between 4. and 5: Weld cross members to heater channels.

Renewing the heater channels using the method outlined is an awful lot of work, and some people take the shortcut of not parting the bodyshell and chassis, preferring, instead, to hack out the heater channels, push the floor edge downward, jam in new heater channels, and weld them in. The problem with this method is that the belly pan gasket will be damaged either when the old heater channel is pulled out, the new one pushed in, or from the heat generated when the new heater channel is welded. The belly pan gasket seals between the floor pans and the heater channels - if it gets damaged, the new heater channels will rust away in record time.

To do the job properly, first strip the interior of the car. Weld braces across the door apertures and between the two 'A' posts so that the shell will keep its shape after the old heater channels have been cut out. Lift off the shell. The shell can be supported on bars between two trestles (which allows the chassis to be rolled out from underneath), or it can be laid on its side on top of lots of padding. Clean all traces of the old belly pan gasket from the chassis assembly.

To cut out the floor pans, an air hacksaw is ideal, but an air chisel could also be used if you can stand the noise! Take care not to cut into, nor distort, the flange between the spine chassis top and base sections. At the rear of the floor pans, take care not to damage, nor distort, the bracket from the damper mounting.

Then, using a 1/8in bit, followed

A floor pan plug welded into place. Note the threaded rod centre picture: this is for the battery clamp bracket. If you have one, run a die up and down the stud to clean off excess paint which might otherwise cause the nut to seize.

Properly executed, plug welds are as strong as the original spot welds. Try to start the weld in the centre of the hole to make sure you have a strong weld to the underlying panel, then move the gun in a small circle to weld to the edges of the upper piece of steel.

This is typical of the state of heater channels. The lumps of MIG weld along the lower edge indicate that a new base has been badly welded on (usually over the original); the step (painted black) is also a cover. Until you cut through the channel, there's no way of knowing how many thicknesses of steel and rust scale there will be.

(if necessary) by a 3/8in bit, drill out the spot welds which fasten the old floor pan edges to the spine flange. These occur approximately every 3/4in on original floor pans. Expect to have to grind out weld at the corners. Clean the flanges.

Prepare the new floor pan by cleaning all edges which are to be welded, then spray a coat or two of weldable, zinc-based paint on the internal faces of the joint. Offer up the floor pans, and bolt them only at the rear damper mounting extension bracket; offer up the heater channels and bolt into position. The two large bolts which pass through the heater channel into the front of the chassis are then fitted, to bring both floor pans and heater channels into the correct positions.

Although the inner top and side of the heater channel are sound, the true state of the assembly is revealed by the rot in the lower part.

How difficult it is to cut off the heater channel depends on how many plates have been welded on over the years.

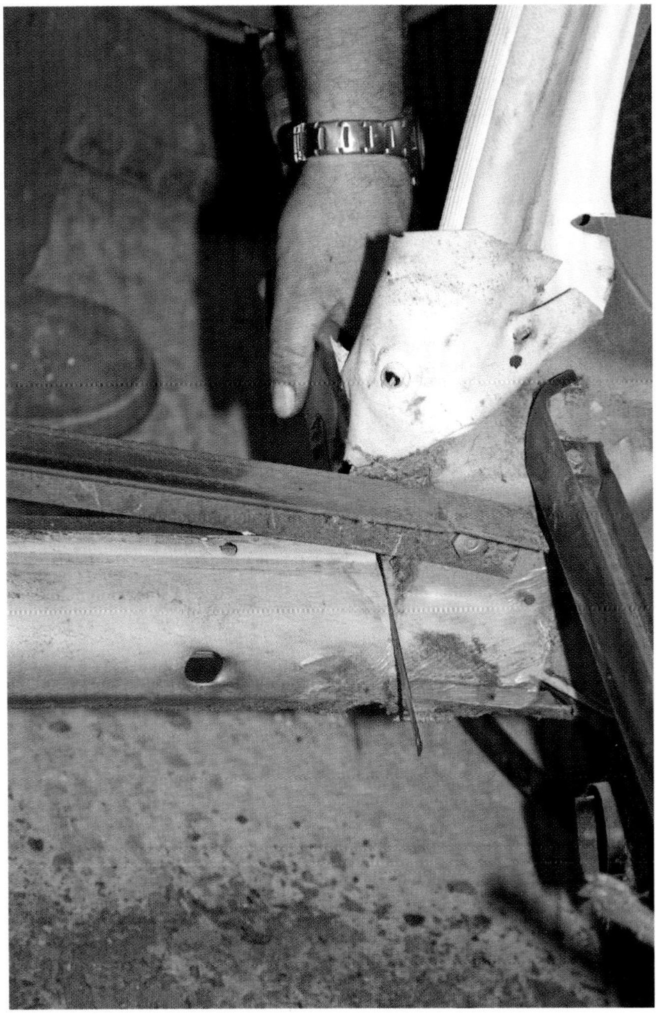

After cutting through the heater channel just behind the 'A' post, cut just in front of the 'B' post.

Left: A section through the heater channel reveals the extent of the rot and bodged repairs.

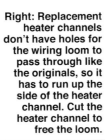

Right: Replacement heater channels don't have holes for the wiring loom to pass through like the originals, so it has to run up the side of the heater channel. Cut the heater channel to free the loom.

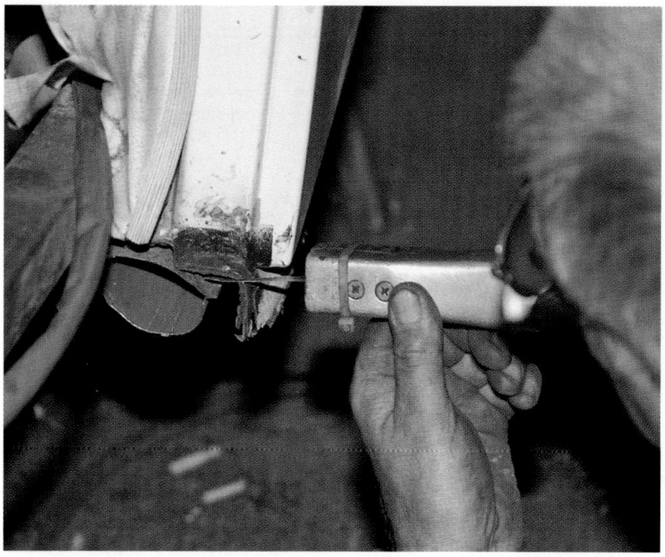

The base of the 'B' post appears sound, so will be retained, if possible. Even if the 'B' post is to be cut away and renewed, leaving the lower flange intact helps placement when the bodyshell is lowered back onto the chassis.

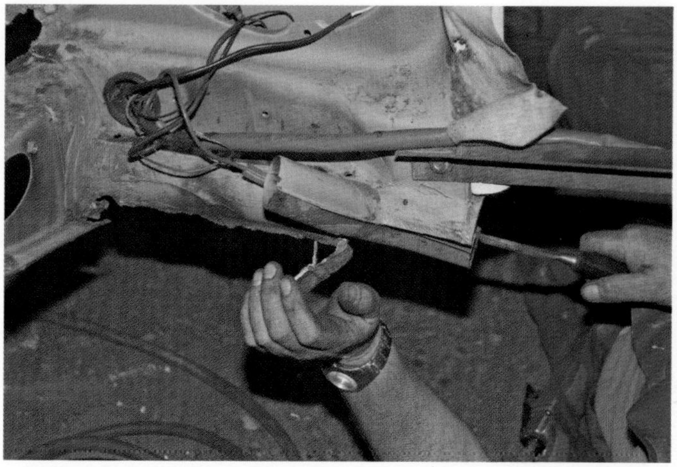

Lever out of the way as necessary the heater channel closing panel and/or welded patches to improve access for further cutting.

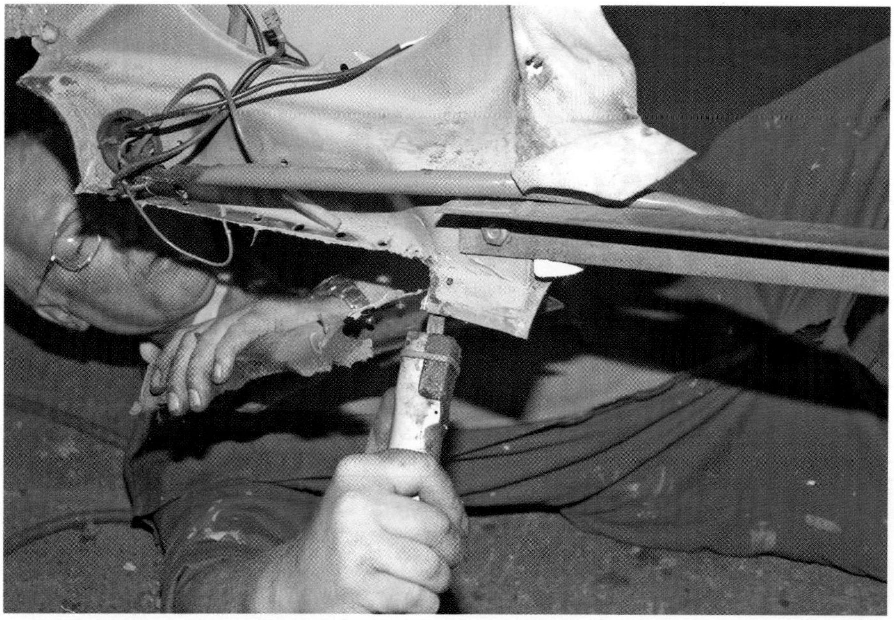

With the spot welds drilled out, the curved portion of the heater channel can be levered off.

Expect spurious floor pans and heater channels to be less than perfect; some tailoring of the floor pan edges might prove necessary, although the most common problem is poor alignment of the bolt holes. On the heater channels fitted to RVJ 403H, the closing (bottom) plate holes did not align with the internal captive nuts, and three of the holes partially obscured the nuts!

Spurious heater channels come with the bottom closing panel already fitted, and OE heater channels have separate closing panels that you have to weld on.

Your typical DIY spot welder will probably not have enough grunt to weld through the two thick spine flanges, plus the floor pan edges (let alone long enough arms), so don't go investing large sums of money on very long arms until you have tested the welder on similar thicknesses of steel! The alternative is to continuously MIG weld the joints, which is not as pretty as spot welds, or to plug weld them, and apply weldable zinc paint before welding.

Now cut out the old heater channels from the bodyshell: this is far easier if the shell is rolled onto its side, with plenty of padding to prevent damage, or if the shell is raised from the ground and supported on axle stands fore and aft - though the shell should only be supported in this way if braces have been bolted or welded onto the 'A' and 'B' posts. Check that your internal bracing is still firmly welded so that the shell cannot distort, before cutting out the old heater channels. Cut carefully along the flitch base, around the 'A' and 'B' post base flanges, and below the rear quarter panel, and cut some way from these at this stage. Some 'persuasion' with a lump hammer may be needed to free the heater channels.

Lift the bodyshell onto the chassis (which now has the new heater channels bolted in place), and carefully manoeuvre it so that the two rear body mounts align with their holes on the damper brackets and the shell sits correctly. Fit the rear body mounting bolts, check again that everything is in line, and fit the doors temporarily to establish that the door gaps are right (you may have to remove the cross brace at this point). Then gas or preferably MIG weld the shell to the heater channels.

When all welding is done, lift the shell from the chassis and fit the belly pan gasket. Some people glue this in place using impact adhesive, but manoeuvring the shell when refitting it can rip the gasket out of position, unless it is securely held by the recommended fixing method of pop rivets. See 'Refit body shell to chassis' later in this chapter for more details.

Refit the shell. The accelerator pedal base has to be welded to the floor pan: it is best to leave this until the engine, clutch/ brake pedal assembly and accelerator cable have been attached. This will allow

When lowering the bodyshell, make sure that the front and rear body mounting holes are aligned with the threaded holes in the beam axle and damper castings. If the bodyshell has not moved, everything else should align - in theory. In practice, the 'A' post, 'B' post/ quarter panel, crossmembers and wheelarch panels might have to be helped into place.

The time to fit the demister down pipes is when bodyshell and chassis are reunites.

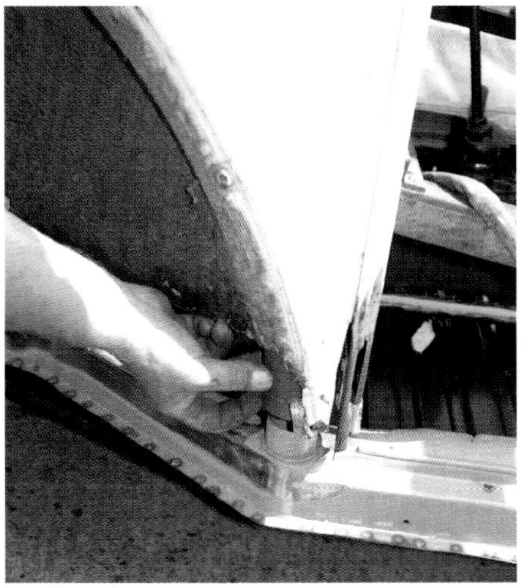

The car hoist used by BSW allows the bodyshell to be held millimetres above the chassis, when it is easy to see whether any panels need adjustment to make them fit. In the absence of a car hoist, try setting the bodyshell on the chassis and raising each end in turn using a trolley jack.

you to check that you have full accelerator lever response to the pedal travel - if you weld the pedal too far away from the lever, you could end up with only a fraction of available throttle lever movement. Equally importantly, the pedals might not line up very well, forcing the driver to lift his right foot a long way when moving from accelerator pedal to brake pedal.

HEATER CHANNEL REPLACEMENT

The first sign of rot here might be that the windscreen stays permanently misted-up because hot air is not reaching it!

Heater channels are normally covered with carpeting. Within each heater channel is a steel tube that carries the hot air, and, in original heater channels, there are two drain holes within the door aperture that allow water to drip onto the inner tube, causing rot. It's possible to renew the heater

This demister down pipe is actually a 50mm fan housing pipe, which does a good job. A short length of the original pipe has been left attached to the three-way manifold, which makes the 50mm pipe a tight fit.

Align the rear body mounting bracket hole (arrowed) with the threaded hole in the damper mounting casting, and loosely fit the bolts.

Ready to lower the bodyshell the last couple of inches. The demister down pipes are in place and fastened so that they cannot be accidentally pulled off the heater channel stubs. Adjustments to wayward panels have been made, and a final check made that nothing (such as wires) is going to be trapped when the shell is lowered.

Expect to have to do some minor trimming to get the bodyshell to sit correctly.

Touchdown. Gravity alone might not be enough to settle the bodyshell correctly - a slight bend in a flange may be holding the bodyshell a fraction too high - so use your weight to push the shell completely down.

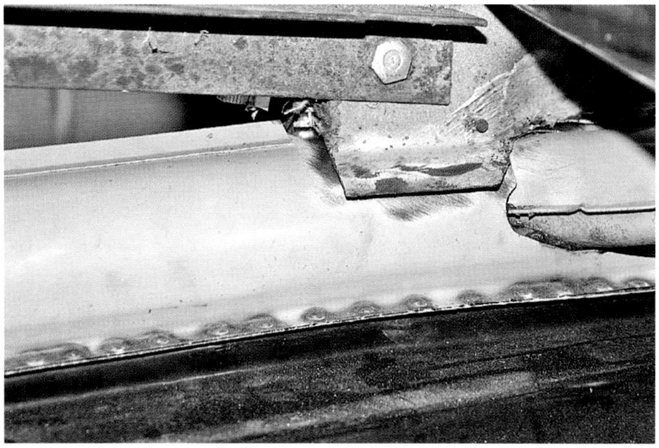

If the base of the 'B' post is not touching the heater channel, use your weight to push it down.

Heater channels. The remains of the heater channel from under the 'A' post. The heating duct is long gone (so the screen demister won't work) and the rest of the assembly is very weak.

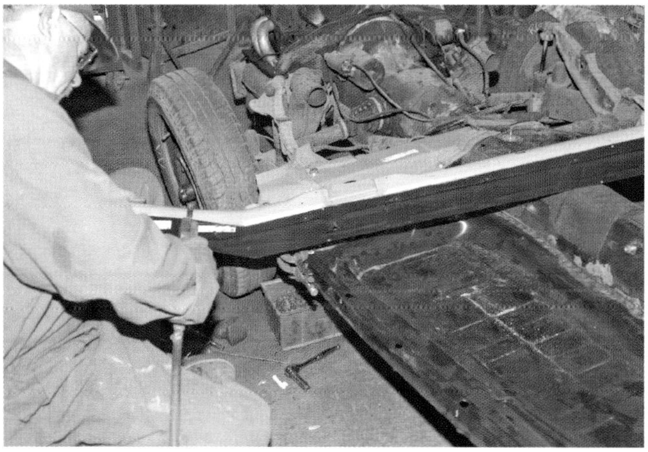

Using original equipment heater channels with spurious closing panels (OE closing panels were out of stock at the time) reveals not only that the spurious panels are thinner gauge steel, but also that they have to be trimmed to fit.

Original equipment heater channels come separate from their closing plates. If you are offered a pre-welded heater channel with closing plate it's not OE.

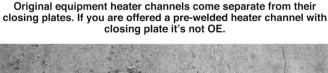

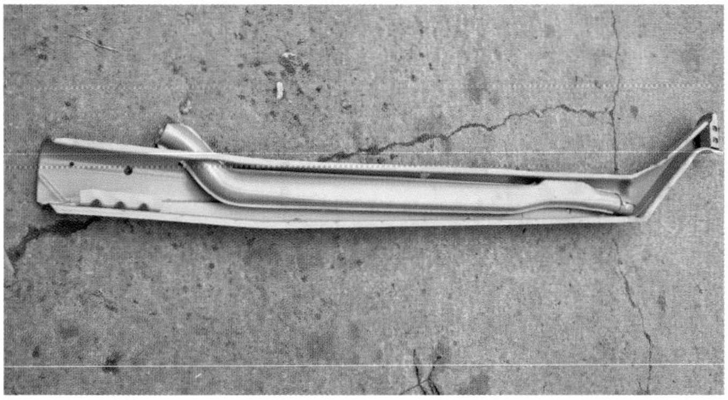

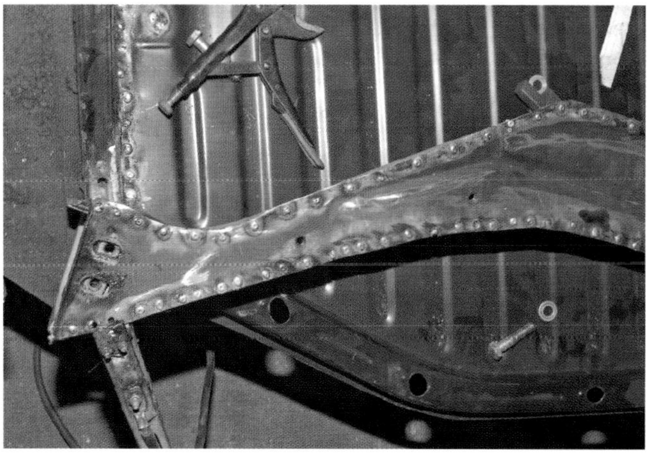

Plug welding is a perfectly acceptable method for joining the upper and lower heater channel sections, and for welding in a floor pan. Just be sure to make plenty of welds and to grind down the surplus.

Don't use a solid grinding disc to grind down surplus plug weld - it's too fierce and easily capable of removing the steel of the panels. Use a 40 grit to 80 grit 'sanding' disc and backing pad.

The paint is being removed in preparation for welding work to the rear face of the front crossmember.

The heater channel welded to the rear crossmember. The assembly will be unbolted later and the underside also welded.

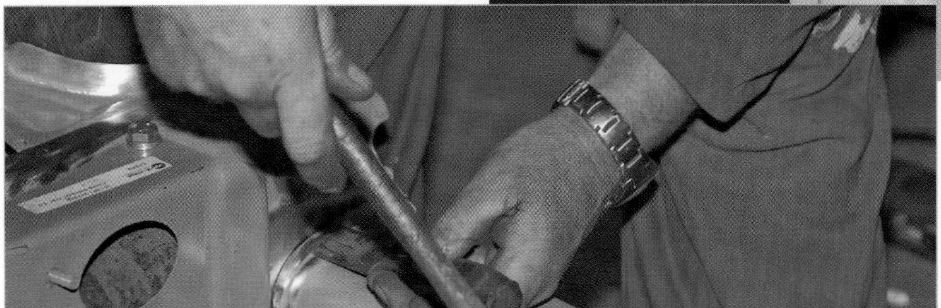

Before performing an edge weld, ensure that the edge actually touches the steel it's being welded to, or the chances are you'll burn away the edge.

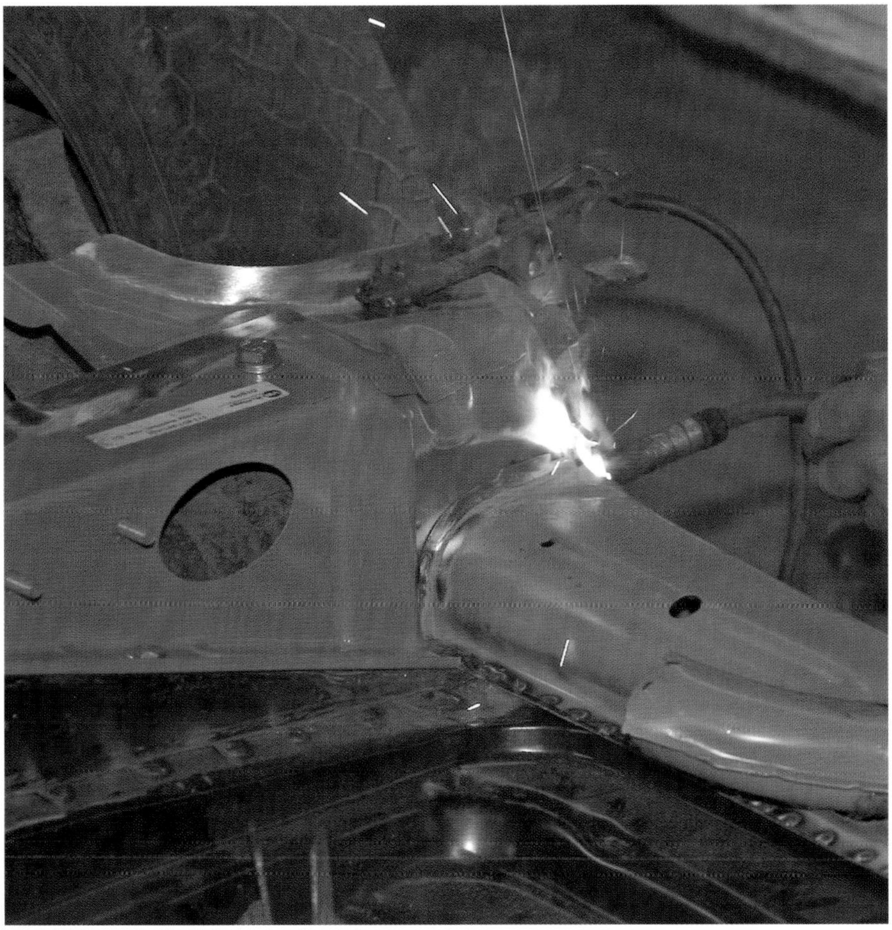

Unless you have an exceptionally high pain threshold, it's advisable to wear leather gauntlets when welding. Here, the heater channel is being welded to the rear crossmember.

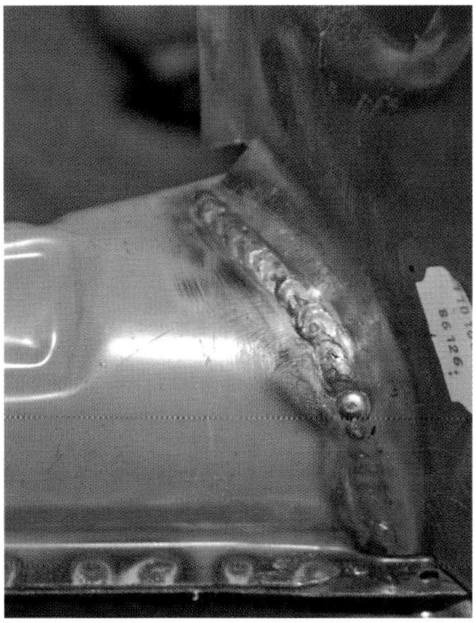

The joins between the heater channels and the front and rear crossmembers must be strong.

channels without taking the body off the chassis, but this will mean fitting new belly pan gasket strips under the heater channel ends, where they would almost certainly be damaged by the heat of welding. This usually means water leaks at the end of the strips, which accelerates new rusting. Far better to remove the body and fit a complete belly gasket as already described, but if you can't lift off the bodyshell, read on.

If the heater channels have rotted badly, it's usual for the floor pan edges to have also, so attend to these first.

The rear seat brace should be kept in position throughout. Cut through the old heater channel just ahead of the 'B' post and behind the 'A' post (take care not to cut into the floor pan edge), then part the welds to the flitch and the inner quarter panel. If the lower part of the flitch is also rotten, cut this away, and weld in new steel after the new heater channels are in place. Cut the rear up to the lower inner wing flange.

Depending on whether the channel has been replaced before, you might also find weld between it and the flitch inner surface and bulkhead panels; this must be ground off, though, in many such cases, you'll have to cut away the base of the flitch. Carefully cut around the bases of the 'A' and 'B' posts. Remove the remaining sections of heater channel; if no welded joints remain then a clout from a hammer will usually do the trick.

Bolt the new channel into position on the chassis assembly; a replacement

When the heater channels have been welded to the crossmembers, unbolt the assembly to weld the underside.

Finally, the complete crossmember/heater channel assembly can be lifted from the floor chassis whilst the latter is cleaned and painted.

The rear crossmember can be plug welded to the heater channel.

Unless you use genuine panels throughout (sometimes not possible as not all panels are available), the fit between genuine and spurious panels might dictate the welding method used to join them. These have been tack welded, because the overlap was too shallow for plug welding.

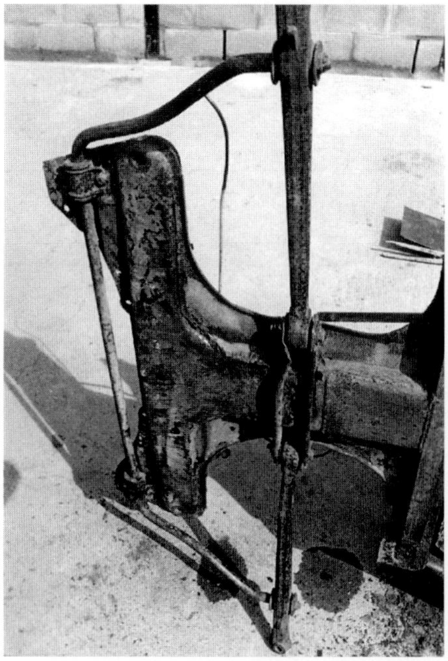

This frame head looks rather sad, and a couple of stabs with a sharp implement revealed extensive rot which substantially weakened it. Normally, this would be cut off and a replacement grafted in - not a job for the amateur - but the owner decided that it had to be repaired.

length of belly pan gasket should have been obtained but not yet fitted, because welding at the ends of the heater channels would burn it away. You may need the help of an assistant to push the floor edges downward as you push the heater channels into position.

Refit the door and check that the gaps are correct front and rear. Tack weld into position the bases of the 'A' and 'B' posts, remove the door, knock down the inner quarter panel and seam weld this to the heater channel. Seam weld the flitch.

Finally, push down the floor edges and fit as much belly pan gasket as possible.

FRAME HEAD

The frame head is the primary location for most of the front suspension/steering mounting points. If this assembly is rotten, handling will be unpredictable and dangerous. The base tends to suffer from rot long before the top section. Because the cost of a replacement frame head assembly is almost as much as that of a new chassis assembly complete with frame head, repair is an attractive alternative. This is a far from easy task which would normally only be undertaken during a full body-off restoration. Access to a spot welder is almost vital.

Strip the car to a bare chassis, then clean off the top of the frame head to check that it is serviceable before turning the chassis upside down. (It's as well to pull the fuel pipe out of the spine before you begin cutting steel.)

Clean the lips of the two halves so that you can see the spot welds, centre punch, then drill out, taking care not to drill through the lip of the top pressing. Split the join as you progress. Cut across both sides of the track control arm pressing, drill out the spot welds holding this to the frame head lower pressing, grind away any MIG or gas weld you find, and finally prise off the pressing.

The repair panel should have captive nuts for the anti-roll bar fixings, intended to replace the two internally threaded rods each side of the upper frame head pressing. If possible, clean, re-tap and use the original fixings, and grind off the captive nuts on the repair panel. The original fixings spread the load from the anti-roll bar between both pressings of the frame head, whereas the captive nuts on the repair panel place all of the strain on the repair panel itself.

Clean the inside of the top frame head pressing and apply a good, rust-proofing primer, then offer the lower pressing into position and bolt down as shown in the photographs. It would be possible to plug or seam weld the two panels together, but strength here is so vital that the author urges the use of a spot welder, even if it has to be hired for the day.

Frame head replacement

This usually becomes necessary on cars which have stood in long, wet grass for some years, or cars that have suffered a heavy front-end collision. In the opinion of the author, it is not a task for the DIY restorer, because the precise positioning of the replacement frame head is critical; if it

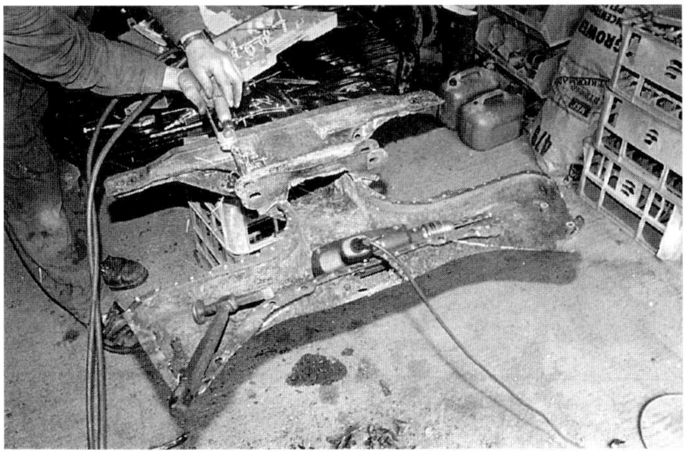

Frame heads are heavy-duty and repairing them is not for the faint-hearted. This McPherson strut car is to have the frame head base renewed. Having drilled out the spot welds, Terry does the fiddly areas with the air hacksaw.

Some sections of the frame head base are best cut with an oxyacetylene torch.

Finally, with the lips cleaned, the repair panel can be bolted down to position it for welding.

The toe board (front crossmember) is best cut out in sections to avoid damage.

is a fraction out, handling and road-holding will suffer.

If you MUST attempt this repair, it's recommended that you begin by making up a welded steel framework (in effect, a crude but accurate jig), which passes from the floor pan to the frame head, and has holes drilled through it to align with the various holes in the existing frame head. This will allow the new frame head to be bolted firmly in the correct position prior to welding.

FRONT CROSSMEMBER (TOE BOARD) REPLACEMENT

For Beetles with torsion bar front suspension, a third party bulkhead panel is available in RHD and a VAG panel in LHD. For cars with MacPherson strut suspension, there doesn't seem to be a panel available. Third party torsion bar crossmember assemblies can be modified to fit McPherson strut cars.

If this is a first-time repair, begin by drilling out the spot welds which hold the old panel in position, then split the welds. If the car has been 'got at' and the panel is plated or has been replaced previously and MIG welded into position, grind away the welds until the panel comes free.

Offer the new panel into position and tack weld it, ensuring that the lower line of the panel matches the profile of the chassis front end. When you are sure that it is correctly positioned, seam weld it in, starting along the top edge, then down

First, the left-hand outer section is cut out, along with the heater channel.

Terry then cuts the bottom seam of the two panels in the toe board assembly.

When cutting steel, always wear eye protection; rust particles can be washed out with minor discomfort, but shards of steel will have to be dug out in hospital, and this - I know from experience - is very painful.

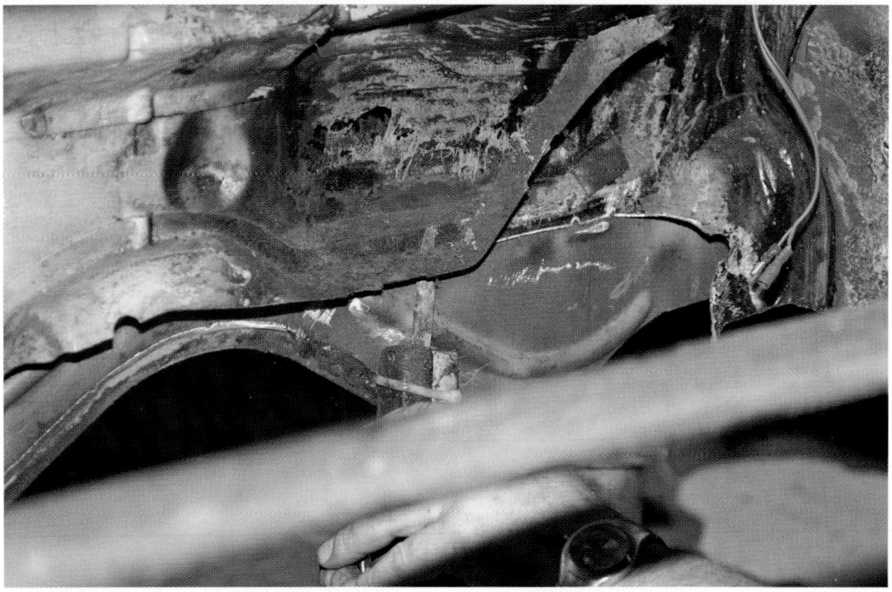

With the bulk of the inner toe board panel cut away, Terry trims the top lip to improve access to the spot welded seam.

both sides. When you come to the lower portions, weld a little, let the metal cool, then weld a little more, before letting the metal cool, to prevent heat build-up from destroying the belly pan gasket.

It is preferable to carry out this work as part of a full body-off restoration and, if this is the case, tack the bulkhead panel securely into position with the body on the chassis for correct alignment, then seam weld with the body raised to improve access.

If you wish to weld the torsion bar version of this panel into a MacPherson strut Beetle, first dolly the edge lips so that they lie flat, then position it correctly and measure the gap between the panel edges and the flitches. Cut strips of steel to fit the gap and weld these to the panel, before offering it for final welding in position. It will also be necessary to weld in plates to cover the gaps from within the front wheelarch.

REAR CROSSMEMBER (HEELBOARD) REPAIRS

The rear crossmember comprises left and right halves which are welded together *in situ*. Because rot is usually confined to

continued on page 187

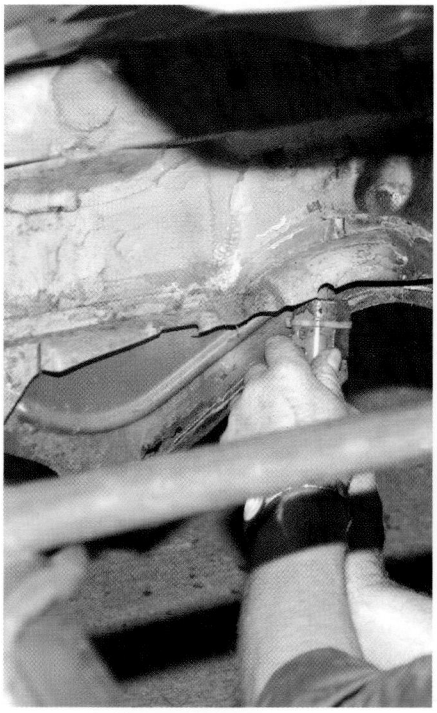

The cut continues, following the line of the panel.

The spot welded seam can now be cleaned to reveal the spot welds.

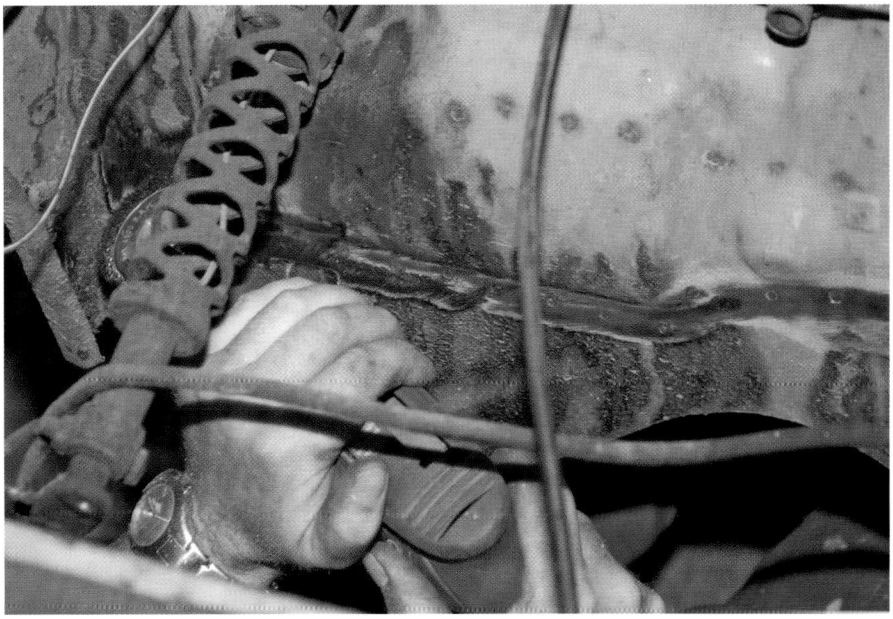

In this case - as sometimes happens - the spot welds cannot be seen clearly from one side of the panel, but cleaning the other side reveals them.

Some of the spot welds are more easily visible from the front.

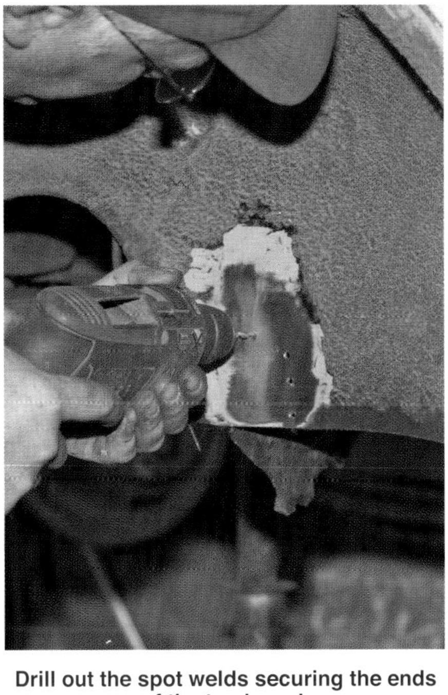

Drill out the spot welds securing the ends of the toe board.

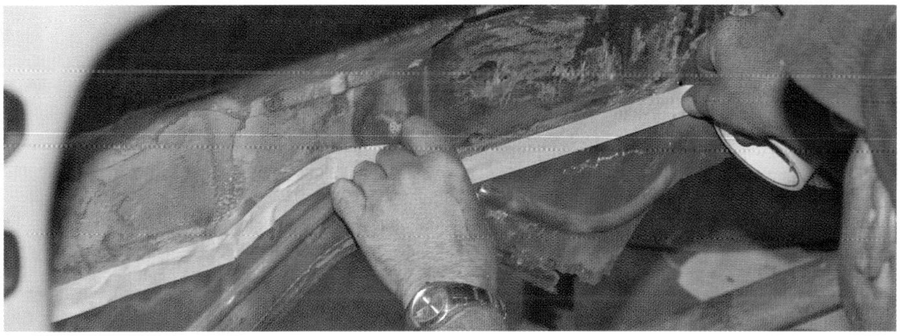

A good way of marking a cutting line is with masking tape, which is easy to see.

Terry is cutting a line up to his marked cutting line.

This area is now ready for uniting with the new toe board, which has been welded to the heater channels. The small amount of surface rust will be cleaned off using a wire brush.

The bulkhead panel should lie on the front side of the crossmember and, if the cut-down bulkhead panel is distorted, you may have to help it into position.

The bodyshell being lowered back onto the new crossmember.

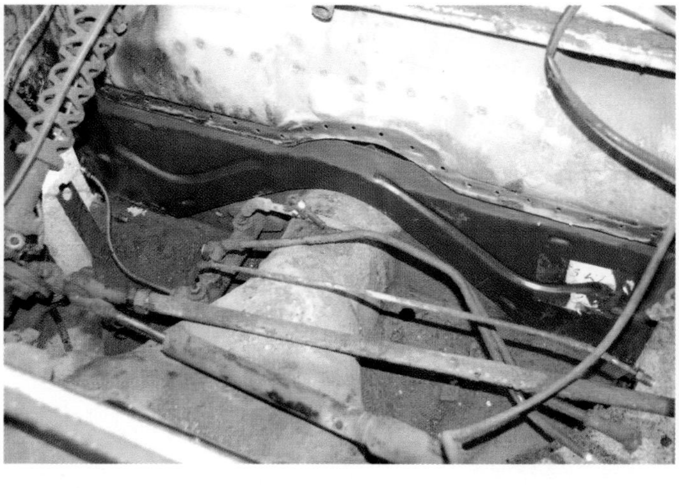

The front crossmember side lip will probably have to be pushed or tapped tight onto the footwell side panel for plug welding from the other side. If the steel is not touching, the edge of the hole will burn, resulting in a weak weld.

The front crossmember front edge is continuous-welded to keep moisture out.

The new heel board is on the chassis, welded to the heater channels. In order to minimise distortion of the adjoining 'parcel shelf' pressing, the spot welds holding it to the heel board are to be drilled out. Clean off the paint first.

Although you can buy various drill bits for removing spot welds, a ⅛in twist bit followed by a bit the size of the individual weld works just as well. Spot welds vary in size, and a range of bits is essential.

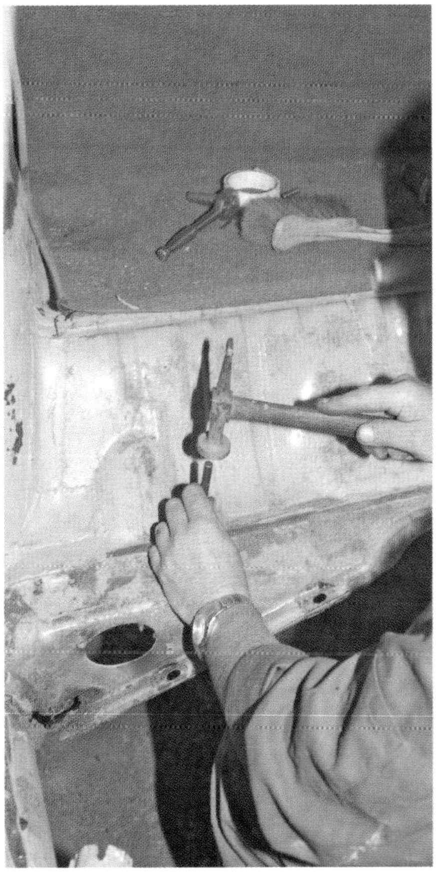

Centre punching all the spot welds takes a while, but saves time in the long run, because the drill bit doesn't wander.

The heel board is held by various cover patches at each end so, in order to remove the heel board, Terry cuts it in half.

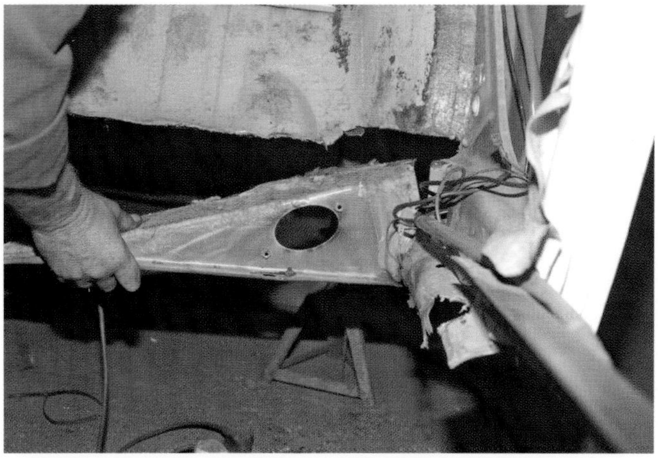

By then lifting and lowering the half heel board, the welds to the cover patches work-harden and weaken.

This is where the painstaking drilling out of all the spot welds pays dividends: the parcel shelf edge has minimal distortion and can be easily trued-up.

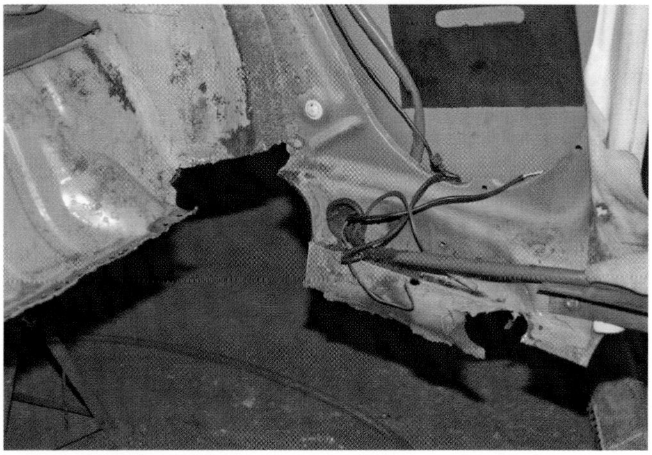

The heel board half is off. The lip visible lower left will have to be dollied flat for welding to the new heel board.

The rear crossmember comes in two halves which have to be welded together. Original panels have a stepped edge so that they lie flush: spurious panels might have to be altered to achieve the same effect.

The heelboard can then be bolted to the floorpans, ready for welding when the bodyshell is reunited with the chassis.

At this point, the bodyshell is almost ready to be lifted, complete with new heater channels and crossmembers, off the chassis.

The leading edge of the boot floor panel is plug welded to the crossmember; again, through the holes made by drilling out the original spot welds.

The two threaded studs found on some rear crossmember panels are to bolt on an ECU - Electronic Control Unit - as found in fuel-injected Beetles. They could be cut off but aren't going to get in the way, tucked under the rear seat as they are.

the outer edges, repairs using home-made panels are common.

Because the crossmember outer ends are welded to the heat channels and strength is vital, it is better to replace the crossmember sections completely rather than patch repair the outer ends.

The crossmember should be replaced with the bodyshell on the chassis because it bolts to the chassis. To remove the old crossmember, drill out the line of spot welds at the front of the parcel shelf; this will provide holes through which you can plug weld in the new panels. Bolt the crossmember halves to the chassis and weld them together. Finally, plug weld the crossmember to the parcel shelf.

'A' & 'B' POST REPAIR

As the heater channels rot, rust spreads up to the bases of the 'A' and the 'B' posts. If the bases have previously been repaired or welded onto new heater channels, it's usual to find that rust has started at the actual weld. Either way, the bases have to be repaired and, as usual, both long and short repair panels are available.

Remove the door. Clean the old paintwork from the post base to determine the true extent of the rot. Decide whether to fit the larger repair panel (which incorporates the lower hinge mounting point), or if you can get away with the shorter version and still find clean, sound steel to weld to on the post. The hinge mounting point must be sound if you are to use the shorter panel and, in this instance, it is as well to take the opportunity to clean

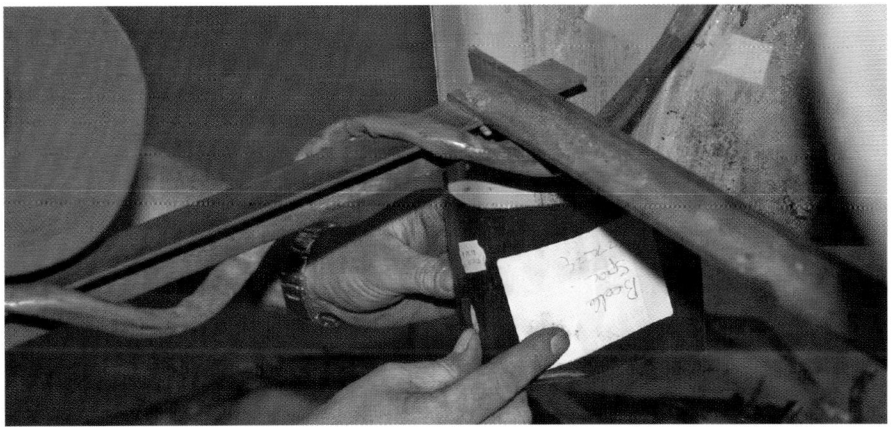

Measuring to fit a new lower 'A' post repair panel.

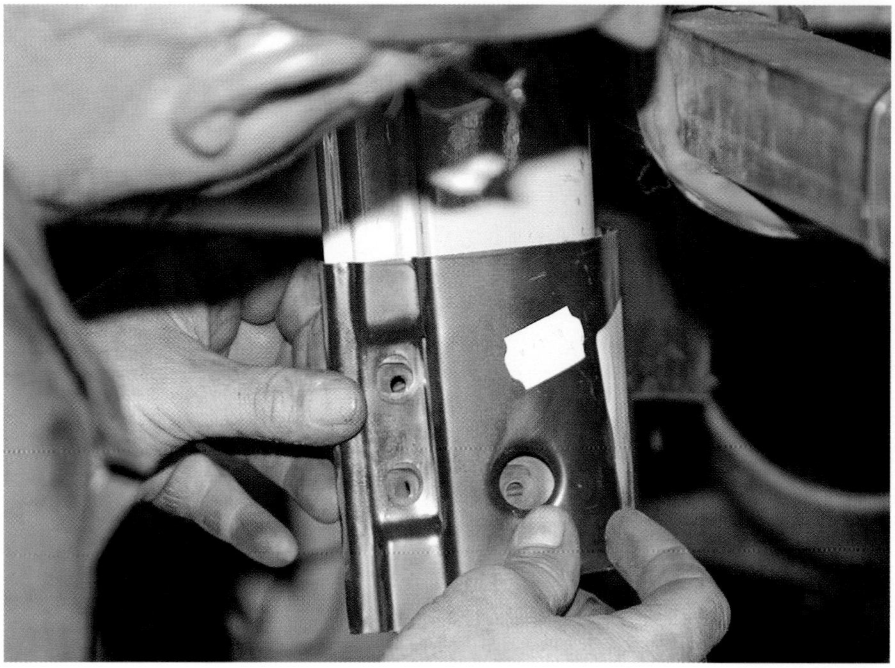

Ensure you have the correct repair panel by checking that the holes line up.

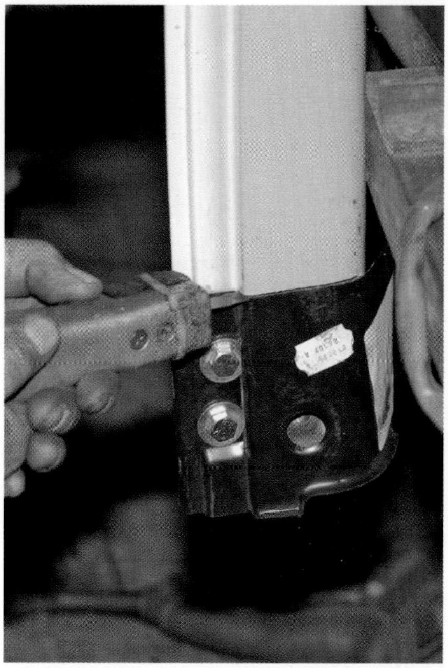

Bolt the panel into the door hinge plate, then cut along the top of it - this will be a butt welded joint.

Cut off the part of the footwell side panel that's to be replaced.

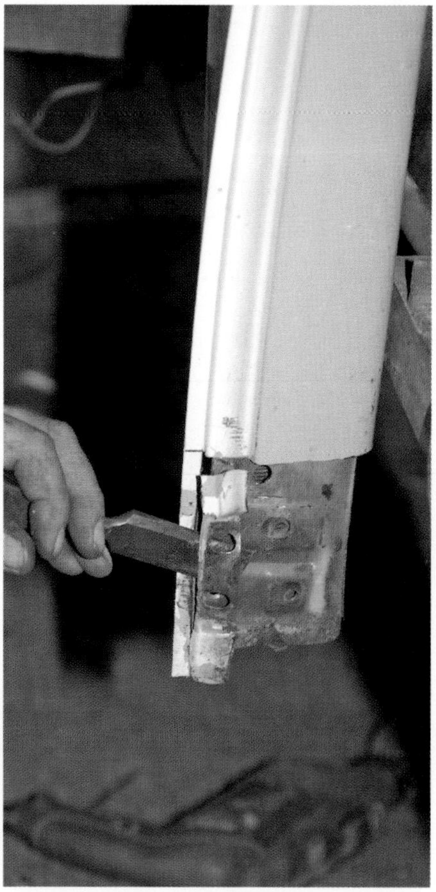

The lower 'A' post is a difficult area to deal with, and you may have to resort to using a chisel on parts of it. Wear leather gloves to prevent cutting your hands on sharp steel edges.

and hand paint the mounting point before covering it with the repair panel.

Prise the folded edge of the old panel from the flitch lip. The rot is best cut out using an air hacksaw, although patience and a junior hacksaw will also do the job - DON'T use a chisel or air chisel, because both will distort the remaining edge and, because the join will have to be butt welded, it will prove difficult to true up the edge sufficiently to get a good result.

Some tailoring may prove necessary to get the repair panel to properly fit the heater channel. If you are fitting the larger panel, have an assistant hold the door whilst you ensure that the mounting built into the repair panels matches the hinge bolt holes, then tack the panel into position and carefully fit the door (supporting the door so that the repair panel does not take any weight), to ensure not only that the hinge holes are aligned, but also that the door shut lines are correct.

If all is in order, butt weld the top join, seam weld the bottom join to the heater channel, and spot weld (if possible) the outer edge. The inside upright joint can be butt welded or overlapped - the former looks neater. Use weldable zinc paint prior to welding, then clean the outside of the joints and apply a good rust-retardant primer.

If you have to fit both 'A' and 'B' post

The 'A' post lower repair panel must be a perfect fit on the heater channels.

Before any welding is done, attend to the door gaps.

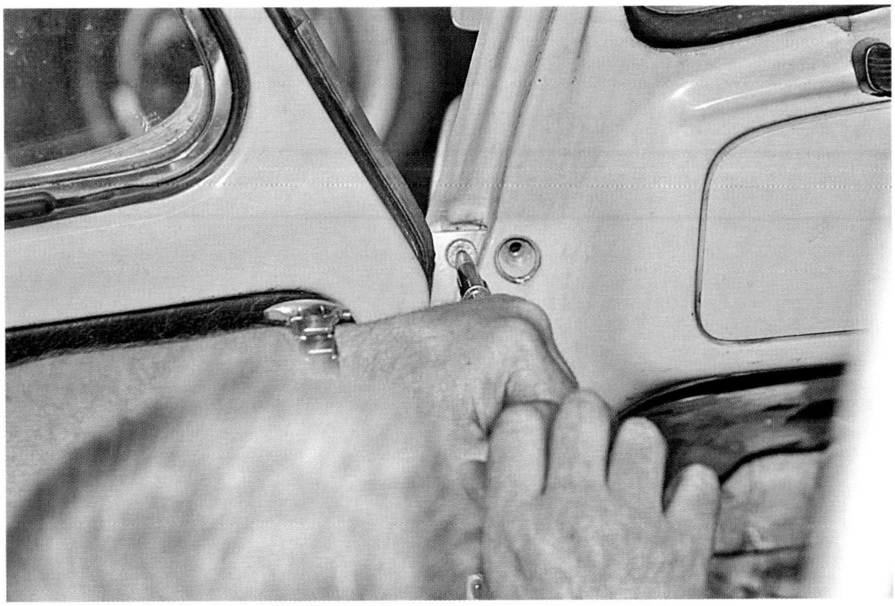

The door must lie flush with adjacent panels, which can be achieved by slackening the hinge screws and pulling the door out, or vice-versa.

When the door aperture has been adjusted for the door, tack the 'A' and 'B' posts, then recheck the door fit.

If the door still fits, weld the 'A' and 'B' posts to the heater channels before anything has a chance to move.

You don't have to fully weld the 'A' and 'B' posts at this stage, just enough to hold them in position.

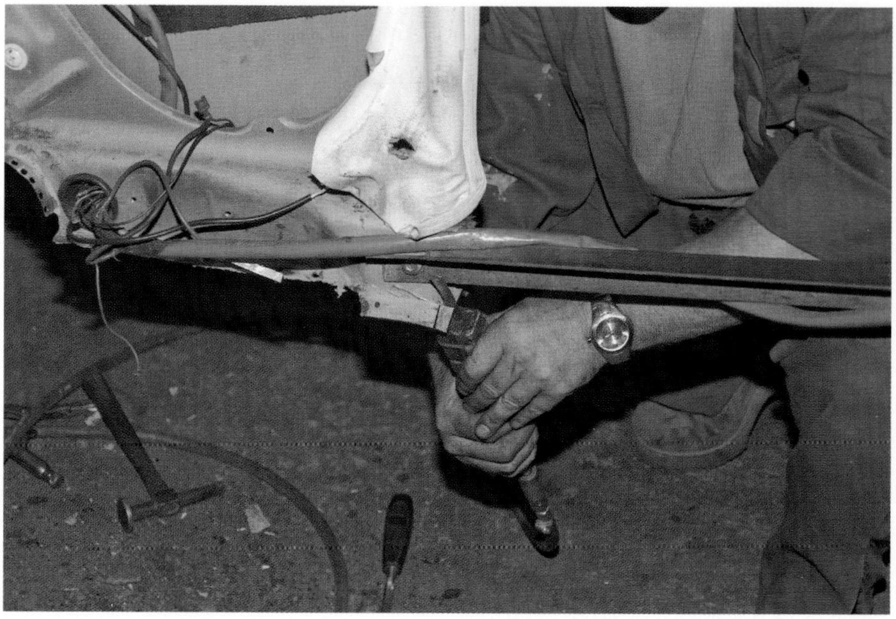

All that remains is to trim the base of the 'B' post so that it sits on its brand-new heater channels.

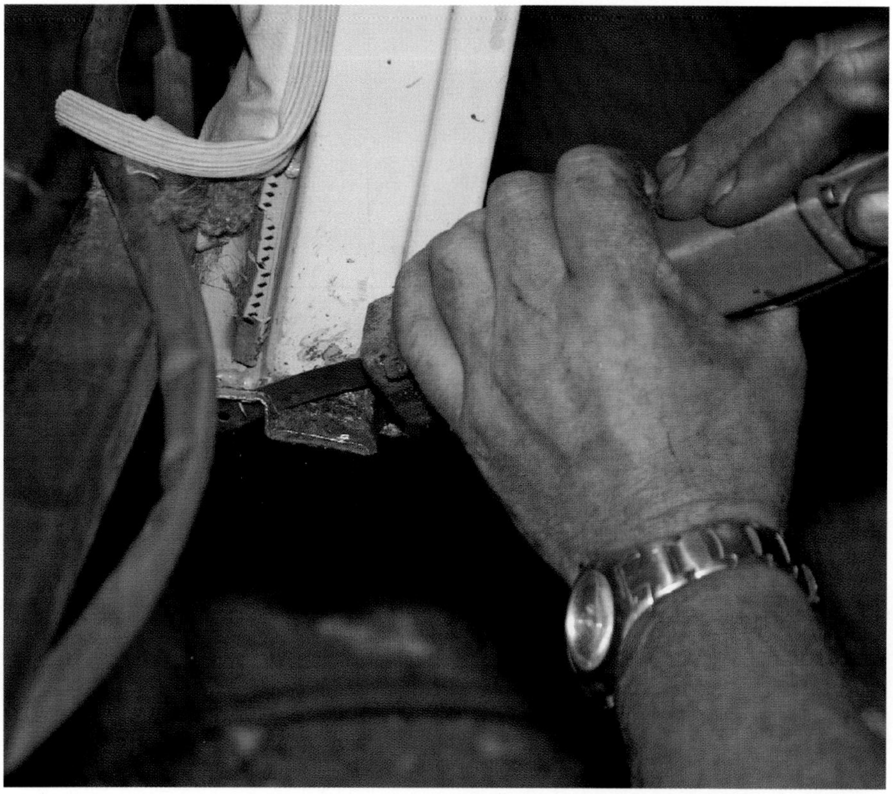

At the front of the 'B' post, trim back to leave a shallow lip to weld to the heater channels. The shallower the lip, the stronger the join.

A small piece of the original heater channel remains under the 'B' post, which must be ground off or the bodyshell won't sit properly on the new heater channels.

lower repair sections and heater channels, fit the 'A' and 'B' post sections while the old heater channels are in place - this will ensure that, when the old heater channels have been cut out and the bodyshell is lowered onto the new heater channels bolted to the chassis, the bodyshell will sit at the correct height.

REFIT BODYSHELL TO CHASSIS

The first stage is to remove and throw away any of the old belly pan gasket which may be stuck to the floor pan edges, and clean (and, if necessary, true up) the edges. Many people try to glue the new seal into position on the floor pan edge, but glue cannot hold the seal strongly enough once you start to manoeuvre the bodyshell into the correct position, so fix it with pop rivets. Don't make the mistake of cutting the new seal into pieces. Begin by laying out the seal along one floor pan edge, starting from a front corner, drilling and pop riveting it in place as you go.

Work across the back, then make

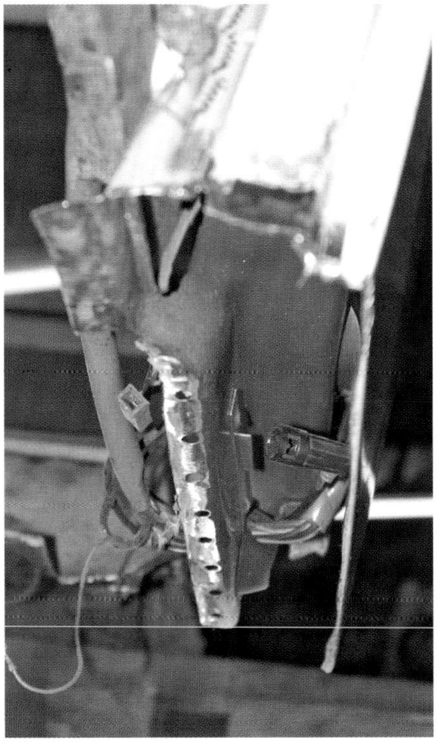

A view inside the rear quarter, now pretty well ready to weld to the new sills.

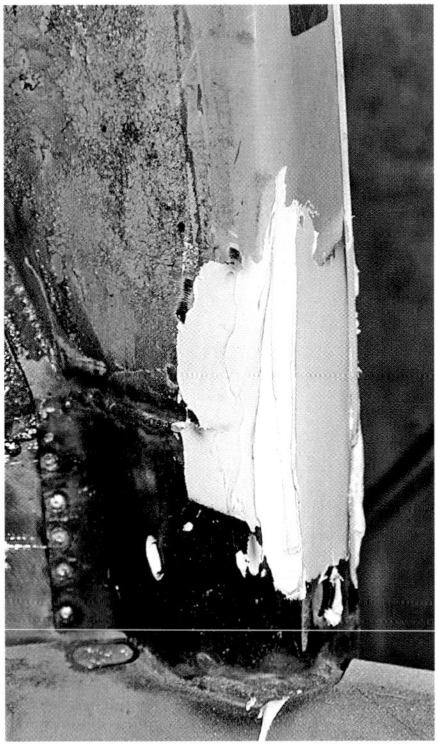

The 'A' and 'B' post repairs will be finished using body filler. This initial application looks on the heavy side, but most of it will be sanded away.

Expect to take some time to sand flat little areas like this. Using a sanding block helps.

When flatted, the base of the 'B' post should have just a very thin layer of body filler.

Schutz is excellent for protecting bodywork on the underside of the car.

another cut at the opposite corner, and start drilling and riveting the other outer edge of the floor pan. Cut off the remaining section of the seal, which will be fitted across the front.

Terry Ball cuts the edges of the front seal strip, then lays one seal partially across the other to give a good seal. The remaining section of the seal is riveted across the front of the floor pan. To improve sealing, Terry then applies a generous glob of windscreen sealant to the

Chassis black not only makes the floor pans look good, it keeps rust at bay, too.

Fixing the belly pan gasket. It might prove necessary to pull or hammer home the tacks used to hold the original gasket.

The gasket could be glued in position, but pop rivets are better, because they prevent the gasket from moving when the bodyshell is manoeuvred back into place.

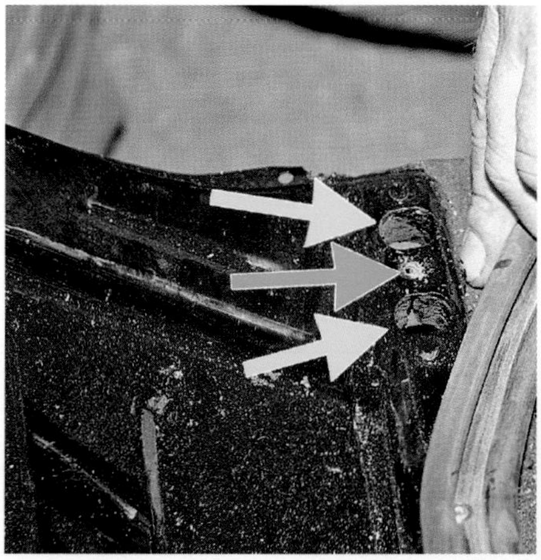

At the front corners, be careful to drill the pop rivet hole in-between the two tubes that prevent the pressing from collapsing when the body mounting bolts are tightened.

four corners of the seal.

With some lifting gear and a great deal of ingenuity, the bodyshell can be manoeuvred onto the chassis by one person, but it's far better to have two strong adults, and preferably three or more (two, three or four to lift and one to check that the mounting bolt holes are aligned). Before lifting on the bodyshell, check that there's nothing lying on the top of the seal or on the frame head to prevent the body from seating properly. Align the rearmost holes first (those on the rear damper bracket); fit the spacers in position and bolt the bodyshell loosely at this stage (remember to use copper grease on all of these bolt threads). Then, move to the front of the car and try to align the two long bolts at the front edges of the frame head. Fit the bolts with new M10 washers, then the four (two each side) smaller bolts which locate further back in the frame head.

If any of these bolts do not align correctly with their respective holes, running a tap through the threads can help, but don't force anything at this stage because you'll get a crossed thread if you do. If you can't get even a tap through a hole, gently lever the bodyshell in the appropriate direction and try again.

Finally, fit the small bolts which run into the sill/heater channel assemblies and, when all are in position, tighten them.

Be sure to space the pop rivets away from where the rectangular washers under the body side mounting bolts will sit.

At the corners, overlap the gasket after cutting away a section of the inner tubing.

You don't need a car hoist to reunite the bodyshell with the chassis. An alternative is to support the bodyshell on a pair of beams and roll the chassis underneath.

QUARTER PANEL REPAIR

The quarter panel runs from the rear of the door to the rear wing, and the lower area is very prone to rot. Both large and small repair panels are available; fit the smaller of the two if possible and, if you have to use the larger panel, cut it to size rather than fit the entire panel. The author has seen quite a few needlessly large repair panels, which means that, the next time the panel rots out, the hapless owner has to patch repair or go to the considerable expense of acquiring and fitting a full side panel. Furthermore, the full repair panel edge runs right across the centre of the panel where welding-generated heat will almost certainly produce corrugations: ALWAYS cut the repair panel to the smallest practicable size.

To fit the repair panel, either cut it slightly oversize and use a joddler to set an edge, which can tuck underneath the

The rear quarter lower repair panel as supplied is quite high, and there are good reasons to cut it down. First, the further away from the centre of this large panel the join is, the less chance of it being distorted by heat during welding. More importantly, by cutting down the panel, the next time a repair is needed, the same panel can be used (but cut down less) rather than a full quarter panel.

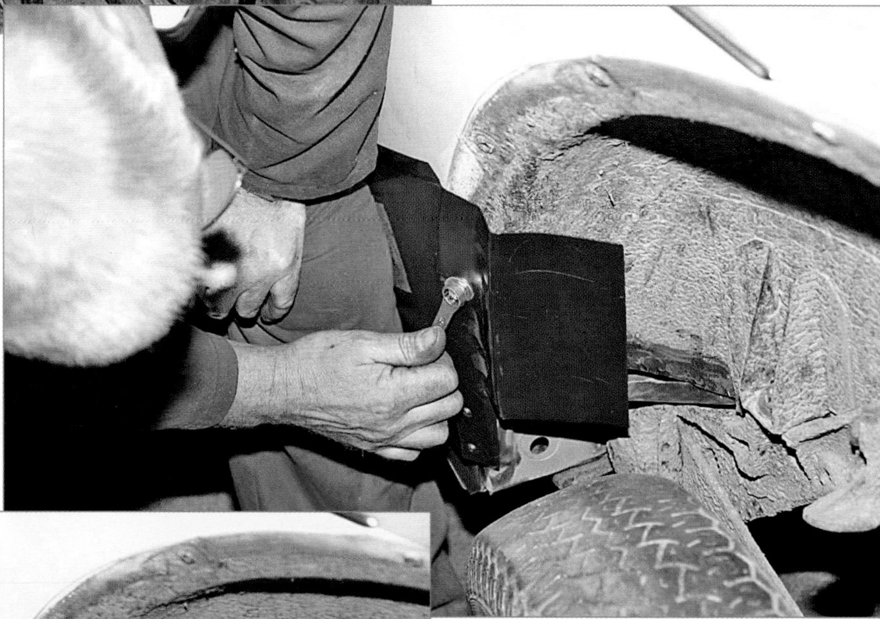

Right: Bolt the repair panel into position using a wing bolt and the captive nut.

If you intend cutting the panel below the level of the wing bolt, drill a hole lower down and fit a self-tapping bolt.

The self-tapping bolt is running into fairly thick steel, so the advice is to use a bolt (which you can turn using a socket) rather than a screw.

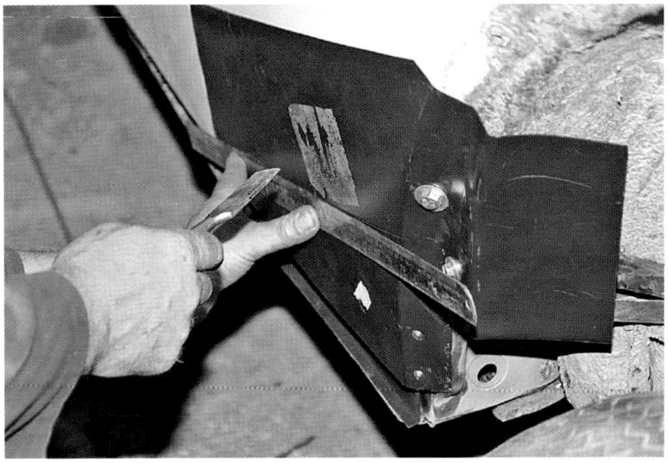

Scribe a cutting line for the repair panel and double-check that there's sufficient overlap between it and the lower cut edge of the original panel.

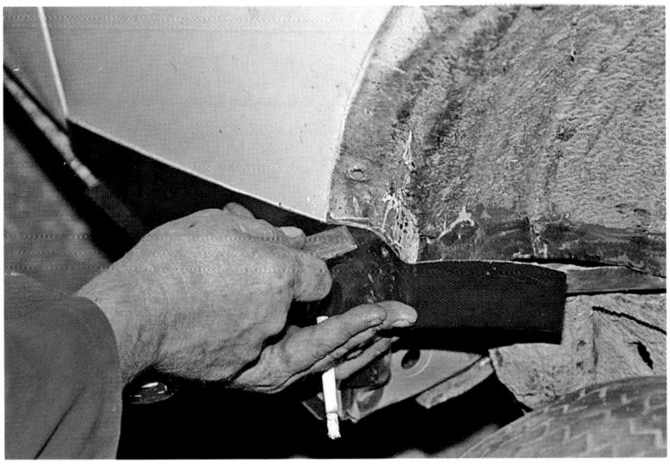

Having cut down the repair panel, Terry scribes a line onto the quarter panel. I'd like to add that smoking is very bad for your health ...

Cut along the edge of the tape, taking care not to cut into the base of the 'B' post.

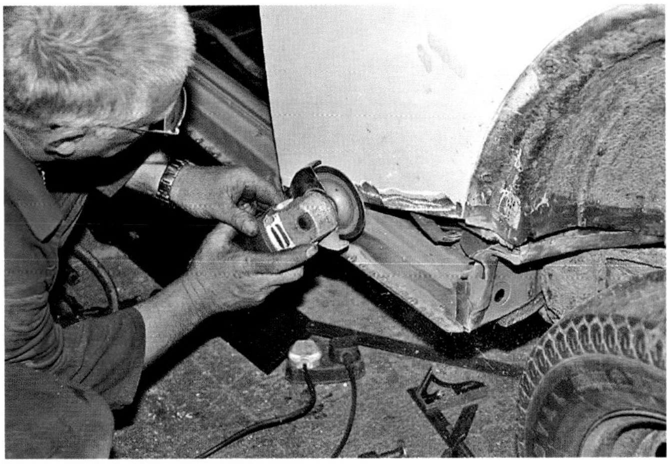

Clean off paint from the area of the overlap.

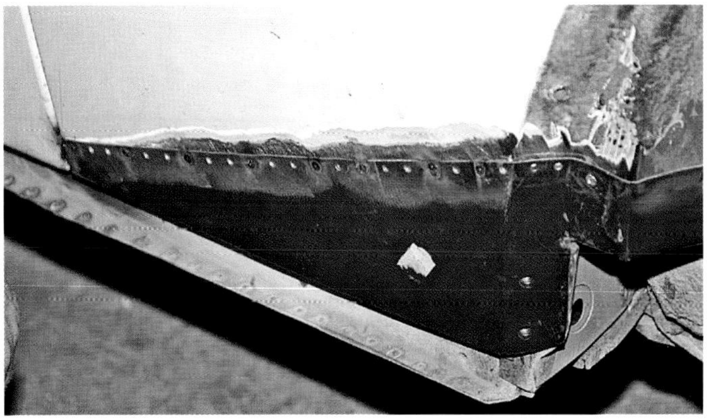

When plug welding on the repair panel, begin by welding every second or third hole. If you weld up all of the holes from one end to the other, the panel might expand a tiny amount with each weld so that it doesn't fit by the time you reach the far end!

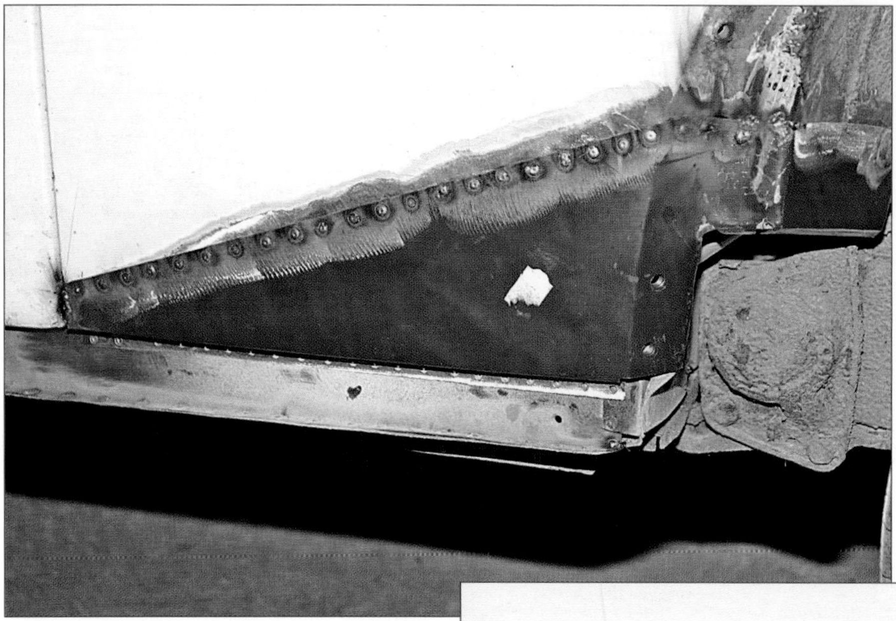

The parts of the repair panel that were discarded can be seen on the floor. If you ever have to repeat the repair (not necessarily because it has rusted - collision damage might be the reason), simply cut off less of the new repair panel.

Plug welding the join reduces the chances of heat buckling occurring, but you need to have plenty of plug welds to give the join the necessary strength.

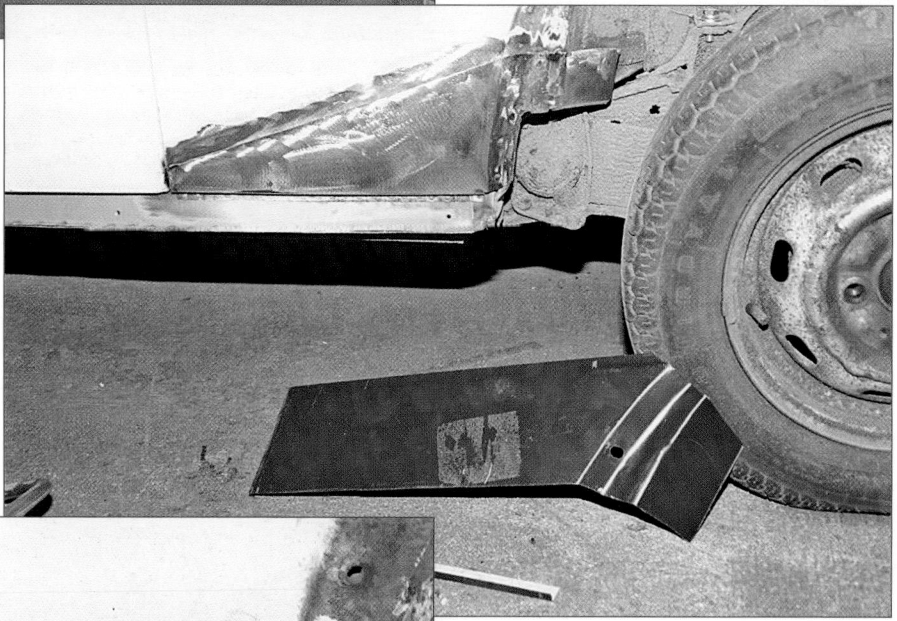

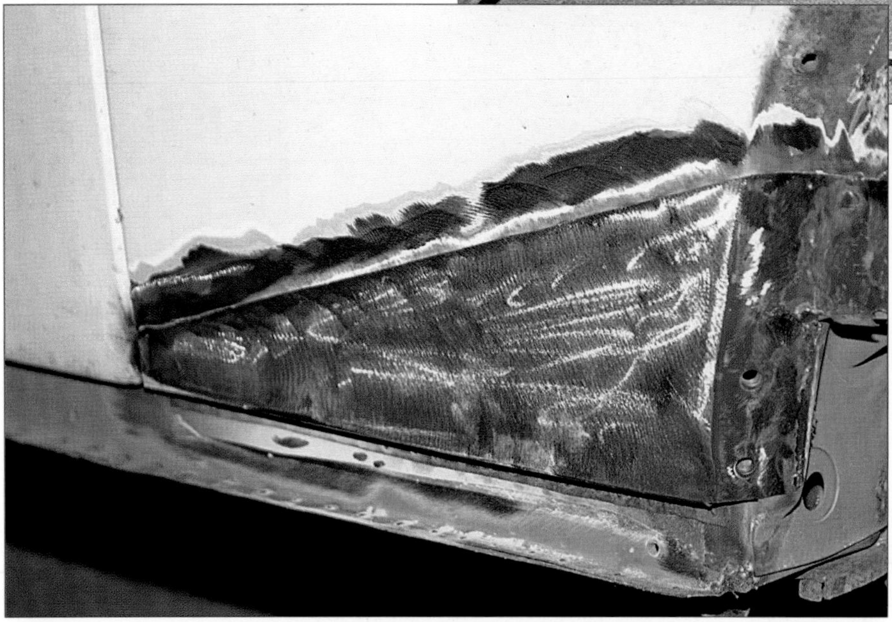

When the surplus weld from the plug welds are ground down, only a thin layer of body filler will be needed to hide the join.

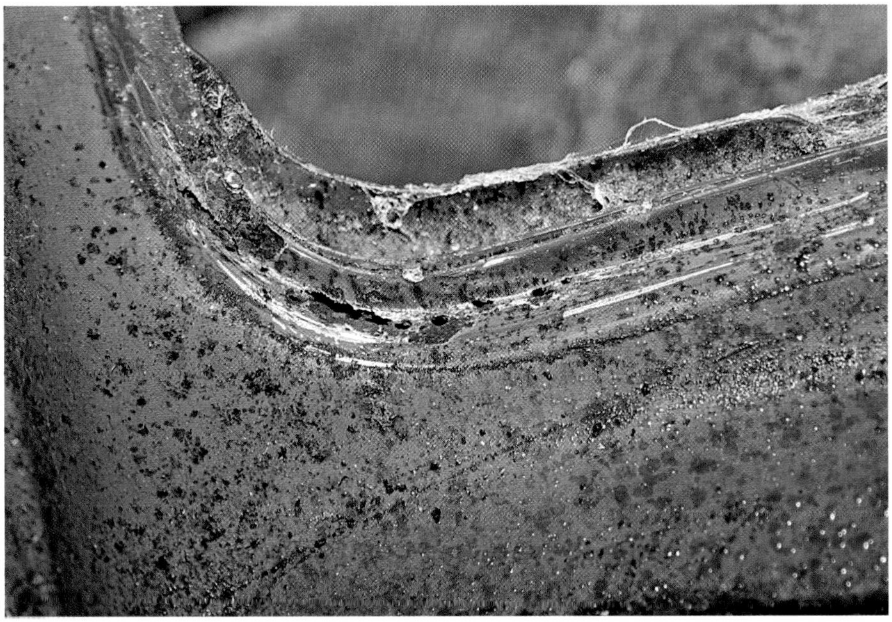

Rot in the window apertures is normally confined to the lower corners, especially in the case of the front windscreen. Repair sections do not appear to be available and, while it is possible to fabricate small repair panels, it's difficult to make them accurately enough for the windscreen seal to sit properly. If the seal does not sit properly it will not seal, and the water it allows in will cause more rot. The alternative is to cut sections from a donor bodyshell.

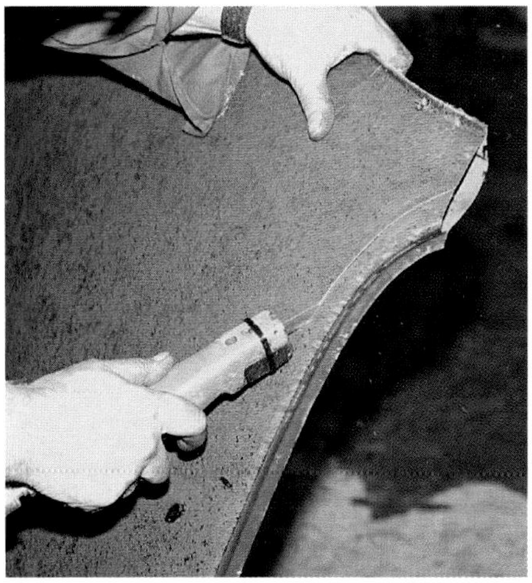

This is the top aperture of the windscreen, which rarely rots. You can use sections cut from this area to repair the lower part of the aperture, which frequently rots.

The air ducting carries warm, moist air, from which water can condense out onto the steel corner air vent, rotting it first and then the adjacent steel. This is the long-term result.

edge of the existing panel or, alternatively, spot weld a strip of steel onto the back of the repair panel to give the same result. In addition to reducing the possibility of buckling, this pulls the two panels into line. Fix the two panels together with pop rivets or self-tapping screws, tack weld them at half-inch intervals, and join the tack welds together with continuous seam welds. By placing so many tack welds on the join and then welding only a short length of steel at a time, the chances of the panels buckling are minimised.

WINDOW APERTURE

Perished or damaged window rubbers allow water to lie against the lip that runs inside the window aperture, causing rust. If rust spreads to in-between the two spot-welded sections that make up the lip, the only solution is to grind away one of the two sections in the effected area, clean off all the rust and coat with weld-through zinc paint, then let in a repair section.

Occasionally, rust in the window aperture extends into a roof pillar or the front scuttle, and this is more serious because repair panels are not available. Because the areas are too complex for the amateur panel beater to replicate, it's tempting to let in a roughly-shaped piece of steel and use lots of body filler to build up to the required level - but there is a better way. If you can find a scrap Beetle on which this section is not rusted, cut it out and weld it into your car.

LUGGAGE/ENGINE BAY SEAL RETAINING STRIPS

It's usual to discover only slight rusting of these thin strips, but don't be fooled more serious rust will be lurking underneath. The recommended option during a full restoration is to drill out the spot welds, remove the strips, clean the underlying metal and apply weldable zinc paint, then spot weld on new strips.

These strips really do need to be spot welded; they are so thin that a MIG will be very inclined to burn through, and cleaning up surplus weld without damaging the lips will verge on the impossible.

FLITCH TOP RAIL REPAIR

When rot under the luggage bay seal retaining strip is left unattended, it results in rot in the underlying flitch tops. Repair panels do not appear to be available for this area so, if practicable, rot can be dealt with by cutting away the weak metal and letting in a strip of new steel. If the rot extends very far down the flitch on torsion bar cars, a replacement flitch panel is the best (although very difficult and fairly expensive) option. On McPherson strut cars, the flitch tops are the location for the strut top mounting; the replacement panels are very expensive.

Plug weld the flange sections and continuous seam weld the butt joint on the roof pillar sections.

The plug welds and proud seam weld will have to be ground down. A solid grinding disc is too fierce for this, so use a 40 grit sanding disc instead.

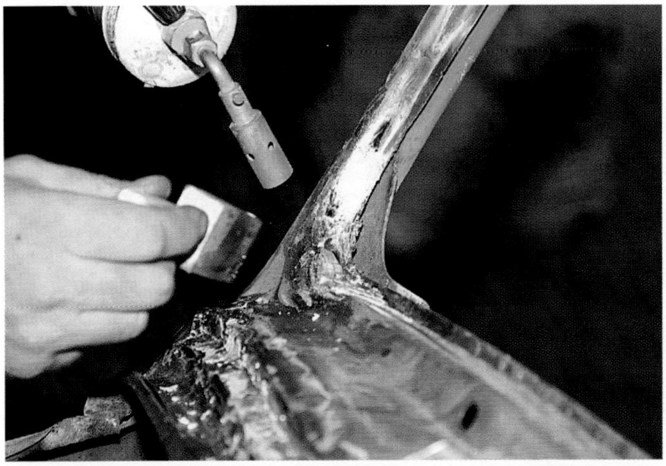

If you make up repair sections for the window aperture it is unlikely they will be accurate enough for the window rubber to sit properly and do its job of keeping out water. Lead loading is the best way to achieve the right shape. Some water will eventually find its way into here, and body filler, being porous, will soak it up and rot the steel underneath. Lead seals the steel.

An alternative to fabricating flitch top rail repair sections is to cut them from a donor shell.

USING 'DONOR' CAR PANELS

Many sections of Beetle bodywork are not available as repair or full panels, and one way to deal with such areas is to cut the same section from a donor car. Because pretty much the same areas rot in different examples of the same car, it's unlikely you'll find a donor car that has any of the common rot-spot sections in good condition. However, donor cars can be a good source for sections of bodywork that are not known for rotting, but which are damaged on your own car.

Beetles that are allowed to tail-slide into a kerb, for instance, often roll onto their side - or even the roof - in both instances, damaging the roof pillars and sometimes the roof. If you can find a non-running Beetle that hasn't been rolled, it is possible to cut some or all of the roof assembly for fitting to your car.

Another reason for cutting up a donor car is to acquire a RHD dashboard for a LHD to RHD conversion, or perhaps just to replace a dashboard that has been butchered in order to fit a modern ICE (in-car entertainment) system or extra gauges,

The difficulty in using panelwork cut from donor cars is that you can rarely cut from an identifiable edge or seam, and the only way to find your cutting lines, or to accurately place the repair section, is by careful measurement.

In the case of a front roof pillar, for instance, you might establish cut lines by measuring from the seam between the

This sorry-looking Beetle is to give its life to save another, as BSW prepares to cut out reusable sections of the bodywork

The body areas that can most usually supply steel in good condition are above the waistline; in this case, areas surrounding the front and rear screens.

Don't expect to find anything worth salvaging in common rot spots!

The most commonly used donor car body panels are the dashboard and top scuttle, which are used not only to replace rotten original steel but also - in the case of the dashboard - for LHD to RHD conversions. Exactly where you cut when salvaging bodywork depends on which sections you need, but, generally, cut the panel oversize and tailor it exactly afterwards.

The dashboard is to be salvaged from this shell. Terry is cutting across the scuttle so that he will have a large but manageable section to take apart in the workshop.

Above: There are no hard and fast cutting lines when the subject is a dashboard, though if any of the steel in the vicinity is rigid through being near a fold (or folds, as arrowed in the photograph) then that's a good place to cut.

Below: Rather than cut along the bottom of the dashboard, Terry has drilled out the spot welds holding it to the scuttle.

However carefully you drill out spot welds in a long flimsy panel like the scuttle, there will be some distortion, which you'll need to clean up using a hammer and dolly.

Offer the replacement dashboard (roughly cut to size) into position to see whether it will fit - often you'll discover small shards of steel on cut edges that still have to be removed.

Clamp the dashboard top edge to the window aperture lip, pull the dashboard into position, and mark lines where old meets new.

The top scuttle and demister duct welded into position. The sequence was: cut the two from the donor shell, part them, weld the demister duct into position, then weld in the top scuttle. A lot of work.

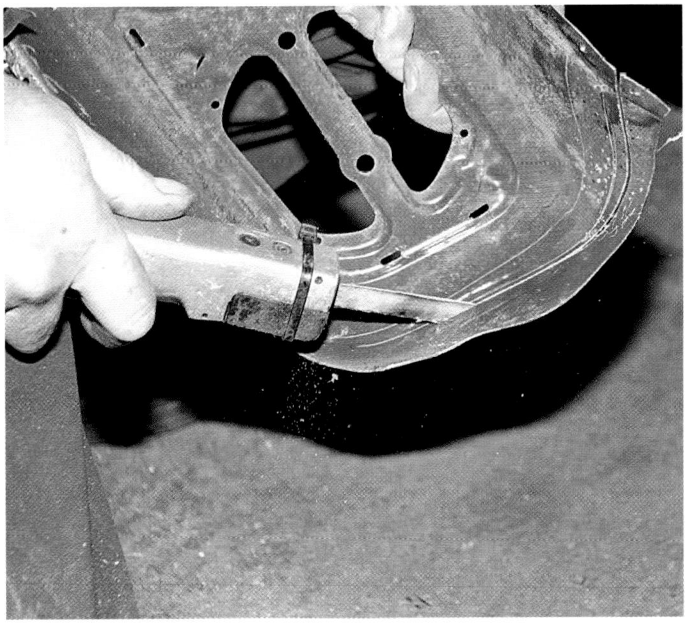

Terry is cutting slightly outside the marked line, intending to overlap the dashboard edge. The alternative is to cut precisely and butt weld them, but the chances of burning through and spoiling the job would be very high.

scuttle and wing. Also take measurements of the depth of the windscreen aperture at set points (which you mark on the top and bottom of the aperture) so you can ensure that the pillar height does not change!

Very few people will be capable of replacing the entire roof section but, if you do, then the rest of the bodywork - especially the heater channels - MUST be sound, because cutting the roof off a Beetle substantially weakens it.

PAINTWORK

Even the most experienced professionals get this wrong from time to time and, in some cases, there's no alternative to removing the topcoat and primer, and starting afresh on bare metal. There's greater potential for things to go seriously and expensively wrong during the painting of the car than at any other time during the restoration. The process involves a considerable investment in paint, which can be wasted because of mistakes during preparation. The tiniest particle of silicone

Terry brazes this joint. Braze is a very good method of joining thin steel that's prone to burning through if electric arc welded, and braze is much easier to grind to shape than weld.

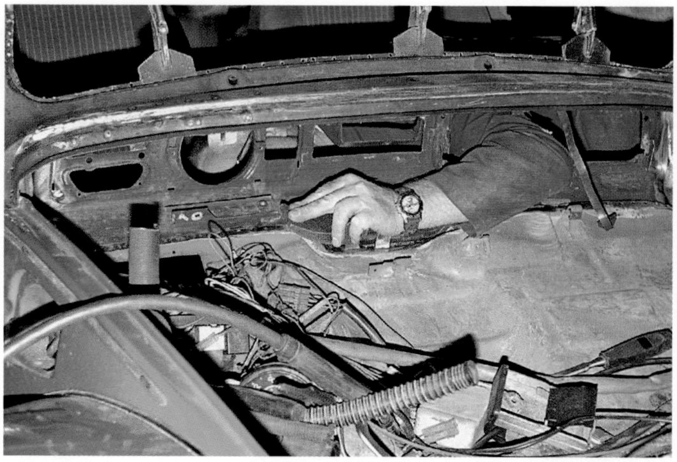

Plug welds will be used to join the bottom edge of the dashboard, so both it and the scuttle edge have to be dollied flat.

You need self-locking wrenches with long jaws to pull the scuttle and dashboard together for spot welding; self-tapping screws are an alternative.

It is imperative that proud plug welds in the window aperture are ground down, or the rubber might leak.

When grinding braze, it's best to use a flexible abrasive disc, because solid discs eat through brass too easily.

The scuttle edges are brazed.

The lower corners of the rear screen are other areas that frequently rot and for which panels cut from donor cars can be used.

Quite how anyone can do so much damage cutting an aperture is not known. One remedy is to cut a complete dash from another car and fit it. In the absence of a donor car, BSW will have to find another solution ...

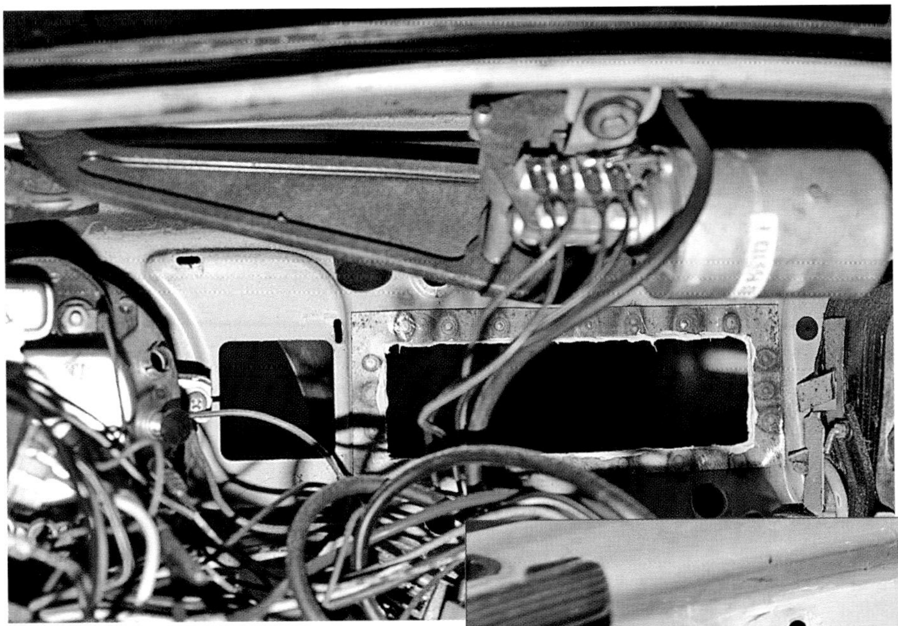

... which was to weld in a new aperture.

The surrounding steel was planished as flat as possible so that a thin skim of body filler restored the smooth surface.

in the atmosphere, dust blowing through a gap in the door, or the paint becoming contaminated by water and/or oil from the compressor: all spell disaster.

There is, therefore, a strong case for having the spraying and paint preparation of your Beetle carried out professionally; the majority of people who do restore their own cars appear to take this option.

Some people prefer to carry out the preparation work themselves and have just the topcoats sprayed by professionals. This approach is fine as long as the preparation is of the highest standard, because shortcomings in the preparation are equally as serious as problems with the application of the topcoats. If you choose to prepare the car for spraying yourself and have the

In between primer and topcoat, remove all masking materials as they will have dry spray on them which will be blown about when the next coat goes on.

topcoats sprayed at a professional spray shop, it's worth asking the person who will be doing the spraying to carry out the final preparation for you.

Before starting spray preparation, stop and consider whether the existing paintwork can be salvaged. If there is a good depth of paint it is often possible to flat, then polish, the most unpromising finish and end up with good-looking results.

The primary objective of painting a car is to prevent the steel of the bodywork from corroding, which paint achieves by insulating the metal surface from the atmosphere. In order for the paint to do this, it must be applied on to corrosion-free, clean, dry and grease-free metal. If paint is applied to metal which has started to corrode, however slightly, that corrosion will spread under the surface of the paint. If paint is applied to a contaminated surface, one of two things can happen; either the contaminant can react with the chemicals in the paint to cause blistering, or one of a dozen different problems, or the paint can fail to adhere properly to the metal. In both cases the paint will sooner or later lift from the surface of the metal and allow corrosion to begin.

The first stage of paint preparation is therefore to remove all traces of rust from exposed metal, and any contaminants (including earlier paint of types which are incompatible with the paint you now wish to spray). In other words, the shell should be taken back to clean, bright metal. This can be achieved using emery paper and much elbow grease, although the modern, dual action and orbital sanding devices speed up and ease the process so much that there can be few today who do this work by hand.

Previous layers of paint and primer do not necessarily have to be removed, as long as they are sanded to provide a key for the new paint, and to remove completely any traces of silicone or other contaminant. Also, the previous paint and primer must be of a type which will not chemically react with the paint you intend to use. Problems can arise if you attempt to spray cellulose over other types of paint, because the powerful cellulose thinners will soften and possibly lift the underlying paint. Before buying your paint, therefore, ascertain which type of paint has previously been used, and ask the paint mixing specialist which paint type can be used over this.

It's best to remove all chrome trim and glass from the car, and thoroughly mask off the interior before you begin to spray. Screen removal is described elsewhere in this chapter; to remove the chrome trim, gently prise away one end with a blunt screwdriver, then use the shaft of a small screwdriver to ease the trim off the clips.

Painting equipmeny and facilities

Three types of equipment can be considered suitable for painting cars. Small, electric sprayers have a very low output and, although they might be ideal for retouching a small area of damaged paint, they will be inadequate for spraying whole cars, or even whole body panels. The recently-introduced warm air sprayers produce a high volume of low pressure air, and are claimed to reduce paint wastage (high pressure compressed air wastes a lot of paint in the atmosphere), and give good results. Unfortunately, an example was not available for testing whilst this book was being prepared.

The traditional equipment consists of an air compressor and spray gun. Air compressors for spraying range from tiny units that have such a short duty cycle (the period of continuous operation) that a roof panel might have to be done in two goes, to giant, floor-standing units with huge air tanks. In-between are a number of compressors which are popular with DIY restorers. The minimum acceptable compressor for serious work would have a 25 litre air tank, although 50 litres is far better, and a 100 litre tank would be by far the best option. Small air tanks rapidly run out of 'puff' when the air pressure drops, and this has to be replenished by the air pump. This puts warmed air into the tank, which can dry the paint in the air before it ever reaches the panel!

In addition to the compressor, you will need at least one - and preferably two - water/oil traps for the outlet connection. When air is compressed, water droplets form in the tank and can be blown through the spray gun to mix with the paint, ruining the painted finish. Also, tiny droplets of oil from the pump will contaminate the air within the cylinder, and both this and the water will have to be filtered before the air reaches the paint gun.

Most spray guns work rather like a carburettor, because as air is forced at high velocity (and hence at low pressure) past a jet of sorts, paint is drawn up to mix with the air in exactly the same way that petrol mixes with air in a carburettor. Other guns have a gravity paint feed and are characterised, not unsurprisingly, by the paint container being mounted on top of the gun. Buy the best spray gun and compressor you can afford, or hire them.

You will also need a mask. Paint which dries in the air forms a fine dust that you should avoid breathing in; because the fumes from thinners are also to be avoided, a respiratory mask is needed rather than a simple dust mask which cannot provide sufficient protection.

It is possible to spray a car outside, given favourable conditions. The weather should not be too hot or too cold, nor wet or windy. A still day is essential, and the temperature should be somewhere in the range of 10-20 degree Celsius. A warmer day may seem a better prospect, but warmer days generate greater winged insect activity, and these are always fatally attracted to wet paint! It is far better to apply paint inside if this is possible, because it allows you some control over the conditions.

The paint should be applied somewhere with a clean, dry atmosphere and good ventilation. The corner of the workshop in which you recently rubbed down body filler is no place for paint spraying unless scrupulously cleaned first. The floor should also be lightly damped down with water to prevent dust from rising into the atmosphere by your movements. You'll require good, even lighting so that you can see which areas you have covered and which you have not.

The temperature and humidity at the time of spraying are important factors. If the temperature is too high, much of the paint can dry in the air before it ever reaches the panel, giving what is known as 'dry spray.' If humidity is too high, water contamination will be apparent as 'bloom.' The surface will be very dull. Avoid very windy days if your workshop is very well ventilated.

Types of paint

Earlier Beetles were finished in cellulose paint. This is quite a good choice for the novice, because it dries fairly rapidly and so reduces the chance of dust falling on to the still-wet, fresh paint surface and spoiling it.

Another beauty of cellulose is that, as long as there is sufficient depth of paint, the surface can be flatted with 1000 or 1200 grit wet and dry, then cut and polished to give a superb finish. Even brushed-on cellulose can be cut and polished to give a top-class finish, provided there is sufficient depth of paint to allow all of the brush marks to be flatted! On the downside, with cellulose there is rather a lot of wastage, and a good thickness is required to produce a luxurious finish as the paint has a low pigment content.

Most body shops today use either synthetic or two-pack paints. Synthetic paints can give an excellent finish but tend to look a little 'plastic' if used on an older car. Synthetic paints have a fairly long drying time, which means a greater chance of airborne dust settling on the surface before it dries. Only two coats of the paint are necessary to produce a gloss finish.

Two-pack paints have a high pigment content and so produce a deep finish. Unfortunately, some of the ingredients of the paints are highly toxic, so they should only be used with proper breathing apparatus, which, in practice, really means an external air supply. Two-pack paints are, therefore, used mainly by well-equipped, professional spray shops.

Preparation

The quality of the paint finish is wholly dependent on the quality of preparation. The entire area to be sprayed should be flatted, using increasingly fine grades of wet and dry, used wet (except on body filler, which would absorb the water). Begin with a coarse grade of 400 grit, and progress through to 1200 grit for the final finish. The surface to be sprayed should be perfectly smooth with no ripples. Use a flexible straight edge to check for unevenness in filled areas.

When the finish is acceptable, begin masking off; masking tape and newspaper is quite acceptable. Avoid using plastic

Vulnerable areas of bodywork can be given protection against flying stones with 'stone chip' paint, which absorbs such impacts. The piece of card is being used as a mask to keep the stone chip paint off the 'A' post.

Floor pans need a tough paint that won't chip easily. Chassis black is the best option.

A 'guide' or 'shadow' coat of black paint has been applied over the high-build undercoat. Flat the guide coat away and you should be left with a smooth surface ready for the topcoats.

When spraying, concentrate on keeping the gun-to-surface distance constant, otherwise you'll get too much paint if you stray too close, too little or dry spray if you stray too far.

sheeting, because the paint will not adhere strongly to this and will quickly dry to a powdery dust, which can be blown around the workshop and on to the painted area before it has dried. Large plastic (dustbin liner) bags are, however, ideal for quickly masking off wheels.

When the masking off is complete, damp down the floor. Clean the metal using a tack cloth, which will remove all traces of paint and filler dust, then finally use spirit wipe to remove any traces of oil or grease.

All types of paint have to be thinned before they can be sprayed; paint manufacturers produce data sheets which will give the correct concentration for the paint used. Strain the primer before thinning it, because even 'new' paint can contain stringy lumps which clog the paint spray gun. An old stocking can be used to strain the paint. After adding the appropriate amount of thinner, stir the mixture well before pouring it into the spray gun. Special cups are available which gauge the paint/thinner solution viscosity by allowing a set amount to drain from a hole in the base of the cup, and timing it. One of these could prove worthwhile for checking the paint/thinner mixture, because the viscosity of the mixture will vary according to temperature. More experienced sprayers can judge viscosity by lifting the stirrer out of the paint and noting how excess paint runs off. In the case of cellulose, aim to get the solution just weak enough for the paint to come off in droplets, rather than in a continuous flow.

You can now set the spray gun controls. There should be one for controlling air flow and one for the paint needle. Set the output pressure from the compressor tank first to 30psi, then fully open the paint and air controls on the spray gun. Make a rapid pass with the gun over a test surface. If large spots of paint can be seen, increase the air pressure at the tank in 5psi increments until a rapid pass produces a suitably fine and even spray. Now adjust the spray gun air and paint controls until the correct size pattern is achieved.

When using the spray gun, the technique is to keep the gun at a constant distance from the surface. Too close and the paint will go on so thickly that runs will develop immediately; too far away, and some of the paint will be air dry before it reaches the surface. Keeping the gun at a constant distance also gives a even spray band width. The gun should have a two-stage 'trigger pull,' whereby stage one allows air to pass through, and stage two opens the paint needle and allows paint into the airflow. The two stages can usually be felt through the trigger, and at the end of the first stage of travel there will be a discernible stop. Further movement of the trigger introduces the paint.

The technique preferred by the author is as follows. When making a pass over a panel, begin to one side of it and start

Always spray the 'awkward' small areas and the edges of a panel first, then move on to the main part.

Below: The tiny paint chip above the chrome trim suggests that the paint went onto a loose surface - probably a solution of paint pigment in water during a flatting operation. This sort of thing is common in nooks and crannies.

Bottom: Removing the side trim reveals a ridge in the underlying paintwork, caused by incomplete rubbing down before a quick respray.

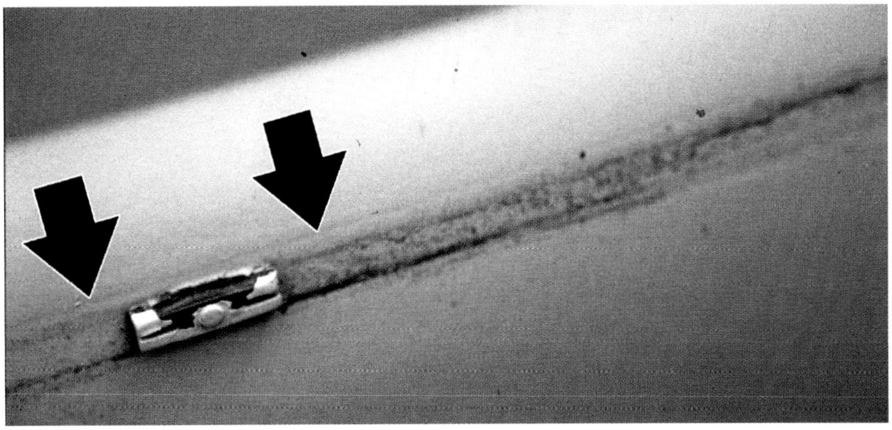

moving the gun with the trigger at stage one, pressing it fully home just before the edge of the panel is reached. Move the gun over the panel in a single, clean movement, and release the trigger back to the first stage when the other edge of the panel is reached, to clear paint from the nozzle. Repeat the exercise until the panel is covered.

Beware 'dry edge,' which is when a band of sprayed paint is allowed to dry before the next band is applied. It could occur if, for instance, you were to begin in the middle of the roof panel and work your way outwards. By the time you came to spray the other half, the first band of paint applied would be thoroughly dry and a visible edge would result. Always begin spraying the roof at an edge.

When you have sprayed your first panel, allow it to dry and inspect it. You are looking particularly for signs of contamination. Small, dark spots surrounded by lighter circles of up to 1 4in diameter are caused by oil/water contamination from the compressor, and another oil and water filter will have to be placed in line. If the surface has paint runs, the gun could be moving too slowly, air pressure could be too high, or the paint too thin. If the paint begins to wrinkle before it dries the underlying surface is contaminated; the primer will have to be removed completely and the surface properly cleaned.

Look closely for scratches, dents and hollows in the underlying surface that the primer may highlight. The problem with matt primer paint is that it can make a rough surface look quite acceptable, even though the final gloss will make every little blemish stick out like a sore thumb. Filler-primers are high-build primers which can be used over areas with small scratches; they lay such a depth of paint on the surface that flatting afterwards can remove many scratches.

The majority of people spray on primer, flat it, and then immediately spray on the topcoats. A friend of the author, Em Fryer, questions the wisdom of being in too much of a hurry to get the topcoats on. Like all paints, primer does not harden fully

Left: When spraying topcoat, spray all the nooks and crannies first ...

Below: ... then spray the larger areas in parallel and overlapping passes.

Bottom: Some people spray on a light coat of paint, wait until it starts to turn 'tacky' and then spray on a heavier coat. The idea behind this is that the first light coat achieves very good adhesion to the undercoats.

for some considerable time after it has been sprayed on and, in the case of cellulose, this usually takes two weeks. If you spray the topcoats over the primer whilst it's still 'soft,' the thinners will have a much more marked affect on the underlying primer than if it had hardened. This manifests itself as marks in the topcoat which show the outline of any body filler used. It's recommended that primer is left to harden for two weeks before being flatted and covered by topcoat.

Some modern primers become inert when they dry, which means they will not react with the thinners used with cellulose paint, and can, in practice, be used as a barrier coat to keep the damaging thinners from underlying paint that is susceptible.

When it has hardened, the primer may be flatted with very fine wet and dry, though a top tip is to first spray on a very light coat in a contrasting colour to the primer, the idea being that the paint will lie in any scratches in the primer. Small scratches in the surface which become apparent after flatting may be filled using body stopper, which should be allowed to cure and then primed. Not even the tiniest scratch should remain if the car is to be painted in cellulose, because this paint shrinks, and the final gloss will show every little flaw, however tiny, in the preparation.

At this stage the author prefers to remove all masking materials and re-mask the car, because over-spray on the masking materials can enter the atmosphere as a fine dust which will contaminate the final finish. Before final masking, go over the primer with 1000 or 1200 grit to get the primer surface really smooth, then examine

It's best to renew masking in-between topcoat layers, because air-dry paint settles on masking materials, and can be blown onto surrounding bodywork, along with the next coat. Note the use of old curtains to mask the road wheels - large plastic bags are an alternative, though, like masking paper, they have to be renewed between coats.

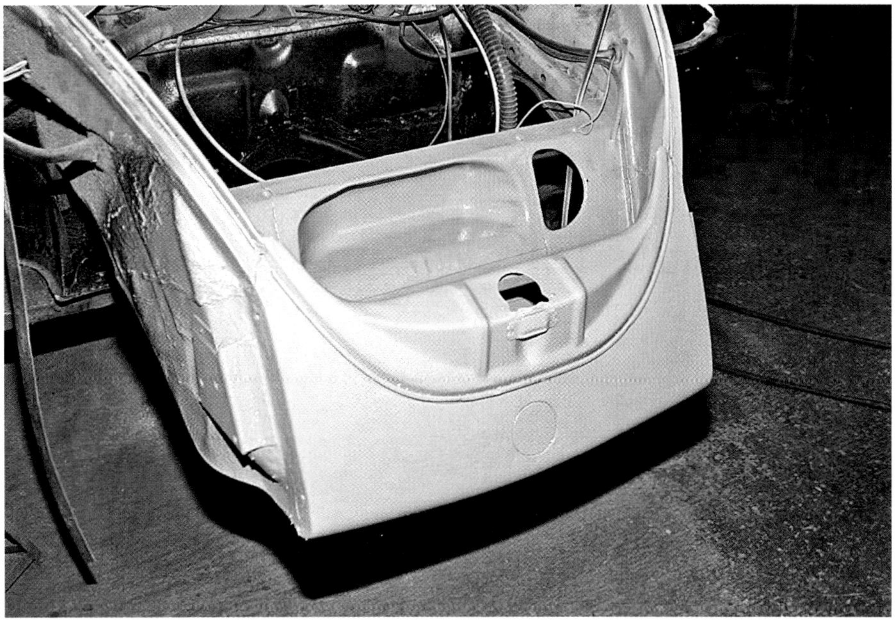

If you're painting parts of a car, remember that paint fades with time, so new paint of the same paint code might not match. Try removing the fuel filler cover, cutting the paint and sending this off for a match.

The petrol flap hinge is held by crosshead set screws. The flap is the easiest piece of bodywork to remove and send off to obtain a matched paint sample.

it minutely - this is your last chance to put right any tiny defects!

Clean the entire surface again, using a tack cloth to pick up any paint and filler dust. The topcoat paint should be strained and thinned, then the surface given a last wipe over with spirit wipe before the first of the topcoats is applied, ensuring there is enough thinner in the paint to allow it to flow by test spraying a piece of scrap hardboard, or similar. The number of topcoats will vary according to the type of paint used. With synthetic paint, two coats will be sufficient to give a good gloss. With cellulose, you could almost apply as many coats as you wish, although three coats should give sufficient depth. With cellulose, coats should be applied at 20 minute intervals, to allow the thinners to evaporate. You can get slow or fast thinners for use in warm or cool conditions.

Remove the masking materials as soon as the paint has dried. If you remove them too soon dry paint dust in the atmosphere will fall on the still-wet surface of the paint. If you remove them too late the paint could have cured to the point where the paint film between the masking tape and the bodywork is so strong that the paint is pulled from the bodywork as the tape is removed.

The preferred order for spraying the car is: roof first, followed by the roof pillars on one side of the car, then the luggage compartment lid, followed by the other roof pillars, and finally the sides, engine bay lid, and valances. If the interior, engine bay and luggage compartment are also being sprayed, it's best to complete these before starting on the outside of the car.

The best advice for the person restoring just the one Beetle, who does not intend to make restoration an ongoing hobby, is have at least the final stages of preparation and application of the topcoats professionally carried out. The cost of paint and reasonably competent equipment can very easily exceed that of a reasonable quality professional respray, and there's great potential for things to go badly wrong for the first-time DIY car sprayer. Even

The engine bay lid spring works even when it's fitted upside-down (as here), but fitting the spring upside-down makes removing the air cleaner very difficult!

Right: Fitting an engine bay lid. Ensuring that the spring is the correct way up, offer the lid into position and locate the spring in the notch provided.

Place the lid on top of the hinges; it should self-support while you fit the bolts (continues on page 212).

if you cut overall outlay by hiring good equipment, rather than buying it, you could still spend almost as much as a reasonable professional respray would cost, but with all the attendant problems of DIY.

Under the wings

The areas underneath the wings are subjected to flying mud and stones when the car is on the move, and so tougher coverings are usually necessary. Underseal can be applied by spray or brush, along with 'stone chip' and other tough paints which absorb some of the knocks and help keep rust at bay.

Still with the wings, the author favours priming these off the car and applying stone chip or similar protection to the inside before bolting them, using small spacers to hold the wings just off the body. The primer is then flatted and the topcoats applied.

Finishing touches

When the spraying is finished, careful examination of the car will usually reveal many small areas which have been missed, or perhaps small blemishes in areas that were not sprayed. These can be dealt with by brushing on paint. On the author's car, the bottoms of the 'A' and 'B' posts, the visible section of heater channel within the door step, and various blemished areas on the doors were hand-painted in this way.

Steel wheels may be stripped (usually they will have plenty of rust which has to be removed) and painted, using a variety of paints. Because the author was building a car to be used rather than for show, he chose to remove loose rust and apply Smoothrite paint - white first as an 'undercoat' followed six weeks later (after this had fully cured) with silver. For show and custom cars, the wheels are best shot-blasted and sprayed with specialist paint, although the after-market offers a wide range of custom wheels which many will find preferable.

You can set the front wheel tracking (the amount by which the wheels should deviate from parallel) roughly by eye, but only to enable you to drive the car to the nearest workshop to set the tracking professionally. This equipment is used by BSW and checks not just the tracking but camber and castor as well.

'BOXING UP'

This motor trade expression (which the author picked up from Terry Ball) basically describes putting the collection of - mainly trim - components back into and onto the completed bodyshell. It can be a time of great frustration or great joy, depending on whether you can remember where you stored each item and how it fits!

Although the restoration is almost at an end, don't rush boxing up. Apart from the risk of damaging paintwork, you also risk damaging the trim items. Do remember that freshly-applied paint stays relatively soft for some time - and that it can easily be damaged until it completely hardens after around two weeks. When leaning over the front wings and working in the luggage compartment, for instance, remove from your pockets sharp objects like keys to avoid damaging the paintwork; if you wear a belt, be aware that the buckle could dent or scratch the paint surface. You can buy specially-made, padded wing protectors to prevent this damage from occurring; an off-cut of carpet, or an old duvet does the same job for nothing.

Carefully examine every component for signs of over-spray, which can be removed with a rag dampened with thinners, mild cutting compound or, alternatively, it may be gently scraped off. A resprayed car looks so much better if all of the external chrome and rubber is free from paint. Pay special attention to the chrome strips and badges, and the wing beading.

CHROMEWORK

Before fitting the bumpers, take time to clean all the old rust from the bumper brackets and paint them, preferably with a rust-resistant primer and a heavy-duty topcoat. The brackets can be seen and rusty old brackets will spoil the look of an otherwise restored car. Put plenty of grease on the bumper bracket bolt threads, so that if the bolts have to come out again they shouldn't shear.

A word of caution: some of the cheaper items of trim which are widely available can turn out to be very poorly made. Don't be surprised if your 'bargain' bumpers are ready-scratched and rusting, and don't be surprised if they are so poorly shaped that fitting them is at best a nightmare and at worst an impossibility. Anticipate finding that bolt holes are in the wrong positions, and that extra holes must be drilled. If you can afford top quality trim, buy it.

An alternative to buying cheap bumpers is to have your own re-chromed, but here again the quality achieved by some chrome plating companies is very poor. As with painting, the most important part of the chroming process is the preparation, and many small companies carry out the preparation themselves, then transport the item elsewhere to have the chrome applied - quite acceptable practice if the results stand the test of time. Use a company which is recommended by previous customers whose chromework has stood the test of time, and always deal with the actual company that carries out at least the preparation - some 'chrome plating specialists' turn out to be no more than agents who send your components away for the entire preparation and chroming process. They are best avoided.

Remove the bumper brackets from the bumpers, fit the brackets loosely to the car and then refit the bumpers - if you try to fit the whole assembly in one go, there's a strong chance that the brackets will scrape new paint from their mounting plates and from the apertures in the wings through which they fit; you don't want the car to begin rusting even before the restoration is finished! If you have new bumpers, firstly drill holes in the front one for mounting the number plate. There is some degree of adjustment in the bumper bracket mounting holes, to allow careful placement; check that the bumpers are parallel to the ground and square to the bodywork before final tightening. If a bumper is not central when fitted (if it sticks out further one side than it does the other), check the mounts, then the symmetry of the mounting holes in the bumpers. If no explanation can be found, the problem could be that the two wings are different shapes!

The chrome strips along each side of the car and down the centreline of the luggage compartment lid simply clip onto their fastenings; if any seem loose, they can be gently pinched up with heavily padded mole grip jaws. If there is paint on these or other items of trim, wipe it off with a rag dampened with thinners, and allow the thinners to fully evaporate before refitting. Allow the paintwork to harden for at least a day or two, and preferably a fortnight, before fitting the chrome trim.

The longer you can leave the paintwork to harden before fitting the lights - especially the headlights - the better. If your car has replacement front wings you might find fitting the headlight units difficult, and possible only after the bowl rim has been gently reshaped with a padded planishing hammer.

The engine lid seal can be fed into its retaining strip, using a little hand soap as a lubricant, if necessary; don't use washing up liquid as a lubricant, as this normally contains industrial salts!

The luggage bay seal is more difficult

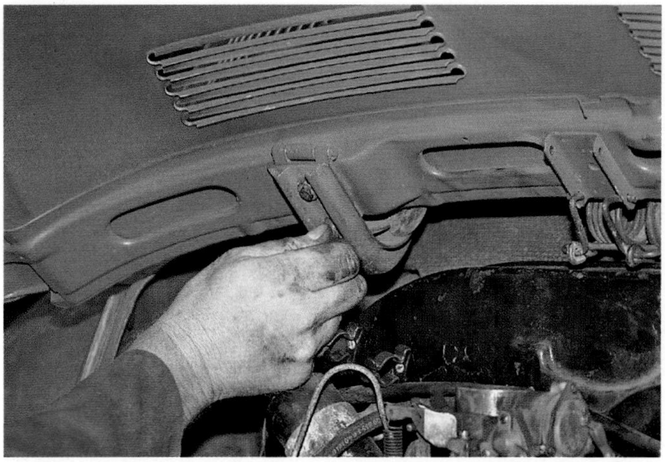

Marks in the paint should show you where the hinge bolts were located. Fit the bolts, manoeuvre the lid so that the washers match the marks in the paint, and tighten the bolts.

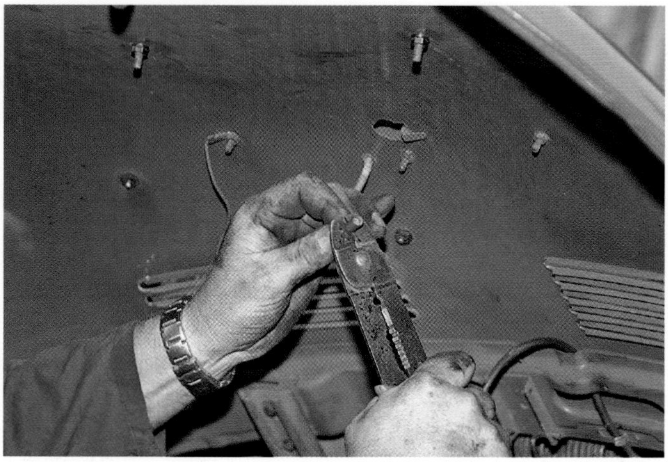

It is probable that the number plate light feed wire had to be cut in order to remove the engine bay lid; fit bullet connectors rather than solder them together.

The heater flap cables pass through separate tubes inside the spine. To remove them, first remove the lever and the tab and washer underneath.

As you pull out the lever and cables, the ends can snag on the ends of their tubes. The new cables will be in two different lengths; the longer one goes to the left hand side heat exchanger, via the upper of the two tubes inside the spine.

When replacing the lever, note which way round the tab goes.

to fit. Push the three moulded rubber fixings each side into their holes and pull from below using long-nosed pliers until they are securely fastened - ensuring that the strip across the back is not twisted. Then ease the strip into its retainers, using a small (blunt) screwdriver and taking care not to puncture it. With both seals, leave plenty of slack at the corners so that the seal is able to lie flat, then trim off the surplus.

Before fitting the luggage compartment handle, ensure that the release cable is doing its job properly: if you close the luggage compartment lid without checking this, you could discover that the only way to reopen it is to grind away the handle ... Adjust the catch using a screwdriver and spanner so that the lid is gripped firmly but not so firmly that the release lever in the glove compartment cannot exert enough pressure to operate it. Start by screwing the catch fully downward, then screw it back in stages until the lid is held firmly and the release lever operates without too much effort.

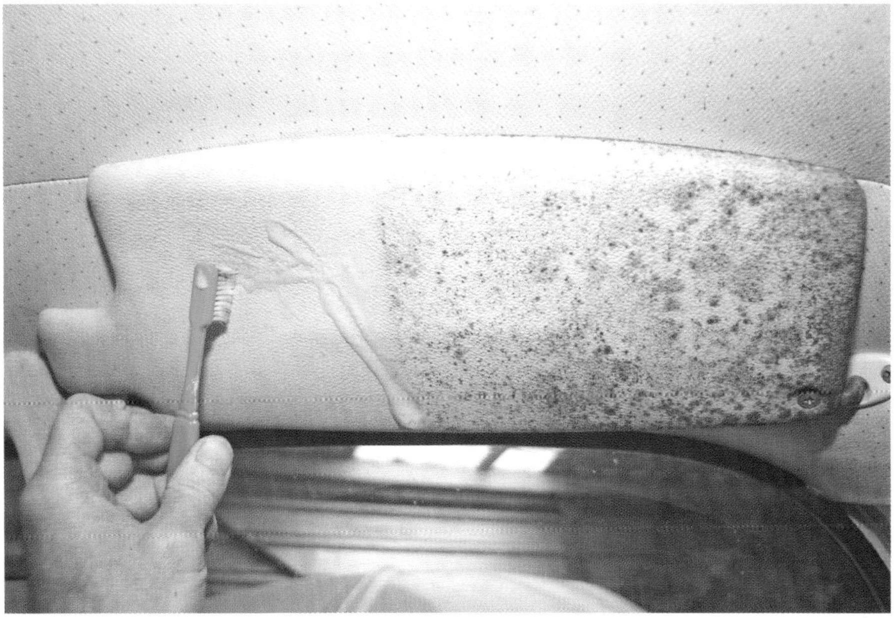

This sun visor was in a dreadful state, but vinyl cleaner should do the trick, as long as you use a brush (an old toothbrush is ideal) to work the cleaning solution into the grain.

INTERIOR

Carpets are generally glued in position along the footwell sides and around the parcel shelf area. The author has tried using many different adhesives but has found that an impact adhesive is essential.

The adhesive usually gives off highly flammable fumes while it is air drying, so be sure there are no potential sources of ignition before starting work. To use an impact adhesive, apply a covering to the carpet backing, then place the section of carpet in position and press down so that some of the glue is transferred to the underlying paintwork. Pull the carpet away. Wait until the glue has apparently dried, then press the carpet into position, being very careful to get the positioning perfect first time, because the carpet will stick instantly and it will not be possible to adjust its position.

Before refitting the pressing which lies under the pedals, check that the pedals are correctly adjusted; the throttle pedal has a full range of travel (it won't if the hinged base has been welded in the wrong position on a new floor pan), and the brake and clutch pedals have reasonable amounts of free travel. The pressing hooks into two slots on the toe board and is held by a single self-tapping screw. This, and the edges of the footwell side carpet, are then covered with the rubber mat.

CASE HISTORY - RVJ 403H

This car was acquired as an MoT failure by Beetle Specialist Workshop on behalf of the author at a price of £200 (spring 1993). The obvious faults which led to the MoT failure included rotten heater channels, rotten rear body mount brackets, and some rot in the floor pans; the rear bumper mountings and the bases of the 'A' posts also required attention. The most attractive aspect of the car - a 1970 1500cc - was that it had not previously had major welded repairs.

Most Beetles of 23 years of age will have either been re-panelled or, more usually, extensively plated. The project car had some body filler, including one huge lump of the stuff, reinforced with chicken wire, around the heel board - but no evidence of welded repairs. Major welded repairs to a car which has not been previously welded are always easier than on a car which has. I have seen no fewer than seven layers of patches (each overlapping the underlying patch) welded

Wipe off the dirty cleaning solution using a clean cloth, and finish with a cloth dampened in water to remove all traces of the cleaning solution.

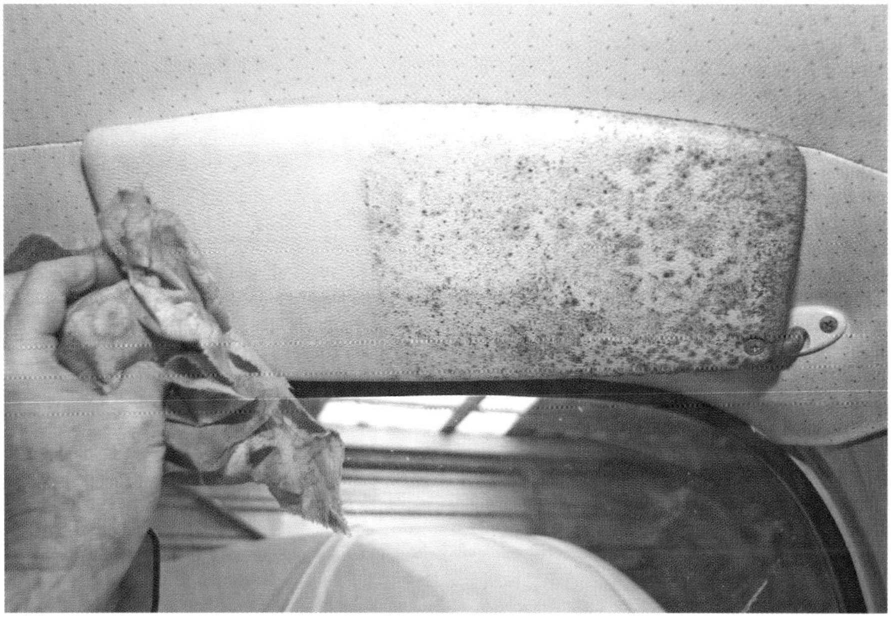

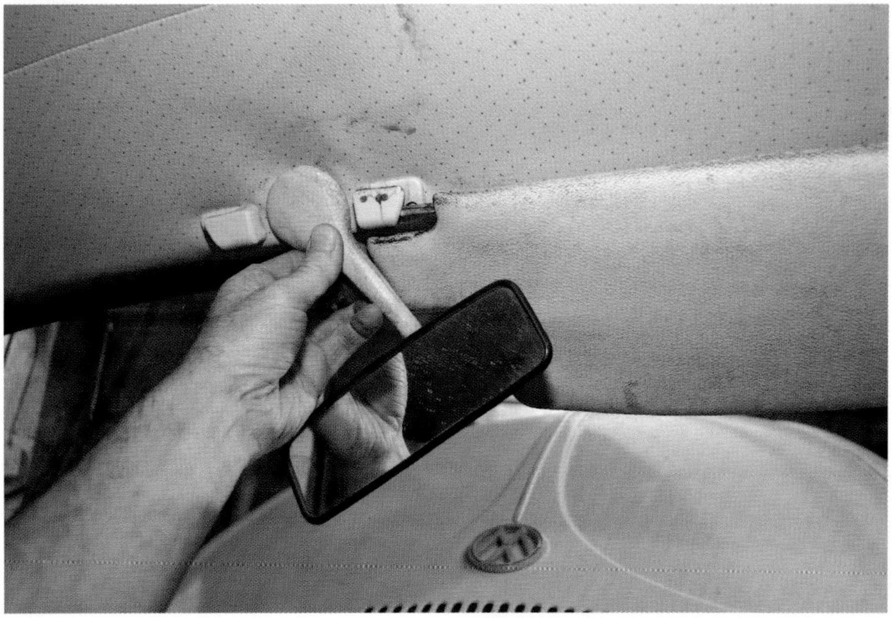

To remove the interior mirror, simply push and turn it anticlockwise.

When refitting the interior mirror, take care not to tear the headlining.

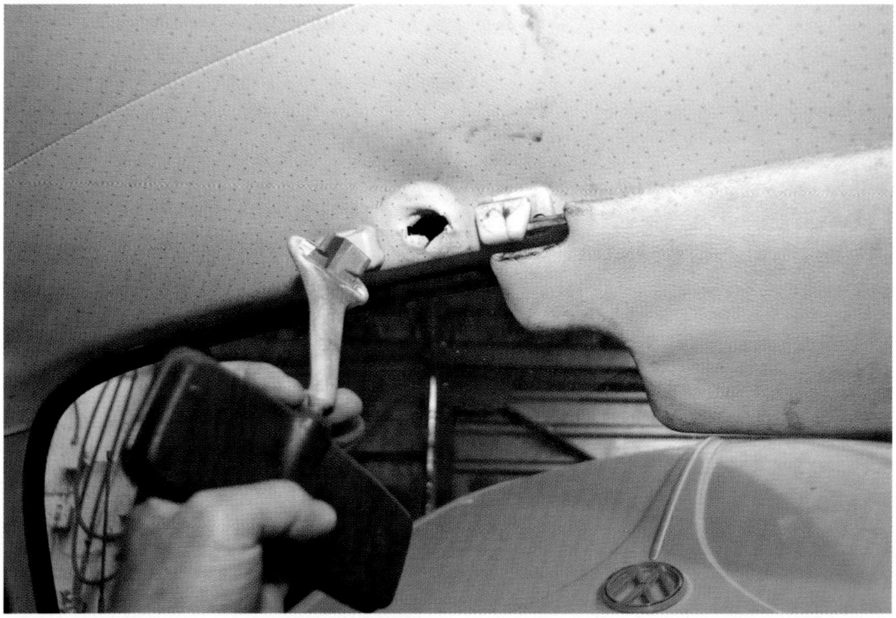

into a Beetle wheelarch, and dealing with that particular car took a very experienced restorer several times as long as did the project car.

The object of the exercise was to combine elements of professional and DIY restoration in order to create a strong and sound car that would not require major attention for many years - but at a budget price. Cost-cutting meant restricting the extent of the professional work to unavoidable and heavy (the author suffers from back problems) tasks such as bodyshell-off work, carrying out the less important but time-consuming work on a DIY basis. Further cost reductions were made by buying second-hand as many spares as possible (seats, etc.), and by utilising various components which the author happened to possess, including an old set of seat belts from an MG Midget, and a battery from a Mini.

It was decided that the serious rot (which meant the body had to be lifted off the chassis assembly) should be dealt with by BSW, and the mechanical and cosmetic aspects of the restoration would be undertaken by the author at home. This type of arrangement is especially worthwhile for anyone working to a tight budget, because it ensures that the important structural work is carried out to the highest standard (so that the car is strong and will not require similar attention for many years), and it allows the remaining build-up to progress as and when funds allow. If you don't set a tight timescale for the rebuild, it's surprising how many spares can be acquired either as special offers, or second-hand at low prices from VW shows, through classified advertisements, or even by buying an MoT failure car with good mechanicals.

The workshop time needed to carry out all structural welding, plus mechanical and boxing up work to MoT standard, was estimated at eighty hours. The author booked forty hours' workshop time, estimated as the minimum time required to complete the body-off structural welding and reassemble the car to a driveable state.

With the major work completed by BSW, the car was trailered home to the author's garage for painting and boxing up. As with previous restorations, the author chose cellulose paint, not only for its relative ease of use but also because it looks right on a car of this vintage.

Two small welded repairs had to be done: the base of the flitch panel was rusted thin and was pulling out from under the 'A' post lip; and the nearside door had an area in the centre which had also rusted thin and was covered in perforations. The flitch repair was easily made up from sheet steel, folded and welded in without mishap, before being 'tinned,' lead loaded and finally flushed over with body filler. The door repair was more problematic.

When a large, flexible panel - such as a door skin - is welded, the heat generated is liable to cause the panel to buckle, and this is what happened. After a rectangular hole had been cut from the panel with an angle grinder, a replacement piece was butt welded in, using the MIG welder at its lowest setting. With the job completed, a concave dent was apparent in the centre of the panel. This was expected, but what was not anticipated was that, when the dent was pushed back out, several new and smaller dents appeared elsewhere in the door skin.

The author beat flat the skin as best he could, then used copious amounts of filler to achieve a fair surface; the idea being to acquire a replacement door at one of the Beetle shows, or perhaps obtain and fit a new skin at a later date.

All areas to be sprayed were taken back to bare metal or sound paint, then treated to two coats of high-build filler-primer. The feathered edges of surrounding paintwork in some instances immediately blistered, indicating one of two things: either the paint was contaminated (possibly with silicone) or, more probably, the car had been given a barrier coat to isolate existing paintwork from new. Barrier coats might typically be used on synthetic-painted surfaces which have been flatted prior to respraying in cellulose, and they keep the powerful cellulose thinners away from the underlying paint. The blistered areas were allowed to harden and flatted back, then given a barrier coat - neat Tractol was ideal - before further (successful) applications of high-build primer.

The primer was allowed to harden and flatted back to give the topcoats something to grip, then the topcoats were applied.

During the spraying, the usual problems of using too-small a compressor and hence getting air-dry spray were encountered. The final coat sprayed on was almost pure thinners, which encourages the surface of the existing paint to 'flow' and give a better finish. Two weeks after the paintwork was completed, it was cut back to reveal fundamental flaws.

The roof section paintwork - apart from a few dents and scratches - was found to be thick enough to simply flat with 1000 grit, cut and polish; the engine lid, much of the sides of the car, and the luggage compartment were similarly dealt with. However, in treating those few small dents and scratches, disaster struck.

At some time, the original topcoat of the car had been over-painted with a bright blue paint of unidentified type. On top of this were further layers of cellulose. In the course of sanding the small repair areas, the author revealed small areas of said blue paint which, when covered with further cellulose, caused an immediate reaction which lifted the cellulose from the surface in a large bubble. In other areas where the blue paint had not been revealed the same thing happened, presumably because either tiny scratches from the flatting had reached the paint, the paint had contaminated the existing topcoat, or the cellulose thinners used had softened the very thin layer of cellulose paint and permeated through to the aforesaid bright blue paint.

Various types of paint which happened to be lying around the workshop were tried as barriers, and eventually the author resorted to neat Tractol. This was sprayed over the problem areas, but caused yet further problems.

The author's spray gun was spitting - giving small areas of over-spray which the author did not attach any significance to. However, when the topcoat had been applied and left for two weeks to harden, initial cutting revealed thousands of tiny red spots in the new surface. Tractol doesn't shrink as much as cellulose when it dries (especially when used neat), and so each tiny spot lay just under the surface of the topcoat, ready to break through the moment cutting compound was wiped over it. The cellulose had to be flatted properly and another coat applied.

Flatting the cellulose revealed more areas of the bright blue paint which reacted so badly when top-coated which were too widespread to be treated individually as before. One possible, though drastic, solution was to take the whole roof back to bare metal and begin again, but this would still leave the problem of the blue paint at the edges - no matter where these were. The chosen solution was to order a proper barrier paint (Bar Coat) from local supplier, Bancrofts, cover the entire roof with this, apply two coats of filler-primer, and finally topcoat it.

A protracted bout of stormy weather put a stop to work before the pre-paint preparations were complete. When a suitable day eventually dawned, the author was in such a bad state of mind that he failed to properly flat some areas, and was rewarded with some very uneven areas around the bases of the quarter panels, which were all too obvious when the topcoats had been applied.

The front valance and luggage lid were blessed with lavish applications of filler where a frontal collision had left small dents. The dents were beaten out and the bare metal sprayed; the results weren't bad, and far better, in fact, than with the filler. The lower portion of the luggage compartment lid was treated to two coats of stone chip - a paint which goes on thick and sets hard so that stone chips don't penetrate through to the metal. This was top-coated, along with the rest of the luggage compartment lid.

With the spraying finally finished, the author spent a couple of days going over the interior and exterior paintwork, cutting back or touching up all of the blemishes in the existing paintwork. Areas which would be tricky to mask off for spraying, such as the bottom of the 'A' posts, and visible portion of the heater channel within the doorstep, were brush-painted. When brushing on cellulose, apply enough thicknesses to cut back to a nice, even surface after the paint has hardened. The author also took the opportunity to clean all external trim items before they were refitted to the car.

The rear wing beading was a nightmare to fit, because the only available beading was intended for a front wing! Some tailoring with a pair of scissors was necessary so that the wing bolts aligned with the cut-aways in the beading; even so, it took two or three attempts to complete the job.

The author had a spare battery which, unfortunately, was the wrong shape to be gripped by the standard fitting. After some deliberation, an extension for the clamp was fabricated which held the battery very firmly. The alternatives, which included welding another length of threaded rod to the floor pan to bring the existing clamp closer to the battery, were ruled out, because they would have been only temporary solutions until the author could afford to buy the correct battery!

With the project car resplendent in its L50B Diamond Blue paint, the old, rusted bumpers looked very out of place, so new bumpers and running boards were ordered, along with black and silver pressed alloy number plates which were appropriate for a car of this age. Again, the new components made other fittings look decidedly tatty, so new screen rubbers, front and back, were acquired and fitted.

The author foolishly decided to economise when buying bumpers, and settled for a cheap, imported variety. These came ready-rusted and with chrome which looked as though it would not see a full year before it started to blister. Worse still, when offered up to the brackets (which were loosely bolted in place on the car), only two bolt holes were anywhere near their corresponding bracket holes. The two centre holes were just under two inches away from the bracket, and had to be pulled in with long bolts and clamped with a G clamp; only then could the standard bolts be fitted. The strain imposed on the brackets by pulling the bumper into shape was huge and, if the author had fastened the brackets to the bumpers before fastening them to the car, there is no way they could have been forced into the wing slots.

Cheap running boards were also acquired, and proved every bit as unsatisfactory as the bumpers. The main problem was the bolt slots which, on one side of the car, were over half-an-inch away from where they should have been, necessitating enlargement of the slots to a ridiculous degree before the boards could fit.

The fuel gauge was not functioning. The first check - earthing the tank terminal via a 6W bulb and then directly - was to no avail, indicating that the actual gauge was the problem. A replacement speedometer - for 1970 cars the fuel gauge is an integral part of this, although the fuel gauge is separate on most earlier cars - was sought. It was eventually established that the fault lay with the fuel gauge voltage regulator (trembler); details are given in the previous chapter.

Finally, it was all down to preparation work for the MoT. This involved setting up the handbrake, checking all electrical equipment, windscreen wipers and washers, and so on. When you have successfully prepared a car for the MoT a few times, the work is a breeze. You obviously cannot properly test the brakes without a set of rollers, but if you jack up each wheel in turn, have a helper apply the brakes, and use your 36mm socket and extension bar to try and turn the lifted wheel, you'll get a pretty fair idea of how effective the brakes are, and will certainly know if any are sticking.

The evening prior to the MoT test, the nearside sidelight refused to work. The lamp unit was removed and the problem revealed as worn spring contacts. Unfortunately, in trying to reshape the contacts, the author inadvertently brought them together, which blew the fuse. It's strange how, when under pressure, you can overlook the most obvious cause of a fault and try to find a cause elsewhere. The author did not even stop to consider whether a blown fuse might be the culprit, and started tracing the feed wire back, testing with a lamp to see whether he could find power.

Then he noticed that the rear light had also stopped working and, after stripping and reassembling the unit, remembered that the sidelight circuit was fused. The 16 amp fuse was replaced, and the project car again had sidelights. However, the brake lights now refused to illuminate. This time, the author began tracing the fault by looking at the fuse, which had blown. The neighbour who had come to the rescue with the 16 amp lights fuse now kindly supplied two 8 amp fuses, the first of which popped as the author re-tested the brake lights. Because the rear lamp cluster had been removed and replaced, the author began by looking here, and discovered that, on replacement, the spade end connector of the stop lamp feed wire had touched and managed to scratch the paint on the wing, causing a direct short to earth.

The remedy was to bend the tab and insulate the spade connector, after which it was all systems go for the MoT test the following morning. The 'fairy tale ending' to this restoration was an MoT pass at the first attempt.

As with any 'new' classic car, the author gave the project car a number of local 'shakedown' runs to discover what problems might be looming. The car had a tendency to jump out of first gear on the overrun (initially thought to be a worn selector mechanism, but happily only a wrongly positioned gear lever plate), and there was a transmission whine in fourth gear. Taken together, the two problems hinted at a gearbox strip down or exchange.

A slow oil leak became apparent as a black patch on the garage floor; this was traced to a leaking rocker tube seal. When accidentally changing from third gear into reverse, rather than second - embarrassingly, right outside the local garage - the author discovered that the flanges on the gearshift plate were a little on the worn side. The plate was replaced to save further embarrassment ...

The project car had its perfect public debut at the 1993 British Volkswagen Festival - a highly recommended annual event. Happily, the venue for this is within ten miles of the author's home, so the journey there and back amounted to little more than another shakedown run.

The author moved to the project car from a 1966 MGB GT, a veritable old warhorse of a sports car which can still show the young colts a thing or two on the open road. Despite fairly harsh treatment (the author drove the Beetle at similar speeds to the MGB GT), the project car regularly returned between 30 and 31 miles to the gallon (87kpl). In daily use, the car is far from perfect, but then, perfect cars attract vandals and thieves. In any case, the author favours comfort over concours. It still goes like a little rocket!

Future projects include transaxle removal and overhaul, plus, perhaps, a few tasteful minor modifications. However, because a 1970 1500cc Beetle is quite a desirable classic car in standard trim, it may well remain so.

Update

After nearly seven years of daily use, and being repaired for no other reason than photographic purposes, the Beetle was sidelined by the acquisition of a 4WD, essential to cope with flooded roads one winter. For three full years the car languished out in a field, used only occasionally for joy-riding in the field, wet grass being the perfect surface on which to practise how to regain control of a Beetle, should the rear end ever decide to slide ...

When the decision was taken to update and reprint my original book, ten years after the restoration work was carried out by BSW, the original bodywork and chassis repairs were still as sound as the proverbial bell, which is remarkable, because the car has outlived many others that were brand new when Terry Ball welded the MoT failure car in 1993. A neighbour's car, which was made in 1993, has just been taken to a workshop for welded repair!

PROFESSIONAL RESTORERS

There are degrees of restoration. The Beetle Specialist Workshop can, for instance, carry out just essential welded repairs to a customer's Beetle for a DIY respray and mechanical rebuild or - if desired - produce a restored Beetle that's re-panelled and fully rust-proofed, which looks and drives like new (with the added bonus that it should outlast many of today's new cars).

However, just as in any other trade, there are good and bad Beetle restorers, ranging from highly regarded companies to the worst examples of backstreet cowboy body shops. It can be difficult for the newcomer to tell which end of the Beetle restorer spectrum he or she is dealing with just by looking at freshly-painted Beetles; the worst restorers are often the most talented body filler sculptors, and a car restored by such a business might look good for a year or two before rust spreads underneath the layers of filler, with the inevitable result that the filler drops out!

The best way to judge a restoration business is by inspecting cars restored by the business, but which were restored two, three, or preferably more, years previously. The best place to see a selection of cars restored by different businesses is at one of the many Beetle meetings.

Few owners of top-quality, professionally restored Beetles will be able to resist showing off their cars if you take an interest, and aggrieved owners of badly-restored cars won't be slow to name the company that bodged their car. Most Beetles are, by now, old enough to have had some body repair or restoration work and, if you attend one of the larger shows which can attract thousands of visitors and their Beetles, you will have a wealth of experience - good and bad - to draw upon!

Begin your search for a restorer reasonably close to home, so that you can easily keep in touch with the workshop staff as the restoration progresses, and perhaps call in once or twice to ensure everything is going smoothly, and your car is actually being worked on. The second rule of choosing a restorer is to only consider Beetle specialists; general restorers - however good - might not be familiar with the Beetle spares scene. They could waste countless hours making up replacement panels which are readily available, or waste a lot of your money by buying overpriced components for which far cheaper sources can be found.

Don't expect to take up too much of the restorer's time. Do remember that all car restorers are plagued by the occasional time-waster who overstays their welcome, asking question after question, requesting endless estimates but never actually getting around to commissioning the work.

Don't turn up to view a restoration business without an appointment, because you probably won't be very welcome for interrupting workshop time booked to and paid for by another customer. However, arriving an hour or so before the appointed time might allow you to see the workshop in its natural state before it's readied for your inspection. If you discover huge tins of body filler lying around, new panels being welded on top of rusted metal, or stored in damp conditions, draw your own conclusions ...

Look at the tools used by the business; poor quality sockets or spanners, for instance, will probably 'round' nuts, and cheap, damaged screwdrivers will distort screw heads. Determine whether there's any semblance of order in the workshop; if tools are strewn about the place the restorer could spend almost as much time trying to find lost tools as in restoring the car.

You then have to discuss with the restorer exactly what work you want done, so arm yourself with a list of jobs that you know are necessary. Some rogues will happily underestimate the amount of work needed in order to present you with an attractively low-priced estimate. The final bill, of course, will be far higher as the company will telephone with the awful news that a lot more panels than originally thought need replacing. Others might try to include work that is not really necessary.

Make certain that both you and the restorer are absolutely clear about the results you expect. If you want absolutely flawless concours paintwork, for instance, then emphasise the fact, because the pre-paint preparation will take far longer (at an obviously increased cost) than for a normal respray, and final examination, cutting, and so on, will also take much more of the restorer's time.

The restorer will examine your Beetle, and draw up an estimate for the work; this should list all components and consumables to be used, and detail labour charges. You won't get the estimate there and then (if you are given an estimate on your first visit it's obviously not going to be very accurate), but the restorer will usually post it to you within the week.

Obtain at least two or three estimates before commissioning any work, just to give yourself a comparison. Unduly high or low estimates should be regarded with caution; there could be a perfectly reasonable explanation why the estimate is so far from the norm, but the chances are that the business is either charging top whack because it does not want to undertake the job, and will only do so if you pay an arm and a leg or, conversely, underestimating in order to secure the business. If one estimate is markedly higher than the average, it's worth discussing why this should be with the restorer; it could be that the estimate is deliberately on the high side to cater for any unforeseen extra work. If this doesn't happen and the job is completed ahead of time, then you could receive a much smaller final bill.

Check the prices quoted for components; you might be able to shop around and acquire these more cheaply to save money. If the estimate from your chosen restorer is still beyond your means, ask whether you can carry out part of the preparation work (initial strip down, etc.) at home and deliver the bodyshell/chassis on a trailer.

Good restoration companies are always in demand, and might not be able to start work on your car for some time because the workshop is booked up for months in advance. If a restorer can take your car at short notice be wary, unless a plausible explanation - such as a cancelled restoration (this does happen) - can be proven.

Payment usually consists of a non-returnable deposit (on commission of the restoration rather than on its commencement), followed - sometimes - by stage payments, and sometimes by a bill on completion. The deposit should not exceed 10 per cent or so of the estimate (if an unduly large deposit is requested there's always a chance that the business is about to go bankrupt and is trying to raise cash by whatever means). Stage payments will usually comprise a third of the money when a third of the work has been completed, and so on.

The deposit should be used by the restorer to buy in components and materials for the restoration, and stage payments should also be used for this purpose. If a large deposit or stage payment is demanded, check that it does not exceed the cost of materials used.

SAD BUT TRUE ...

Many DIY restorations end up with a professional restorer for finishing for a number of reasons. Not all restorers will be happy to pick up the pieces of a failed or terminated DIY restoration, and the prices quoted will usually reflect this. From experience, restorers know that putting right someone else's mistakes always takes longer than doing the job properly in the first place, so, if you're in this situation, expect to have to pay the price.

Chapter 4
About the Beetle

The Beetle has had literally many tens of thousands of factory modifications throughout its 50-plus year production life. The following is an abridged production history of the car, for the interest of the newcomer to the Beetle scene, and intended as a guide for those readers seeking a particular year and model. It applies to UK imported cars; cars sold in other Volkswagen export markets may differ in many respects.

Designed by Ferdinand Porsche during the years 1934-1938, the 'Type 60' proved the ideal car to meet the requirements of German Chancellor Adolf Hitler, who had a vision that, one day, every German would own his own motorised transport. The Volkswagen (People's Car) Beetle was intended to enter production in 1938 and, on 26th May of that year, the Volkswagen plant was officially opened.

Up until 1946, the Volkswagen plant (called 'Strength Through Joy Town') was owned by the National Socialist (Nazi) political party and was not a commercial company as such but a political creation. During the war years, the Volkswagen factory was used for the manufacture of a limited number of Beetles (some authorities place war-time production at 1500 cars), and also several types of military vehicle based on the Beetle platform and sharing its engine and running gear, the best known of which is the *Kubelwagen*. The factory was intensively bombed and nearly destroyed by the Allies as the war neared its end.

After the cessation of hostilities, a group of British Army personnel from the Royal Electrical and Mechanical Engineers (REME) was dispatched to the plant to salvage what they could, and - if possible - to re-establish the production of cars. A single Beetle survived in the wreckage of the factory. The British Army personnel sent to the plant knew that the occupying forces were desperate for immediate and low cost motorised transport. They painted the surviving Beetle in military colours, demonstrated it to the military governments, and were rewarded with an order for 20,000 Beetles. A production target of 1000 cars a month was set - for a factory which did not even have a roof - and through a combination of hard work, innovative use of military and other available resources, and suffering (the first winter's production took place under a temporary tarpaulin roof), the 1000th Beetle was produced in March of 1946.

A German management team, headed by Heinz Nordhoff, was assembled during the latter part of 1947, and in 1949 the factory was handed over to the regional government of Saxony.

By 1947, production had risen to 2500 cars a month, and the factory slowly gained momentum over the following years, in 1950 celebrating completion of the 100,000th Beetle. Thereafter, production accelerated, and the one millionth Beetle milestone took only another five years to reach. It's easy to gloss over the one millionth Beetle production landmark without properly appreciating its significance. In the mid-fifties, total production figures of most cars were limited to a few thousand, those of a small number of cars reached tens of thousands, and only a few particularly successful cars went on to hundreds of thousands; million-sellers were as rare as hen's teeth. If ever a company could be said to have risen, pheonix-like, from the ashes, it was surely Volkswagen during the 1950s.

Despite attempts by the British Society of Motor Manufacturers and Traders to prevent Beetle exports (the car must by now have been seen as a serious threat to perhaps previously complacent UK manufacturers), exporting began. The Beetle was not introduced to the UK until 1953 (fitted with a 1131cc engine, and until late 1953 characterised by a split rear window) but, although over 500,000 examples of this version were manufactured, UK sales did not really begin in earnest until the following year with the introduction of the Type 1 (1200).

Sold in both Standard and Deluxe versions, this model had an enlarged 1192cc engine which delivered 30bhp. The new model featured vacuum ignition advance and improved cooling for the cylinder head. In total, in excess of seven million examples of the 1200 Standard and De-Luxe were sold worldwide.

A 1958 vintage right hand drive Beetle is quite a rarity today. Like many, this example is far from original, housing a 1600cc, fuel-injected Mexican engine.

A 1960s Beetle is also fairly rare nowadays, especially in such good condition. This example richly deserves its place in a Pembrokeshire motor museum.

In 1955, the first Karmann Cabriolet was offered on the UK market, four years after its introduction elsewhere. The following year, the exhaust system was altered to the now-familiar twin tail pipe set-up and the cars offered relative luxury with adjustable front seat backs. Battery capacity was increased to 66 amp hours and, along with interior cosmetic improvements, the bumper had overriders.

In 1957, tubeless tyres were fitted in place of crossply. The following year, the front and rear screens were enlarged and larger drum brakes were fitted.

In 1959, the chassis was strengthened, and, in the following two years, the Beetle enjoyed a host of improvements and modifications. In 1960, a front anti-roll mechanism was fitted, along with external door push buttons, and the generator output was increased. In 1962, the engine power was boosted to 34bhp by increasing the compression ratio. An automatic choke and a windscreen washer were fitted. The fuel tank was altered. The De-Luxe even had an all-synchromesh gearbox. In 1964, a folding rear seat appeared, and the Beetle became available in a new range of colours.

In 1965, the 1200A was introduced. The size of windscreen front and rear increased. Late that year, the 1300 was introduced; basically, a 1200 fitted with a 1285cc, 40bhp engine. Production of the 1300 ran to some 2.7 million examples. The following year, a convertible became available for a short time.

1967 was a busy year. The 1200A acquired a reserve fuel tank, and the 1300 rear suspension was altered to give a wider track. Late in the year, the 1500 was introduced with a 1493cc engine delivering 44bhp. In four years of production, some 1,800,000 1500s were manufactured.

In 1968, the 1200 gained fully independent suspension, some cosmetic improvements, and an external fuel cap. The 1300 made the switch from 6 volt to 12 volt electrics, had dual circuit braking, and a fuel gauge. The 1500 shared these improvements and had carburettor modifications.

In 1969, the 1200 also received 12 volt electrics, plus hazard warning lights and a locking fuel cap. In addition, the 1300 was available with a semi-automatic gearbox and radial ply tyres. The 1500 also acquired a steering column lock.

As the 1970s dawned, the 1200 received a modified carburettor and dual circuit braking, plus new-style glass. The 1500 was discontinued.

In 1971, the 1200 gained a larger windscreen. The 1300 also received more power and was fitted with larger brakes. The 1600 Super was introduced late in '71 as the 1302S, fitted with the 1584cc unit. This car was the first to feature the new diagonal rear suspension, with double jointed drive shafts, and a Mcpherson strut front suspension. It also had front disc brakes.

The following year, the 1200 gained a larger rear window. The 1300 and 1302S were fitted with an electronic diagnostic socket, but both 1300 models were discontinued in late '72. One point of special note is that, in 1972, the Beetle took the all-time car production record (15,007,034) from the Model T Ford, and this was celebrated with a limited edition 'World Champion' version.

In 1973, the gear lever and handbrake levers were re-positioned. The 1300A was introduced as an economy version, and was essentially a 1200 car with 1300 engine. The 1303 (1285cc) and 1303S (1584cc) were introduced with the same basic bodyshell as the 1302S, but with a curved windscreen. The rear wings were enlarged, and disc brakes were fitted at the front end of the 1303S. The gear ratios were altered. A special Limited Edition GT Beetle was sold with a 1584cc engine.

In 1975, the 1303 and 1303S were fitted with rack and pinion steering, but, that same year, UK imports of both versions ceased. The following year, the 1200 became the 1200L. The extra De-luxe features were all in the interior of the car. In 1977, a convertible version of the 1303 made by Karmann was sold as the 1303 LS, and appears to have been imported into the UK until 1979.

Saloon sales to the UK ended in 1977. European production of the saloon continued to 1978, and of the cabriolet until 1980. Of course, production of the Beetle did not stop, but was merely transferred to other countries: Peru, Nigeria, Brazil, the Philippines and Mexico. In its place, Volkswagen offered the ill-fated K70 series for a short period before hitting gold again with the amazingly successful Golf series.

By the 1990s, the Beetle was still being manufactured in Mexico at the rate of 450 a day, and was, in fact, that country's best-selling car. In June of 1992, the twenty-one millionth Beetle rolled off the

Mexican production line - an achievement met by resounding indifference from the British motoring press. Perhaps this lack of recognition is not so surprising when you consider that the Beetle overtook the previous all-time production record (Model T Ford) twenty years previously, and that every single Beetle manufactured after that time sets a new production record! The Beetle's production record is almost certainly unassailable now, because all manufacturers change their models substantially every few years, whereas the Beetle was made in more or less the same form over 57 years.

The Beetle then returned to the shores of Britain as Mexican-built cars, imported in small numbers to sell to enthusiasts who wanted a new car, but one with more character than the efficient but often bland offerings of the 1990s. One apparent side-effect of the availability of brand-new Beetles was a reluctance amongst enthusiasts to pay as much as (if not more than) the price of a new Mexican Beetle for a restored Beetle, which hit the UK restoration trade. To make matters worse, a convertible was also available (Bieber Cabriolet), giving the enthusiast the opportunity to acquire - at a far lower price than that of the Escort or Golf convertible - a brand-new, open four-seater with bags of character but without any of the drawbacks inherent in running a classic.

Finally, in 2003, Beetle production in Mexico ended. Interest in restoring old Beetles is bound to rise as a result.

The Beetle formed the basis for a range of other vehicles. On the surface, this Karmann Ghia looks nothing like a Beetle ...

... but look under the engine bay lid and you'll find an air-cooled flat four. The early Karmann Ghia was based on the chassis of the 1200cc Beetle.

LIVING WITH A BEETLE

The first thing you tend to notice when driving a Beetle is that you have enrolled - automatically - into the great and very friendly family of Beetle enthusiasts. The driver of virtually every other Beetle you see on the roads will acknowledge you with a wave or a flash of the headlights. This camaraderie extends to drivers of other air-cooled Volkswagens; drivers of Karmann Ghias, campers and vans, type 3s and 4s, will also almost always acknowledge you. Before long you'll find yourself drawn into the spirit of things, and will wave back without conscious effort.

If you are unfortunate enough to suffer a roadside breakdown, it would be almost unthinkable for a driver of an air-cooled VW to pass by without stopping to offer assistance. Likewise, you will feel under an unofficial obligation to stop and help if you see a fellow air-cooled VW driver in difficulty.

Something else noticed on your first Beetle drive is that it's fun! Cars today are smooth and quiet, with free-revving engines; the Beetle offers none of the attributes that modern drivers deem so essential, yet, driving along with that torquey flat four chugging away in the 'boot,' and making its presence felt in the passenger compartment both in vibration and decibels, is actually a refreshing experience.

In these days of lean-burn engines and catalytic converters, some environmentally aware types might look upon the Beetle with some concern. The fuel consumption is hardly frugal by today's standards, and the pollution from the average Beetle exhaust is higher than environmentalists would like to be the case. Yet, in reality the Beetle is both economical and surprisingly 'green.'

The economy stems from the fact that, compared to almost any recent vehicle, the Beetle (new imported cars excepted) is essentially a non-depreciating car, so that, irrespective of fuel consumption, repair and other costs, Beetle ownership over a period of years is relatively cheap. For the price of two or three years' depreciation on a new, modern family saloon car, you can buy and run a Beetle. For the price of five years' depreciation on the modern car, you should be able to buy, restore and run a Beetle: after the five years are up, the modern car will have depreciated to the extent that it is practically worthless, but the Beetle will still probably be worth a good percentage of its purchase price.

The Beetle is also far more user-repairable than most - if not all - more recent cars, a fact which the DIY-inclined owner can use to bring down servicing and repair costs dramatically. Apart from any other consideration, all new cars sold on the UK market from January 1993 must be fitted with catalytic converters, which effectively means that the simple and easily repaired carburettor has been supplanted by sophisticated - and anything-but-user-repairable - fuel injection. The flat four engine can be removed in a fraction of the time it takes to remove the engines of most other cars (minutes instead of hours), and the engine can be test-run on any suitably flat, hard surface before it is placed back in the car.

The car is ecologically 'friendlier' than many would have you believe. Most Beetles enjoy longer working lives than the average car, and many Beetles out-last ordinary cars by a factor of two, three, or even more. Since between 20 and 40 per cent of the energy consumed by a vehicle occurs during its manufacture, the saving in pollution is obvious - catalytic converters and fuel consumption notwithstanding. In fact, back in the early 1990s, ecologists were waking up to the idea that all cars should be manufactured to give longer working lives in the interest of reduced pollution. Of course, the mighty motor manufacturers continued to concentrate on making cars that customers would want to upgrade to and, in time, from ...

The Beetle can be a very reliable car, simply because there's less to go wrong than with almost any other road car. The fact that the engine is cooled by air means that there won't be any cracked engine blocks and cylinder head problems in cold weather due to the expansion of frozen liquid coolant, no leaking radiators and hoses, or non-functioning water pumps; all of which can occur with liquid-cooled engines and wreck certain of them in a very short space of time.

Compare the Beetle with the average modern car. The modern car has by law to be fitted with a catalytic converter, and hence fuel injection, and also have to be fitted with electronic 'brains' (the dreaded Engine Control Units), which meter out the fuel precisely in order to avoid damaging the catalytic converter. All of this technology should pose no problem when the car is new, but when the same car is a few years old, each extra component is something else which is likely to go wrong and cause a breakdown. Those electronic components, in many instances, are the most fault-prone parts of the modern car.

VW has produced two vehicles which truly deserve their cult status, and joining the Beetle on the sun 'n surf scene is the Type 2, universally referred to as the 'Bus.'

What is perhaps worse is that today's mechanic is no longer dealing with repairable components, but is very often faced with sealed units or electronic components which are so sophisticated that it takes a degree in computer science in order to understand how they function! In other words, problems within some of these units can only be dealt with by replacement. Even worse, despite the availability of computerised diagnostic equipment, many faults can only be identified by substituting components, one-by-one, until the fault disappears. This increases repair costs but, more importantly, means that a modern car that breaks down miles from anywhere, due to a problem with one of its electronics systems, cannot be repaired there and then. It must either be towed away or stay where it is until the necessary component can be sourced and transported to it.

Many qualified mechanics (or technicians, as they are called today) can only trace faults using computer diagnostic equipment; if the computer can't diagnose the fault, the technicians lack the experience to find it themselves. One trained and qualified modern technician admitted to the author that he would not be able to fault-find problems on Beetles and, in fact, would not even know where to begin! Because the fuel delivery and ignition systems are, to all intents and purposes, integrated on modern cars, and many faults could equally be caused by fuel or ignition components, fault-finding by substitution can be a lengthy process. This is exacerbated by economics, which dictate that spares are no longer held in dealerships but ordered as and when needed. Modern car components include throttle position sensors, inlet air mass flow sensors (and temperature sensors), crankshaft position sensors, camshaft position sensors, lamba (oxygen) sensors, coolant temperature sensors, engine bay temperature sensors, exhaust gas recirculation systems (vales, regulators, secondary electronically operated valves and yet another temperature sensor) and more all of which are capable of causing a range of faults.

The Beetle is so simple that most roadside breakdowns can be dealt with there and then without the need of special equipment beyond a normal motorist's tool kit.

DRIVING

Driving a Beetle is very different to driving a more modern car. The seemingly lazy, slow-revving engine which lacks straight bhp, in fact, delivers sufficient torque to get and keep you on the move without ever breaking into a sweat. Although nought to sixty mph times for Beetles are anything but impressive, the torque always seems to be there when needed for overtaking. Ignore the speedometer reading at your peril; the slow engine revolutions are deceptive and can lull inexperienced Beetle drivers into driving far more quickly than they realise.

The interiors of all Beetles are spartan in comparison with most modern cars. The seat bases are passably comfortable, but the seat backs lack proper support, most noticeable when cornering. Instrumentation is kept to a bare minimum, displaying the speed and fuel tank level but not the revs, oil pressure or engine temperature; quite in keeping for a car which revelled in being an anachronism in its own lifetime. Driver visibility is generally excellent, although all four wings are hidden from view which, perhaps, explains the large number of town Beetles with dented wings!

The unnecessarily huge steering wheel, coupled with the massive rear weight bias of the car, makes the steering so light - even when manoeuvring at car park speed - you could be forgiven for wondering whether Herr Porsche had cunningly hidden a power steering pump within the steering box. Put a few too many psi in the front tyres, though, and the car feels as though the dampers at the front have failed; the eccentric bush-induced understeer is also increased which, coupled with the bouncing of the front end, can make cornering a little too exciting ...

Correctly shod and with no weak points in the suspension, and especially the dampers, Beetles can go around tight corners at considerable speed as sure-footedly as if they were - excuse the cliche - running on a pair of rails. Push the car a fraction too hard, though, and the rear end can break away into massive oversteer - or in extreme cases a spin - so quickly and viciously that even the most experienced driver can have trouble regaining control of the car.

The problem is one of weight distribution. Having the weight of the transaxle and engine over the rear wheels gives plenty of traction to get you moving on slippery surfaces, but when centrifugal forces become great enough during hard cornering, this mass has much potential energy, which makes its presence felt the moment the rear wheels lose traction. Few, though, ever drive so close to the limit for this - the so-called 'dumbell effect' - to be a problem.

Swing axle cars are more prone to snap into oversteer than more recent diagonal arm suspension cars because their rear wheels suffer constantly variable camber. Unlike later Beetles which had universal joints at either end of their drive shafts, early 'swing axle' car drive shafts possessed only one UJ at the differential end. Because the transaxle which houses the differential rises and falls relative to the road (and thence the wheels), its angle alters that of the drive shafts, and the hubs and wheels which were fixed to them. When the rear centre of gravity of these cars rises on a tight bend, the heavily loaded outside wheel develops a positive camber angle (which gives very poor grip). This rise in the centre of gravity is exacerbated if, for some reason, the driver lifts off the accelerator pedal - or worse, applies the brakes - partway through the corner. When that happens at speed, the dumbell effect is very evident.

Beetles with diagonal arm rear suspension might be less prone to the dumbell effect, but this just means that, when it happens, the cars are travelling at a higher speed and the consequences are potentially more dangerous. Going one stage further, the author has even experienced (from the passenger seat) a 270 degree spin in a Porsche 911 being driven at very high speed; not an experience he ever wishes to repeat ...

Experienced Beetle drivers will be mindful of the potential dumbell effect, and not rush headlong into blind corners which could conceal some obstacle that would force them to take avoiding action while the rear suspension was loaded.

The fact that the engine and gearbox of the Beetle are situated over the driving wheels brings one huge benefit; their weight gives those wheels excellent traction, and the car excels when used on slippery surfaces and off-road. The Beetle will go where most other cars simply sit still and spin their driving wheels, and even the front-engined, front wheel drive car takes second place to the Beetle because, although its engine and gearbox might place weight over the driving wheels, the rearward transfer of mass which occurs when torque is applied to the wheels reduces tyre grip.

So, the Beetle is not especially rapid, comfortable or well-behaved on the road when compared to modern cars: why then, do Beetle owners derive so much pleasure from driving their cars? The simple answer is that the Beetle driver can enjoy the Beetle experience, savouring the sensations that only the Beetle can provide.

Index